W9-BRO-124

Pro CSS Techniques

■ ■ ■

Jeff Croft, Ian Lloyd, and Dan Rubin

Apress®

Pro CSS Techniques

Copyright © 2006 by Jeff Croft, Ian Lloyd, and Dan Rubin

ISBN-13 (pbk): 978-1-59059-732-3

ISBN-10 (pbk): 1-59059-732-X

eISBN-13: 978-1-4302-0335-3

Printed and bound in the United States of America 9 8 7 6 5 4 3 2

Trademarked names may appear in this book. Rather than use a trademark symbol with every occurrence of a trademarked name, we use the names only in an editorial fashion and to the benefit of the trademark owner, with no intention of infringement of the trademark.

Lead Editor: Chris Mills
Technical Reviewer: Wilson Miner
Editorial Board: Steve Anglin, Ewan Buckingham, Gary Cornell, Jason Gilmore, Jonathan Gennick, Jonathan Hassell, James Huddleston, Chris Mills, Matthew Moodie, Dominic Shakeshaft, Jim Sumser, Keir Thomas, Matt Wade
Project Manager: Beth Christmas
Copy Edit Manager: Nicole Flores
Copy Editor: Liz Welch
Assistant Production Director: Kari Brooks-Copony
Production Editor: Katie Stence
Compositor and Artist: Kinetic Publishing Services, LLC
Proofreader: Lori Bring
Indexer: Broccoli Information Management
Cover Designer: Kurt Krames
Manufacturing Director: Tom Debolski

Distributed to the book trade worldwide by Springer-Verlag New York, Inc., 233 Spring Street, 6th Floor, New York, NY 10013. Phone 1-800-SPRINGER, fax 201-348-4505, e-mail orders-ny@springer-sbm.com, or visit http://www.springeronline.com.

For information on translations, please contact Apress directly at 2855 Telegraph Avenue, Suite 600, Berkeley, CA 94705. Phone 510-549-5930, fax 510-549-5939, e-mail info@apress.com, or visit http://www.apress.com.

For Haley, because everything I do is dedicated to you.
—Jeff Croft

For Manda. Thanks for the continued support—lloydi loves ya!
—Ian Lloyd

For Mum, Dad, and Alex—friends, till the end.
—Dan Rubin

Contents at a Glance

Contents

About the Authors

JEFF CROFT is a web and graphic designer focused on web standards–based development who lives and works in Lawrence, Kansas. As the senior designer at World Online, Jeff works on such award-winning standards-based sites as http://lawrence.com and http://LJWorld.com. Jeff also runs a popular blog and personal site at http://jeffcroft.com, where he writes about many topics, including modern web and graphic design.

In addition to his work with World Online, Jeff has worked at two major universities in an effort to bring web standards to the education sector, and he has completed many freelance and contract jobs for various clients.

When he's not hunched over a computer, Jeff enjoys photography, music, film, television, and a good night out on the town.

IAN LLOYD runs Accessify.com, a site dedicated to promoting web accessibility and providing tools for web developers. His personal site, Blog Standard Stuff, ironically, has nothing to do with standards for blogs (it's a play on words), although there is an occasional standards-related gem to be found there.

Ian works full-time for Nationwide Building Society, where he tries his hardest to influence standards-based design ("to varying degrees!"). He is a member of the Web Standards Project, contributing to the Accessibility Task Force. Web standards and accessibility aside, he enjoys writing about his trips abroad and recently took a year off from work and all things web but then ended up writing more in his year off than he ever had before. He finds most of his time being taken up by a demanding old lady (relax, it's only his old Volkswagen camper van).

Ian is married to Manda and lives in the oft-mocked town of Swindon (where the "boring lot" in the UK version of *The Office* are from) next to a canal that the locals like to throw shopping carts into for fun.

Ian is the author of *Build Your Own Web Site the Right Way with HTML & CSS* (SitePoint, 2006), which teaches web standards–based design to the complete beginner. He has also been technical editor on a number of other books published by Apress, friends of ED, and SitePoint.

DAN RUBIN spends his days blending music, design, typography, and web standards with the sunny beaches of South Florida. From vocal coaching and performing to graphic design and (almost literally) everything in between, Dan does his best to spread his talent as thin and as far as he possibly can while still leaving time for a good cup of tea and the occasional nap.

His passion for all things creative and artistic isn't a solely selfish endeavor either—you don't have to hang around too long before you'll find him waxing educational about a cappella jazz and barbershop harmony (his design of roundersquartet.com is just one example of these two worlds colliding), interface design, usability, web standards, graphic design in general, and which typeface was on the bus that just drove by.

In addition to his contributions to sites including Blogger, the CSS Zen Garden, and Microsoft's ASP.NET portal, Dan is a contributing author to *Cascading Style Sheets: Separating Content from Presentation* (2nd Edition, friends of ED, 2004), a technical reviewer for *Beginning CSS Web Development: From Novice to Professional* (Apress, 2006), and coauthor of *Web Standards Creativity* (friends of ED, 2007). He writes about web standards, design, and life in general on his blog, `http://superfluousbanter.org` and publishes podcasts on `http://livefromthe101.com`, and his professional work can be found at his agency's site, `http://webgraph.com`.

About the Technical Reviewer

 **WILSON MINER** is a designer and web developer based in San Francisco. He works at Apple and he's also the designer for Django, an open source Python web framework. He publishes occasionally at www.wilsonminer.com.

Acknowledgments

Thanks to everyone who helped make this book possible—and there are a lot of you.

To Chris Mills, for giving me this wonderful opportunity and for guiding me through it every step of the way. To Beth Christmas, for managing the project and keeping on me when I slipped behind (and God knows I did). To Liz Welch, for keeping our grammar, tone, and spelling in check. To Katie Stence, for her wonderful production work. And to everyone else at Apress who worked long and hard to get this book published. You guys have been tremendous.

To my long-distance friends and coauthors, Ian Lloyd and Dan Rubin. It's been a joy working with you both. I can't wait until we can celebrate in person. To my good friend and colleague Wilson Miner, who, in addition to doing the book's technical editing, put a great deal of effort into the early planning stages of this project. And to design rockstar Bryan Veloso for his early contributions. It wouldn't have been possible without all of you.

To my friends and colleagues at World Online, especially Dan Cox, Nathan Borror, Jacob Kaplan-Moss, Matt Croydon, David Ryan, James Bennett, and Tom Tobin for their encouragement and feedback throughout this process. Working with you guys is at once a challenge, an education, and a great source of entertainment. Also to my friends at Kansas State University, especially Janelle Corkill and Neil Erdwien, for not being afraid of my big ideas and believing in me as much as you did. I miss you guys.

To Jeffrey Zeldman, for being the inspiration to me and many others to get on board with web standards, and to Dave Shea, for creating the resource that ultimately proved CSS could really work—and also for giving me some personal opportunities that helped me through a trying time.

To the many great minds in the web standards community who share their ideas, discoveries, and wonderful personalities with us through blogs and other online resources. All of you are constant sources of inspiration and motivation. Among you: Cameron Adams, Faruk Ates, Ryan Brill, Mark Boulton, Douglas Bowman, Andy Budd, Dan Cederholm, Tantek Çelik, Jared Christensen, Joe Clark, Andy Clarke, Simon Collison, Mike Davidson, Dustin Diaz, Garret Dimon, Todd Dominey, Derek Featherstone, Andrei Herasimchuk, Jon Hicks, Molly Holzschlag, Shaun Inman, Roger Johansson, Jeremy Keith, Dirk Knemeyer, Ethan Marcotte, Drew McLellan, Eric Meyer, Cameron Moll, Paul Nixon, Dunstan Orchard, John Oxton, Mike Papageorge, Veerle Pieters, D. Keith Robinson, Mike Rundle, Richard Rutter, Jason Santa Maria, Ryan Sims, Nathan Smith, Steve Smith, Jonathan Snook, Greg Storey, Jeffrey Veen, Khoi Vinh, Russ Weakley, Rob Weychert, and Simon Willison. There are more of you—you know who you are.

To Sue Jarchow at Washburn University, for (quite literally) showing me the door to freedom, respect, and opportunity. Thanks for the enormous kick-start you gave to my career.

To everyone who visits jeffcroft.com and posts an occasional comment. I owe this opportunity to you as much as anyone.

To all my friends, who've seen a lot less of me in the past seven or eight months. I'm looking forward to hanging out with you all regularly again.

To Michelle, who spent many nights on the couch alone while I hacked away at this book. Thanks for all your support and understanding. I love you, Meesh.

To my whole family, especially my Mom, who was as excited about this opportunity as I was, and my Dad, whom I look to as a role model and an inspiration far more than he knows. You guys have supported me through everything, good and bad, and in more ways than any child should even dream of. Words cannot express how much I love you and need you, and nothing I will ever be able to do will be a suitable way to thank you.

To my beautiful daughter Haley, who is the reason I do everything I do. I love you, sweetheart, and the moments I spend with you are truly the ones I value more than any other.

And of course to you, for reading.

Jeff Croft

Beginning with the obligatory group hug, thanks to my fellow authors Jeff and Dan. Without you guys . . . erm . . . well, I'd have had a lot more to write. Lifesavers. Seriously, though, you were all quick to respond to queries about your respective chapters so we all knew what was going on despite a sometimes tight time frame. We got through it—will have to down a beer or two with you in Austin next March!

Thanks to Wilson for the tech editing and for not being too brutal. He never threw any major curve balls in my direction for which I was truly thankful!

Thanks to all the people at Apress who were flexible enough to accommodate me when I couldn't quite meet the deadlines (on account of doing other work for the publisher at the same time). It was a juggling act at times, so flexibility was a good thing!

And finally, thanks to the other half, the missus, 'er indoors—whom I never refer to in those terms but it seemed like fun to do so in print!—for giving me the OK to take on these chapters, knowing full well that it would mean times when I would lock myself away for hours and communication would involve little more than the odd grunt or head nod. Wait, that's just a normal day. My bad.

Ian Lloyd

Writing a book is an adventure. To begin with, it is a toy and an amusement; then it becomes a mistress, and then it becomes a master, and then a tyrant. The last phase is that just as you are about to be reconciled to your servitude, you kill the monster, and fling him out to the public.

—Winston Churchill

Churchill's words accurately describe the process, and I would not have been able to make it through without the help, love, and encouragement of some truly amazing people.

First and foremost, I owe a massive debt of gratitude to the entire team at Apress, specifically Chris Mills, Beth Christmas, Liz Welch, Kylie Johnston, and Katie Stence. You are all wonderful, caring, and patient people, and it has been a pleasure working with you over these last few months. I would not have been able to "kill the monster" without you.

To my coauthors, Jeff and Ian: you guys are talented, knowledgeable writers, even if your headshots aren't as nice as mine. It is an honor to have my name share the cover with you both.

This book could not have been written without years of experience, but not simply in the design or web standards fields. Everyone who has had an impact on my thought process, writing style, and the long and constant learning process that is the Web has contributed in some way. During the course of writing this book, however, I would be remiss in not thanking certain individuals for their support: to Brad Tuckman, KSC Studio, Pixel Logo and MusicAlly, my clients over the last few months, for being so understanding; to Bryan Veloso, Jeremy Hubert, Mark Hornsby, Jina Bolton, Kris Rector, Lauren Grant, Brean Thibodeau, and Stephanie Ditchfield for their tireless encouragement, moral support, and late-night insanity phone calls and IMs; to Anton Peck for his support and the wonderful logo design used for one of the examples in this book; to Garrett Dimon for some CSS brainstorming and being cool in general (Vince Vaughn and Ben Stiller have *nothing* on us!); to Ryan Brill for helping out with some Windows-related development tidbits; to my brothers in harmony, Alex, Sean, Myron, and the rest of the Rounders family for putting up with my lack of focus on singing for a while; to the members of my chorus for the same—I know it's difficult when the director misses rehearsals; to Kristina Horst, for taking such a wonderful photo of me for use in this book; to Dinah, Kit, and Tana, the three most awesome, wonderful, and inspirational people I know; to the entire crew at Starbucks on US1 and Broward Blvd. for the steady stream of caffeine, the smiling faces, and for always remembering my name and drinks when I walk in the door; to Tetley for the many boxes of British Blend tea I consumed during the course of this project; to cows and dairy farms, for the milk in my tea; and to Big Sugar (with the amount of tea I drank, I should either invest in sugar futures or a better dental plan).

And finally, I owe more than I can possibly express to my family. Mum and Dad, you are inspiration personified. Now we can put this book on the shelf next to yours. Bro (aka "Alex"), thanks for everything, and then some, and for taking care of me and the business while I was distracted by all this darned writing . . . as busy as we both are, you're always on top of things, constantly amazing and impressing me with more moral fiber and strength of character than anyone I've ever met.

Dan Rubin

Introduction

This book is a collection of proven, professional, modern techniques that you can use every day to get the most out of the time you put into your projects, from start to finish.

As it has finally come to pass that CSS (Cascading Style Sheets) and other web standards are useful, real-world tools as opposed to idealistic goals, more and more professional web developers are moving to CSS from older approaches. Web browsers that support CSS well are now the default for the vast majority of web surfers. Additionally, a whole new generation of web developers are appearing on the scene, many of whom have never had the grave displeasure of dealing with nested table layouts and spacer GIFs.

So how are these web developers learning CSS? Most often, they are self-taught. They've picked up bits and pieces from online articles and blog posts, they've scoured other people's code to dissect how someone achieved a particular style or layout technique, and they've read other CSS books on the market.

Like blog posts and online tutorials, most of the CSS books currently available are focused on specific principles and techniques out of context. *Pro CSS Techniques* focuses on context, and how each of the techniques presented fits into the lifecycle of a real-world project.

What This Book Is Not

This book is not an introduction to CSS. Although we'll provide an overview of the basics, we'll assume you have a simple understanding of what CSS is and how it works.

This book is not a comprehensive reference guide, either. Reference guides can be very useful (and CSS references already exist on the market), but they don't usually deal with context, best practices, and issues of practicality.

This book is also not a preachy bible for web standards. We'll assume you've already had at least one zealot preach at you about the importance of standards, and that if you're reading this book, that zealot has already won you over. Or maybe you've already discovered the benefits of web standards on your own. Either way, you're a convert. We believe strongly in web standards, but we also believe in doing what's practical and effective above all else. We try to be 100 percent standards compliant where possible, but aren't afraid to deviate from that goal slightly if it's more practical to do so.

This book is not a gallery of clever, experimental CSS techniques. We're focusing on techniques you can use today in the real world, on real projects, for real clients.

The Goals of This Book

This book is focused on four key goals:

- *Maintainability*: We'll provide suggestions on how you can easily write, organize, and store your code in ways that makes it simple to maintain—by you or by someone else.

- *Compatibility*: We'll show you how you can avoid browser compatibility issues before they crop up, and how you can work around them when they do.

- *Reusability*: We want you to get the most out of your styles by taking advantage of the inheritance and specificity built into CSS.

- *Practicality*: We'll remind you not to get too hung up on any of these ideals. It's always smart to try to do something the "right" way, but if the "right" way proves to be impractical, use what works in the real world and move on. The ink is never dry on a web site—you can always optimize later.

Who This Book Is For

Pro CSS Techniques will be useful to anyone with a basic understanding of (X)HTML and CSS, who wants to take their knowledge and technique to the next level. We'll focus our attention on web designers and developers who are building professional sites for general audiences. We know that not everyone who works in web development spends their time off reading web design magazines, blogs, and other people's code. If you want to get up to speed on modern CSS development without reading hundreds of blogs posts all over the Internet, this book is your ticket home.

The Structure of This Book

Although this book is about CSS, it's essential that you understand and provide clean, semantic (X)HTML to hang your CSS styles upon. Therefore, the first chapter of this book, "The Promise of CSS," includes a review of modern (X)HTML markup. Next comes "The Language of Style Sheets," a chapter that, along with its follow-up, "Specificity and the Cascade," provides all the dirty details on how CSS actually works. We then discuss "The Browsers," including their inconsistencies, which you likely already know is the bane of CSS development.

We move on to cover the practical management of your CSS development workflow. In "Managing CSS Files," you'll learn best practices for writing CSS selectors and declarations, how to best organize your selectors in multiple CSS files, and how to optimize your style sheets for bandwidth and speed. In "Hacks and Workarounds," we explain how you can avoid over-complicating your CSS by building to the most reliable browsers first, when you'll need to use CSS "hacks" or "filters," and how to use them in the cleanest way possible. We also outline the most useful CSS filters.

Following these early chapters, the meat of the book shows you specific CSS styling techniques that you can use in your projects. We start with "CSS Layouts," explaining effective ways for creating many common layouts, and then move on to "Creating Common Page Elements," which covers such goodies as navigation tabs, drop-down menus, and rounded-corner boxes. We have a chapter dedicated to CSS "Typography," the subtle art of fine-tuning text for readability and aesthetics. We then move on to specific chapters on the visual formatting of (X)HTML tables, forms, and lists, and close with a chapter on "Styling for Print and Other Media."

We finish the book with a troubleshooting guide we call "Everything Falls Apart." It will help you get through the inevitable cases when things don't go as planned. We discuss how you can figure out which components of your CSS are causing problems, some common CSS mistakes, and fixes to common CSS browser bugs.

Finally, we include useful references in appendices at the end of the book.

A Note About Internet Explorer 7

At the time of this writing, IE 7 was in beta, so we referred to it as such throughout this book; however, by publication it will be available as a full release.

Conventions Used in This Book

Throughout the book, we'll use the following terms:

- (X)HTML refers to both HTML and XHTML.

- CSS refers to the CSS 2.1 specification, unless otherwise stated.

All (X)HTML examples in this book are assumed to be nested in the <body> tag of a complete (X)HTML document. For the sake of brevity, we will often not show the entire (X)HTML document but only the relevant code snippet. Similarly, all CSS examples are assumed to be in the <head> of an (X)HTML document (usually by way of a link to an external style sheet).

Now, let's get started.

■ ■ ■

CHAPTER 1

The Promise of CSS

The ideal that Cascading Style Sheets (CSS) strives to attain is the complete separation of content from presentation. In other words, you build, maintain, and store the core *content* of your web page, web site, or application (the text, related images, forms, and so forth) separately from the *visual* presentation (such as the layout, typography, and decorative images).

Those of you moving to CSS from the world of old-school web development may find this approach quite different from what you're used to. You may be accustomed to using (X)HTML tables as layout grids, creating margins between items by including img elements in your (X)HTML that serve up one-pixel transparent GIF images, and specifying typefaces using the (X)HTML font element. "Freeing your mind" from relying on those approaches isn't easy, but most people who do are glad they did. For those of you who have used CSS since the day you started building web sites, consider yourselves blessed—learning CSS from scratch is easier than changing the way you think about web design.

■Note Most discussion points and examples in this book apply to both HTML and XHTML. We will use the notation (X)HTML to indicate these cases. When things do apply specifically to HTML or XHTML and not both, we will use the appropriate name alone, without the parenthetical (X).

The Advantages of Using CSS for Style

There are numerous real-world advantages to separating content and style, and most of you are probably already aware of them. We'll recap, just in case.

By separating the two layers of your document, you make it simple to add, remove, or update content without having to worry about botching up your layout. You also make it easy to change the font used for the entire site without having to dig through your content in search of every single <font> tag. Separating the two layers allows a web team to work efficiently; your visual designers can focus on design while your content producers focus on content—and neither has to worry about the other getting in their way. If you're a solo developer, you'll find that the separation of content and presentation allows you to keep your "frames of mind" separate as well. When you need to make a change to content, you won't have to dig through a bunch of style code to find what you're looking for.

In addition, separating the two layers makes it possible to do an entire site redesign without touching the content at all—you only need to create a new CSS style sheet. By using external style sheets, separate from your HTML structure, you can make all modifications to the visual presentation of the site by editing just *one* file rather than the numerous files (possibly numbering in the hundreds!) that make up your content.

As we move along, you'll find that the complete separation of content and presentation doesn't always pan out in the real world, but it's still an important goal. Trying to attain it—even if you don't make it 100 percent of the way—will pay off for you in efficiency and simplicity. If you shoot for the moon and don't make it, you'll still end up in the stars.

Semantic (X)HTML: Markup with Meaning

Before we can start working with CSS, we need to be sure we are able to adequately structure our (X)HTML documents in a modern fashion. Contrary to what you may have learned in the earlier years of web development, (X)HTML should not define the look and presentation of a web page (that's the job of CSS). Instead, the purpose of (X)HTML is to provide context and meaning to the content of the document—this is referred to as *semantic markup*.

What Is Semantic Markup?

CSS relies completely on the (X)HTML that references it. If you want to use CSS to its fullest potential, it's imperative that you provide it with clean, structured content marked up with (X)HTML. Before you can do that, you need to understand (X)HTML's purpose in life. According to the World Wide Web Consortium (W3C), an organization that develops specifications for many of the interoperable technologies used on the Web, "HTML is the *lingua franca* for publishing hypertext on the World Wide Web . . . HTML uses tags such as `<h1>` and `</h1>` to structure text into headings, paragraphs, lists, hypertext links etc." (`www.w3.org/MarkUp/`).

In simpler terms, (X)HTML is a way of adding structure and meaning (or "semantics") to textual content. It's a way of saying, "This line is a header, and these lines make up a paragraph. This text is a list of items, and this text is a link to another document on the Web." Note that it is not the job of HTML to say, "This text is blue, and this text is red. This section is a column that is to the right of everything else, and this line is in italics." That presentational information is CSS's job. When developing for the modern Web—especially if you come from the old school—always remember this: *(X)HTML tells us what a piece of content is (or what it means), and not what it looks like.*

When we refer to "semantic markup," we are talking about (X)HTML that is free of presentational information and chock-full of meaningful tags that define the structure of the document.

(X)HTML VALIDATION

(X)HTML validation, the process of checking your markup for errors against the specifications the W3C has created, is an invaluable tool for modern web developers. Oftentimes, when it seems something isn't working properly, it's because you have an error in your code that a validator script (such as the one at `http://validator.w3.org/`) can easily find and point out to you.

However, it's also important to note that validation and clean, semantic markup are not one and the same. It's possible to write very poorly structured markup that will pass the validation test with flying colors. Likewise, it's possible to write very good, semantic (X)HTML and still find that you have a validation error or two.

Remember: both validation and solid semantics are important goals, but neither one necessarily leads to the other. A proper (X)HTML document will be semantic in nature *and* validate. It's important to ensure you are striving to meet both of these goals and not just one or the other.

How Does Writing Semantic Markup Help You in the Real World?

Good semantic (X)HTML markup helps to promote the accessibility of your site to visitors. Not all visitors to your site will be able to "see" your CSS and JavaScript, but they'll all get your (X)HTML. Therefore, it's essential that your markup provide the semantic context necessary for comprehension of your content.

Screen readers (for visitors who are visually impaired) "read" your page based on the markup. For example, if you use the semantic `<acronym>` tag, a screen reader may "spell out" your word rather than trying to pronounce it. You'll learn how to create semantically rich markup in the next section.

Personal digital assistants (PDAs), cell phones, and other devices may not render your page in the same way a desktop web browser does (usually because these devices have reduced support for CSS). Using semantic markup ensures that these devices render your page in a way that makes sense. Ideally, it is the job of the viewing device to render the content as appropriate to the context of that device. Starting with semantic markup gives the device the information it needs to make contextual decisions, and saves you from having to think about all the possible contexts where your content will be consumed (now or in the future). For example, a cell phone may choose to render text marked up with a header tag in bold. A PDA may display the same text in a larger font. Either way, by marking up your text as a header, you've made sure the reading device will act accordingly, based on what it feels is appropriate for the context in which the page is being viewed.

Search engine crawlers also rely on your markup to determine context and weight of various keywords. You may not have considered search engine crawlers and bots as "visitors" to your site in the past, but they are actually extremely valuable users. Without them, search engines wouldn't be able to index your sites, and human users would be less likely to find them. It's in your best interest to make your pages as easy to understand as possible for crawlers, which largely ignore presentational markup and pay attention only to semantic markup. Therefore, if the name of your web document is marked up in a `<font size="7">` tag instead of an `<h1>`, your site's position in search engine results could suffer.

Besides promoting accessibility, semantic markup facilitates the proper use of CSS and JavaScript by providing many "hooks" on which to apply styles and behaviors.

Creating Semantically Rich (X)HTML Markup

Now that you understand the benefits of semantic markup, how can you go about creating (X)HTML that is as structured and meaningful as possible?

Start by using the right (X)HTML elements for your content. If it's a paragraph, put it in a `<p>` tag. If it's a header, put it in an `<hx>` tag. If it's a list of links, use `<a>` tags inside of list elements. This may sound simple, but it's astonishing how many sites you'll find on the Internet that don't bother with these details at all. They choose to put two `<br>` tags after some text rather than using the paragraph element, or they use `<font size="5">` instead of a header element.

To help you decide on the right elements for your content, become familiar with some of the lesser-used (X)HTML tags. There are a whole host of useful elements out there that many web developers seem to completely forget about. By simply adopting some of these tags as your own, you can quickly add structure, context, and styling hooks to your documents. We'll be using many of these tags later in the book as we get into styling various page elements. In the meantime, you may wish to brush up on your (X)HTML if these are not elements you are familiar with. Table 1-1 lists some of the lesser-used tags you may want to get to know.

Table 1-1. *Semantic (X)HTML Elements That Are Often Underused by Designers and Developers*

Element	Purpose
address	Allows you to mark up addresses
dl	Indicates a definition list (especially for term/definition pairs, but can be used for other key/value pairs as well)
dt	Indicates a definition term within a definition list
dd	Indicates the definition of a term within a definition list
blockquote	Indicates extended quotes
q	Indicates inline quotes
label	Labels form elements
th	Marks headers of columns and rows within a table
thead	Marks table headers
tfoot	Marks table footers
fieldset	Groups form elements
button	Creates form buttons
cite	Specifies citations or references to other sources
samp	Indicates sample output of scripts, programs, etc.
kbd	Indicates text to be entered by the user
abbr	Specifies abbreviated forms or words or phrases
acronym	Indicates acronyms

It should be obvious by now, but when creating semantic markup, you want to avoid presentational tags such as `<font>`, `<i>`, `<b>`, and `<u>`. The sole purpose of each of these tags is to create a visual effect, which in the modern world of web development is the job of CSS, not (X)HTML. You should use elements like em and strong to define the meaning of the content, and then use CSS to specify your desired presentation for those elements (such as underlined, bold, or italic).

Also, do not repurpose structural tags for presentational effect. Before browsers supported CSS, many a web developer (including the authors of this book!) found creative ways to use tags for purposes other than their intended ones. For example, developers used the `table` element—designed for displaying tabular data such as spreadsheets and invoices—as a layout grid for their pages. They used the `<blockquote>` tag to create indentions. This sort of repurposing, while clever, is simply not necessary on the modern Web. Using CSS, you can style any element to look any way you'd like. There's no need to use an `<li>` tag just to get a bullet to appear next to some content. Use the list item element (`li`) if it really is a list item, but if it's not, simply use CSS to restyle the appropriate element with a bullet. Remember, the (X)HTML should tell us *what it is*, not what it looks like.

Avoiding Nonstructural Tags

To provide as much structure as possible, limit your use of (X)HTML's nonstructural tags as much as possible. `<div>` and `<span>` are incredibly useful—and absolutely necessary for CSS development—but they have no semantic meaning. Always check for an appropriate semantic tag you could use instead before resorting to `<div>` and `<span>`.

The `div` element serves as a unit for grouping structural areas of your web document—for example, lumping together all of the primary content and then all of the secondary content. The purpose of the `span` element is to set apart inline content within a parent element. For example, consider the header text "Chapter One: Modern Markup." If you consider the phrase "Modern Markup" emphasized, then you should mark it up like so:

```
<h1>Chapter One: <em>Modern Markup</em></h1>
```

If, on the other hand, you wish to set "Modern Markup" apart for some nonsemantic reason (perhaps because you want to style it differently), use `<span>`:

```
<h1>Chapter One: <span>Modern Markup</span></h1>
```

`div` and `span` should not be used to replace more appropriate elements. For example, there is no reason to do this:

```
<div>This is a paragraph of text.</div>
```

when you could simply do this:

```
<p>This a paragraph of text.</p>
```

The first example is meaningless, whereas the second provides the paragraph structure to the browsers and other devices reading it.

Avoiding "Divitis" and "Classitis"

Often, developers who are accustomed to using the `table` element for layout will be inclined to create markup with lots of nested `<div>` tags, effectively replicating their `table` layouts with the `div` element. This practice, which has been dubbed *divitis*, should be avoided.

Similarly, be careful about "wrapping" single elements in `<div>` tags. This is often done for styling purposes—and it is sometimes necessary to create a particular effect—but usually it is wasted markup. For example, why do this:

```
<div id="menu">
  <ul>
    <li>First item</li>
    <li>Second item</li>
    <li>Third item</li>
  </ul>
</div>
```

when this provides as much structure and uses less code:

```
<ul id="menu">
  <li>First item</li>
  <li>Second item</li>
  <li>Third item</li>
</ul>
```

Less code is always a good thing.

Like divitis, it's also possible (and very common) for developers to overuse (X)HTML's class attribute. This has been deemed *classitis*. The class attribute exists so that you can add some semblance of semantics if no appropriate (X)HTML element is available and so that you can create "hooks" for CSS styles and JavaScript behaviors to act on. But developers often use classes instead of more appropriate tags, like this:

```
<p class="address">
  John Smith<br />
  1234 Rolling Rock Rd. <br />
  Albany, NY, 12345<br />
</p>
```

Instead of using (X)HTML's address element, like this:

```
<address>
  John Smith<br />
  1234 Rolling Rock Rd. <br />
  Albany, NY, 12345<br />
</address>
```

developers also tend to use a class over and over again on repeated elements when they could simply apply it once to a parent element. Consider this:

```
<ul>
  <li class="cheese-type">Cheddar</li>
  <li class="cheese-type">Mozzarella</li>
  <li class="cheese-type">Parmesan</li>
  <li class="cheese-type">Swiss</li>
</ul>
```

Here's a much cleaner approach:

```
<ul class="cheese-types">
  <li>Cheddar</li>
  <li>Mozzarella</li>
```

```
  <li>Parmesan</li>
  <li>Swiss</li>
</ul>
```

So, when dealing with div, span, and the class attribute, be sure you aren't using them instead of more appropriate (X)HTML elements, and be sure you are using as few of them as possible. They're useful when used properly, but they can clutter up your document and cause a great deal of confusion if you're not careful.

Choosing Your Markup Language and DOCTYPE

HTML isn't the only game in town when it comes to web markup. XHTML has hit the ground running and is now very popular among many web designers and developers. Even after you choose one of the two, you'll still have to decide exactly which version you intend to write against. There are several factors to consider, and it's important to think them through and choose the right markup language for your project—changing down the road may prove tedious and time consuming.

HTML vs. XHTML: Why the Decision Does—and Doesn't—Matter

HTML was the original language of the Web, and it continues to be the most widely used. HTML 4.01 is both the most recent and last version of HTML—it is the final W3C specification for HTML. XHTML 1.0 was created after HTML 4.01 to encourage a transition to a new genre of markup languages. XHTML is a reformulation of HTML in XML. Because of this, XHTML documents are both hypertext documents and XML documents.

As far as the users of your web site are concerned, there is almost no real-world benefit to using XHTML over HTML. However, there are still a few compelling reasons why you, as a developer, may prefer XHTML.

XHTML, because of its XML roots, has far more rigorous syntax rules than HTML. Although this may seem like a bad thing at first glance, it actually forces authors to be more precise, which in turn makes XHTML documents easier to maintain than their HTML counterparts. The most relevant examples of XHTML's more particular syntax requirements include insisting that all element and attribute names be lowercase, requiring that all attribute values be quoted, and demanding that all elements—even empty ones—be properly closed.

As valid XML, your XHTML documents can theoretically be parsed by XML utilities that would choke on HTML pages. Also, as valid XML your XHTML documents are ready to be manipulated by Extensible Stylesheet Language Transformations (XSLT). While we don't discuss XSLT in this book, you may find it to be relevant in your organization, and preferring XHTML to HTML will give you this extra layer of compatibility.

Note If you want to find out more about using XML and XSLT in your work, check out *Beginning XML with DOM and Ajax: From Novice to Professional,* by Sas Jacobs (Apress, 2006, ISBN 1590596765) and *Beginning XSLT 2.0: From Novice to Professional,* by Jeni Tennison (Apress, 2005, ISBN 1590593243).

You will run across people who will argue very strongly for both XHTML and HTML. The authors of this book tend to prefer XHTML, but we also recognize that HTML is every bit as valuable to your users. In the end, writing clean, semantic markup is the most important thing, whether you choose to do it in HTML or XHTML.

DOCTYPE: The Most Underappreciated Tag of All

All modern, valid (X)HTML documents must open with a DOCTYPE declaration. DOCTYPE is an (X)HTML string created primarily as a validation mechanism. It indicates to the browser, validator, or other reading device what sort of document you are writing, as well as which specification, or set of rules, you are writing it against. Most modern browsers actually display the page differently based on what DOCTYPE is declared (we'll cover the specifics of how different DOCTYPEs affect browser display in Chapter 4). When you declare a DOCTYPE, you are effectively saying to the browser, "I, the developer of this site, have chosen to write my code against the following specification, and I'd really appreciate it if you'd use the same specification to render it."

So what are these specifications? There are many possible DOCTYPEs, but for the purposes of this book, only four are significant:

- HTML 4.01 Strict

- HTML 4.01 Transitional

- XHTML 1.0 Strict

- XHTML 1.0 Transitional

Let's take a look at each in turn.

HTML 4.01 Strict

HTML 4.01 Strict allows for a trimmed-down version of HTML 4.01. HTML 4.01 Strict emphasizes structure over presentation. It does not contain deprecated and presentational elements (such as font, center, or u), nor does it allow for frames or link targets. Use a strict DOCTYPE when you intend to write only 100 percent clean markup, free of presentational clutter. To declare HTML 4.01 Strict, the first line of your markup document should be

```
<!DOCTYPE HTML PUBLIC "-//W3C//DTD HTML 4.01//EN" ➥
   "http://www.w3.org/TR/html4/strict.dtd">
```

HTML 4.01 Transitional

HTML 4.01 Transitional includes all elements and attributes of HTML 4.01 Strict but also supports older presentational attributes, deprecated elements, and link targets. Use a transitional DOCTYPE when dealing with legacy files that may still contain some presentational markup (you can always change the DOCTYPE to Strict once you completely clean up your legacy code). To declare HTML 4.01 Transitional, make the following the first line of your document:

```
<!DOCTYPE HTML PUBLIC "-//W3C//DTD HTML 4.01 Transitional//EN" ➥
   "http://www.w3.org/TR/html4/loose.dtd">
```

XHTML 1.0 Strict

Similar to HTML 4.01 Strict, the Strict version of XHTML 1.0 emphasizes structure by remov-ing all presentational tags and attributes, and being XHTML, it also enforces the strict rules of XML on your markup, as detailed in the section "HTML vs. XHTML: Why the Decision Does—and Doesn't—Matter." Use a Strict DOCTYPE when you intend to write only 100 percent clean markup, free of presentational clutter. To declare XHTML 1.0 Strict, use the following as the first line of your document:

```
<!DOCTYPE html PUBLIC "-//W3C//DTD XHTML 1.0 Strict//EN" ➥
  "http://www.w3.org/TR/xhtml1/DTD/xhtml1-strict.dtd">
```

XHTML 1.0 Transitional

Similar to HTML 4.01 Transitional, the XHTML 1.0 Transitional specification allows for some presentational markup, although again, the XML rules are enforced. Use a Transitional DOCTYPE when dealing with legacy files that may still contain some presentational markup (you can always change the DOCTYPE to Strict once you completely clean up your legacy code). To declare XHTML 1.0 Transitional, use the following as the first line of your document:

```
<!DOCTYPE html PUBLIC "-//W3C//DTD XHTML 1.0 Transitional//EN" ➥
  "http://www.w3.org/TR/xhtml1/DTD/xhtml1-transitional.dtd">
```

The Three Layers of a Modern Web Document

Modern, well-constructed web documents have three distinct layers of data (see Figure 1-1). The first is the *structure layer*, which is (at least for the purposes of this book) a text document marked up in HTML or XHTML. It contains the content of your document, along with the seman-tic information that indicates what each bit of text is (headers, paragraphs, lists, and so forth).

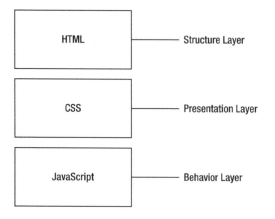

Figure 1-1. *The three-layer model of modern web development*

The second layer is the *presentation layer*, which is the core focus of this book. It describes how your document will be presented to the visitor, including such details as layout, typography, colors, decorative images, and even nonvisual presentations like the voice family a screen reader may use. Generally, the presentation layer of a web document is written using CSS.

Besides these two layers, you'll also find references to the *behavior layer* of a web document. We don't discuss this layer in depth, but you should understand that it refers to using scripting (usually JavaScript for manipulating the Document Object Model, or DOM) to update, add, or remove items from the document based on the user's behavior.

■**Note** For more information about JavaScript and the DOM, check out *Beginning JavaScript with DOM Scripting and Ajax: From Novice to Professional*, by Christian Heilmann (Apress, 2006, ISBN 1590596803).

For a simple example of how the three layers work in conjunction with one another, consider a basic "contact us" form on a company's web site. The form itself is marked-up text, produced in (X)HTML. That text is then styled into the aesthetic presentation you see on screen using CSS. After you fill out the form and click the Submit button, JavaScript steps in to validate your input and lets you know that you skipped a required field. After you fix that oversight, you hit Submit again. JavaScript then disables the button and displays a simple animation to let you know something is happening before returning a message such as "Thank you! We'll get back to you as soon as possible."

Summary

In this chapter, we've covered the basics of modern (X)HTML markup. Because CSS expects you to have written clean, valid, and semantic markup for your documents, it's essential to have this piece of the equation in great shape before moving on to the presentation layer of your page or site. Many CSS headaches can be solved simply by getting your (X)HTML right. Speaking of CSS, let's move on to Chapter 2, where we'll cover the basics of what CSS is and how it works.

CHAPTER 2

■ ■ ■

The Language of Style Sheets

OK, now we've had a look at modern web design, and how CSS fits into that, let's turn our attention to recapping the basics of CSS to make sure we are all on the same page before we start immersing ourselves in all the exciting techniques and productivity-improving tips that make up the rest of the book. Even if you think you have a good handle on the basics of CSS, at least skim through the chapter anyway. Specifically we cover the following:

- Adding style to your document

- Creating a style sheet and declarations

- Choosing selectors to apply styles to your markup

- Understanding XHTML and how it can be represented as an element node tree

- Daisy-chaining and grouping selectors

Adding Style to Your (X)HTML Document

In this section we'll explore the various ways in which you can add CSS styles to your (X)HTML document. We'll cover several approaches, and offer some best practices for making your markup and presentation information work well together.

The <link> Tag

There are a few ways to add CSS style information to an (X)HTML document, but it's almost always a best practice to use the `<link>` tag. The tag's purpose is simple: to associate one document with another. For our purposes, let's use it to associate a CSS document with an XHTML document, like so:

```
<link rel="stylesheet" type="text/css" href="styles.css" media="all" />
```

This simply tells the XHTML document to use the file `styles.css` as a source of CSS information. We call CSS documents referenced in this way *external style sheets*. Link tags that reference external style sheets must be placed inside the `head` element of your (X)HTML document (but not inside any other element).

The attributes of the `<link>` tag are fairly straightforward. The `rel`, or relation, attribute, describes the sort of relationship the linked file has to the (X)HTML file calling it. For CSS style sheets, its value will always be `stylesheet`. The `type` attribute defines the file type of the linked file, and its value should always be text/css for CSS style sheets. As you might expect, the href attribute declares the URL of the style sheet file you'd like to attach to your document. This URL may be absolute or relative. The final attribute, media, states for which presentation media the styles contained in the external style sheet should be applied. As Table 2-1 shows, several possible media types are defined in CSS—and they have varying degrees of browser support (more on this in Chapter 13).

Table 2-1. *Available CSS Media Types*

Column Heading 1	Column Heading 2
all	Applies styles for all media types
aural	Applies styles when listening to the document with a screen reader or similar audio-rendering device
braille	Applies styles when presenting the document with a Braille device
embossed	Applies styles when printing the document with a Braille device
handheld	Applies styles when viewing the document with a handheld personal device, such as a cell phone or PDA
print	Applies styles when printing the document (or when displaying a print preview)
projection	Applies styles when using a projection medium, such as a digital projector
screen	Applies styles when presenting the document on a screen, such as that on a typical desktop computer
tty	Applies styles when displaying the document in a fixed-character width setting, such as Teletype printers
tv	Applies styles when the document is being presented on a television-style screen

It's up to each viewing device that supports CSS—be it a desktop computer's web browser, a cell phone, a PDA, or a web TV device—to render the styles appropriate for the context in which it's being used. Desktop browsers, for example, know to use styles destined for the "screen" media type when they display web sites normally but to use those defined for the "print" type when you are printing; cell phones and PDAs know they should use styles for the "handheld" type; and so on.

You can use a single style sheet in multiple media by setting the value of the media attribute to a list, separated by commas. For example, to use the style sheet named styles.css in both screen and projection media, you'd use the following:

```
<link rel="stylesheet" type="text/css" href="styles.css" ➥
media="screen, projection" />
```

We'll cover using CSS media types in much greater detail in Chapter 13.

Using Multiple Style Sheets

You can also attach multiple style sheets to a single (X)HTML document with the <link> tag. The browser will use all linked style sheets and render the page accordingly.

Also, there exists the concept of an *alternate style sheet*. In some browsers (notably those powered by the Gecko rendering engine, such as Mozilla, Firefox, and recent versions of Netscape), these alternate visual presentations of your document will appear in a menu for the visitor to select between. For example:

```
<link rel="stylesheet" type="text/css" href="styles.css" ➥
media="all" title="Default" />
<link rel="alternate stylesheet" type="text/css" ➥
href="low_vision_styles.css" media="all" title="Low vision" />
```

Here, we've defined references to two different style sheets. Because the second one has the value `alternate stylesheet` for the `rel` attribute, it will not be used when the page is first presented but will be offered to the user as a choice (only in those browsers that support it, though). Note the use of the `title` attribute to give each style sheet a name (which will appear in the visitor's menu of choices). Alternate style sheets are not widely used, probably because of their limited browser support.

It's important to note that any `<link>` tag with both a `title` attribute and a `rel` value of `stylesheet` will be considered a preferred style sheet. Only one preferred style sheet will be used when the page is initially loaded. Therefore, it's important that you don't assign multiple `<link>` tags both a `title` attribute and a `rel` attribute value of `stylesheet`. `<link>` tags *without* a `title` attribute are designated as persistent style sheets— which means they'll *always* be used in the display of the document. More often than not, this is the behavior you'll want. Because of this, you should only apply a `title` attribute to your `<link>` tags if you are referring to an alternate style sheet.

The style Element

The `style` element is an (X)HTML element that allows you to embed CSS style information directly in the page you're working on, rather than abstracting it out to an external style sheet. Although this may sound like a convenience at first, it's almost always a hindrance in the real world. One of the major benefits of CSS is the ability to have all of your style information in a single external style sheet that many pages refer to. That way, when you want to change something, you only have to change it one time. In the case of embedded style sheets created with the `style` element, the style information applies only to the (X)HTML document you're working with. It's possible this behavior is what you want, but more often than not it's beneficial to have the style information abstracted.

If you do want to embed a style sheet, use code like this in the head element of your (X)HTML document:

```
<style type="text/css" media="screen, print ">
...
</style>
```

The practical applications of embedded style sheets are few. If you are making a simple, one-page site, it may be more convenient to keep your style information embedded in your (X)HTML document. You may also have one page within a larger site that needs additional or overriding styles along with the styles applied to the rest of the site. In this case, you can get by with an embedded style sheet, but it still may be a best practice to abstract the styles into their own file. You never know when you may need to add another page utilizing those styles, or reuse them in another section of the site. Having them in their own file provides this additional flexibility.

Creating a Style Sheet

CSS syntax is quite simple: we're dealing with nothing more than a list of rules. A simple style sheet might look something like this:

```
h1 {
  color: blue;
}
h2 {
  color: green;
}
```

Save those two lines into a text file and give it a name ending in .css, and you've got yourself a perfectly valid (albeit simple) external style sheet. Put those two lines in a <style> element within the head of your (X)HTML document, and you've made an embedded style sheet.

Each style rule is made up of two parts: a *selector* and one or more *declarations*—each of which consists of a property and a value.

Declarations

Let's go about this in reverse order. Declarations are property/value pairs that define visual styles. *Properties* are things like background color, width, and font family. *Values* are their counterparts, such as white, 400 pixels, and Arial—or, in the proper syntax:

```
background-color: white;
width: 400px;
font-family: Arial;
```

Declarations are always formatted as the property name, followed by a colon, followed by a value, and then a semicolon. It is common convention to put a space after the colon, but this is not necessary. The semicolon is an indication that the declaration is concluded. Declarations are grouped within curly brackets, and the wrapped group is called a *declaration block*.

Selectors

Selectors define which part(s) of your (X)HTML document will be affected by the declarations you've specified. Several types of selectors are available in CSS. Note that some of them are not supported in all browsers, as you will learn in Chapter 4.

Element Selectors

The most basic of all selectors is the *element selector* (you may have heard them called *tag selectors*). It is simply the name of an (X)HTML element, and—not surprisingly—it selects all of those elements in the document. Let's look again at the previous example:

```
h1 {
  color: blue;
}
h2 {
  color: green;
}
```

We've used h1 and h2 as selectors. These are element selectors that select h1 and h2 elements within the (X)HTML document, respectively. Each rule indicates that the declarations in the declaration block should be applied to the selected element. So, in the previous example, all h1 elements in the page would be blue and all h2 elements would be green. Simple enough, right?

Note Although this book is about using CSS to style (X)HTML documents, CSS can be used for other types of documents as well (notably XML). Therefore, it's entirely possible that you will run across element selectors that are not valid (X)HTML elements.

Class Selectors

So far we've been assigning styles exclusively to (X)HTML elements, using element selectors. But there are several other types of selectors, and the *class* and *ID selectors* may be next in line as far as usefulness. Modern markup (as discussed in Chapter 1) often involves the assigning of classes and IDs to elements. Consider the following:

```
<h1 class="warning">Be careful!</h1>
<p class="warning">Every 108 minutes, the button ➡
must be pushed. Do not attempt to use the computer ➡
for anything other than pushing the button.</p>
```

Here, we've specified a class of warning to both the h1 element and the p (paragraph) element. This gives us a hook on which we can hang styles that is independent of the element type. In CSS, class selectors are indicated by a class name preceded by a period (.); for example:

```
.warning {
  color: red;
  font-weight: bold;
}
```

This CSS will apply the styles noted in the declaration (a red, bold font) to all elements that have the class name warning. In our markup, both the h1 and the p elements would become red and bold. We can join an element selector with a class selector like this:

```
p.warning {
  color: red;
  font-weight: bold;
}
```

This rule will assign the red color and bold weight *only to paragraph elements* that have been assigned the class warning. It will not apply to other type elements, even if they have the warning class assigned. So, the h1 in our previous markup would be ignored by this style rule, and it would not become red and bold. You can use these rules in combination to save yourself some typing. Take a look at this block of CSS code. We've got two style rules, and each has several of the same declarations:

```
p.warning {
  color: red;
  font-weight: bold
  font-size: 11px;
  font-family: Arial;
}
h1.warning {
  color: red;
  font-weight: bold
  font-size: 24px;
  font-family: Arial;
}
```

A more efficient way to write this is

```
.warning {
  color: red;
  font-weight: bold;
  font-size: 11px;
  font-family: Arial;
}
h1.warning {
  font-size: 24px;
}
```

Class selectors can also be chained together to target elements that have multiple class names. For example:

```
<h1 class="warning">Be careful!</h1>
<p class="warning help">Every 108 minutes, the button ➡
must be pushed. Do not attempt to use the computer ➡
for anything other than pushing the button.</p>
<p class="help">The code is 4-8-15-16-23-42.</p
```

A .warning selector will target both the h1 and first p elements, since both have the class value warning. A .help selector will target both p elements (both have a class value of help). A chained selector such as .warning.help will select only the first paragraph, since it is the only element that has both classes (warning and help) assigned to it.

ID Selectors

ID selectors are similar to class selectors, but they are prefaced by a pound sign (#) instead of a period. So, to select this div element:

```
<div id="main-content">
  <p>This is the main content of the page.</p>
</div>
```

we would need a selector like this:

```
#main-content {
  width: 400px;
}
```

or this:

```
div#main-content {
  width: 400px;
}
```

Note You may ask yourself why you'd ever need to join an element selector with an ID selector, since IDs are valid only once in each (X)HTML document. The answer lies in the fact that a single style sheet can be used over many documents. So, while one document may have a div element with the ID of content, the next might have a paragraph with the same ID. By leaving off the element selector, you can select both of these elements. Alternatively, you can ensure that only one of them is selected by using the element selector in conjunction with your ID selector.

ID selectors cannot be chained together, since it is invalid to have more than one ID on a given element in (X)HTML. However, it is possible to chain class selectors and ID selectors, such as div#main-content.error.

(X)HTML's Family Tree

(X)HTML documents are hierarchical in nature. Nearly every element in your (X)HTML document is the child of another element. For example, head and body are children of the html element. A ul element will likely have children li elements.

Another way to describe the parent and child relationship is as *ancestor* and *descendant*. Although they may seem alike, there is a vital difference: an item's parent element is exactly one level up the family tree from it. While the parent is an ancestor, there are likely additional ancestors two or more levels above it. Consider the following (X)HTML code:

```
<body>
  <h1>This is a <em>really</em> important header</h1>
  <p>This is a <strong>basic</strong> paragraph</p>
</body>
```

The top-level element in this example is body. Below it, there is an h1 element, which has a child em element. The em is a descendant of body, but body is not its parent (h1 is its parent). The h1 element is both a child and a descendant of body, and it is the parent of em. Similarly, there is a paragraph element that has body as a parent and strong as a descendent. Therefore, the XHTML code can be represented using the element node tree seen in Figure 2-1.

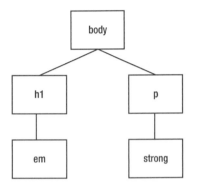

Figure 2-1. *An XHTML element node tree*

As you might have guessed, the reason for the quick family tree lesson is CSS's ability to piggyback on this inherent structure of (X)HTML.

Descendant Selectors

Descendant selectors, sometimes called *contextual selectors*, allow you to create style rules that are effective only when an element is the descendant of another one. Descendant selectors are indicated by a space between two elements. As an example, you may want to style only li elements that are descendants of ul lists (as opposed, say, to those who are part of ol lists). You'd do so like this:

```
ul li {
  color: blue;
}
```

This rule will make li text blue—but only when the li is contained within a ul element. So, in the following code, all li elements would be blue:

```
<ul>
  <li>Item one</li>
  <li>Item two</li>
  <li>Item three</li>
  <li>Item four has a nested list
    <ol>
      <li>Sub-item one</li>
      <li>Sub-item two</li>
    </ol>
  </li>
</ul>
```

Even though the nested list in item four is an ol element, the blue color will still be applied to its list items because they are the descendants of a ul.

Descendant selectors can be useful in targeting items deep in your (X)HTML structure, even when they don't have an ID or class assigned to them. By stringing together many elements, you can target strong elements inside cite elements inside blockquote elements inside div elements:

```
div blockquote cite strong {
  color: orange;
}
```

You can combine these with your class and ID selectors to get even more specific. Perhaps we want only li elements in ul elements with a class of ingredients inside our div with the id value recipes:

```
div#recipes ul.ingredients li {
  font-size 10px;
}
```

As you can imagine, descendant selectors are powerful, and it's no coincidence that descendant selectors are among the most-used types of CSS selectors.

Child Selectors

Child selectors are similar to descendant selectors, but they select only children rather than all ancestors. Child selectors are indicated by a greater-than sign (>).

■**Note** Microsoft Internet Explorer 6 and below does not support child selectors.

Consider our example markup from earlier:

```
<ul>
  <li>Item one</li>
  <li>Item two</li>
  <li>Item three</li>
  <li>Item four has a nested list
    <ol>
      <li>Sub-item one</li>
      <li>Sub-item two</li>
    </ol>
  </li>
</ul>
```

Whereas our descendant selector, ul li { color: blue; }, targeted all li elements in this example, a similar child selector would only select the first four li elements, as they are direct children of a ul element:

```
ul > li {
  color: blue
}
```

It would *not* target those li elements in item four's nested ol list.

Adjacent Sibling Selectors

Adjacent sibling selectors allow you to target an element that immediately follows—and that has the same parent as—another element.

■**Note** Microsoft Internet Explorer 6 and below does not support adjacent sibling selectors.

The concept of adjacent sibling selectors may sound a bit convoluted at first, but consider this example:

```
<body>
  <h1>This is a header</h1>
  <p>This is a paragraph.</p>
  <p>This is another paragraph.</p>
</body>
```

Paragraphs, by default, have a margin of 1 em above and below them. A common style effect is to remove the top margin of a paragraph when it is immediately after a header. The adjacent sibling selector, which is indicated by a plus sign (+), solves this problem for you:

```
h1 + p {
  margin-top: 0;
}
```

Although this is incredibly useful in theory, it's not so useful in the real world. Internet Explorer version 6 and older doesn't support this selector (Internet Explorer 7 does offer support for it, though). Including it in your styles doesn't hurt anything—IE will simply ignore it. But those visitors using IE won't see your adjacent sibling style rules, either.

This selector doesn't do a lot for you in the real world at the time of this writing, but it's still smart to be aware of it, as someday it will come in handy.

Attribute Selectors

While we're covering things that Internet Explorer doesn't support, let's talk about the humble *attribute selector*. This selector, which is indicated by square brackets ([ ]), allows you to target elements based on their attributes. You can select elements based on the presence of

- An attribute in an element

- An exact attribute value within an element

- A partial attribute value within an element (for example, as a part of a URL)

- A particular attribute name and value combination (or part thereof) in an element

In this section we will go into greater detail about these possibilities.

■**Note** Microsoft Internet Explorer 6 and below does not support attribute selectors.

Presence of an Attribute

Consider anchor tags as an example of how simple attribute selection works. They are used both for links and for anchors within the page. Perhaps you want to style the two differently? You could select based on the presence of the href attribute, right? For example:

```
a[href] {
  color: red;
}
```

will select all anchor (<a>) elements that have an href attribute. The code

```
a[href][title] {
  color: red;
}
```

will select all anchor elements that have both href and title attributes. You can also use the universal selector, *, to target all elements that have a particular attribute. The code

```
*[src]
```

will select any element with an src attribute, which may include img, embed, and others.

Exact Attribute Value

You can also select based on the value of an attribute. For example, you may want to have links to your homepage appear differently than the rest of the links on your site:

```
<a href="http://ourcompany.com/" title="Our homepage">Home</a>
```

You could accomplish this in either of two ways:

```
a[title="Our homepage"] {
  color: red;
}
a[href="http://ourcompany.com"] {
  color: red;
}
```

Using this format matches attribute values exactly. In order for selection to occur, the match must be exact, even including case.

Partial Attribute Values

For attributes that accept a space-separated list of words (notably, the class attribute), it is possible to select based on the presence of a word within the list, rather than the exact match earlier. Remember our multiple-class example:

```
<p class="warning help">Every 108 minutes, the button ➥
must be pushed. Do not attempt to use the computer ➥
for anything other than pushing the button.</p>
```

To select this paragraph with the exact match selector earlier, you'd need to write: p[class="warning help"]. Neither p[class="warning"] nor p[class="help"] would match. However, by using the tilde-equal (~=) indicator, you can select based on the presence of a word within the space-separated list, like so:

```
p[class~="help"] {
  color: red;
}
```

Note that this is functionally equivalent to the class selector (p.warning or p.help) we introduced earlier, and the class selector is far more widely supported. However, the partial attribute selector also works for attributes other than class.

Particular Attribute Selector

Perhaps better named the "equal to or starts with" attribute selector, the *partial attribute selector*—with its pipe-equal (|=) syntax—matches attribute values that either match exactly or begin with the given text. For example:

```
img[src|="vacation"] {
  float: left;
}
```

would target any image whose src value begins with vacation. It would match vacation/photo1.jpg and vacation1.jpg, but not /vacation/photo1.jpg.

Attribute selectors, like adjacent sibling selectors, would be more valuable if Internet Explorer 6 and lower supported them (again, they are supported in IE 7). Since it doesn't, many web developers are forced to admire them from afar.

Pseudo-Classes and Pseudo-Elements

And now for something completely different. OK, not completely—but close. Pseudo-class and pseudo-element selectors allow you to apply styles to elements that don't actually exist in your (X)HTML document. These are structures that you may have explicitly added to your (X)HTML document if you'd been able to predict them—but you can't. For example, it's often helpful to style the first line of a paragraph differently than the rest. But, given the vast array of devices, browsers, and screen sizes your site will be rendered on, there's simply no way to predict and define ahead of time what text encapsulates the first line.

Pseudo-Classes

Pseudo-classes are best understood by way of the anchor element, typically used for links between (X)HTML documents. It is commonplace for links to documents a user has visited in the past to be displayed differently than ones they haven't visited. But there's simply no way for you, as the web developer, to predefine this, because you haven't a clue what documents your visitor may have already hit.

To compensate for this, CSS 2.1 defines two pseudo-classes specifically for hyperlinks. Pseudo-classes are indicated by use of a colon (:). The two link-specific (with *link* defined as an anchor element with an `href` attribute) pseudo-classes are

- `:link`, which refers to links that point to documents that have not been visited. Some browsers interpret this incorrectly and apply it to all links, visited or not.

- `:visited`, which refers to hyperlinks to an address that has already been visited.

Using these pseudo-classes, you can make unvisited links blue and visited ones purple like so:

```
a:link {
  color: blue;
}
a:visited {
  color purple;
}
```

A couple of other common pseudo-classes are `:hover` and `:focus`. These are activated based on the current state an element is in with regard to the user's interaction with it. The hover state is activated when a user hovers on an element. Most typically, the hovering behavior is rolling over the element with a mouse. However, it's important to note that users on alternate devices may hover in a different manner. The focus state is activated when a user gives a particular element (especially a form field) focus by selecting it. In the typical desktop browser environment, this is done by tabbing to the element, or by clicking in a form field. Using these two pseudo-classes, you can easily change the display of an element only when these states are activated. For example:

```
a:hover {
  color: red;
}
tr:hover {
  background-color: #dfdfdf ;
}
input:focus {
  background-color: #dfdfdf ;
}
```

■**Note** Microsoft Internet Explorer 6 and below supports pseudo-classes only on links (anchor elements with an `href` attribute). It does not allow for `:hover`, `:focus`, and so forth on arbitrary elements.

There are a handful of other pseudo-classes, all of which are covered in detail in Appendix A of this book.

Pseudo-Elements

As mentioned earlier, it is sometimes useful to style the first line of a paragraph or first letter of a header. These are examples of pseudo-elements. These work in a fashion similar to pseudo-classes:

```
p:first-line {
  font-weight: bold;
}
h1:first-letter {
  font-size: 2em;
}
```

In addition to `first-line` and `first-letter`, CSS offers `:before` and `:after` pseudo-elements, which let you generate content to be displayed just before or just after a particular element. For example, you may want to insert a comma (,) after every `<li>` element. Pseudo-elements are a topic of their own (and aren't very well supported across browsers); we cover them in detail in Appendix A.

Daisy-Chaining Selectors

It's important to note that all types of selectors can be combined and chained together. For example, take this style rule:

```
#primary-content div {
  color: orange
}
```

This code would make for orange-colored text in any `div` elements that are inside the element with an `id` value of `primary-content`. This next rule is a bit more complex:

```
#primary-content div.story h1 {
  font-style: italic
}
```

This code would italicize the contents of any `h1` elements within `div`s with the `class` value `story` inside any elements with an `id` value of `primary-content`. Finally, let's look at an over-the-top example, to show you just how complicated selectors can get:

```
#primary-content div.story h1 + ul > li a[href|="http://ourcompany.com"] em {
  font-weight: bold;
}
```

This code would boldface all `em` elements contained in anchors whose `href` attribute begins with `http://ourcompany.com` and are descendants of an `li` element that is a child of a `ul` element that is an adjacent sibling of an `h1` element that is a descendant of a `div` with the `class` named `story` assigned to it inside any element with an `id` value of `primary-content`. Seriously. Read it again, and follow along, right to left.

Grouping Selectors

You can also group selectors together to avoid writing the same declaration block over and over again. For example, if all your headers are going to be bold and orange, you could do this:

```
h1 {
  color: orange; font-weight: bold;
}
h2 {
  color: orange; font-weight: bold;
}
h3 {
  color: orange; font-weight: bold;
}
h4 {
  color: orange; font-weight: bold;
}
h5 {
  color: orange; font-weight: bold;
}
h6 {
  color: orange; font-weight: bold;
}
```

Or, for more efficiency, you could comma-separate your selectors and attach them all to a single declaration block, like this:

```
h1, h2, h3, h4, h5, h6 {
  color: orange; font-weight: bold;
}
```

Obviously this is much more efficient to write, and easier to manage later, if you decide you want all your headers green instead of orange.

Summary

CSS selectors range from simple to complex, and can be incredibly powerful when you begin to understand them fully. The key to writing efficient CSS is taking advantage of the hierarchical structure of (X)HTML documents. This involves getting especially friendly with descendant selectors. If you never become comfortable with the more advanced selectors, you'll find you write the same style rules over and over again, and that you add way more classes and IDs to your markup than is really necessary.

Another key concept of CSS is that of specificity and the cascade. We'll cover that topic in our next chapter.

CHAPTER 3

■ ■ ■

Specificity and the Cascade

In the first two chapters, we reviewed the basics of writing proper (X)HTML and gave you a general overview of CSS. You learned how to attach style sheets to your documents, but now it's time to put on your work clothes, head to the garage, and rip apart the engine to find out exactly how the darn thing runs. In this chapter, we'll take a quick look at CSS selectors and then dive into the guts of *specificity* (determining which selector overrides another, and how to take advantage of this knowledge) and the cascade (the method used by browsers to calculate and assign importance to each rule in your style sheet).

CSS 2 AND IE/WIN

It's worth noting here that the most widely used browser on the planet as of this writing (IE 6) doesn't support some of the cooler selectors in the CSS 2.1 specification, which are used throughout this book. The situation improves with IE 7 (see Appendix C for more details; there are also numerous mentions of IE 7 support throughout this book—look to the index for specifics), but you're better off having the latest version of Firefox, Safari, or Opera available to view all the examples in this chapter. And don't worry, if you absolutely *must* provide a high level of support for IE/Win versions 6 and earlier, Chapter 6 provides the CSS therapy you crave.

Selectors

You already know what a selector is from reading Chapter 2, so rather than giving you a detailed description of every possible selector, we're going to provide an overview of selector types, and then move on to the examples.

Selectors: Simple and Combined

Officially, there are two categories of selectors: *simple* and *combined* (also known as *contextual*). The W3C (`www.w3.org/TR/CSS21/selector.html#q2`) provides a rather wordy description of a simple selector:

> *A simple selector is either a type selector or universal selector followed immediately by zero or more attribute selectors, ID selectors, or pseudo-classes, in any order. The simple selector matches if all of its components match.*

If your head hurts after reading even small portions of W3C recommendations, you're not alone. Let's make things easier by looking at some basic examples.

Simple Selectors

The following is easy enough, and probably familiar territory for you, but as you will see later on, even simple selectors can become complex under the right circumstances:

body {...} matches **\<body>...\</body>**.

h2.first {...} matches **\<h2 class="first">...\</h2>**.

div#logo {...} matches **\<div id="logo">...\</div>**.

a:visited {...} matches **\<a href="link.html">link\</a>** in its visited state.

The members of the W3C aren't prone to underachievement, so they follow the description of simple selectors with information about the creatively named "selectors" (many developers prefer combined or contextual):

A selector is a chain of one or more simple selectors separated by combinators. Combinators are: whitespace, ">", and "+". Whitespace may appear between a combinator and the simple selectors around it.

Once again, examples make the heart grow fonder.

Combined Selectors

As you can see, various combinations of simple or combined selectors and *combinators* target specific elements within your (X)HTML document:

body p {...} matches \<body>**\<p>text\</p>**\</body>.

h2.first > span {...} matches \<h2 class="first">**\text**\</h2>.

div#logo + h3 {...} matches \<div id="logo">\</div>**\<h3>text\</h3>**.

div > ul + p em {...} matches \<div>\<ul>\</ul>\<p>**\text**\</p>\</div>.

■**Note** Whitespace surrounding the *child* and *adjacent sibling* combinators (> and +) is optional, but keep in mind that removing the whitespace may make your selectors more difficult to read. The benefits of clarity can outweigh the minor optimization gained by removing the whitespace.

Now let's take a quick look at the specific types of selectors available (attribute and pseudo-class selectors are covered in detail in Chapter 2). If you are used to coding by hand using a text editor, and you know your selectors after reading Chapter 2, you can skip this part and head straight to the section titled "The Cascade: Calculating Specificity," later in this chapter. However, those of you who have been relying on visual development tools (such as

Adobe's Dreamweaver or GoLive products) and who wish to learn more about the nuts and bolts of CSS in order to free yourself from your programmatic shackles, read on.

■**Tip** Have you ever been reviewing someone else's style sheet and found yourself wondering what that strange, long selector actually does? Paste the selector into the SelectORacle (`http://gallery.theopalgroup.com/ selectoracle/`) and in return you'll receive a plain-text translation in English or Spanish.

Universal "Star" Selector

Something many developers are not aware of is the universal (or "star") selector, otherwise known as the asterisk (*). This selector will match any single element in your (X)HTML document.

■**Note** If you've been using CSS for a while and you've taken advantage of some of the IE/Win hacks on the Web, it's likely you've seen this selector before in the Star HTML hack, covered in Chapter 6. But that use is purely a side effect of a bug in the IE rendering engine, and this selector has practical uses beyond fooling IE/Win.

A popular technique that uses the universal selector is setting global, default styles at the beginning of your style sheet. To set margins and padding on all elements to zero (an approach used by many developers when starting a project to cut down on browser-rendering weirdness), simply use the following:

```
* {
  margin:0;
  padding:0;
}
```

This is certainly a handy trick to have up your sleeve. But what about some more creative uses? Well, the universal selector allows you to target all items within a certain element:

```
div#header * {...}
```

This code selects any element contained by `<div id="header">`. If you prefer, you can even target the *grandchildren* of a particular element:

```
div#header * p {...}
```

This will style any p (the *grandchild*) contained within any element (the *child*) that is contained by `<div id="header">` (the *parent*). This trick can be quite useful for targeting groups of elements that have only their level of ancestry in common. And because the universal selector can also be used more than once in a combined selector, its uses are fairly limitless. One great example of this is Eric Meyer's Universal Child Replacement technique, which you can read about at `www.meyerweb.com/eric/thoughts/2005/05/31/universal-child-replacement/`.

Element Selectors

If you've ever written even a single rule in a style sheet, you've used an *element selector* (listed as *type* selectors in the W3C spec, and sometimes called *tag* selectors), which simply describes any element name used as a selector. For example, h1, p, strong, ul, and div are all element selectors. It's probably safe to assume you don't need a specific example, so let's move along to the more interesting selectors.

Descendant, Child, and Adjacent Sibling Selectors

Specific levels of ancestry and the relationships between elements are the cornerstones of CSS. But when it comes to selectors, the family connection between elements can be strong. These selector types allow you to take advantage of those relationships, just like that aunt of yours who's always spreading rumors at family cookouts. Again, this stuff has been covered in Chapter 2 to a large extent, but we're giving you a recap here that will prove useful when we explain inheritance and the cascade.

Descendants

Perhaps the most common family relationship is the more generic *descendant* selector. These selectors consist of two or more elements separated by whitespace (which is *technically* a CSS combinator, according to the W3C). Descendants are any elements contained at any level below another element, like so:

```
div h2 {...}
```

This selector will style any h2 contained within any div. Any h2s just sitting within the body or any other container will not be styled by this rule.

Children

Again, as we saw in Chapter 2, the *child* selector consists of two or more elements separated by a greater-than character (>). The child selector allows you to cast a smaller net: only style elements that are descendants of another element without any other elements in between the parent and child. For instance, where the descendant selector targets *any* level beneath the specified parent element:

```
div h3 {...}
```

which will style any of these h3s:

```
<div>
  <h3>Heading</h3>
</div>

<div>
  <ul>
    <li>
      <h3>Heading</h3>
    </li>
  </ul>
</div>
```

the child selector is much more particular about its lineage:

```
div > h3 {...}
```

and will only target h3s that are *children* (the first descendant of their parent), like so:

```
<div>
  <h3>Heading</h3>
</div>
```

Siblings

The *adjacent sibling* selector type works similarly to the child selector, but instead of targeting a direct descendant, it allows you to style elements that are next to each other in the document flow and that share the same parent element by joining two simple selectors with a plus sign (+).

This type comes in quite handy when, for example, you need to give the first p immediately following an h2 a smaller margin than all other paragraphs:

```
<h2>Heading</h2>
<p>some text</p>
<p>some more text</p>
```

Without the adjacent sibling selector, you would have to assign a class or ID to the first paragraph, but thankfully this selector does the job for us:

```
h2 + p { margin-top: .25em; }
```

Pseudo-Class Selectors

Although both Chapter 2 and Appendix A contain details on pseudo-classes, there's one aspect worth mentioning here that deals with specificity—ordering link rules within your style sheet.

Link and Dynamic Pseudo-Classes: A LoVe/HAte Relationship

Styling links is fairly straightforward, but it's helpful to know the correct order to place the various pseudo-classes within your style sheet in order to see the correct behavior in the browser. The correct order is :link, :visited, :hover, and :active (or LoVe/HAte), like so:

```
a:link {
  color:blue;
}
a:visited {
  color:purple;
}
a:hover {
  background-color:black;color:white;text-decoration:none;
}
a:active {
  background-color:red;color:white;text-decoration:none;
}
```

Using this order ensures that your :hover styles will work whether a link has been visited or not, and that your :active styles will be used even when a user is hovering over a link.

For more on link specificity, check out Eric Meyer's write-up on the subject (which also includes some great points about calculating specificity in general): www.meyerweb.com/eric/css/link-specificity.html.

Pseudo-Elements

In what is one of the shortest (but still confusing) descriptions in the CSS specification, the W3C has this to say about *pseudo-elements* (www.w3.org/TR/CSS21/selector.html#pseudo-elements):

> *Pseudo-elements create abstractions about the document tree beyond those specified by the document language.*

Well, now, that sums it up nicely, don't you think?

Pseudo-elements can be powerful weapons in your CSS arsenal, and include the following four gems:

- :first-line

- :first-letter

- :before

- :after

Their use is similar to that of pseudo-classes; however, pseudo-elements may only be attached to the last simple selector in a combined selector (the element is targeted by the selector, referred to by the W3C as the "subject").

■**Caution** The :first-line and :first-letter pseudo-elements are supported by IE 6 (:before and :after are still not supported by *any* version of IE/Win including IE 7 as of this writing), but there are some pitfalls. For an up-to-date list (including IE 7 issues), visit Ingo Chao's site at www.satzansatz.de/cssd/pseudocss.html.

:first-line

As you might guess, the :first-line pseudo-element targets the first line of the element to which it is attached, and that element must be defined or styled as block-level, inline-block, table-caption, or table-cell. There is also a restricted list of properties that may be used:

- font properties

- color

- background properties

- word-spacing

- letter-spacing

- text-decoration

- vertical-align

- text-transform

- line-height

These properties can be useful when you're styling opening paragraphs—for instance, the code

```
p:first-line {
   text-transform:uppercase;
}
```

makes the first formatted line (meaning the first line as it is rendered by the browser, based on the layout, font size, and other variables, rather than how the line breaks in your markup) all uppercase. Simple, yes?

In addition, the :first-line pseudo-element is intelligent and will style the text of an element nested within the target element, as long as both are block-level and the nested element is not positioned or floated. For example, this means that the following rule:

```
div:first-line { font-weight:bold; }
```

will style the text within this markup, even though the p element isn't targeted:

```
<div><p>Some line of text</p></div>
```

Since the text is still the first line, it matches the selector.

:first-letter

Similar to the :first-line pseudo-element, :first-letter selects the first alphanumeric character of the targeted element, as long as there is no other content (such as an image) preceding it. The target element must also be defined or styled as block-level, inline-block, list-item, table-caption, or table-cell.

The main purpose of this pseudo-element is to allow you to style drop caps and initial caps; as with :first-line, there is also a restricted set of properties that you can use:

- font-properties

- text-decoration

- text-transform

- letter-spacing

- word-spacing

- line-height

- float

- vertical-align (when not floated)

- margin properties

- padding properties

- border properties

- color

- background properties

Let's say we want to create a two-line *drop cap* for the following paragraph:

```
<p>Gorillas don't always eat bananas, all cows eat grass, good boys do fine➥
always, and fat cops get donuts after every bust.</p>
```

To style the paragraph and the G accordingly, all we need is this:

```
p {
  font-size:100%;
}

p:first-letter {
  font-size:300%;
  font-weight:bold;
  float:left;
}
```

This gives us the result shown in Figure 3-1.

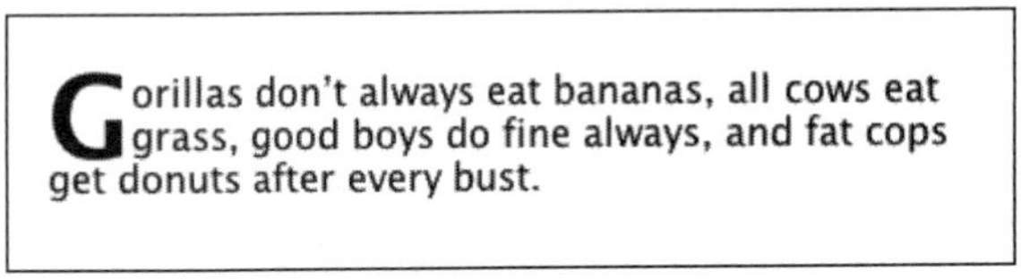

Figure 3-1. *Our drop cap, as rendered by Firefox*

If we decide we'd rather style the G as a larger *initial cap*, we only have to adjust the p:first-letter rule by removing the float declaration and increasing the font-size (as seen in Figure 3-2):

```
p:first-letter {
  font-size:400%;
  font-weight:bold;
}
```

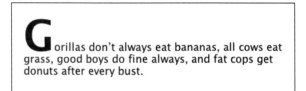

Figure 3-2. *Our initial cap displayed in Firefox*

It's worth noting that Safari does some strange things with our very straightforward examples (see Figure 3-3); your mileage may vary when using this pseudo-element, so remember to test and adjust the font-size as needed.

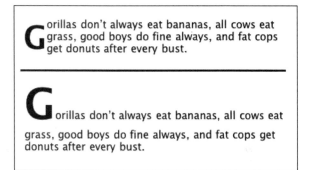

Figure 3-3. *Surfin' Safari, Batman! Browsers interpret the specifications differently, so you may have to try different font sizes and line heights in order to get the same result.*

:before and :after

These final pseudo-elements, :before and :after, allow you to insert generated content *before* or *after* the element they are attached to, as opposed to simply altering the display of the element's content. The content property is the key to their success.

Let's start with a simple example using both :before and :after. Say you want to enclose all paragraphs assigned class="note" within square brackets, in addition to changing the text size and color, but you want to keep the brackets out of your markup. First, we add the class to our paragraph:

```
<p class="note">Gorillas don't always eat bananas, all cows eat grass, good➡
boys do fine always, and fat cops get donuts after every bust.</p>
```

Next, we add styles for the .note class (to set the font-size and color properties), then the pseudo-element rules to generate our square brackets:

```
p {
  font-size:85%;
  color:#666;
}
```

```
p.note:before {
  content:"[";
}

p.note:after {
  content:"]";
}
```

The result (Figure 3-4) is a smaller, lighter, bracketed block of text, without those silly brackets sitting in our markup. The content property simply contains the character(s) we want to display *before* and *after* the p element. The sky is essentially the limit for what can be generated (to explore the possibilities, check out the W3C's reference on generated content: www.w3.org/TR/CSS21/generate.html).

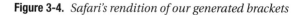
[Gorillas don't always eat bananas, all cows eat grass, good
boys do fine always, and fat cops get donuts after every bust.]

Figure 3-4. *Safari's rendition of our generated brackets*

One popular (and more complex) use of the :after pseudo-element is to display the URI for all external links when a page is printed, following the actual link text. This can be accomplished by placing the following rule (which combines the :after pseudo-element with an attribute selector) in your print style sheet:

```
a[href^='http://']:after {
  content:" [" attr(href) "]";font-size:90%;
}
```

In cooperation with the attribute selector, this rule tells the browser, "If the href attribute of an a element includes http://, place the content of the href attribute after the a element and reduce its font size to 90 percent." This selector shows how combining different selectors gives you a greater amount of control while keeping your markup uncluttered.

The :before pseudo-element works the same way, but inserts the generated content *before* the attached element. This can come in handy when, for instance, you want to display an alternate character (in this example, a right arrow, →) instead of the default bullets on unordered list items (Figure 3-5):

```
ul li {
  list-style:none;margin:0;text-indent:-1em;
}
ul li:before {
  content:"\2192 \0020";
}
```

The first rule disables the default bullets, and then we assign our generated version. The content property requires escaped hex equivalents for special characters like this, so we use \2192 to generate the right arrow (\0020 inserts a space). For a complete list of ASCII codes, check out www.ascii.cl.

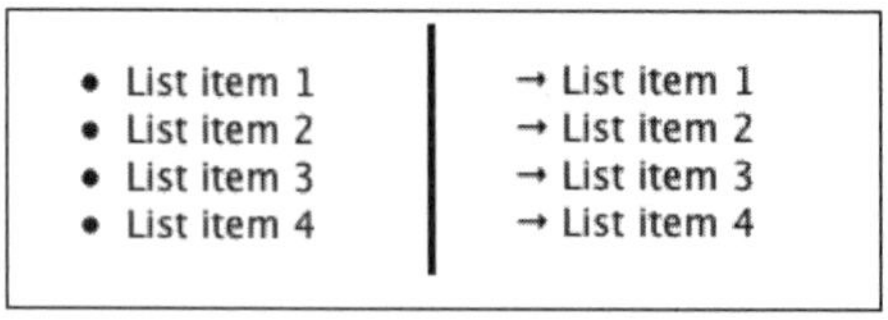

- • List item 1   → List item 1
- • List item 2   → List item 2
- • List item 3   → List item 3
- • List item 4   → List item 4

Figure 3-5. *On the left, Safari's default list rendering; on the right, our generated replacement*

The Cascade: Calculating Specificity

Now that we're all on the same page regarding selectors, let's explore the laws of specificity and the cascade. Basically, in CSS every rule is assigned a specificity value based on the composition of its selector, its location within a style sheet, and the location of that style sheet relative to other style sheets. *Specificity* is how rules interact with each other, and which rules have more importance than others (and therefore, override them). In other words, specificity is what helps the browser determine whether p#description carries more weight than p.description, or if a rule with the selector ul#nav li a:hover should override another rule with ul li a:hover. Understanding how this works is key to mastering CSS.

There is a fairly straightforward system that governs the order of priority of one selector over another, but the trick is understanding the way the browsers assign importance to selectors—and that's what we're going to discuss next.

How the CSS 2.1 Specification Describes the Cascade

The key to comprehending the cascade lies (almost surprisingly) within the actual W3C specification (www.w3.org/TR/CSS21/cascade.html#cascading-order). The description of the cascading order is perhaps the most clearly written part of the entire specification, which is good news for us all, since it might otherwise be quite difficult to understand:

6.4.1 Cascading order

To find the value for an element/property combination, user agents must apply the following sorting order:

1. Find all declarations that apply to the element and property in question, for the target media type. Declarations apply if the associated selector matches the element in question.

2. Sort according to importance (normal or important) and origin (author, user, or user agent). In ascending order of precedence:

    1. user agent declarations — browser

    2. user normal declarations

    3. author normal declarations

    4. author important declarations

    5. user important declarations

3. Sort rules with the same importance and origin by specificity of selector: more specific selectors will override more general ones. Pseudo-elements and pseudo-classes are counted as normal elements and classes, respectively.

4. Finally, sort by order specified: if two declarations have the same weight, origin and specificity, the latter specified wins. Declarations in imported style sheets are considered to be before any declarations in the style sheet itself.

Translating the Spec

While the W3C's cascading order is fairly straightforward, let's further simplify their list, translating item by item (our numbers coincide with the quoted specification):

1. Find the matching target element(s), and apply the styles.

2. The browser (or user agent) should apply its own default styles first, then apply rules from a user-specified style sheet (if one exists), followed by author style sheets (applying !important declarations last), and finally !important rules from a user-specified style sheet (again, if it exists).

3. Rules with more specific selectors override less specific selectors (the part about pseudo-elements and pseudo-classes applies to Table 3-1 later in this chapter).

4. If two or more selectors match the same target element and have the exact same score, whichever comes later in the style sheet gets the girl (or guy), and any rules within style sheets imported into *other* style sheets are sorted earlier.

@IMPORT AND THE CASCADE

The @import rule exists to allow users to import style sheets from within other style sheets. Although this rule is widely used to hide style sheets from older browsers (see Chapter 6), it can also be used to help manage multiple CSS files (as noted in Chapter 5). Because the Cascade assigns a lower importance to rules within imported style sheets, it's worth understanding how it will affect your styles should you use @import in your projects.

For example, let's say you have a default style sheet (base.css) that imports a second style sheet for your typography. The following @import statement would be located at the top of your default style sheet, prior to any rules:

```
@import url("typography.css");
```

If within typography.css you have a rule setting the font-size for all h3 elements to 12px, but if somewhere in base.css you happen to have a rule targeting h3s and assigning them font-size:14px; the latter rule will override the rule set in your imported typography style sheet.

The cascade assigns importance to rules within imported style sheets based on the order they are imported (style sheets imported earlier have lower importance)—something to be aware of if you import multiple style sheets (or if you import style sheets recursively).

Keeping Score

The specificity of a rule is based on a "score" assigned to each part of its selector. This score is in turn based on the importance of each *type* of selector (see Chapter 2 or the beginning of this chapter for selector types), in the following order, from least important to most important:

1. Element selectors (including pseudo-element selectors)

2. Class selectors (including attribute and pseudo-class selectors)

3. ID selectors

4. Inline styles

Dizzy yet? Don't worry, it gets easier, and we'll take it slow. It's less difficult to understand how browsers calculate specificity when you can see the results, so let's step through a few basic examples showing progressively more specific rules (a commented version can be found in ch3_specificity_basic.html in the Source Code/Download section for this book at the Apress web site), and then we'll compare the specificity and score of each selector side by side.

A Series of Basic Examples

Our guinea pigs for this process will be a pair of poor, unassuming h1 and p elements:

```
<h1>Page Title</h1>
<p>Lorem ipsum dolor sit amet, consectetur adipisicing elit, sed do eiusmod➡
tempor incididunt ut labore et dolore magna aliqua.</p>
```

Figure 3-6 shows the standard but boring result with Safari's default styles.

Page Title

Lorem ipsum dolor sit amet, consectetur adipisicing elit, sed do eiusmod
tempor incididunt ut labore et dolore magna aliqua.

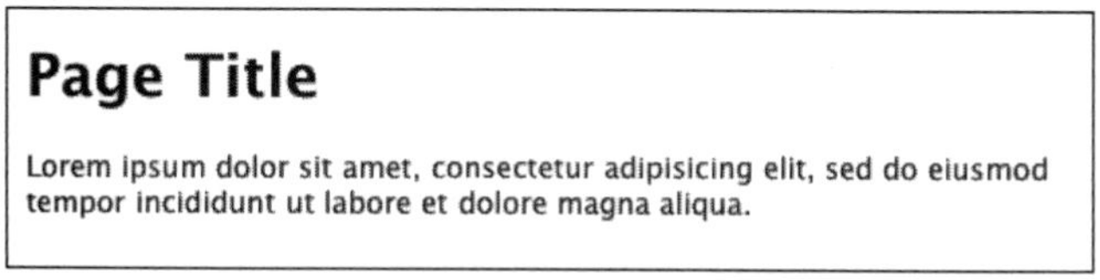

Figure 3-6. h1 *and* p *using Safari's default styles*

Let's start with some basic styles, using element selectors to assign colors to our text:

```
h1 {
  color:#000;
}
p {
  color:#000;
}
```

We've now styled our elements using the selectors with the lowest specificity—element selectors—which also means they cast the widest net; any h1 or p elements in our markup will use these styles. Figure 3-7 shows the result, which doesn't look any different from the default rendering because we've used the same color as the browser default.

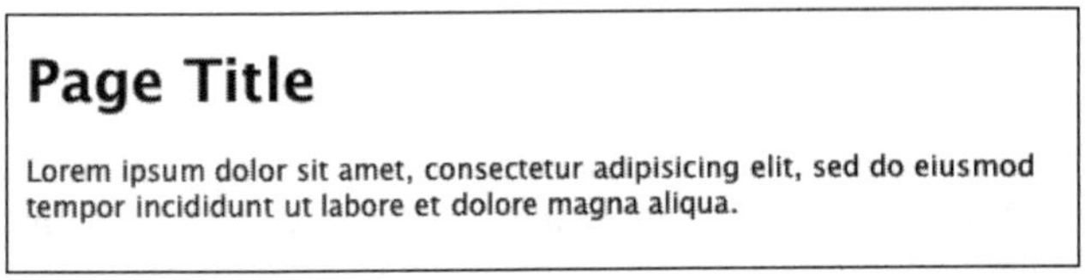

Page Title

Lorem ipsum dolor sit amet, consectetur adipisicing elit, sed do eiusmod
tempor incididunt ut labore et dolore magna aliqua.

Figure 3-7. *Our example styled with element selectors*

Next, let's duplicate our guinea pigs and wrap them in a div, allowing us to use a more
specific selector to style only the new pair (without the added rule in the CSS, the second set
of elements would look the same as the first). Our document and style sheet now contain the
following (the addition is shown in bold):

Markup

```
<h1>Page Title</h1>
<p>Lorem ipsum dolor sit amet, consectetur adipisicing elit, sed do eiusmod➥
tempor incididunt ut labore et dolore magna aliqua.</p>

<div>
  <h1>Page Title</h1>
  <p>Lorem ipsum dolor sit amet, consectetur adipisicing elit, sed do eiusmod➥
  tempor incididunt ut labore et dolore magna aliqua.</p>
</div>
```

CSS

```
h1 {
  color:#000;
}
p {
  color:#000;
}
div h1 {
  color:#333;
}
div p {
  color:#333;
}
```

The new selectors are more specific, and thus apply only to the second set in our markup
(Figure 3-8).

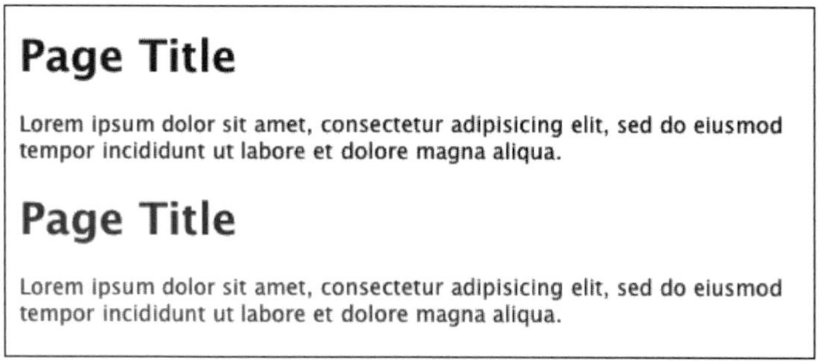

> **Page Title**
>
> Lorem ipsum dolor sit amet, consectetur adipisicing elit, sed do eiusmod
> tempor incididunt ut labore et dolore magna aliqua.
>
> **Page Title**
>
> Lorem ipsum dolor sit amet, consectetur adipisicing elit, sed do eiusmod
> tempor incididunt ut labore et dolore magna aliqua.

Figure 3-8. *The more specific selector only affects the tags wrapped in a* div.

Now let's create a third instance of our h1 and p, this time assigning a class to the div and adding a new, more specific rule to our CSS. Even though our third pair is contained within a div, the addition of a class to the selector increases its specificity.

Markup

```
<h1>Page Title</h1>
<p>Lorem ipsum dolor sit amet, consectetur adipisicing elit, sed do eiusmod➥
tempor incididunt ut labore et dolore magna aliqua.</p>

<div>
  <h1>Page Title</h1>
  <p>Lorem ipsum dolor sit amet, consectetur adipisicing elit, sed do eiusmod➥
  tempor incididunt ut labore et dolore magna aliqua.</p>
</div>

<div class="module">
  <h1>Page Title</h1>
  <p>Lorem ipsum dolor sit amet, consectetur adipisicing elit, sed do eiusmod➥
  tempor incididunt ut labore et dolore magna aliqua.</p>
</div>
```

CSS

```
h1 {
  color:#000;
}
p {
  color:#000;
}
div h1 {
  color:#333;
}
div p {
  color:#333;
}
```

```
div.module h1 {
  color:#666;
}
div.module p {
color:#666;
}
```

Our newest page output is shown in Figure 3-9.

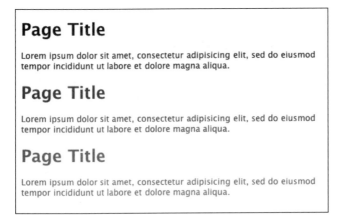

Figure 3-9. *Our new selector only targets the* `<div class="module">`, *ignoring the others.*

For our fourth pair, let's add an ID to the div, and another set of rules with more specific selectors to our style sheet. Even though the class remains on the div, the new selectors are more specific due to the ID (which is more important than elements and classes, as noted at the beginning of this example), and thus override the other rules (see Figure 3-10):

Markup

```
<h1>Page Title</h1>
<p>Lorem ipsum dolor sit amet, consectetur adipisicing elit, sed do eiusmod➡
tempor incididunt ut labore et dolore magna aliqua.</p>

<div>
  <h1>Page Title</h1>
  <p>Lorem ipsum dolor sit amet, consectetur adipisicing elit, sed do eiusmod➡
  tempor incididunt ut labore et dolore magna aliqua.</p>
</div>

<div class="module">
  <h1>Page Title</h1>
  <p>Lorem ipsum dolor sit amet, consectetur adipisicing elit, sed do eiusmod➡
  tempor incididunt ut labore et dolore magna aliqua.</p>
</div>
```

```
<div id="content" class="module">
  <h1>Page Title</h1>
  <p>Lorem ipsum dolor sit amet, consectetur adipisicing elit, sed do eiusmod➥
  tempor incididunt ut labore et dolore magna aliqua.</p>
</div>
```

CSS

```
h1 {
  color:#000;
}
p {
  color:#000;
}
div h1 {
  color:#333;
}
div p {
  color:#333;
}
div.module h1 {
  color:#666;
}
div.module p {
  color:#666;
}
div#content h1 {
  color:#999;
}
div#content p {
  color:#999;
}
```

■Note A little specificity can go a long way: while `div#content` and `#content` may target the exact same element in the markup, a rule with `div#content` is more specific, and will override any rule using just `#content` (without the preceding `div`). This applies to IDs (as in this example), classes, attribute selectors, pseudo-classes, and pseudo-elements.

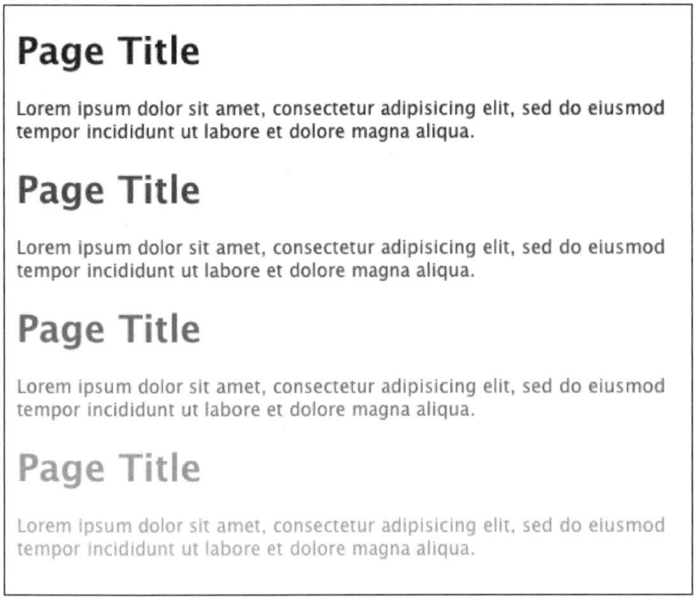

Page Title

Lorem ipsum dolor sit amet, consectetur adipisicing elit, sed do eiusmod tempor incididunt ut labore et dolore magna aliqua.

Page Title

Lorem ipsum dolor sit amet, consectetur adipisicing elit, sed do eiusmod tempor incididunt ut labore et dolore magna aliqua.

Page Title

Lorem ipsum dolor sit amet, consectetur adipisicing elit, sed do eiusmod tempor incididunt ut labore et dolore magna aliqua.

Page Title

Lorem ipsum dolor sit amet, consectetur adipisicing elit, sed do eiusmod tempor incididunt ut labore et dolore magna aliqua.

Figure 3-10. *The ID selectors override the previous three.*

Our fifth pair demonstrates the power of inline styles. By adding `style="color:#ccc;"` directly to the opening `<h1>` and `<p>` tags, we override all the styles set in the style sheet (the style sheet does not change from the previous example, only the markup). Inline styles are given more importance by the browsers than any of the selectors in the style sheet, and therefore override even the ID selector.

Markup

```
<h1>Page Title</h1>
<p>Lorem ipsum dolor sit amet, consectetur adipisicing elit, sed do eiusmod➥
tempor incididunt ut labore et dolore magna aliqua.</p>

<div>
  <h1>Page Title</h1>
  <p>Lorem ipsum dolor sit amet, consectetur adipisicing elit, sed do eiusmod➥
  tempor incididunt ut labore et dolore magna aliqua.</p>
</div>

<div class="module">
  <h1>Page Title</h1>
  <p>Lorem ipsum dolor sit amet, consectetur adipisicing elit, sed do eiusmod➥
  tempor incididunt ut labore et dolore magna aliqua.</p>
</div>

<div id="content" class="module">
  <h1>Page Title</h1>
```

```
<p>Lorem ipsum dolor sit amet, consectetur adipisicing elit, sed do eiusmod➡
tempor incididunt ut labore et dolore magna aliqua.</p>
</div>

<div id="content" class="module">
  <h1 style="color:#ccc;">Page Title</h1>
  <p style="color:#ccc;">Lorem ipsum dolor sit amet, consectetur adipisicing➡
  elit, sed do eiusmod tempor incididunt ut labore et dolore magna aliqua.</p>
</div>
```

The result is shown in Figure 3-11.

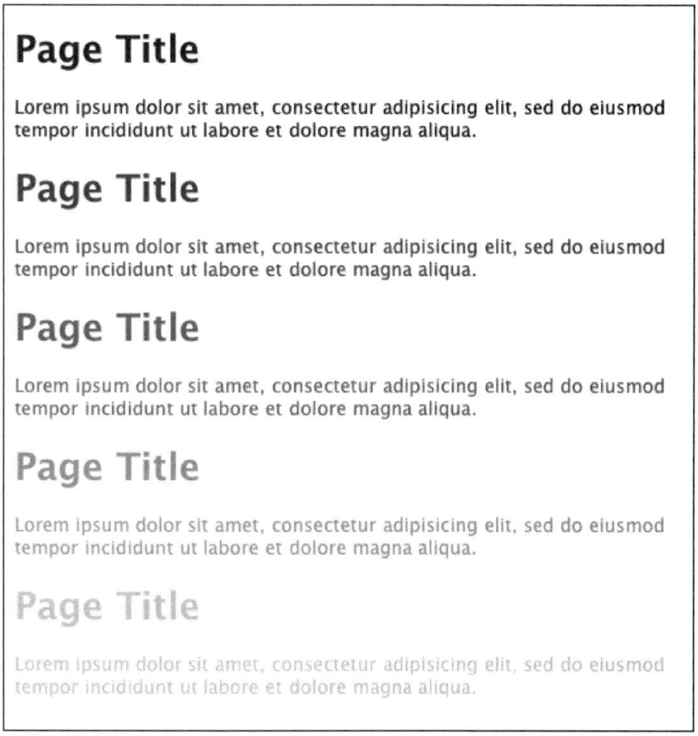

Page Title

Lorem ipsum dolor sit amet, consectetur adipisicing elit, sed do eiusmod
tempor incididunt ut labore et dolore magna aliqua.

Page Title

Lorem ipsum dolor sit amet, consectetur adipisicing elit, sed do eiusmod
tempor incididunt ut labore et dolore magna aliqua.

Page Title

Lorem ipsum dolor sit amet, consectetur adipisicing elit, sed do eiusmod
tempor incididunt ut labore et dolore magna aliqua.

Page Title

Lorem ipsum dolor sit amet, consectetur adipisicing elit, sed do eiusmod
tempor incididunt ut labore et dolore magna aliqua.

Page Title

Lorem ipsum dolor sit amet, consectetur adipisicing elit, sed do eiusmod
tempor incididunt ut labore et dolore magna aliqua.

Figure 3-11. *Inline styles override all rules in the style sheet.*

Finally, the !important declaration has the power to override everything used in our example style sheet, even when used within the original element selectors. So, using the same markup, let's make one small change at the top of our style sheet.

CSS

```
h1 {
  color:#ccc !important;
}
p {
```

```
  color:#ccc !important;
}
div h1 {
  color:#333;
}
div p {
  color:#333;
}
div.module h1 {
  color:#666;
}
div.module p {
  color:#666;
}
div#content h1 {
  color:#999;
}
div#content p {
  color:#999;
}
```

With the addition of !important, what was once the *least* important rule in the style sheet is now the *most* important (see Figure 3-12).

Figure 3-12. *The* !important *declaration struts its stuff.*

Understanding the Scoring

Now that you've witnessed the effects of specificity firsthand, let's examine the parts that make up the specificity score for each of the selectors used in our examples (see Table 3-1, adapted from http://molly.com/2005/10/06/css2-and-css21-specificity-clarified/).

Table 3-1. *Calculating Selector Specificity*

Selector	Inline Style	# of ID Selectors	# of Class Selectors	# of Element Selectors
h1	0,	0,	0,	1
p	0,	0,	0,	1
div h1	0,	0,	0,	2
div p	0,	0,	0,	2
div.module h1	0,	0,	1,	2
div.module p	0,	0,	1,	2
div#content h1	0,	1,	0,	2
div#content p	0,	1,	0,	2

The selectors in Table 3-1 are listed in order from lowest specificity to highest, top to bottom. The score is the total number of a given selector type within each combined selector.

Note When calculating specificity, remember that attribute selectors and pseudo-classes are counted as classes, and pseudo-elements are calculated as elements.

It's important to think of these scores in columns; thus, commas should be used to separate the individual scores when writing them out inline (as opposed to the tabular form above) rather than combining the numbers into base-10 (e.g., "11" or "111"), because it's possible (although unlikely) to have more than nine matches in a given column (e.g., 0,0,1,12). Using comma-delimited notation to keep score will help reduce any possible confusion (and when it comes to specificity, there's lots of confusion to be had—beware of the many resources available on the Web that describe specificity using base-10, for their authors are living reckless and dangerous lives). For a downright fun example, check out Malarkey's (Andy Clarke) Star Wars specificity chart (www.stuffandnonsense.co.uk/archives/css_specificity_wars.html).

Note The universal selector (*) has a value of 0 when used within a combined selector (such as #content * p, which targets any <p> elements that are grandchildren of #content), or a score of 0, 0, 0, 0 when used on its own. Basically, its use doesn't affect the score one bit.

How the Cascade, Inline Styles, and !important Affect Our Scoring

When browsers calculate specificity, the selector with the highest score takes precedence, no matter where in the style sheet that selector is located.

However, there are three exceptions to this pattern:

- When two or more selectors of the same specificity match the same target element

- If inline styles are applied to an element targeted by selectors within a style sheet

- If the !important declaration is used

Matching Selectors

When two or more selectors of the same specificity match the same target element, the last matching selector takes precedence. This behavior is due to the rules of the cascade, covered earlier in this chapter. Let's use the following markup as an example:

```
<div id="main">
  <div id="content">
    <p class="note">This paragraph has class.<p>
  </div>
</div>
```

Although the following two selectors both match the same target (`<p class="note">`), only the last rule will be applied:

```
#content p.note {
  font-size:small;
}
#main p.note {
  font-size:x-small;
}
```

Inline Styles

Inline styles (styles applied directly to an element using the style attribute) are the reason for the first column in our scoring table: an inline style overrides *any selector* that matches that specific element (with the exception of !important declarations, covered in a moment). Let's say we have a fairly specific selector in our style sheet to change the color of text within an li when it is assigned class="current":

```
#wrapper div#content ul#subnav li.current {
  color:red;
}
```

Normally, this would color any `<li class="current">` red. However, in our markup, there exists an inline style:

```
<div id="wrapper">
  <div id="content">
```

```
  <ul id="subnav">
    <li class="current" style="color:blue;">Current subsection</li>
  </ul>
</div>
</div>
```

Because the inline style on the li (our target element) is more important than the selector in our style sheet, the inline style wins and the list item text will be blue.

!important

This is the ultimate heavyweight: an !important declaration within a rule will override that same property within *any other rule of equal or higher specificity* (as demonstrated earlier in this chapter), with the exception of another !important declaration within a rule of higher specificity anywhere in the style sheet, or equal specificity later in the style sheet. You should generally leave such rules out of your style sheets, since they are intended to offer more control to users (allowing users to override author styles within a user style sheet), but it's useful to understand how they work. Here's a quick example:

```
p {
  color:red !important;
}
p {
  color:blue;font-size:90%;
}
```

Both selectors have the same specificity, so normally the second rule would win based on the rules of the cascade (as the last matching rule), but since the first rule includes !important in the color declaration, the paragraph will be red instead of blue. However, font-size will still be 90%, since that declaration is not being overridden.

Tip Although the !important declaration's intended use is allowing users to override styles set by a site's author, it's an incredibly useful tool for debugging styles when they are being difficult. Think of it as sending a misbehaving property in your style sheet to its room to contemplate what it's done.

Real-World Examples

But aside from all these crazy calculations and talk of base-10 and comma delimiters, how does knowing all this help us in real projects? Thankfully, it isn't all theoretical nonsense, so let's consider some practical examples.

Navigation Menu Hover Effect

Let's start with a basic (in terms of specificity usage) but real-world example. On his personal web site (http://superfluousbanter.org), one of the authors, Dan Rubin, wanted to create some nifty effects for his sidebar's navigation items. His goal was to mimic a transparency effect and at the same time reveal a hidden text element, along with changing the colors, all on :hover (see Figure 3-13).

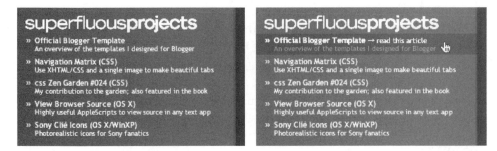

Figure 3-13. *Simulating transparency and changing visibility on* :hover

Let's start with the (X)HTML for the Projects links (for reference, this snippet is contained within <div id="sidebar">). We've simplified some of the URLs for this example:

```
<h4>superfluous projects</h4>
<ul>
  <li>
    <a href="/archives/2004/05/">Official Blogger Template
      <span>&rarr; read this article</span>
      <em>An overview of the templates I designed for Blogger</em>
    </a>
  </li>
  <li>
    <a href="/archives/2004/05/">Navigation Matrix (CSS)
      <span>&rarr; read this article</span>
      <em>Use XHTML/CSS and a single image to make beautiful tabs</em>
    </a>
  </li>
  <li>
    <a href="http://www.csszengarden.com/024/">css Zen Garden #024 (CSS)
      <span>&rarr; visit this site</span>
      <em>My contribution to the garden; also featured in the book</em>
    </a>
  </li>
  <li>
    <a href="http://webgraph.com/resources/">View Browser Source (OS X)
      <span>&rarr; visit this site</span>
      <em>Highly useful AppleScripts to view source in any text app</em>
    </a>
  </li>
  <li>
    <a href="http://webgraph.com/icons/">Sony Cli&eacute; Icons (OS X/WinXP)
      <span>&rarr; visit this site</span>
      <em>Photorealistic icons for Sony fanatics</em>
    </a>
  </li>
</ul>
```

As you can see, the base markup is simply an unordered list (ul) with list items (li), each containing a (the link), span (the text only visible on :hover), and em (the link description). No IDs, no classes—just the bare markup and content.

The CSS uses the enclosing <div id="sidebar"> to target the elements in the list, since Dan has more than one ul in his sidebar (one list for each category of link). This way, he doesn't have to assign specific IDs or classes to the uls or enclose them within more specific wrapper divs. The aim is to get your documents as lean as possible when it comes to IDs and classes, rather than littering your document with unnecessary markup.

```css
#sidebar ul {
  list-style:none;
  margin:0 0 12px;
  padding:0;
  font-size:11px;
}

#sidebar ul a {
  display:block;
  background:url(../i/icon_bullet_sidebar.gif) no-repeat 12px 7px;
  padding:3px 0 3px 25px;
  color:#cb5100;
  font-weight:bold;
  text-decoration:none;
}
#sidebar ul a span {
  color:#333;
  font-size:10px;
  font-style:normal;
  font-weight:normal;
}
#sidebar ul a em {
  display:block;
  color:#808080;
  font-size:10px;
  font-style:normal;
  font-weight:normal;
}
#sidebar ul a:hover {
  background-color:#262626;
  background-image:url(../i/icon_bullet_sidebar_hover.gif);
  color:#6cf;
  border-right:3px solid #221C18;
}
#sidebar ul a:hover span { color:#fc3; }
#sidebar ul a:hover em { color:#4d4d4d; }
```

The selectors needed to create our effects are those targeting a, span, and em. Let's look at each part of the effect, and then compare the specificity of the selectors used.

span

First, we set `visibility:hidden;` for the span, effectively making the text invisible to the user. We chose this approach rather than using `display:none;` to avoid strange positioning issues that might arise on `:hover`, since the text is already being rendered by the browser rather than replacing empty space. By simply switching to `visibility:visible;` on `:hover`, we ensure that the text will seem to magically appear to the user; the `:hover` pseudo-class counts as a class selector in the specificity calculation, giving the second span selector a higher score than the first selector and thus allowing us to override the visibility of the text (see Table 3-2).

Table 3-2. *Specificity Effect: Span Visibility*

Selector	Inline Style	# of ID Selectors	# of Class Selectors	# of Element Selectors
`#sidebar ul a span`	0,	1,	0,	3
`#sidebar ul a:hover span`	0,	1,	1,	3

a and em

Finally, our effect relies on changing the a and em styles to mimic transparency using colors to achieve the desired result:

- On `:hover`, we set the background-color of a to a slightly darker gray than the sidebar background, but it still sits beneath our em text.

- To get our transparent look, we change the color of the text contained within the em elements, also to a darker gray (from #808080 to #4d4d4d).

In the end result, it appears as if the background of the link area is transparent and sitting closer to the viewer than the description text (em). Once again, this works because the first selectors for a and em have lower specificity scores than the `:hover` selectors (see Table 3-3).

Table 3-3. *Specificity Effect: Faking Transparency*

Selector	Inline Style	# of ID Selectors	# of Class Selectors	# of Element Selectors
`#sidebar ul a`	0,	1,	0,	2
`#sidebar ul a em`	0,	1,	0,	3
`#sidebar ul a:hover`	0,	1,	1,	2
`#sidebar ul a:hover em`	0,	1,	1,	3

Styling Links in a Footer

A common requirement in many site designs is alternate link or text styling for a certain area within a layout, and frequently that area is the footer. Thanks to selector specificity, we can override generic styles set elsewhere in our style sheet, and get even more specific with the help of a few strategically placed IDs. The result (Figure 3-14) is quite nice, but how do we get there?

Figure 3-14. *Styled footer links on PixelLogo.com*

It all starts with the markup, of course, since we need to give unique IDs to each of our lists:

```
<div id="footer">
  <ul id="nav-a">
    <li><a href="#">Logo Catalog</a></li>
    <li><a href="#">Web Templates</a></li>
    <li><a href="#">Logo FX</a></li>
    <li><a href="#">Stationery</a></li>
  </ul>

  <ul id="nav-b">
    <li><a href="#">Contact Us</a></li>
    <li><a href="#">Terms of Use</a></li>
    <li><a href="#">Privacy Policy</a></li>
    <li><a href="#">FAQ</a></li>
    <li><a href="#">About Us</a></li>
  </ul>

  <ul id="nav-c">
    <li><a href="#">Affiliates</a></li>
    <li><a href="#">Logo Design Resources</a></li>
    <li><a href="#">Logo Design Samples</a></li>
    <li><a href="#">Logo Templates</a></li>
    <li><a href="#">Logo Design</a></li>
  </ul>
</div>
```

So we have three lists, each with a different ID, and all three contained by a div. Let's apply some styles:

```
#footer ul {
  float:left;
  margin:30px 0 0 20px;padding:0;
  font-size:85%;
  list-style:none;
}
#footer ul li { line-height:1.4; }
#footer ul li a {
```

```
  background-repeat:no-repeat;
  background-position:0 50%;
  padding-left:10px;
  color:#ddd;
  text-decoration:none;
}
#footer ul li a:hover {
  color:#fff;
}
#footer ul#nav-a li a {
  background-image:url(../i/bullet_footer_blue.gif);
}
#footer ul#nav-b li a {
  background-image:url(../i/bullet_footer_orange.gif);
}
#footer ul#nav-c li a {
  background-image:url(../i/bullet_footer_green.gif);
}
```

These rules highlight a few different techniques that take advantage of specificity (and also the cascade):

- First, the `uls` are all styled with one rule, taking care of the basic characteristic, and using a selector that makes the rule specific to `uls` within the `#footer`.

- Next, common properties are assigned to the a elements—since the only thing different about the three lists is the bullet color, we can even set `background-repeat` and `background-position` globally for all links within the three lists.

- The list IDs are only used to give a higher specificity score to the last three rules, which set `background-image` for the links within each of the lists.

There's nothing to override in this case; we're simply sharing styles among similar elements (cutting down on the number of rules in our style sheet and thus making maintenance easier) and using IDs to create rules that will target elements more specifically (see Table 3-4).

Table 3-4. *Specificity Effect: Targeting Specific Elements*

Selector	Inline Style	# of ID Selectors	# of Class Selectors	# of Element Selectors
#footer ul li a	0,	1,	0,	3
#footer ul#nav-a li a	0,	2,	0,	3
#footer ul#nav-b li a	0,	2,	1,	3
#footer ul#nav-c li a	0,	2,	1,	3

Creating Alternate Layouts

Another useful technique is changing the positioning, color, or any other properties of elements for different sections of your site. By setting specific IDs on the body element based on the location of the page within your site (the Homepage, About, or Contact sections, for example), you can create selectors with higher specificity to override generic settings.

Take for example a basic, two-column layout with a footer. The markup might look like this:

```
<body>
  <div id="content">
  ...
  </div>

  <div id="sidebar">
  ...
  </div>

  <div id="footer">
  ...
  </div>
</body>
```

All we need next are a few basic rules to send the sidebar to the right and set a few other defaults, and we have our standard layout (see Figure 3-15):

```
#content {
  float:left;
  width:74%;
}

#sidebar {
  float:right;
  width:25%;
}

#footer {
  clear:both;
}
```

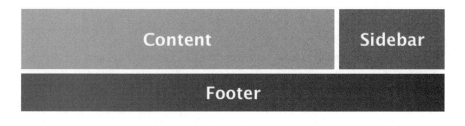

Figure 3-15. *A basic, two-column layout with a footer*

Now, let's say that on the homepage we want to have the sidebar on the left (Figure 3-16), and on our contact page, we don't want a sidebar at all (Figure 3-17). To accomplish this, we simply assign an ID to the body element on those pages (`<body id="homepage">` and `<body id="contact">`), and then create alternate rules with higher-scoring selectors:

```
body#homepage #content {
  float:right;
}
body#homepage #sidebar {
  float:left;
}
body#contact #content {
  width:100%;
}
body#contact #sidebar {
  display:none;
}
```

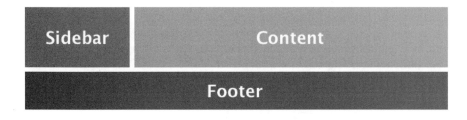

Figure 3-16. *Our basic layout, with the sidebar moved to the left*

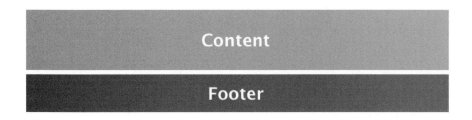

Figure 3-17. *The same layout, with the sidebar hidden thanks to specificity*

Our default selectors each include an ID, but our alternate styles include two IDs and thus have a higher specificity. The body element selector at the beginning of our alternate rules is simply there for clarity; the addition of an element selector to the score doesn't make a difference in this case because the IDs are more important (see Table 3-5).

Table 3-5. *Specificity Effect: Alternate Layouts*

Selector	Inline Style	# of ID Selectors	# of Class Selectors	# of Element Selectors
#content	0,	1,	0,	0
#sidebar	0,	1,	0,	0
body#homepage #content	0,	2,	0,	1
body#homepage #sidebar	0,	2,	0,	1
body#contact #content	0,	2,	0,	1
body#contact #sidebar	0,	2,	0,	1

Using specificity in this manner gives us lots of flexibility with our layouts, without having to adjust the markup one bit.

Summary

The depths of the cascade, specificity, and importance can be confusing at first, so the best way to truly understand how rules and selectors interact with each other is to experiment. Take the knowledge you've gained in this chapter, and try a simple example to make sure the logic works for you. Then create some strange and complicated selectors and see what happens when you change and reorder them in your style sheet. The interactions become easier to recognize and manipulate the more you play with them, and that's the fun part, especially when dealing with the various quirks and oddities associated with browser types and versions, as we'll review next in Chapter 4.

CHAPTER 4

■ ■ ■

The Browsers

There are a lot of great things about developing web sites using CSS. The browsers are not one of them. Unfortunately, quite a few inconsistencies exist among common browsers when it comes to how they render CSS styles. For the most part, these inconsistencies fall into two distinct categories: unsupported selectors or attributes, and bugs.

A Little History

The great tale of the so-called browser wars has been told many times before (read more at http://en.wikipedia.org/wiki/Web_browsers), but somehow it never gets old.

In the beginning, there was Netscape (actually, there were a handful of browsers before Netscape, but this is the place where our story begins). Netscape was a pioneering Internet company that manufactured a web browser—software for viewing web sites on a personal computer. At the time, there was no CSS or JavaScript—there was only HTML. As you know, HTML defines the structure of a document, not its presentation. As such, Netscape was left to its own devices regarding visual display. They made several very reasonable choices: headers would be displayed bigger, and bolder, than other text. Paragraphs would have a small margin above and below them. Unordered lists would have bullets next to each list item. And so on.

Things went quite well until Microsoft saw a market they weren't dominating and decided to enter the space with their own web browser, which they deemed "Internet Explorer." By and large, Internet Explorer rendered pages just as Netscape did, but there were minor differences. As Microsoft began making inroads into the web browser market share, both companies realized they needed a competitive edge if they were to be the browser of choice for most users. To achieve this, both companies appealed to web designers and developers by adding extensions to HTML that only worked in their browser. Oftentimes, each company added features that were very similar but required different HTML code from the other one. This created havoc for web designers, as we were forced to decide which browser we would target with our code (or ignore the nifty new features altogether). What's worse, it wasn't only Netscape and Microsoft; other smaller players entered the browser space as well. Trying to make a web site that worked well in all browsers was an exercise in frustration.

As browser makers first began to implement CSS, the issue didn't get any better. Some browsers had support for CSS and some didn't. Some supported just a few small pieces of the CSS spec, so it was difficult to remember which browsers supported which. Some browsers claimed to support CSS, but their implementations were so buggy that they were unusable.

Rather than support the CSS (and HTML) specs the way they were defined by the W3C, browser manufacturers simply made their browser do things the way they thought it ought to—which led to massive inconsistencies.

The Standards Movement

In the early 2000s, web designers and developers began to pressure browser manufacturers, demanding that they change their rendering engines to display pages as the specs recommended. This was a bit easier said than done; simply changing the browsers would have "broken" most of the sites on the Internet, since their code was written for the inconsistent browser landscape rather than for the HTML and CSS specs as outlined by the W3C.

But change they did, and through some clever mechanisms (including DOCTYPE switching, which we'll discuss later in this chapter), they even managed to do so without breaking the Internet.

Well, mostly. Several browser inconsistencies still exist, and this chapter will help you understand them. Without question, the most difficult thing we as web designers and developers do is make our projects work equally well across all browsers and platforms. Things are looking up, but it's still a challenge.

The bottom line, though, is that we are in the best place we've ever been as far as consistency across browsers goes, thanks to the web standards movement. If you develop using CSS and modern (X)HTML markup and follow some best practices, you'll find that the vast majority of your code "just works" across the board.

The Current (Desktop) Browser Landscape

While mobile devices like phones and PDAs are becoming more popular, the desktop computer remains the primary place in which people use the Web. As such, understanding the available browsers available in this context and the way they impact your web development process is key.

Firefox

Often looked upon by web designers and developers as the "gold standard" of web browsers, The Mozilla Corporation's Firefox (www.mozilla.org) is an open source browser that began life as a fork of the Mozilla Suite but has since become the primary development focus for the company. At the time of this writing, the latest version of Firefox is 1.5, and a 2.0 beta has been made available. Firefox is available for Windows, Mac OS X, and Linux.

Besides providing several popular end-user features (such as pop-up blocking, tabbed browsing, and extensibility via a plug-in system), Firefox is known for its outstanding support of web standards, including (X)HTML and CSS. Most web designers consider it to be the most reliable and accurate available browser when it comes to rendering things according to the specifications. It also includes some built-in tools (such as the DOM Inspector) and some freely available extensions (such as Firebug, covered more in Chapter 14) that are handy in debugging your web work. For these reasons, we highly recommended that you use Firefox as your main development browser.

At the time of this writing, Firefox's market share is estimated to be about 12 percent of all web users.

Like all browsers, Firefox has a "rendering engine" as one of its components. This is the part of the browser that actually renders web pages (handling (X)HTML, CSS, JavaScript, and more). Firefox's rendering engine, called Gecko, is available separately with an open source license so that enterprising folks can build other browsers on top of it. Some other Gecko-based browsers include Netscape (versions 6 and higher; previously released for several operating systems but no longer available), Camino (Mac OS X only; see `www.caminobrowser.org`), Flock (Windows, Mac, and Linux; see `http://flock.com`) Mozilla Application Suite (available for several operating systems; see `www.mozilla.org`), and Minimo (for small devices such as cell phones and PDAs; see `www.mozilla.org/projects/minimo/`). Generally speaking, you can count on all Gecko-based browsers to render your (X)HTML and CSS the same. Thus, it is probably unnecessary (although it never hurts!) to test your sites in all of these alternative browsers.

Safari

Another popular web browser for designers and developers is Safari (`www.apple.com/macosx/features/safari`), Apple Computer's Mac-only application that has shipped as the default browser on every Mac since version 10.3 (Panther). The current version of Safari at the time of this writing is 2.0.

While Mac users are much less numerous than their Windows-based counterparts, Mac sales have been on the rise for several years, and Safari is now estimated to account for over 5 percent of all web traffic. This might not seem like a lot, but it certainly is a percentage large enough for most web developers to sit up and take notice. Safari usage has been on the rise since its release, and doesn't show any signs of slowing down.

Safari is also known among standards-oriented web designers as a star citizen of the Internet, handling CSS and (X)HTML as well as Firefox, and even besting Firefox by supporting a few more CSS 3 properties. Safari's JavaScript engine has been the subject of many complaints— and deservedly so—but when it comes to rendering CSS, you can rely on Safari to treat you pretty well. If you are not doing a lot of JavaScript, Safari can be a good primary development browser for designers.

As Mozilla did with Firefox, Apple has released the rendering engine for Safari, which it calls WebKit, under an open source license. WebKit itself is based on another open source project called KHTML, a rendering engine with its roots in Linux, the KDE desktop environment, and the Konqueror web browser. A handful of Mac-only browsers are based on WebKit, including OmniWeb (`www.omnigroup.com/applications/omniweb/`) and Shiira (`http://hmdt-web.net/shiira/en`). WebKit also powers the web browser built into Nokia's latest line of cell phones, as well as other mobile devices. In addition, many popular Mac programs whose primary purpose is something other than web browsing use WebKit to render (X)HTML, CSS, and related content. Programs that use WebKit generally render content identically to Safari.

Opera

Opera (www.opera.com) is an Internet suite that, in addition to web browsing, handles e-mail, online chat, and more. Developed by Opera Software, it is a commercial project available free of charge, and runs on many operating systems, including Windows, Linux, Mac OS X, Solaris, and FreeBSD. It is also a very popular browser for mobile devices, such as cell phones, PDAs, and game consoles. In development since 1994, Opera is a relatively old browser, and the version number shows it. The most recent version of Opera at the time of this writing is version 9.

Opera is a small player when it comes to market share—the latest stats indicate the browser is in use by less than 1 percent of all web surfers. However, it is notable in that support for web standards, including CSS, has long been a priority at Opera. Although earlier versions of Opera do have minor quirks in the way they render some web pages, it's safe to say the most recent versions have very good support for (X)HTML and CSS, and are unlikely to cause you any major headaches as you build CSS-based sites.

Internet Explorer

Microsoft's Internet Explorer (www.microsoft.com/windows/ie/) is the most widely used web browser in the world, no doubt in large part due to the fact that it is the default browser for Windows, the most popular operating system in the world. The current version of IE is version 6, which was released in the summer of 2001. Version 7 should be available by the time you read this (although if Microsoft's history with shipping products on time is an indication, we probably shouldn't count on that).

Although Microsoft created versions of Internet Explorer for several platforms, including Windows, Mac OS X, Classic Mac OS, and Solaris, only the Windows version remains in active development.

After having won the browser wars of the late 1990s, Internet Explorer's market share was up to around 96 percent in 2002. Since the releases of Firefox and Safari, it has steadily declined, but it remains the dominant browser by a large margin. At the time of this writing, IE accounts for about 85 percent of web traffic.

And yet, most standards-aware web designers and developers have a strong distaste for Internet Explorer. While Microsoft has been criticized for several problems in IE, notably security issues, the one that irks people building web pages is frustrating gaps in support for modern web standards, especially CSS. Internet Explorer 6 was actually quite advanced in terms of CSS support when it was released, but no significant enhancements have been made since 2001, and other browsers have steadily gotten better and better. Web designers and developers are frustrated at the time they spend working around IE's bugs, missing support, and proprietary feature set when simple, clean, standards-based code should work across the board. Thankfully, the release of Internet Explorer 7 should solve the vast majority of these issues, as Microsoft seems to be placing a major focus on providing strong support for standards. However, it will be a good while before most users have migrated from version 6 to 7, so we will certainly need to deal with the frustrations of IE 6 for some time to come.

In this section, we'll detail some notable CSS support issues in IE 6. We'll show you how to address these issues using a combination of sensible planning, workarounds, and hacks. (See Chapter 6 for more on hacks and workarounds.)

Box-Model Discrepancy

The CSS box model, which allows block-level elements to be drawn with margins, padding, and borders, is a key concept in CSS-based design, and one we'll learn more about in several chapters of this book. As defined by the CSS specifications, the width of a block-level element, when it is explicitly stated by the CSS author, defines the width only of the content of the block—not including and padding (the whitespace inside the block), margin (the whitespace outside the block), or border. However, Internet Explorer's flawed box-model implementation includes the margin, padding, and border in the specified width, resulting in a narrower box when displayed. For example, the CSS code

```
div#content {
  width: 300px;
  margin: 10px;
  padding: 10px;
  border: 1px solid #fff;
}
```

should result in an element that takes up 342 pixels of horizontal space (the 300-pixel-wide content area plus 20-pixel-wide padding (10 pixels on both the left and the right) plus a 20-pixel-wide margin (10 pixels on both the left and the right) plus 2 pixels of border (1 pixel on both the left and the right). This is demonstrated in Figure 4-1.

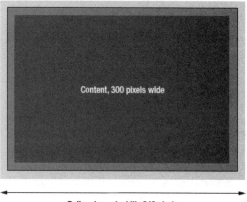

Entire element width: 342 pixels

Figure 4-1. *Correct box-model behavior, resulting in a total element width of 342 pixels*

However, older versions of Internet Explorer will display the entire element at 300 pixels wide, subtracting the size of margins, padding, and borders from the content area's width, as Figure 4-2 illustrates.

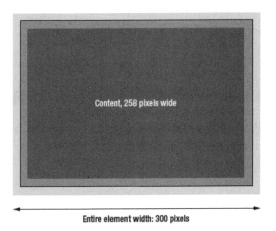

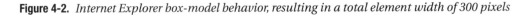

Figure 4-2. *Internet Explorer box-model behavior, resulting in a total element width of 300 pixels*

Internet Explorer 6 added support for a concept known as DOCTYPE switching, wherein the rendering of the page changes based on the DOCTYPE of the document. IE 6 has two rendering modes: standards compliance mode is enabled when a strict DOCTYPE is used and quirks mode is enabled when a strict DOCTYPE is not used. IE 6 uses the correct box-model implementation when in standards compliance mode and the incorrect one when in quirks mode. This is one of several reasons why it is always preferable to use strict DOCTYPEs—rendering engines in standards compliance mode produces much more predictable and consistent behavior than those in quirks mode.

Inconsistent Support for :hover

The :hover pseudo-class (first discussed in Chapter 2) allows CSS authors to define different CSS properties for an element when that element is "hovered," or "moused-over." Usually this is done to indicate that the element the visitor has rolled their mouse over is a clickable, linked element. Per the CSS spec, CSS authors should be able to assign :hover to any element. However, IE only supports the use of :hover on anchor elements (a). One example of a common use for :hover is to highlight rows of a table that are hovered, often by changing their background color. This usability aid is not possible in IE without the use of JavaScript because of IE's limited support for :hover.

Missing Support for position: fixed

When positioning elements in CSS, an author may choose to use the fixed positioning model. Fixed positioning works in a similar way to absolute positioning, except that when a visitor scrolls the page the element does not scroll with it (it is "fixed" in place). IE 6 and lower do not support fixed positioning and display elements whose position property is set to fixed as static instead.

Incomplete Support for PNG Images

Although this topic is not directly related to CSS, it is also notable that IE 6 and lower do not fully support the PNG image file format. One exciting feature of PNG is its support for alpha channel transparency (as opposed to the binary transparency of, say, the GIF image file format). IE 6 does not natively support this type of transparency when using PNG images (although some workarounds make it possible).

It's Not All Bad

Despite the ominous tone of the preceding paragraphs, it is possible to wrangle IE 6 into behaving fairly well, if you follow the best practices outlined in this book. A site without a few IE workarounds is a very, very rare commodity, but the workarounds do work, and aren't particularly hard to implement.

Other Browsers

There will always be other browsers (you can find an exhaustive list of web browsers at http://en.wikipedia.org/wiki/List_of_web_browsers). There are less commonly used browsers out there now; niche players will always enter the marketplace, and new alternative devices will be born with browsers of their own. The goal of web standards is to make this fact irrelevant. If these new browsers properly implement the standards set forth by the W3C (including (X)HTML and CSS)—and you write your code to those specs—you should be able to count on your sites displaying as you expect on all browsers. The open sourcing of great rendering engines like Gecko and WebKit is making this more possible than ever before.

However, expecting all web browsers to render pages identically is an idealistic view of the world, and probably won't be reality any time soon. The best you can do, as a web designer or developer, is to write standards-based code, apply workarounds where necessary to make your sites work in the major browsers, and test in as many browsers as you can get your hands on.

Dealing with Older Desktop Browsers

Unfortunately for us web designers and developers, not all web surfers use the latest and greatest versions of their browsers. Some folks are hesitant to upgrade, others don't know they should upgrade, and yet others have hardware that is outdated to a point where upgrading is not an option.

One fear organizations often have when they consider moving to a CSS-based approach is whether doing so will alienate these users. The reality, though, is that a properly implemented web-standards method of web development will actually make your site *more* accessible to users with older browsers.

You see, in the first era of web development (which lasted throughout the '90s), we were forced to make hard choices about which browsers we would support. The vast differences between browsers meant we needed to rewrite most aspects of each site for each one, and this was only practical to do for a few choice browsers.

Modern web development (using web standards), on the other hand, allows us to support all browsers—at least in some capacity. And when we refer to all browsers, we mean *all*. This includes the version of Mosaic released in the early '90s all the way up to today's browsers, browsers on alternative devices (cell phones, PDAs, game consoles, etc.), and even browsers that haven't been imagined yet and that will show up on the devices that reach the public in 2009. Whether to exclude a browser is not a choice we have to make.

Instead, we need to consider what "support" actually means. In the past, people have taken "support" to mean "everybody gets the same thing." If we support Internet Explorer 6 and Netscape 4, then the site will look virtually identical in both browsers—and so on. Thus, web designers and developers learned to use a "lowest common denominator" approach, using only the features of XHTML, CSS, JavaScript, and so forth that worked well in the oldest, poorest browser they'd chosen to support. But this thinking is flawed in that it offers benefits to no one.

Nate Koechley, a Senior Web Developer at Yahoo!, gave this example on the Yahoo! Developer Network (`http://developer.yahoo.com/yui/articles/gbs/gbs.html`):

> *Consider television. At the core: TV distributes information. A hand-cranked emergency radio is capable of receiving television audio transmissions. It would be counterproductive to prevent access to this content, even though it's a fringe experience.*
>
> *Some viewers still have black-and-white televisions. Broadcasting only in black-and-white—the "lowest common denominator" approach—ensures a shared experience but benefits no one. Excluding the black-and-white television owners—the "you must be this tall to ride" approach—provides no benefit either.*
>
> *An appropriate support strategy allows every user to consume as much visual and interactive richness as their environment can support. This approach—commonly referred to as progressive enhancement—builds a rich experience on top of an accessible core, without compromising that core.*

Broadcast television offers full color. It offers Dolby Pro Logic surround sound. It offers high-definition resolution and clarity. If your television supports these technologies, you get the richest TV experience possible. If it doesn't, your experience will not be enhanced—but you *will* still get the core content of the television program.

This is very much the same approach the web standards movement applies to the Web. All browsers, no matter what device they're on, how old they are, or how technologically inferior they are, ought to get the core content of the page (in most cases, this means text, images, etc.). The latest and greatest browser will get the richest experience. Everything else will be somewhere in between.

Graded Browser Support

In February 2006, the Yahoo! Developer Network (`http://developer.yahoo.com/`) introduced the concept of *graded browser support*. This wasn't actually a new idea, but it may have been the first time it was ever written down and presented in a palatable way to the masses, and it also offered evidence that major Internet companies (such as Yahoo!) were thinking along these lines.

Yahoo!'s approach, which has since been adopted by many web designers and developers, was to inspect each browser and grade it. They based their grades on characteristics such as

- *Identified versus unknown*: There are over 10,000 browser brands, versions, and configurations and that number is growing. It is possible to group known browsers together.

- *Capable versus incapable*: No two browsers have an identical implementation. However, it is possible to group browsers according to their support for most web standards.

- *Modern versus antiquated*: As newer browser versions are released, the relevancy of earlier versions decreases.

- *Common versus rare*: There are thousands of browsers in use, but only a few dozen are widely used.

The result of their work is a three-grade system: *C-grade*, *A-grade*, and *X-grade*. Yahoo! defines each as follows:

C-grade

"C-grade is the base level of support, providing core content and functionality. It is sometimes called core support. Delivered via nothing more than semantic HTML, the content and experience is highly accessible, un-enhanced by decoration or advanced functionality, and forward and backward compatible. Layers of style and behavior are omitted.

C-grade browsers are identified on a blacklist. Approximately 3% of our audience receives a C-grade experience.

Summary: C-grade browsers are identified, incapable, antiquated and rare. QA tests a sampling of C-grade browsers, and bugs are addressed with high priority."

A-grade

"A-grade support is the highest support level. By taking full advantage of the powerful capabilities of modern web standards, the A-grade experience provides advanced functionality and visual fidelity.

A-grade browsers are identified on a whitelist. Approximately 96% of our audience enjoys an A-grade experience.

Summary: A-grade browsers are identified, capable, modern and common. QA tests all A-grade browsers, and bugs are addressed with high priority."

X-grade

"X-grade provides support for unknown, fringe or rare browsers. Browsers receiving X-grade support are assumed to be capable. (If a browser is shown to be incapable—if it chokes on modern methodologies and its user would be better served without decoration or functionality—then it is considered a C-grade browser.)

X-grade browsers include all browsers not on the C-grade blacklist or the A-grade whitelist. Approximately 1% of our audience receives the X-grade experience.

Summary: X-grade browsers are generally unknown, assumed to be capable, modern, and rare or fringe. QA does not test, and bugs are not opened against X-grade browsers."

The Relationship Between A- and X-grade Support

"A bit more on the relationship between A and X grade browsers: One unexpected instance of X-grade is a newly-released version of an A-grade browser. Since thorough QA testing is an A-grade requirement, a brand-new (and therefore untested) browser does not qualify as an A-grade browser. This example highlights a strength of the Graded Browser Support approach. The only practical difference between A and X-grade browsers is that QA actively tests against A-grade browsers.

Unlike the C-grade, which receives only HTML, X-grade receives everything that A-grade does. Though a brand-new browser might be characterized initially as a X-grade browser, we give its users every chance to have the same experience as A-grade browsers."

This is a terrific approach to determining browser support for your organization. It ensures that all visitors get the core content of your site. It ensures that those users who live on the bleeding edge aren't penalized for their use of the latest beta release of their favorite browser. It ensures that the visitors using Netscape 4 on an old 486 PC with Windows 95 doesn't see a broken layout that obscures their ability to read the text. And it gives you, the web designer/developer, a steady target to shoot at when it comes to browser support.

Yahoo!'s browser grading chart has been made public, and you can find it at `http:// developer.yahoo.com/yui/articles/gbs/gbs_browser-chart.html`. While using their chart directly may work fine for your organization, you may also find that you need to come up with your own chart, grading the browsers based on the criteria that matter most to you so that you can draw your own lines between grades. The beauty of this sort of system is that no matter where you draw those lines, you won't be cutting off anyone—now or in the future—from receiving the content of your site. Just like television.

Appendix C includes a version of the browser-grading chart that we think is appropriate for most general-use web sites and applications. It may not work for your organization without some modifications, but it should at least provide you with a good start toward your own grading system.

On Choosing a Development Browser

Deciding which web browser you will use as you develop CSS-based sites is a significant choice. Although different schools of thought exist, most web designers agree that developing in a solid, reliable, standards-compliant browser (such as Firefox or Safari) is best. This lets you focus on doing things the "right" way through most of your development. Then, you can go back after the fact and provide workarounds for less-ideal browsers (such as Internet Explorer). Trying to develop to the lesser browsers as you go tends to result in more workarounds than necessary and code that is less clean.

Your mileage may vary, but we recommend using Firefox as your primary development browser, not only because of its great standards support, but also because of the many great extensions available for web developers.

Browsers for the Mobile Web

Estimates are there will be over 3 billion cell phone users worldwide by 2009. That's a staggering number, and especially so for you, the web developer, when you consider that the vast majority of those phones will have web browsers running on them.

Besides cell phones, handheld game consoles like the Sony PlayStation Portable and the Nintendo DS have web-browsing capabilities, as do many PDAs, such as those powered by Palm OS, Windows Mobile, and PocketPC.

If you thought the landscape of desktop web browsers was fragmented and confusing, prepare yourself for an even bigger shock. There are over 200 models of cell phones in use today from over 25 different major manufacturers with over 30 different web browsers installed.

This new and incredibly fragmented landscape of web browser and devices only further strengthens the demand for web standards–based development. If you've created your page or site with clean, semantic (X)HTML and styled it with CSS, you optimize your options for dealing with those visitors hitting your corner of the Web from a phone or other mobile device.

Brian Fling, of the great Seattle-based web studio Blue Flavor (`http://blueflavor.com/`), proposes the following four options for the mobile "version" of your site (which may not actually be a different version at all) in his presentation from WebVisions 2006 (`www.blueflavor.com/ed/mobile/designing_for_mobile.php`):

Use Small Screen Rendering (SSR): Some mobile browsers, such as Opera Mini and Blazer, automatically optimize your pages for smaller screens, reformatting them where necessary. This technique requires no effort from you, the designer, but also has the significant disadvantage of only being of service to the relatively small percentage of users who have these SSR-enabled browsers. Also, from a performance perspective, this method is quite slow, as it takes time for the SSR processing to occur in these browsers.

Programmatically reformat: Using various server-side techniques, it's relatively simple to strip (X)HTML of superfluous elements (such as images and styling) on the fly, serving a bare-bones version of the site to mobile users. Doing so doesn't require a whole lot of effort from your organization, but the result is still less than ideal. You don't have fine-grained control over what mobile visitors see and don't see, and you may never be able to trust that your reformatting algorithms are doing exactly what you'd like. Although faster than SSR, this approach is still quite slow from a performance perspective.

Use "handheld" style sheets: As mentioned in Chapter 3, CSS defines a `media` attribute for style sheets so that you can serve a particular style sheet only to mobile, or handheld, devices. This technique offers you a great deal of control over the visual presentation of your content on mobile devices, but not so much control over the context itself. It takes some work on the part of your organization to get these handheld style sheets ready, but once they are, they'll serve you well. Because there is no request-time processing being done, this method is considerably faster than SSR or stripping elements from (X)HTML.

Create a mobile-specific site: You can create an entirely separate version of your site for mobile devices (the convention is to house these at `mobile.yourdomain.com`). While this is obviously quite a lot of work, the result is that you have fine-grained control over every aspect of the mobile display of your site, including the context. You can pick and choose to display only the content that is *contextually relevant* to the mobile user (for more on contextual relevance, see `www2.jeffcroft.com/2006/mar/16/on-mobile-web-contextual-relevance/`). Generally this will be the fastest option, performance-wise, as it requires no request-time processing and usually results in smaller (X)HTML and CSS files than the other methods.

Put simply, how to support mobile devices is not a binary matter—"do we support mobile devices or not?" It should actually be a *continuum* of support, in which you can offer some support with little to no effort, or great support with added effort. Fling sums this up with a great graph, as shown in Figure 4-3.

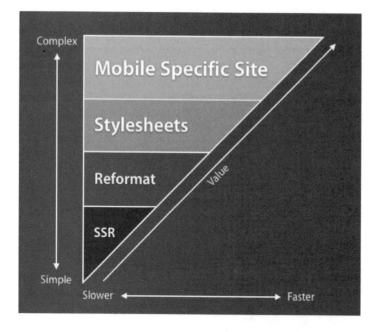

Figure 4-3. *Fling's graph shows how each option for mobile versions of your site relate with regard to complextibly of creation, value to the end user, and speed of download and rendering.*

Whatever options you choose for mobile web support, the most important thing is that you don't ignore it. The mobile Web is here, and it's here to stay.

Summary

While all web designers definitely have frustrations in dealing with web browser inconsistencies, the truth is that using web standards, including CSS, actually minimizes these when done correctly. By following the best practices outlined in this book, you'll be able to create sites that work well across the board. But before we get too deep into that, let's talk about the management of your CSS files. Chapter 5 covers this important, if often overlooked, process.

CHAPTER 5

■ ■ ■

Managing CSS Files

At this stage in the book, you should be well on your way to creating professional-level websites and applications using modern techniques. You've got semantic, clean, and valid (X)HTML under your belt; you've had a refresher course on the basics of how CSS works; and you've seen how the varied browser landscape can be tamed with a good grading chart and some policies regarding the level of support you'll give to each grade of browser. Now we'll move on to the practical, production-time aspects of CSS—starting with how you manage the style sheet files themselves.

As you delve into bigger projects, you'll find that CSS files can become unwieldy if they're not well managed. There are several reasons why thinking ahead of time about where you'll store style sheets, how you'll keep them readable, and how they can be optimized will increase efficiency:

- Whether you're a solo developer or part of a team, it's important that your files be readable by someone other than you—and this is doubly true for teams in which more than one CSS author works on the same project. Although it may be tempting to obfuscate your work for the sake of "job security," the honest, transparent, and right thing to do is prepare your style sheets for the day when you no longer maintain them.

- Developing a set of consistent standards for yourself or your team will make you work faster from project to project. If you do things the same way you did the last time, and the time before that, you'll start to develop habits that will increase efficiency.

- Style sheet files can be large, and it may be in the best interest of your server and budget to optimize them for minimal bandwidth use by compressing the files into the smallest possible format.

This chapter shows you how to approach these considerations. Whether you adopt the suggestions we make in this chapter is a matter of personal preference. We'll provide you with some options for managing files, and reasons why we personally prefer one or the other, but ultimately you'll need to establish which methods work best for you on your own. The key thing to take away from this chapter is not so much the techniques themselves but the fact that giving CSS file management some forethought will pay off for you in the long run.

Style Storage

Deciding how you will store your CSS declarations is a two-part question:

1. Where on the server will the files live?

2. How many style sheets will you have, and what exactly goes in each one?

The Path to Your CSS

The answer to the first question may depend, to some degree, on the back-end server and application configuration you are using. In some web server setups, the server path to the CSS files have a direct relationship with their URLs. In other setups, including several of the modern web application frameworks like Django (http://djangoproject.com) and Ruby on Rails (http://rubyonrails.com), the URL structure is different from the server directory structure. In either case, you'll want to consider both the ease of access for you and your team, as well as the URL itself.

Although it's certainly not necessary, it is an established convention to store all CSS files in one directory, often named css, styles, or something similar. Many times, this directory is accessed at a URL directly off the root level of the site, as in http://yoursite.com/css/ or http://yoursite.com/styles/. Some designers and developers prefer to maintain a directory that contains all the linked resources of the site (such as CSS, images, or JavaScript), sometimes called resources, media, or site. In this case, the URL structure often looks like http://yoursite.com/media/css/, http://yoursite.com/resources/images/, or http://yoursite.com/site/js/. Where you store your CSS files, in terms of both the path on the server and the URL path relative to your domain root, is entirely up to you, but we do recommend keeping all CSS files together in one directory and sticking with a structure once you've chosen one. Doing so will help you develop habits that increase your production effectiveness.

Using Multiple Files As One Style Sheet

Deciding how many style sheets to maintain and what they should contain is more difficult. In a small, simple site it may be fine to keep all of your declarations in one file. But as sites grow larger, there seems to be a point at which it becomes simpler to deal with multiple files than it is to find the declaration or attribute you're looking for in a mile-long single style sheet.

Because CSS includes the ability to import other style sheets, it's relatively simple to link to one style sheet from your (X)HTML file, and then import additional style sheets from that one. Take a look at the following example:

index.html:

```
<!DOCTYPE html PUBLIC "-//W3C//DTD XHTML 1.0 Strict//EN" ➥
"http://www.w3.org/TR/xhtml1/DTD/xhtml1-strict.dtd">
<html xmlns="http://www.w3.org/1999/xhtml" xml:lang="en" lang="en">
  <head>
    <meta http-equiv="Content-Type" content="text/html; charset=utf-8"/>
    <title>untitled</title>
    <link rel="stylesheet" type="text/css" ➥
      href="http://yoursite.com/media/css/base.css" />
```

```
  </head>
  <body>
  <p>The content of our page.</p>
  </body>
</html>
```

base.css:

```
@import url("layout.css");
@import url("typography.css");
```

Here, our linked style sheet, `base.css`, imports two additional style sheets, `layout.css` and `typography.css`. We've split our CSS into three separate files, but the browser will treat them as if they were one long style sheet.

Personal preference is involved in deciding which is easier to wrap your brain around—one file or multiple files. Oftentimes, the scope of the project will dictate your methodology. A small project with only a few pages may have far fewer styles, and thus be quite manageable in a single file. Larger projects are more likely to get complex, and breaking their style into multiple files may help you keep track of things more efficiently. You also may find special cases that warrant their own style sheet, such as groups of hacks and workarounds to compensate for browser bugs or styles specifically for a particular media type (such as `print` or `handheld`).

Whether you decide to break up your styles into multiple files is entirely up to you. With a little experimenting, you'll find methods that make sense for you and your team.

Conventions for class and id Names

Another common point of debate among CSS pedants is the style in which you write your CSS `class` and `id` names. Many CSS writers are familiar with programming languages of various types, so it's natural for them to use conventions similar to those they're familiar with. The Python language, for example, encourages the use of the underscore (_) character for variable names with more than one word (for example `comment_form` or `main_content`.) JavaScript programmers tend to use what's commonly referred to as "camel case"—in which the first letter of any word(s) after the first one is capitalized (like `commentForm` and `mainContent`). Still other people prefer the hyphen (-) character to separate words (`comment-form` or `main-content`).

CSS itself is not particularly picky. Any of these notations are valid, and it's up to you to choose the one that works best for your workflow. If your developers commonly work in another language, it may be wise to pick a convention similar to the one that language prefers. You may want to consider readability when you choose (it can be argued that the underscore makes for the most readable names). And finally, you may wish to consider ease of typing; for example, using the hyphen character prevents you from having to press the Shift key, as you would have to when producing an underscore character or capital letter. This can be more efficient, especially in reducing typos.

As with most of the suggestions in this chapter, what you choose isn't as important as taking the time to make a conscious choice.

Formatting CSS Declarations

Formatting what comes in between those brackets is perhaps even more important than any `class` and `id` outside them. There are countless ways of formatting your CSS files, and it's important for you to adopt a process that will provide a style sheet that is easy to read, interpret, and edit—both by you and other members of your team.

One Line vs. One Property Per Line

Because CSS itself doesn't care how whitespace is used in style sheets, it's up to CSS authors to determine what works best for them. Some designers prefer to list all of the properties and values for each selector on one line, while others favor a vertical, one-property-per-line approach. The following CSS declarations are functionally equivalent:

```
#footer {
  clear: both;
  height: 204px;
  margin: 0 auto;
  padding: 26px 20px 20px;
}
```

```
#footer { clear: both; height: 204px; margin: 0 auto; padding: 26px 20px 20px; }
```

Most people immediately find one or the other of these styles to be considerably more readable and manageable. Some believe it's easier to quickly scan through one style, and some think the other style makes the CSS more easily parsable. The majority of web designers and developers use one style or the other, although there are some who mix them—typically using the single-line approach for shorter declarations and the vertical method for longer ones. As with most of file-management issues, which you choose isn't as important as picking a style and then sticking to it. You'll want to figure out which method is simpler for your team and roll with it.

There are a few real practical benefits to each method, though. Most syntax validators you use on your CSS code will reference line numbers when they find errors. If you have used a one-property-per-line coding style, that line number will translate directly to a single property that is in error. If you're using multiple properties per line, it may not be as simple to find the error that the validator is referring to. On the other hand, the multiple-properties-per-line method results in much shorter files, which have a smaller file size. This translates to saved bandwidth, which means faster downloading for the end user and saved money on your hosting bill.

Note You'll have probably noticed that we've used the one property per line style throughout this book. This is because we want to make it as easy as possible for you to follow along with the examples.

Beyond Organized: Ordering Your Properties

Some CSS authors meticulously order the individual properties within each CSS rule (although probably only a handful of CSS developers and designers are organized enough to maintain it!). Some adopt a particular order that "fits their brain," such as margin, then padding, then border, then background, then font styles, and so forth. Others order their properties alphabetically. The benefit to doing this is that you can easily keep track of which rules have been applied to avoid duplication. It's a handy trick—if you can keep on top of it.

The vast majority of style sheets on the Web, though, do not have a specific order for individual properties. If it helps you to maintain an order, by all means do it. For most of us, it's probably more trouble than it's worth.

Saving Time with Shorthand

CSS allows for the use of several *shorthand properties,* a way of combining several properties into one property/value pair. The advantages of shorthand are the time savings, as well as a very slight reduction in file size, which saves you a bit of bandwidth and increases the download speed for your visitors. Some CSS authors find shorthand more difficult to parse when they're quickly trying to locate and change a single property, and they may accidentally modify something other than what they intended to change. Others find the shorthand easier to read and don't seem to have any trouble with editing these properties. Again, you should experiment and decide whether or not shorthand works for you.

All of the shorthand properties are listed in Appendix A; a few examples follow:

Standard CSS:

```
border-width: 1px;
border-style: solid;
border-color: #dfdfdf
```

Shorthand CSS:

```
border: 1px solid #dfdfdf;
```

Standard CSS:

```
background-color: #dfdfdf;
background-image: url('/img/background.png');
background-position: 15px 5px;
background-repeat: repeat-x;
```

Shorthand CSS:

```
background: #dfdfdf url('/img/background.png') 15px 5px repeat-x;
```

Standard CSS:

```
margin-top: 20px;
margin-right: 20px;
margin-bottom: 20px;
margin-left: 20px;
padding-top: 20px;
padding-right: 10px;
padding-bottom: 20px;
padding-left: 10px;
```

Shorthand CSS:

```
margin: 20px 20px 20px 20px;
padding: 20px 10px 20px 10px;
```

Even-shorter-hand CSS:

```
margin: 20px;
padding: 20px 10px;
```

Note Remember that whenever you're writing shorthand for any CSS property that deals with length, the directions go in a clockwise manner: *top, right, bottom, left.*

FOR MORE ON SHORTHAND

Perhaps the most comprehensive resource on CSS shorthand properties ever written exists at the personal web site of Dustin Diaz (www.dustindiaz.com). His CSS Shorthand Guide (www.dustindiaz.com/css-shorthand/) covers all the properties that accept shorthand notation, examples of each, and some "gotchas" to watch out for when using shorthand.

Grouping and Notating CSS Rules with Comments

If you build web sites of substantial depth, you will no doubt discover that your CSS rules can become unmanageable without an organizational system in place. Every CSS author or team of authors will find what works best for them individually, but we can offer several suggestions.

Like most markup and programming languages, CSS supports the concept of *comments,* snippets of text that are ignored by the browser (or other rendering device). These can be useful for several distinct purposes.

CSS Comment Syntax

Before you can make use of comments, you must understand how they are indicated in the CSS files. CSS uses the "slash-star, star-slash" syntax for comments, in which a comment block is opened with a slash (/) followed by an asterisk (*) and closed by its opposite—an asterisk followed by a slash. Comments can span multiple lines.

```
/* This is a CSS comment */
/* This is a CSS comment
    that spans multiple lines */
```

Code Notations

The first, and perhaps most obvious, use of comments is to leave contextual notes to yourself or members of your team. For example, you may do something like this:

```
h3 {
    color: #666; /* I switched the h3 color to this lighter ➠
 gray for increased contrast - jcroft, 06/14/2006 */
}
```

It's a good idea to sign and date your comments, especially if you're working on a team. It's always nice to be able to ask the person in the cubicle next to you why he or she did what they did when you're trying to make sense of code you didn't write. Another helpful concept is that of standardizing on several comment openers that have meaning to you or your team. For example, you may start a comment with TODO for pieces of code that need to be completed, or BUG for pieces of code you know need fixing. These types of flags create an easy way for you or your team members to search for specific tasks within the code. Here are a few more examples of this type of notation:

```
/* TODO: The h1s need further styling, but this gets us started. */
h1 {
  color: #333
}

/* BUG: This doesn't seem to work as I intended. ➠
 Anyone have ideas on how to fix it? */
h2 {
  float: left;
  width: 200px;
  margin-right: 20px;
  font-family: Georgia, serif;
}

/* KLUDGE: It's not a very elegant solution, but I used ➠
the negative margin here to achieve ➠
the positioning I wanted. It works, but if someone else ➠
has a better way, go for it. */
h3 {
  display: block;
  margin-left: -11px;
}
```

Comments for Metadata

A great practice to get into the habit of is saving a chunk of *metadata* (literally "data about data") at the top of your CSS files so that anyone else who sees the file will have a bit of context to go on while parsing it. An example might look something like this:

```
/* ------------------------------------
Filename: base.css
Title : Primary CSS file for jeffcroft.com
Author : Jeff Croft, jeff@jeffcroft.com
URL : http://media.jeffcroft.com/css/base.css
```

```
License: Copyright 2006, Jeff Croft, All Rights Reserved. ➥
Feel free to read and learn from this, but please don't steal.

Description : This base style sheet imports other style sheets and ➥
provides basic styling for XHTML elements for the personal web site ➥
and blog of web designer/developer Jeff Croft.
-------------------------------------- */
```

It's far more common than you might imagine for humans to read your CSS files. Web designers and developers are constantly looking at other people's code for ideas and clues on how you achieved a particular effect. Be aware that your code is being read and provide the context necessary to make sense of it. Adding license information ensures you have some ground to stand on when someone steals your site's design—and trust me, *they will*.

Comments for "Code Glossaries"

Another great use for CSS comments is for storing *glossaries* of those style bits you'll find yourself using over and over again throughout the site. Color schemes and typeface selection are especially good examples. For instance, you may find it useful to include something like this at the top of your style sheet:

```
/* --------------------------------------
Main Purple: #50017C
Lighter Purple: #732799
Accent Orange: #ff8800
Accent Green: #99cc00
Accent Blue: #6699cc
Beige: #A5A48C
Light Beige: #C7C3B3

Serif fonts: Georgia, "Times New Roman", serif
Sans-serif fonts: Verdana, Arial, Helvetica, sans-serif
-------------------------------------- */
```

Having this in the style sheet as a reference makes it simple to copy and paste your colors, fonts, and anything else you might need regularly, which saves you a lot of time guessing at colors (or opening up Adobe Photoshop).

Comments for Grouping

Comments can also be handy for creating section delimiters within your CSS files that you'll see easily as you quickly scroll through a document. It can often be helpful to group like rules together. For example, you may wish to collect all of your rules related to a particular navigation menu together. Or, maybe you want all of your header styles to be grouped.

By putting an easily visible *flag* in the middle of your document, perhaps with a few lines of whitespace above and below it, you can achieve an effect similar to that of the "page break" in your favorite word processing application:

```
/* ---------------------------------------------------------------------
   NAVIGATION STYLES
   --------------------------------------------------------------------- */
```

This is a fairly extravagant example, and you can feel free to create whatever delimiter style you like, but there's no doubt this would get noticed among a sea of CSS rules as you scroll through your style sheet.

It is important to note that comments still get sent to the site visitors. Because of this, fancy flags with many characters will slightly increase the file size of your style sheets. Also, a savvy web user can view your style sheets and read these comments, so be sure not to include anything that is private.

Perhaps an even more novel way to use these sort of comment flags is by creating a unique string of characters within them that you can search on within your text editor. Doug Bowman of Stopdesign popularized this idea in a 2005 blog post (`www.stopdesign.com/log/2005/05/03/css-tip-flags.html`) with the following flag:

```
/* =NAVIGATION STYLES */
```

By using a flag like this, it's simple to "tab through" your groupings simply by searching for `/* =` over and over again. Or, if you are looking specifically for the navigation style section, you can perform a search for `/* =NAV` to jump very quickly to this part of what promises to be a long document. Or, you could repeatedly search for `=` (which is almost certainly not going to show up elsewhere in a CSS document) to tab through your sections. It's a clever, creative use of CSS comments, and has since been adopted by many designers and developers.

Ordering CSS Rules

There are several schools of thought on the ordering of your CSS rules within a style sheet. There's no "right" way to do it, so like with many things in this chapter, you'll need to figure out what works best for you. We'll outline a few common techniques here.

General to Specific

One common approach is to start with rules that are more general (i.e., will apply to more elements or to the entire page) and follow those up with rules that are more specific (applying to fewer elements). For example, you may start with a bunch of rules using element selectors to style (X)HTML elements like body, header, paragraphs, lists, tables, forms, and so forth. These general rules will apply throughout your document(s). Then, you can get a bit more specific, perhaps styling (X)HTML elements within certain divs using descendant selectors. Finally, you could get quite specific, styling things like individual tables (by their id) or types of lists (by their class).

By Order in Which They Appear

Some designers like to order rules in relation to the order they will physically appear on the final page—for example, starting with styles for the header, followed by styles for the main content area, and finishing up with styles for the footer. Note that this method can break down somewhat when you start creating style sheets for alternate devices, such as print and mobile, particularly when you are hiding some elements of the page for those mediums.

By Page or Section of the Site

Another common technique is to order rules by page, section, or page type within the site. For example, a style sheet for a newspaper site may include a grouping of rules for the homepage, followed by a grouping for front pages of each section (sports, opinion, etc.), followed by rules for individual story pages. A personal site may contain a group of rules for the homepage, then one for the "about me" page, and then one for the blog.

Note that all of these techniques can be combined as well. You may wish to group your rules by section of the site, and arrange those sections by the order in which they appear within the site, and order rules within the sections from most general to most specific.

Creating a Reusable Framework

As you develop sites using CSS, you will undoubtedly find yourself doing the same things over and over again. You'll separate your CSS into the same four or five files, you'll use the same handful of flags for grouping your rules, and you'll store everything in the same basic directory structure.

Frameworks are all the rage these days, with application frameworks like Django and Ruby on Rails and JavaScript frameworks like Prototype and the Yahoo! User Interface Library (also referred to as the YUI library.) But what is a framework, really? At the most basic level, it's nothing more than a collection of useful bits of code that encourage best practices and make it faster and easier for you to get a web site bootstrapped and up and running.

You can do the same thing with CSS. Create site-agnostic, generic versions of the core files and rules you find yourself using repeatedly. Save them in the directory structure you usually use for a site. Then, simply copy the directories into your latest site and modify them accordingly. This sort of reusable package can save you from having to perform a lot of the mundane tasks required to get a site started.

The Mass Reset

If you've used CSS for web development in the past, you've probably noticed that some inconsistencies exist between the various browsers with regard to the way they display elements by default (i.e., without CSS styles applied). Certain things are pretty reliable: paragraph elements can usually be counted on to have `margin: 1em 0` applied by default, and you can safely expect the strong element to get `font-weight: bold`. However, several elements are styled inconsistently across browsers, especially in certain areas such as forms.

A technique most CSS designers and developers seem to be adopting is the "mass reset," in which default styles are eliminated before any of your custom styles are applied. This, of course, forces you to explicitly style things that might otherwise have been done for you, but it also gives you a clean slate to work with—one that you can count on to be the same across all browsers.

This technique was popularized by Eric Meyer when he wrote about it in his blog (http://meyerweb.com/eric/thoughts/2004/09/15/emreallyem-undoing-htmlcss/), following up Tantek Çelik's similar entry (http://tantek.com/log/2004/09.html#d06t2354).

Some designers take the approach of unstyling only those elements that are normally styled. For example, designer/developer Faruk Ates made the following file, which he calls `initial.css` (available at http://kurafire.net/log/archive/2005/07/26/starting-css-revisited). According to Faruk, the "file neutralizes a lot of default (browser) quirks."

```
/* =INITIAL
   v2.1, by Faruk Ates - www.kurafire.net
   Addendum by Robert Nyman - www.robertnyman.com */

/* Neutralize styling:
   Elements we want to clean out entirely: */
html, body, form, fieldset {
  margin: 0;
  padding: 0;
  font: 100%/120% Verdana, Arial, Helvetica, sans-serif;
}

/* Neutralize styling:
   Elements with a vertical margin: */
h1, h2, h3, h4, h5, h6, p, pre,
blockquote, ul, ol, dl, address {
  margin: 1em 0;
  padding: 0;
}

/* Apply left margin:
   Only to the few elements that need it: */
li, dd, blockquote {
  margin-left: 1em;
}

/* Miscellaneous conveniences: */
form label {
  cursor: pointer;
}
fieldset {
  border: none;
}

/* Form field text-scaling */
input, select, textarea {
  font-size: 100%;
}
```

The Yahoo! User Interface library (which was originally just a JavaScript toolkit but has recently added some CSS pieces as well) includes a file called reset.css that takes a similar, but slightly more heavy-handed, approach. It looks like this (code reproduced here exactly as it appears in the file):

```
/*
Copyright (c) 2006, Yahoo! Inc. All rights reserved.
Code licensed under the BSD License:
http://developer.yahoo.net/yui/license.txt
version: 0.11.0
*/
body,div,dl,dt,dd,ul,ol,li,h1,h2,h3,h4,h5,h6,pre,form, ➥
fieldset,input,p,blockquote,th,td{margin:0;padding:0;}
table{border-collapse:collapse;border-spacing:0;}
fieldset,img{border:0;}
address,caption,cite,code,dfn,em,strong,th,var ➥
{font-style:normal;font-weight:normal;}
ol,ul {list-style:none;}
caption,th {text-align:left;}
h1,h2,h3,h4,h5,h6{font-size:100%;}
q:before,q:after{content:'';}
```

Other CSS authors have taken an even more dramatic approach, turning off absolutely every possible default style the browser may have applied. For a more minimal approach to resetting, you can get a lot of mileage out of simply zeroing out margins and padding on all elements, like so:

```
* {
margin: 0;
padding: 0;
}
```

Whether you build your own mass reset file or use a publicly available one like Yahoo's or Faruk's, you'll find that the mass reset will save you lots of headaches. Probably the simplest way to incorporate a mass reset is to store the resetting rules in their own file and then use @import to include that file in the style sheet you've linked to your (X)HTML document:

```
@import url("reset.css");
```

Summary

Management of CSS rules and files may seem like a mundane and tedious task—and it definitely can be. It is difficult to provide you with the "right" way to do this sort of thing, because every project, designer, developer, and team is different. But taking the time to think about the best way to handle these things for you or your organization and implementing a common workflow (or even a reusable framework) will no doubt save you many headaches in the long run.

Now that you're familiar with modern markup and how CSS works, and you've thought through the management of your CSS files, it's time to move on to a topic that shouldn't really be necessary but is: hacks and workarounds for CSS rendering bugs and inconsistencies in web browsers.

CHAPTER 6

■■■

Hacks and Workarounds

Hacks are like the significant other you've broken up with, but keep going back to on those cold, lonely nights because you just can't live without them. You want to forget about them, to never call or see them again, to just *move on*, but they continue to haunt your dreams. OK, so maybe that's just our point of view after spending countless hours over the years searching for and applying various hacks in the late stages of projects, fighting to keep designs looking exactly the way we intended in all current browser versions on all platforms.

The point is this: if you're developing sites using CSS for positioning, it's likely you have already come across (and been frustrated by) some of these odd and sometimes-unexplainable behaviors exhibited by some browsers. It's an unfortunate reality, brought about in large part by the poor standards compliance in IE/Win (as discussed in Chapter 4), but a reality we must deal with nonetheless.

In this chapter, we'll examine the correct methods for using hacks during development to help you avoid common problems. We'll also discuss best practices for keeping hacks organized and out of the way, review the hacks that are handy to have around just in case—including the Star HTML and "Holly" hacks (for IE versions prior to 7), a quick approach to horizontal centering, easy float clearing (for all browsers!), and filters to help you avoid older browsers. In addition, we've included some notes about changes in IE 7 that will affect your hacks, and what you can do to avoid any negative effects. While we're at it, we'll show you how to make a nice apple crumble for dessert. OK, we lied about that last part. Let's move on . . .

■**Note** Though the term *hack* is used in this chapter, *workaround* is equally interchangeable. Anything that involves nonstandard uses of CSS or markup (or a combination thereof) in essence equals a "hack" no matter how you slice it. From Wikipedia: *In modern computer programming, a "hack" can refer to a solution or method which functions correctly but which is "ugly" in its concept, which works outside the accepted structures and norms of the environment, or which is not easily extendable or maintainable* (http:// en.wikipedia.org/wiki/Hack_%28technology_slang%29).

Using a "Standards First" Approach

The best, most headache-free way to construct layouts using CSS is to get everything working properly in a standards-compliant browser *first*, and then test in other browsers and apply hacks when needed. For the time being, the best browser to start with when putting together your web site (no matter which operating system you use for development) is Firefox. Its rendering engine is the most accurate of all modern browsers, and as an added bonus, you can take advantage of Chris Pederick's incredibly useful (and free!) Web Developer extension (`http://chrispederick.com/work/webdeveloper/`), which will save you countless hours and many sleepless nights while massaging your markup and styles.

Leave IE/Win for Last, Then Hack Like a Surgeon

Once your layout is working perfectly when viewed in Firefox, it's a quick task to test in Safari and Opera (the current versions of both should require no adjustments when following this process), and testing in IE/Win (6/5.*x*) will be nearly painless (though it's best to expect a few problems and layout weirdness, since that's the fun of dealing with IE/Win). This process results in fewer hacks, and those you *do* use can be applied with surgical precision (using more specific selectors), with no collateral damage from cascading hacks. The example project at the end of Chapter 14 gives a step-by-step walkthrough, showing how this approach simplifies testing and bug fixing.

Wait, You Forgot a Few Browsers!

Now, if you haven't passed out from the effort of reading this book thus far, you'll notice we've failed to mention testing on IE/Mac (and a few similarly ancient user agents). This is because we don't believe any time should be wasted developing for a dead browser (and by "dead" we mean "no longer being developed"—Microsoft ceased all work on IE/Mac in late 2005, and stopped distributing it altogether in January 2006), unless you *absolutely must* because of your intended audience. Now, if you fall into that category, fear not: though your situation is unenviable, and likely unavoidable, there are a few hacks targeted specifically at IE/Mac later in this chapter. If you eagerly flip ahead hoping to find hacks for Netscape Navigator 4, or hacks targeting early versions of IE or Opera, you won't find them (aside from a quick tip to hide styles from older browsers completely), and are probably reading the wrong book (you'll want one that went out of print a few years ago, around the time those browsers should have been mothballed).

Note Though CSS hacks exist for Safari, Opera, and even Firefox and Mozilla (usually to correct rendering bugs that have been fixed in subsequent versions, or even to "fix" problems introduced by developers coding for IE/Win), you'll have no need for them if you follow the standards-first approach (if you still need to satisfy your curiosity, Google "css hack *browsername*").

To Hack or Not to Hack

The key to using hacks successfully is knowing when, how, and why to apply them, and *where* (as Chapter 5 suggests, it can be good for your organization in larger projects to keep different aspects of your CSS separated into separate files, and then import them into your base style sheet—a separate file to keep your hacks grouped together is a great idea). If you follow the standards-first approach outlined in this chapter, you'll find that the need for hacks for *any* modern browser diminishes dramatically.

So When Should You Use a Hack?

Sure, we'd all love to enforce a "Zero Hack Policy," but the reality is there are plenty of situations when using a hack is your only option. In fact, as you'll see later in this chapter, almost any CSS layout will require at least one or two hacks to ensure proper display in IE/Win versions 5 and 6. So while hacks tend to leave a slight smell hanging around your code, for the time being you'll need to use at least a few on a regular basis (unless you're one of those few lucky folks who only develop for an intranet with non-IE browsers).

Typically, the process might go something like this:

- Develop and test using Firefox. Everything looks fine and dandy.

- Test in Safari and Opera. Still dandy.

- Test in IE/Win; commit hara-kiri after seeing the result.

No Need to Get Dramatic

OK, so self-disembowelment-by-sword may be an exaggeration in this case, but seeing your nice layout being messed with can definitely make you feel a bit ill to say the least. This is where hacks can bring some sunshine into your life.

WITHER IE 7?

As of this writing, IE 7 beta 3 has been released, and by the time you read this, the final version may well be winging its way onto Windows users' hard drives via Windows Update. This is a *Good Thing,* because IE 7 brings us a big step closer to a more standard browsing environment between browsers, but it also underscores the need for minimizing the number of hacks you use, being as specific as possible when applying those hacks, and keeping browser-specific workarounds separate from your default style sheet.

The reason is that hacks that developers have been using for years to target and correct bugs in IE/Win (specifically versions 5, 5.5, and 6) will not work in IE 7, thus breaking many layouts in the new browser—in addition, most of the bugs targeted by those hacks have been fixed in IE 7, and the new version also supports many CSS 2 selectors that have been used in conjunction with the hacks to send correct styles to non-IE browsers, meaning that IE 7 can now "see" rules that were not intended for its rendering engine. You can almost hear the web development community letting out sighs of relief and screams of agony simultaneously; luckily, IE conditional comments (covered later in this chapter) allow targeting of versions less-than-or-equal-to IE 6, which should ease the pain significantly if your hacks are kept in separate style sheets (they also have Microsoft's official stamp of approval for this very purpose).

Keep Hacks Separated and Commented

So you built your site using web standards, validated all of them, and carefully applied a few hacks to keep IE 6 in line. Then you realize that your layout breaks in IE 7, because the new browser is being sent multiple (and often conflicting) rules between the hacks and rules previously intended for other browsers. This sort of epiphany can give a developer serious stomach pains.

However, some forward-thinking web developers are not quivering at the sight of IE 7. These smart folks use IE conditional comments to deliver separate style sheets to IE/Win (sometimes even specific versions of IE), and in so doing, have saved themselves a lot of trouble now that IE 7 is upon us.

IE Conditional Comments

Most of the time, proprietary browser features are considered a bad thing, but *conditional comments* are one notable exception that, especially with the release of IE 7, we can be thankful for.

Microsoft's special addition to IE (versions 5 and higher) allows you to use a specially formatted HTML comment (`<!-- comment here -->`) to send markup to (or hide it from) IE, while other browsers ignore it completely.

There are a few ways you can use conditional comments to your advantage (for the complete list, see `http://msdn.microsoft.com/workshop/author/dhtml/overview/ccomment_ovw.asp`), but for our purposes we're interested in hiding our IE hacks from IE 7 (and future versions). The conditional comment for this purpose looks like this:

```
<!--[if lte IE 6]>
  <link rel="stylesheet" type="text/css" href="css/IEhacks.css" />
<![endif]-->
```

The `if` statement at the beginning of the comment says, "If the version of IE is less than or equal to 6, display the following markup," thus preventing IE 7 or newer from reading the style sheet containing our hacks.

Gotta Keep 'Em Separated

The key to success lies in confining hacks to separate style sheets *specifically for hacks*. Isolating CSS hacks makes them much easier to troubleshoot (simply comment out the `<link>` or `@import` that loads the hack style sheet) and you can also remove them from your site entirely in the future by just deleting the appropriate reference. So when the day finally comes when you can stop supporting IE/Win versions 6 and older (and it will come, the prophets have foreseen it!), you can gleefully erase all signs of those IE hacks from your site forever, without having to search through your entire style sheet line by line. And even if you *don't* use IE conditional comments (why wouldn't you?), your hacks are still separate from your primary styles, and thus easier to maintain overall.

You Might Not Even Need a Hack!

The fewer hacks you employ, the better, and one benefit of using IE conditional comments is that you can take advantage of *source order* within the cascade. By importing or linking your

IE-specific style sheet *after* your primary style sheet, you can simply send alternate values and properties to IE without using *any* hacks! If you haven't already, you'll want to dog-ear this page, because it's important.

For example, to send alternate styles to IE 6 and earlier, in a separate style sheet a portion of your document's <head> might look like this:

```
<link rel="stylesheet" type="text/css" href="c/styles.css" media="screen" />

<!--[if lte IE 6]>
  <link rel="stylesheet" type="text/css" href="c/IEbugs.css" media="screen" />
<![endif]-->
```

Non-IE browsers will only load styles.css, but IE versions "less than or equal to" 6 will also load IEbugs.css, and apply those rules after the rules from the first style sheet, thus overriding specified values for any duplicate selectors.

Note The if statement at the start of conditional comments can target other browsers, such as <!--[if IE 5]> to catch IE versions 5 and 5.5 (both start with "5"), or the all-encompassing <!--[if IE]>.

So, where you might have used a hack in the past to, say, specify an alternate line height for lists in IE, you can now have a default rule in your primary style sheet:

```
ul li {
  line-height:1.4;
}
```

and override it in your IE-only style sheet:

```
ul li {
  line-height:1.6;
}
```

IE versions targeted by your conditional comment will use the second value, because it comes later in the source order. No hacking necessary!

Hmm, What Does This Bit of Code Do?

There's nothing worse than revisiting a rule months after writing it, only to be stumped at its purpose. It doesn't need to be a complicated hack either: even the simplest hack can be a mystery when enough time has passed. The solution is to comment *everything*, even if you know what function the hack performs—comments provide *context*, and context is an essential element of understanding.

Say for example you have a client's logo positioned near the top left of a layout using an absolutely positioned h1 heading within a relatively positioned <div id="container">, which works perfectly in non-IE browsers. Your (X)HTML looks like this:

```
<h1 id="logo">
  <a href="/" title="return to the homepage">My Snazzy Logo</a>
</h1>
```

and your rules something like this:

```
#container {
  position:relative;
}

h1#logo {
  position:absolute;
  left:15px;
  top:20px;
  margin:0;padding:0;
}
```

but for some strange reason known only to the developers of IE 6 (and possibly not even them), the logo vanishes from the screen entirely when viewed in that browser (it happens). You don't have time to figure out *why* IE is shifting your client's logo into space—you just need to get it fixed and move on.

After a few rounds of trial and error, you discover that changing to position:relative and using a bottom margin of negative-170px puts the logo back in its proper place in IE. Weird. Confused but satisfied, you drop the IE-specific rule (using the Star HTML hack, covered later in this chapter) in your hack style sheet like this:

```
* html #logo {
  position:relative;
  margin-bottom:-170px;
}
```

Your work is done. You forget about the hack and IE's strange behavior, and you move on with your life. Seven months later, the client decides he wants the logo on the site to be bigger and lower on the page. "No problem!" you say with confidence, and you make the change. Only now the logo doesn't position properly in IE. Rather than rely on your memory (or more trial and error) to figure out what's going wrong, let a few simple comments do the work for you.

Here's the original h1#logo rule, with an added comment referencing the hack:

```
/* this positioning does not work in IE6, hack used */
h1#logo {
  position:absolute;
  left:15px;
  top:20px;
  margin:0;padding:0;
}
```

and now the commented version of the hack itself:

```
/* this corrects a strange positioning behavior in IE6
(the logo vanishes from the screen without it). Surprise surprise... */
* html #logo {
```

```
  position:relative;
  margin-bottom:-170px;
}
```

The comments remind you that you used a hack in the first place, and then why you used the hack. It doesn't hurt to be specific when documenting your hacks, because you never know when someone who *isn't you* will have to work with the styles you've created. Comments provide everyone with a roadmap.

A Few Good Hacks (and Workarounds)

OK, so there's no such thing as a "good" hack, but there *are* a few that it's useful to know about, especially as long as IE 6 continues to command a large portion of the browser market. Just remember, the fewer hacks you use, the better off we'll all be down the road.

May I Have the Envelope Please?

What follows is a selection of the must-have hacks that can save you time, effort, and frustration. Dog-ear these pages now, as you'll likely refer back to them many times (for a more comprehensive—nay, *exhaustive*—list of browser hacks, visit www.positioniseverything.net). We also cover some more useful hacks in the "Hacking a Real-World Layout" section later in this chapter.

Star HTML Hack

IE has an interesting quirk (prior to version 7, where this bug has been fixed): it recognizes an additional, unnamed element outside the outermost element in the document (html). This element is represented by the universal selector (or "star"), and allows the html element to be targeted as a child, rather than the document's parent element (this is not supported anywhere in the CSS specifications, nor by any other browser). This bug can be used to target IE (Mac or Win), and because it uses a parent element in the selector that no other browser recognizes, it also has higher specificity (meaning it can be located anywhere in the cascade's source order, and will still override selectors meant for other browsers).

For example, to hide something from IE—say, a transparent PNG background image that adds to the visual presentation but doesn't take anything away when missing—you can set the value to none and just feed that to IE (because IE 6 and earlier can't display PNGs with alpha transparency):

```
body {
  background:#f90 url(bg_gradient.png) repeat-x;
}

* html body {
  background-image:none;
}
```

Only IE recognizes the * html selector, so in IE versions 6 and earlier, the image will not display (see Figure 6-1). And again, since the selector has higher specificity, the hack can be placed anywhere in the source order and will still override the simple selector.

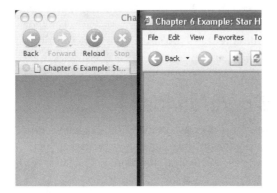

Figure 6-1. *On the left, Camino on OS X displays the transparent PNG, but it is hidden from IE 6 on the right by the Star HTML hack.*

Holly Hack (and an IE/Mac Filter)

Many display issues in IE/Win are the result of oddities in its rendering engine, specifically whether an element has "layout," which is the source of much consternation among web standards developers (read all about IE's hasLayout property at www.satzansatz.de/cssd/onhavinglayout.html if you *really* want to know more). Elements behave quite differently when they have "layout" compared to when they do not, and usually the desired behavior results from a box "having layout," which is triggered by applying any dimension to the box.

Named after the incredibly intelligent woman who discovered it, Holly Bergevin (www.positioniseverything.net), the Holly hack builds on the Star HTML hack, using it to deliver a very small height to specified containers in IE, which tells IE's rendering engine to give the targeted element "layout." Thanks to another bug in IE (which causes the browser to ignore a specified dimension and instead expand a box to contain its contents), this height is ignored and the box expands.

Because IE/Mac does not suffer from the same float bug as its Windows counterparts but does process the Star HTML hack, a filter is used to hide the hack from that browser. The combination of the three parts—Star HTML hack, the IE/Mac filter, and the Holly hack itself (the {height:1%;} declaration)—looks like this:

```
/* Hides from IE5-mac \*/
  * html .floatcontainer { height:1%; }
/* End hide from IE5-mac */
```

When fixing strange display behavior in IE/Win, this hack is often your best starting point for a quick solution (see the next section for an example of the Holly hack in use).

Easy Float Clearing

If you've worked with CSS layouts for any length of time, you've probably encountered the issue of float clearing, especially for columnar layouts. Until recently, the standard method involved inserting something like `<div style="clear:both;"></div>` as the last element within a container `div` surrounding the floats, but that's a nasty way to accomplish the task. Now, thanks to Tony Aslett (`http://csscreator.com`) and the fine folks at `positioniseverything.net`, we have a better way.

Here we have a container `div`, a floated box, and a few block elements following the float:

```
<div class="container">
  <div class="floatedbox">
    <p>floated box</p>
  </div>
  <h3>Container 1</h3>
  <p>(<em>without</em> easy clearing)</p>
</div>
```

And let's add a few styles for visual clarity:

```
.container {
  padding:1em;
  background-color:#eee;
  border:3px solid #ddd;
}

.floatedbox {
  float:left;
  width:125px;
  height:125px;
  margin-right:1em;
  padding:0 10px;
  background-color:#fff;
  border:3px solid #bbb;
}
```

This gives us the result shown in Figure 6-2. Since the float isn't cleared and is taller than the containing element, it extends below the bottom border of its container `div`.

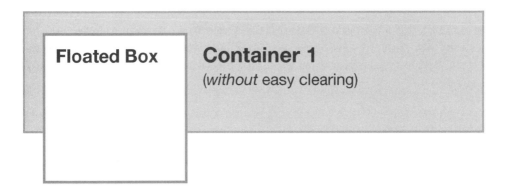

Figure 6-2. *Our noncleared float ignores the container borders.*

Clearly this doesn't work (no pun intended . . . well, mostly), so let's examine our "easy clearing" solution:

```
.clearfix:after {
  content:".";
  display:block;
  height:0;
  clear:both;
  visibility:hidden;
}

/* Hides from IE-mac \*/
  * html .clearfix { height:1%; }
/* End hide from IE-mac */
```

Let's review what's going on under the hood. The first rule (.clearfix:after) uses the :after pseudo-element to generate content *after* our containing block, and the declarations create the content (a period in this case), change the display from the default inline to block (the clear property cannot be applied to inline elements), make the generated content disappear (height:0; and visibility:hidden;), and of course, clear any floats no matter which side they are on. The last part should be familiar from the Holly hack (because it *is* the Holly hack), and sends IE/Win a height to give the container element "layout," which causes IE to expand the container div to surround the floated box.

The only change needed in our (X)HTML is adding the class clearfix to the container div, like so:

```
<div class="container clearfix">
```

The result keeps the markup clean, works in all modern browsers, looks exactly how you might expect it to (see Figure 6-3), and is a much cleaner way to clear those floats of yours.

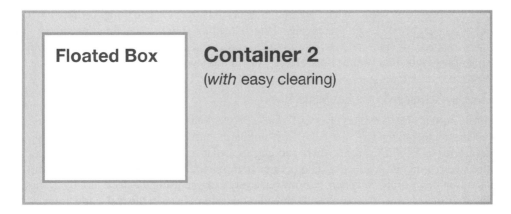

Figure 6-3. *With easy clearing, our float no longer colors outside the lines.*

Horizontal Centering

Another frequent need is to center an entire layout horizontally within the browser window. While you might think this should work without resorting to CSS trickery, you would be wrong. Happily, the workaround is a quick and easy one (and you can use it to center other elements within your layout, not just the entire page—bonus!).

The only requirement is that you have a wrapper around your entire layout. For this example, we'll call our wrapper element #wrapper:

```
<body>
  <div id="wrapper">
    ...
  </div>
</body>
```

Take a few seconds to imagine all your other layout elements where the ... is in the previous code. Done? OK, now on to the CSS:

```
body {
  text-align:center;
  min-width:800px;
}

#wrapper {
  margin:0 auto;
  width:800px;
  text-align:left;
}
```

Setting text-align:center; on the body element centers the layout in IE/Win, thanks to another one of its rendering bugs, while the min-width dimension (which should match the dimension on #wrapper) corrects a strange behavior in some slightly older versions of Mozilla and Netscape browsers. The auto left and right margins on #wrapper keep things centered in other browsers, and text-align:left; realigns the text within your layout (without setting it again, all your text would be centered thanks to the earlier rule). The hack-less example layout (see "A Sample Layout That Doesn't Need Hacks" later in this chapter) shows this method in use.

A Hack-less Alternative to the Box Model Hack

For a while now, the Box Model hack (www.tantek.com/CSS/Examples/boxmodelhack.html) has been a required tool in the virtual shed of most standards-based developers. It fixes a glaring rendering error in IE/Win 5 and 5.5, where padding applied to a box is *subtracted* from the box's specified width rather than added to it, as defined in the specification, resulting in messed-up dimensions in those browsers. There is, however, a way to avoid using the hack, as long as the thought of using an extra div doesn't make you ill (and it shouldn't—in the real world, things are never ideal, and adding an extra element here or there is the lesser of two evils when compared with a browser hack).

The hack-less way around this problem is simple: nest an extra div for padding inside your div with assigned dimensions, like so:

```
<div id="container">
  <div id="container-padding">
    <p>some content</p>
  </div>
</div>
```

We prefer to give an ID to the nested div so it is clearly labeled, but you can choose to leave it out and just use a simple descendent selector instead (as long as you know there won't be any other divs within your container).

The CSS looks like this:

```
#container {
  width:200px;
  height:150px;
}
#container-padding {
  padding:10px;
}
```

Because #container-padding doesn't have any stated dimensions, the incorrect math of IE/Win 5 and 5.5 is no longer a factor. No hacks, no complicated mess—and it works the same in all modern browsers.

Filters: The Sophisticated, High-Society Hacks

Though quickly becoming a thing of the past (thanks in part to more standards compliance across the browsers), *filters* are hacks that don't actually *fix* anything, but rather allow you to target or exclude specific browser versions (similar to IE conditional comments, but they can be used to target almost any browser and version). Though we recommend *against* relying on filters by default (you shouldn't have to if you follow the standards-first process), they can come in handy, especially when you have to support an older browser (some popular hacks even incorporate filters, like the earlier example targeting IE/Mac). And because filters can be kept in separate style sheets just like any other hack (some filters actually *control* which browsers can "see" a style sheet to import), you can properly isolate them, continuing to keep your primary style sheet clean and crisp.

Covering all available filters and variations could take an entire book (and this isn't it), but thankfully Kevin C. Smith maintains a very up-to-date browser compatibility matrix of known filters (`www.centricle.com/ref/css/filters/`), which should provide you with all the information you need if you absolutely *must* filter your styles. For quick access to a few de facto filters, check out Tantek Çelik's list (`www.tantek.com/CSS/Examples/`).

IE 7 "Fixes" You Need to Be Aware Of

Although IE 7 is a huge improvement over previous versions (serious kudos to the IE 7 development team for all their hard work, and for listening to the web standards community throughout the process), some of the fixed bugs and changes to the rendering engine mean some of the most popular hacks still in widespread use today *will not work*.

The most important of these is the Star HTML hack, which takes advantage of a bug in the rendering engines of older versions of IE, and is used by many developers, including your esteemed authors. This hack does not work in IE 7 (this has been confirmed by the IE 7 development team), so if for some reason you are not using IE conditional comments to separate your hacked styles, expect to spend some time working around this issue for your existing sites (but we *know* you'll be separating your hacks like the good web developer that you are after reading this chapter).

In the event you would still like to explore the possibility of hacks that specifically target IE 7, take a look at Brothercake's Triple-X hack (which works as of IE 7 beta 2; see `http://brothercake.co.uk/site/resources/reference/xxx/`) and remember to check everything once IE 7 has officially shipped.

Hacking a Real-World Layout

As we mentioned at the beginning of this chapter, hacks are a necessary evil employed to ensure cross-browser layout equality, or more simply, hacks help us make things look right for everyone. One basic example is the "Thisaway" template series one of the authors, Dan Rubin, designed for Blogger, Google's popular weblog application. We'll look at some layout issues Dan encountered with it, and how he solved them (for another example using multiple hacks to solve a variety of layout problems, see Chapter 14).

The Layout

The templates are used by hundreds of thousands of users around the world, using many different browsers and operating systems, so browser compatibility was essential. The layout Dan designed is fixed width, with pixel-precise widths for the columns (which are created using Dan Cederholm's excellent "Faux Columns" method; you can read the original article at www.alistapart.com/articles/fauxcolumns/; it's also covered in Chapter 7). The (X)HTML/CSS was developed using the standards-first approach explained earlier, and the result (Figure 6-4) looked great in Firefox, Safari, and pretty much any browser that wasn't IE (typically, layouts developed using this method won't require much bug fixing at all, even in IE).

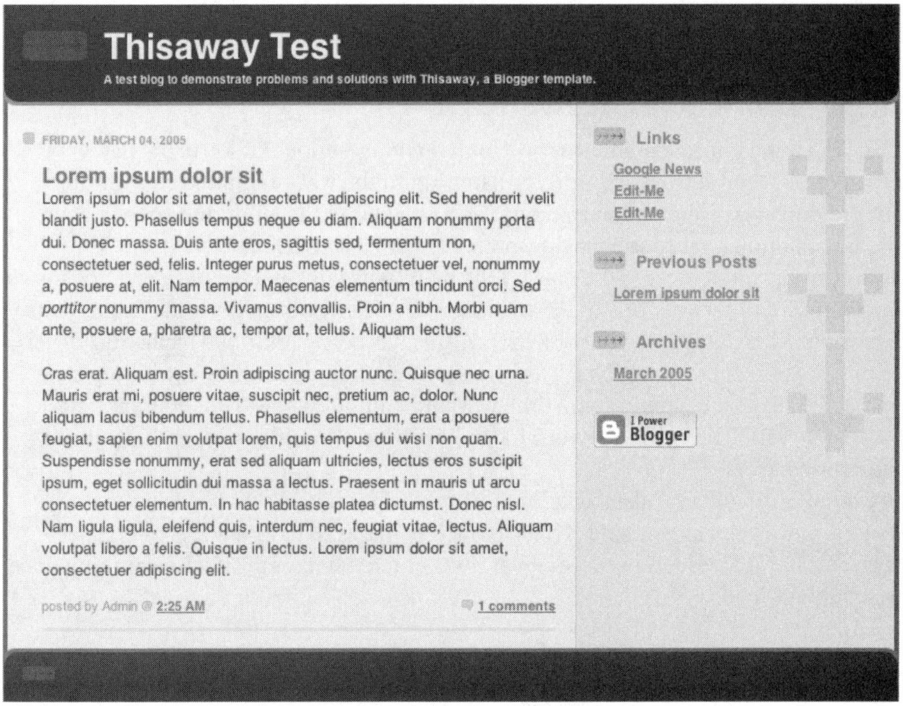

Figure 6-4. *Ooh, that design's so pretty I think I'll blog about my cats.*

However, when viewed in IE/Win, there was a slight problem with the sidebar display (Figure 6-5). When we say "slight" we mean "OMG, the layout's ruined!"

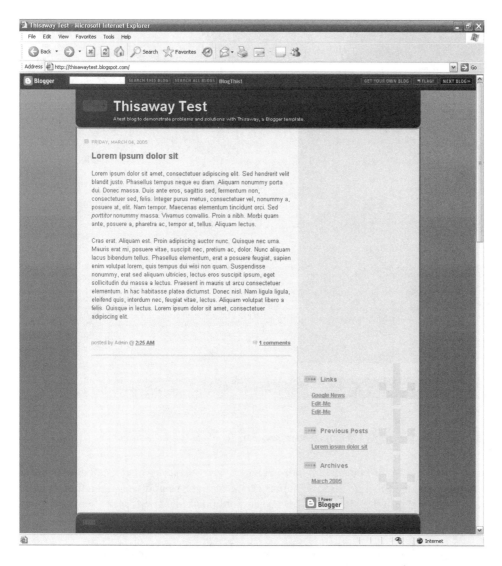

Figure 6-5. *IE/Win and this author have differing opinions on where the sidebar should be.*

The culprit here is another strange bug in IE, where the margin of floats becomes doubled (www.positioniseverything.net/explorer/floatIndent.html), which can wreak havoc with pixel-perfect layouts. If not for the existence of a hack, IE would force rethinking the layout, or changing measurements just to accommodate that browser.

The Hack

As it turns out, the solution also takes advantage of yet another IE rendering oddity: when a floated element is also set to display:inline, IE changes the way that element is rendered (when it should actually ignore the inline value altogether, which other browsers do correctly). The result, after applying display:inline to the left and right column wrappers (which are both floated, and both have margins), is a properly behaved IE (Figure 6-6).

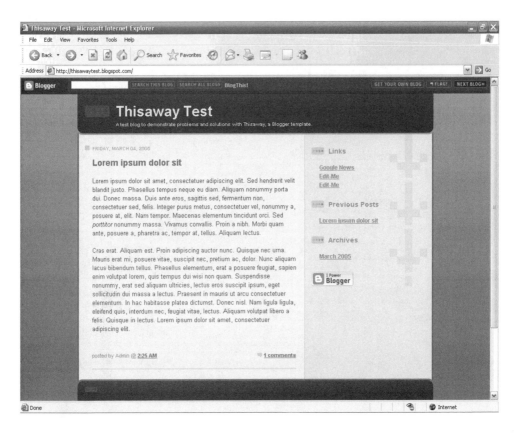

Figure 6-6. *Thanks to a quick hack, IE now remembers its place (and the sidebar's).*

To see the full example code, take a look at `ch6_example_thisaway.html` located in the Source Code/Download section for this chapter at `www.apress.com` and see what happens in IE when you remove `display:inline;` from `#main-content` and `#sidebar-wrapper`.

A Sample Layout That Doesn't Need Hacks

Although hacks have their place (and are required to render most complex layouts across multiple browsers), it is still possible, with a little planning and compromise, to achieve a nice, not-too-basic layout without the use of any hacks at all.

You accomplish this goal in part with good planning and forethought, and by using the IE conditional comments. By sending a few minor corrections to IE 6 and earlier (but no hacks), we can make sure everything is hunky-dory in IE, without using any real hacks (there are some who might cry foul, but the fact is conditional comments are a supported, if proprietary, function of IE, and this is one of their intended purposes).

Although there are live sites that don't use hacks (`http://momcbloomington.org` is a good example), they are difficult to track down, and we'd rather show you a live site with a little more to the layout than the examples we could find online. And since we can't find a live site with those qualities, we've decided to design and build one from scratch for this section.

The Design

The goal for this example is to design a simple personal site as a sort of "portal" to this author's various interests, which he can keep separate from his blog. To do this, we'll use four major areas (design, programming, singing, and writing) along with a few links to favorite online destinations.

■**Note** This layout can be seen in action at `www.danielrubin.org/procss/nohacks/`.

We can't use any complex floats (the easy float clearing method includes a hack, so it doesn't qualify for this example), perform any real multiple-column trickery, or do anything that might trigger IE's strange layout rendering (using the Holly hack is not an option either). That said, we don't want boring, so after spending a little time in our sketchbook and Photoshop (plus a nice logotype courtesy of the amazing Anton Peck), we've settled on a layout that we're happy with (Figure 6-7).

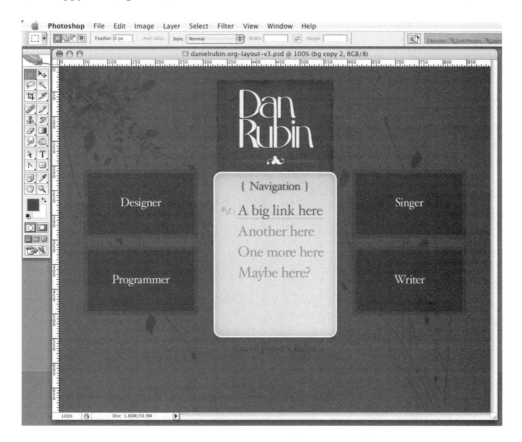

Figure 6-7. *Our proposed layout (complete with dummy link text) in Photoshop*

The Markup

Now that we have a design, we need to figure out how to structure the information within our (X)HTML document. The obvious elements we need to account for are the four boxes, the logotype, and the list of links in the middle. We've decided to make this a fixed-width layout, with the content elements centered in the browser.

After a little thought, we can see the four boxes are in two columns of two boxes each, with the link list as a third, center column. We can float the two outer columns to the left and right, and center the link list in between, as long as the center column comes last in the source (which is perfectly fine in this case, since we'd like the other content to display first for users viewing the site without styles or on an alternate browsing device). That only leaves the logo-type: we'd prefer to have an h1 with the site title before all our other content in the source, and replace that with the logo graphic. That means the h1 cannot be located in the center column (since it's going to be last in the source). We can move it to the top by adding a header div to enclose the site title, and then align it with the center column.

We now have the following markup for the layout elements (we've omitted some of the extra markup used for the contents of the four outer boxes, since it doesn't affect the layout—the full source file is included in the downloads for this chapter, and no hacks are used to style the extra elements):

```
<div id="superfluous">
  <div id="wrapper">
    <div id="header">
      <h1>Dan Rubin</h1>
    </div>

    <div id="col1">
      <p id="top1">...</p>
      <p id="bottom1">...</p>
    </div>

    <div id="col2">
      <p id="top2">...</p>
      <p id="bottom2">...</p>
    </div>

    <div id="content">
      <div id="navigation">
        <ul>
          <li><a href="http://superfluousbanter.org/">Read my blog &raquo;</a></li>
          <li><a href="http://webgraph.com/">See my work &raquo;</a></li>
          <li><a href="http://roundersquartet.com/">Hear me sing &raquo;</a></li>
          <li><a href="http://flickr.com/photos/danrubin/">Browse my pics➡
            &raquo;</a></li>
          <li><a href="http://myspace.com/danielstephenrubin">My MySpace➡
            &raquo;</a></li>
          <li><a href="mailto:dan@danielrubin.org">Send me email &raquo;</a></li>
        </ul>
    </div>
```

```
      </div>
      <p id="footer">&copy; 2006 <a href="http://superfluousbanter.org/">Daniel S.➥
        Rubin</a>. Logo by <a href="http://antonpeck.com/">Anton Peck</a></p>
    </div>
  </div>
</div>
```

As you can see, we've filled out the link list, and also added a footer paragraph within the center (third) column. The footer paragraph will follow the list in the flow, and its default position should be exactly what we want.

You might also have noticed two outer `div`s surrounding the other elements. These will allow the layout to be centered in the browser window (#wrapper), as well as add the gradient and background artwork anchored to the top of the browser in our design (#superfluous—the gradient and artwork at the bottom of the design will be assigned to the body). Without styles, this displays in a fairly orderly manner (Figure 6-8, with actual content included).

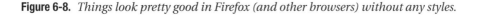

Dan Rubin

I am a Designer I design beautiful, usable interfaces for screen, plus some print work

I am a Programmer I use web standards to promote forward-compatibiltiy and accessibility

I am a Singer I sing a cappella, barbershop harmony, and even some solo stuff

I am a Writer I write about design and code for Apress, friends of ED and on my blog

- Read my blog »
- See my work »
- Hear me sing »
- Browse my pics »
- My MySpace »
- Send me email »

© 2006 Daniel S. Rubin. Logo by Anton Peck

Figure 6-8. *Things look pretty good in Firefox (and other browsers) without any styles.*

The Style Sheet

At this stage, we have a good idea of how we're going to position and style the various elements of the layout, including applying a few background images to incorporate the purely visual parts of the design (shown here minus styles used for visual effects on the four boxes; as with the markup, this extra code is included in the downloadable source, and is hack-free):

```
body {
  background:#930 url(bg_body.gif) no-repeat center bottom;
  margin:0;padding:0;
  text-align:center;
  min-width:832px;
  font-family:'hoefler text', georgia, serif;
}
```

```
#superfluous {
  background:url(bg_superfluous.gif) no-repeat left top;
  height:594px;
}
#wrapper {
  width:800px;
  margin:0 auto;
  padding:25px 0 0;
}

#header {
  margin:0 0 -20px;
}
#header h1 {
  background:url(logo.gif) no-repeat;
  width:245px;
  height:195px;
  margin:0 auto;padding: 0;
  text-indent:-5000px;
}

/* the third, centered column */
#content {
  width:280px;
  margin:0 auto;
}

#navigation {
  background:url(bg_navigation.png) no-repeat center top;
  height:360px;
}
#navigation ul {
  list-style:none;
  margin:0 auto;padding:2.5em 0 0;
  font-size:30px;
  line-height:1.4;
  letter-spacing:-1.5pt;
  text-align:left;
}
#navigation ul li {
  margin:0 0 0 22px;padding:0;
}
```

```css
#navigation a {
  background:url(list_hover.png) no-repeat 0 -100px;
  padding:0 0 0 32px;
  color:#996;
  text-decoration:none;
}
#navigation a:hover {
  background-position:0 50%;
  color:#663;
}

#footer {
  margin:0;
  color:#6d1800;
  font-size:75%;
}
#footer a {
  color:#6d1800;
  text-decoration:none;
}
#footer a:hover {
  border-bottom:1px solid;
}

#col1 {
  float:left;
  width:240px;
  margin:30px 16px 0 0;
}
#col2 {
  float:right;
  width:240px;
  margin:30px 0 0 16px;
}

#col1 p,
#col2 p {
  margin:0 0 16px;padding:0;
  font-size:24px;
}
```

```
#col1 p a,
#col2 p a {
  display:block;
  background-color:#661600;
  border:8px solid #842800;
  padding:1.1em 0 0em;
  color:#ffc;
  text-decoration:none;
}
```

The left and right columns (#col1 and #col2) are containers for the paragraphs, which hold the as that create the actual boxes (the as are set to display:block so they fill the entire width of each p). Phew. The center column (#content) is positioned using the same method that our outer #wrapper uses to center the entire layout. Also, note the #superfluous outermost element needs a height because the background image assigned to it is taller than all the elements within the layout (without the height, the background image would be cut off at the point at which the contained elements finished rendering).

Everything looks good in Firefox so far, but before we move on to testing in IE, we must correct one small issue with the positioning of our bottom background image (Figure 6-9).

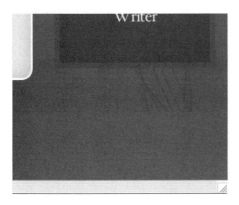

Figure 6-9. *Firefox doesn't expand the* body *to the full height of the browser window.*

As it turns out, assigning height:100% to the html element fixes this Firefox problem and doesn't affect other browsers, so after adding that to the top of our style sheet, we're ready for IE.

Adjusting for IE 6

As luck would have it, our layout barely suffers when first viewed in IE (Figure 6-10).

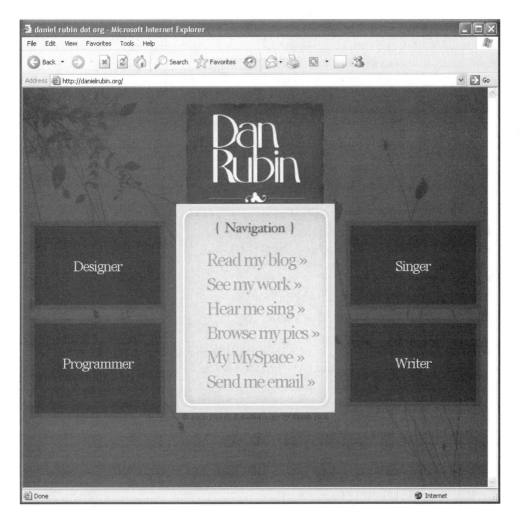

Figure 6-10. *IE is already quite close, leaving us with just a few tiny adjustments to make.*

Comparing IE's rendering with Firefox, we only have to make a few margin adjustments on the left and right columns (they are further down the page than they should be), reduce the size of the footer text, and of course correct the background image in the center column.

Fixing the margins ends up involving adjustments to multiple rules: the #header receives a shorter negative bottom margin, the padding on top of #navigation ul is reduced, and the top margins of the left and right columns are cut in half. Reducing the size of the footer text is a simple matter of setting a smaller font-size.

That leaves the background image behind the link list. Because our design uses a drop shadow around the entire menu, we decided we wanted that to be a transparent PNG so the artwork further in the background would be able to show through. Unfortunately, IE 6 doesn't support 8-bit transparency in PNGs, so we're going to let IE users see an alternate image (a GIF) that doesn't include the shadow.

These adjustments can all be placed within an IE conditional comment, targeting IE 6 and earlier:

```
<!--[if lte IE 6]>
  <style type="text/css" media="screen">
    #header { margin-bottom:-10px; }
    #navigation { background-image:url(bg_navigation.gif); }
    #navigation ul { padding-top:2em; }
    #footer { font-size:65%; }
    #col1, #col2 { margin-top:15px; }
  </style>
<![endif]-->
```

These IE-specific styles could also be placed in an external style sheet and the style sheet linked within the conditional comment. The final layout looks great across browsers and platforms (Figure 6-11), with no hacks in sight.

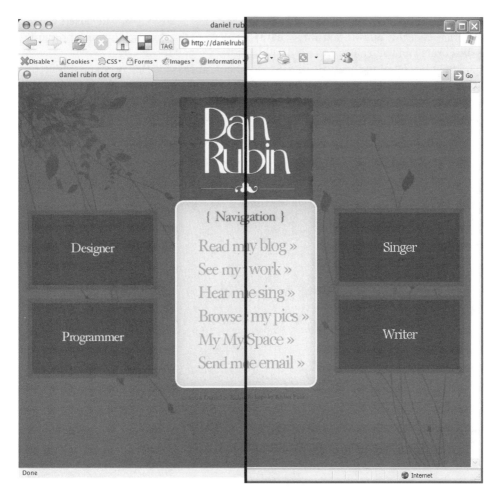

Figure 6-11. *Firefox on OS X (left) and IE 6 on Windows XP display everything just as intended.*

Summary

In the end, get the job done—that's the best philosophy to adopt with web design. When dealing with browser problems in the real world, you'll find the process is best summed up by a time-tested quote from one of history's great leaders:

Perhaps it is better to be irresponsible and right, than to be responsible and wrong.

Winston Churchill

In the quest for browser and platform compatibility, we are often forced to strike a balance between clean markup and a few extra wrappers, and between totally valid styles and a few necessary hacks. In the long run, if your goal is to have a working layout on all major browsers, a little "irresponsible" code that perfectly serves the needs of your site's users is better than perfect code that doesn't. You always have to remember that you are designing primarily for the site's users, not yourself.

Thankfully, by planning ahead, using a development process focused on standards first, and having a few necessary hacks in our back pocket, we can make the process of dealing with these browser oddities (almost) completely painless. This method will be especially useful when you start working with complex CSS layouts in the next chapter.

CHAPTER 7

■■■

CSS Layouts

For the longest time, the majority of web developers looked at CSS as something that was useful primarily for maintaining a consistent look for typography across a web site and such aspects as background colors, but not much else. At some point, people started to make greater use of the styling of block-level elements—and by that we mean putting everything in boxes with styled borders (some styles were more successful or tasteful than others!). This practice was carried through to the early full CSS layouts. But the site that really showed that a full layout with CSS was possible *without* being boxy and ugly was the famous CSS Zen Garden (www.csszengarden.com/). Designer Dave Shea did a fantastic thing with that site by taking all the theory and the practical-but-essentially-ugly examples of CSS and coming up with a handful of showcase CSS designs that proved what was possible; that handful of examples eventually spawned hundreds of amazing entries.

Now we're at a stage in the game where true web professionals understand not only that a CSS layout is possible to do (and do well) but also that it's a task they can carry out in a wide number of ways. Each method has its fans and detractors, though, and no one method is right or wrong; your decision obviously depends on the audience and content of your web site. In this chapter we'll look at various CSS layout methods that are available to you as a web developer, and we'll assess the benefits of each method and the various "gotchas" that you may run up against.

The Never-Ending Debate: What's the Perfect Page Width?

Don't expect us to settle the debate of the perfect width here—we're going to sit on that proverbial fence and simply present the evidence before you. Here are the issues:

- *Readability*: How easily can a block of text be read on screen, and what effect does resizing the screen or font size have?

- *Adaptability/portability*: How easily can the design be used on a small screen (e.g., a small PC monitor or a device such as a PDA)?

- *Future maintainability*: The more technically clever the design, the greater the difficulty in building something that another developer could later take on and support (if they are not at the CSS ninja status that you are soon to achieve!).

The argument about what constitutes the best page width is all about these factors. A web page (or site) can be a fixed width, which might mean that at the default font size the line length (as in the distance from left to right of the content that you're reading) is easy to read. This is because as your eye reaches the end of the line, you can easily scan back to the next line without losing your place. But what if you increase the font size in a fixed-width layout? Figure 7-1 shows a good example from `http://lost.cubit.net/` (Sledgeweb's Lost … Stuff, a popular fansite for the TV program *Lost*). As you can see, at the default font size the site scores high on the readability scale but not so high on the adaptability scale (Figure 7-2).

Figure 7-1. *At default text size, this popular Lost fansite—which is styled with CSS—is perfectly readable. (Screen shots from Sledgeweb's Lost … Stuff,* `http://lost.cubit.net`*. Reprinted with permission.)*

Figure 7-2. *With the text notched up a few sizes, it soon runs out of room in the fixed-width layout.*

A solution to this type of problem might be to enable the page to be more flexible; we could, for example, have a fixed left navigation area but a flexible content area. However, this approach presents its own problems: if you maximize the browser window, the line length of the text becomes long and harms readability. See, it's not easy, is it? In this section, we'll look at some examples. Which method is best is up to you to decide; they all have their own respective merits. To aid with the comparison, we'll use an example page design—a simple, two-column design with a header—and apply the various treatments.

The Fixed-Width Layout

The fixed-width layout is arguably the easiest of the layouts to achieve. You can, to some extent, remove some of the what-ifs associated with web page design. A print designer knows what dimensions they are designing for, but on a screen can you be so sure? Deciding on a fixed width can level that playing field somewhat. The first issue to address is the page width you should design for. We recommend aiming for a width of 770 pixels so that a browser running full screen in a monitor at 800×600 pixels will be able to display the page without also showing the Ugly Horizontal Scroll Bar of Doom.

Why 800×600? There are still many people out there who are running that resolution, though admittedly the most common at the time of this writing is 1024×768 pixels. Given that, if you make the layout work for 800×600, it's going to play nice on 1024×768. However, if you design for 800×600 and someone with a monitor the size of a cinema screen and with a super-high resolution is viewing your site, it may resemble a postage stamp. The key to getting it right is this: know your audience. Get some stats and base your design decision on those. We'll assume that 800×600 is what your stats people are telling you for now.

■**Note** Usability expert Jakob Nielsen (www.useit.com/alertbox/screen_resolution.html) suggested in June 2006 that "optimizing" for 1024×768 was the way to go since it involves designing for the majority while taking steps to accommodate users with lower screen resolutions. An example is having the bulk of page content visible in the 800-pixel width area, with related links (or other "nonessential" content) the only parts missing from the default view. We hate to see horizontal scrollbars and favor making the layout work in 800×600 wherever possible. But as we said, base your decision on the stats and facts available to you.

Trust us when we say that you will make mistakes with your first (unaided) CSS layouts. Rather than take you straight into the utopian world of "perfect-layout-first-time," we'll demonstrate some of the pitfalls that we have experienced along the way. That way, you'll be better armed to deal with similar problems with your projects.

So, try not to skip ahead just yet—we want you to ride through some of these potholed roads with us for a while!

Using Absolute Positioning

A fairly simple method for positioning elements on a page is to use absolute positioning. Using this scheme, you remove sections of the document from the normal "flow." To explain this concept, we'll use an analogy. Imagine the document as if it were a roll of paper towels. Now think of each tear-off section as a clearly defined area of your web page: sheet 1 = the header section, sheet 2 = content, sheet 3 = navigation elements. By default, the running order is to have one after the other. However, in CSS you can break those sections out from the prescribed running order and place them where you want. Back to the paper towel analogy again: imagine tearing off each sheet and then placing each square on top of each other (triple thickness!). This is basically what you are doing if you specify in your CSS that those three page elements should be absolutely positioned: the browser removes them from the flow of the document and simply places them at the top- and leftmost positions in the browser window. What you need is a method for fanning those pieces of the web pages back out so that they sit in the correct place and so that one piece is not obscuring another. You can accomplish this by specifying some x and y coordinates for each piece. Here's the basic (X)HTML for our example page (truncated somewhat):

```
<body>
  <div id="wrapper">
    <div id="header">
      <img src="swanky-header-graphic.gif" alt="Swanky header graphic"➥
        width="377" height="41" />
    </div>
    <div id="content-wrapper">
      <div id="content-inner">
        <p>We flew with Czech Airlines ...  </p>
      </div>
    </div>
    <div id="navigation">
```

```
    <ul>
      <li><a href="day1.html">Day 1 (arrival)</a></li>
      <li><a href="day2.html">Day 2 (kutna Hora)</a></li>
      <li><a href="day3.html">Day 3 (Prague Castle)</a></li>
      <li><a href="day4.html">Day 4 (up the towers, Karlstejn Castle)</a></li>
      <li><a href="day5.html">Day 5 (Metro tour)</a></li>
    </ul>
  </div>
 </div>
</body>
```

This page has an outer container (`wrapper`), which contains a header (for the header graphic) and then the page content (`content-wrapper`). The `content-wrapper` div contains two child elements: one for the content itself and one for the navigation section. All of these elements are distinct and unique, and as such have been given `id` attributes, which we can refer to in the CSS accordingly in order to style and lay out the page. For the purposes of these examples, we're going to focus on the layout and positioning aspects and not get hung up on the styling of the text (Chapter 9 will go into more detail about styling text).

Here is the CSS that will set the specific areas of the page where we want them. Note the parts in bold that show the layout aspects at play here:

```
body {
  margin:0;
  padding:0;
  text-align:center;
  background: #f0f0f0 url(body-bg.gif) repeat-x top;
}
#wrapper {
  text-align:left;
  width:770px;
  margin:10px auto 0 auto;
  position:relative;
}
#header {
  background: #272727 url(header-bg.gif) repeat-x bottom left;
  padding:10px 15px 10px 13px;
}
#content-wrapper {
  width:570px;
  background:#fff url(nav-to-content-trans.gif) repeat-y left;
  position:absolute;
  left:200px;
}
#content-inner {
  padding:5px 15px 0 15px;
}
```

```
#navigation {
  position:absolute;
  width:200px;
  padding-top:15px;
  background:#dade75;
}
```

Note You can find the code for the HTML and CSS for this chapter in the Source Code/Download section of the Apress web site.

Please, please don't use a `<center>` tag on your web page. You center a layout in the CSS, not in the web page markup. In our example, you'll see mechanisms in place to do this:

- For the more standards-compliant browsers out there, you use the `margin` property on the element that needs to be centered and give it a value of `auto`. So, the `wrapper` div had `margin:10px auto 0 auto`, where the left and right values were set to `auto`. This causes the browser to calculate equal margins on either side, thus centering the `wrapper` div.

- For IE/Windows version 6 (if running in quirks mode) or earlier, the previous technique is not recognized, so the `body` element is given a `text-align` value of `center`. This causes anything in the body, regardless of whether it really is text, to center on the page. That leaves us with something to clean up, though.

- Because of inheritance, every element below the `body` element in the document (basically, everything!) will also center text, so we need to reset the normal appearance of text and other elements by reapplying a `text-align` value of `left` in the newly centered `wrapper` div.

In our CSS example, you'll note that some items are positioned using the value `absolute` and some with `relative`. What's the difference and which one should you use?

When you specify that an element is to be positioned absolutely, the browser needs to know "in relation to what?" If you state that it should be absolutely positioned 0 pixels from the top and left, the browser treats that as 0 from the browser viewport, regardless of what container that element sits in or how far down the document tree that is—unless you tell the browser to use a different starting point.

If the element you are trying to position is contained in one that is itself already positioned (as the `wrapper` div is), then the x and y coordinates (or left and top properties) start from that point. This is a tricky concept to explain with words alone, so refer to Figure 7-3, which explains it visually.

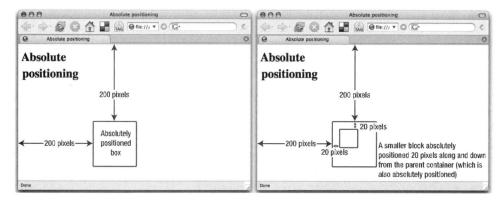

Figure 7-3. *Absolute and relative positioning explained*

So, how does the CSS transform the (X)HTML you saw earlier? Well, the site now looks something like Figure 7-4.

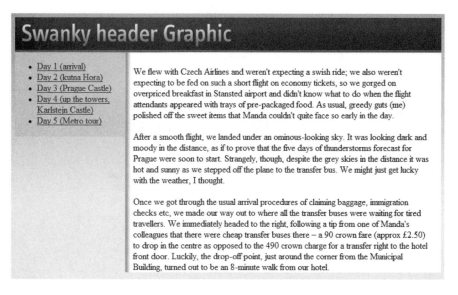

Figure 7-4. *Absolutely positioned content and navigation areas*

Ahem, something's not quite right here. The problem lies in the fact that the navigation on the left is much shorter than the content and only takes up as much space as it needs. That's resulting in an ugly effect not unlike a Tetris piece waiting to land. You could specify in the CSS that the navigation have a certain height, but what height should that be? Ideally, it needs to match up with the content to the right of it. But then if you do that—say, set both to 600 pixels height—it *might* be fine for a navigation area but content varies wildly. If the size is too small, your text will burst out of the space you make available; if you set a value too high in the hope that the main page content has enough space—for example, 2,000 pixels—you're creating a design that might be fine on some pages but massively oversized for other pages with minimal content (which means a whole lot of scrolling for no good reason). One method you could employ is to use JavaScript to calculate the height required for each column. If you are a confident JavaScripter, this may be a practical solution, but it may go against your principles of markup and code purity. (The solution would require the JavaScript to calculate the heights of two elements after page load and then adjust the height attribute of whichever element is shorter.) Besides, what happens to your layout if you use such a technique but the user has JavaScript disabled? And it's another thing to maintain, remember!

Instead of setting a height for both the navigation div and the content div, you could specify a set height for the container that holds both of these elements. In this case, we mean the wrapper. This approach results in a slight improvement, but we still have the same issue regarding the height. Here is an example; we've used a repeating background image that is set in the outer wrapper container div to create a column effect:

```
#wrapper {
  text-align:left;
  width:770px;
  margin:10px auto 0 auto;
  position:relative;
  height:600px;
  background:#fff url(nav-bg.gif) repeat-y left;
}
```

You can see the result in Figure 7-5.

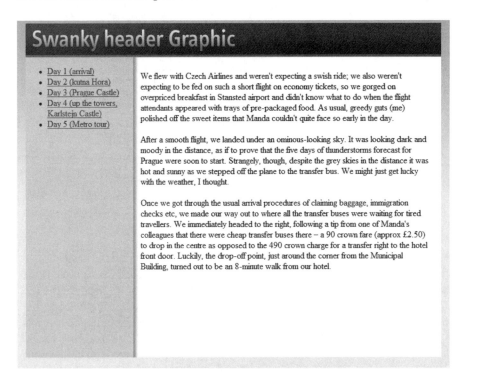

Figure 7-5. *We've fixed the left column by applying a height to the outer container and using a tiled background image.*

The problem with this approach to layout (and the horrible workarounds that we've suggested might be solutions) involves the way that absolutely positioned items work. As we mentioned earlier, when you set something to be positioned absolutely, you remove it from the flow of the document. This has the effect of making containing elements pay no attention to the dimensions of the items that are inside it, because you've effectively taken them out.

Imagine, if you will, three balloons. Somehow you've managed to place two balloons inside the third balloon so that you can still get to the necks of those two inner balloons. Not only are you a genius for managing to do that, but you also have a powerful set of lungs and can blow both of those balloons up quite easily. What happens? The outer balloon stretches as the inner ones are inflated. This is what happens in a "normal" web page (think containing div element = balloon skin, content = air). When you *absolutely position* those inner elements, the outer element won't stretch to fit. Phew, was that a whole load of hot air on our part or did that expand your understanding of the issue?

So, it's one thing to understand the idea behind absolute positioning, but there are other (usually better) ways of doing things. Let's show you one of them.

Using Floated Positioning

We're still looking at a fixed-width design, but this time we'll take the content and "float" it over to the right of the page, and we'll take the navigation and float it to the left. If you are familiar with some of the old-school methods of web page building and design, this strategy is similar to applying the align="left/right" attribute to tables or images (you shouldn't use that approach any longer, by the way, folks). When you use align="left/right", content flows around it, not under it, thus creating an L-shape.

The outer container is 770 pixels wide; we'll split the page so that the navigation takes up 200 pixels and the content has the remaining 570 pixels. Here's the CSS that achieves this layout scheme (the relevant parts are highlighted in bold); the (X)HTML is identical to the first fixed-width examples:

```
body {
  margin:0;
  padding:0;
  text-align:center;
  background: #f0f0f0 url(body-bg.gif) repeat-x top;
}
#wrapper {
  text-align:left;
  width:770px;
  margin:10px auto 0 auto;
  background:#dade75;
  border:1px solid silver;
}
#header {
  background: #272727 url(header-bg.gif) repeat-x bottom left;
  padding:10px 15px 10px 13px;
}
#content-wrapper {
  width:570px;
```

```
  float:right;
  background:#fff url(nav-to-content-trans.gif) repeat-y left;
}
#content-inner {
  padding:5px 15px 0 15px;
}
#navigation {
  width:200px;
  float:left;
  padding-top:15px;
}
```

Figure 7-6 shows the effect.

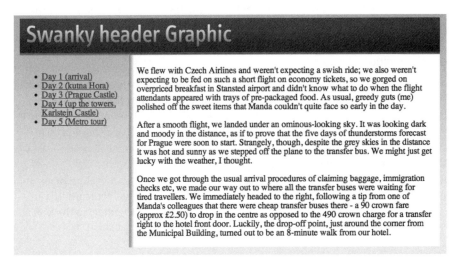

Figure 7-6. *The background image in the body shows through as the outer container has collapsed down.*

What's happened this time? Notice that the left column is missing the background color; the fade image set on the body element is showing through. Don't worry, though, it's easily fixed. Besides, we think it's only fair to take you through the pain that other CSS layout newbies have to endure so that you know how to put things right!

The problem here is similar to what happened with the absolutely positioned scheme: when the items were floated, the outer container effectively collapsed in behind those floated items. The simplest way to solve this problem is to insert a div element after the two floated items and add some CSS to clear any floated elements, which restores the normal document flow. We'll give this div an id of footer (even though there's currently no footer text or information in there; think: future-proofing!). This has the effect of dragging the outer container back out to where the floated items finish. (Clearing float collapse problems can get a little troublesome but don't worry—this thorny topic is covered later in this chapter in the section "Managing Floats.")

Note Actually, the quick-and-dirty method is to place a break tag with a `clear:both` style attribute in there: `<br style="clear:both;" />`. It's common to see this but it's a bad practice; you can end up with hundreds or thousands of pages that you may need to change later. Therefore, it's always better to put clearing instructions for the browser in an external CSS file, however tempting the quick-and-dirty approach may seem at the time.

Here's the amended (X)HTML:

```
<div id="wrapper">
  <div id="header">
    <img src="swanky-header-graphic.gif" alt="Swanky header graphic"➥
      width="377" height="41" />
  </div>
  <div id="content-wrapper">
    <div id="content-inner">
      <p>We flew with Czech Airlines ... </p>
    </div>
  </div>
  <div id="navigation">
    <ul>
      <li><a href="day1.html">Day 1 (arrival)</a></li>
      <li><a href="day2.html">Day 2 (kutna Hora)</a></li>
      <li><a href="day3.html">Day 3 (Prague Castle)</a></li>
      <li><a href="day4.html">Day 4 (up the towers, Karlstejn Castle)</a></li>
      <li><a href="day5.html">Day 5 (Metro tour)</a></li>
    </ul>
  </div>
  <div id="footer"> </div>
</div>
```

And the CSS addition is here:

```
#footer {
  clear:both;
}
```

Figure 7-7 shows the effect on the layout. As you can see, the left column background is once again showing, as is the subtle one-pixel gray border around the layout. (If you cannot see the effect in this figure, you might want to download the source code for this book and try this technique for yourself.)

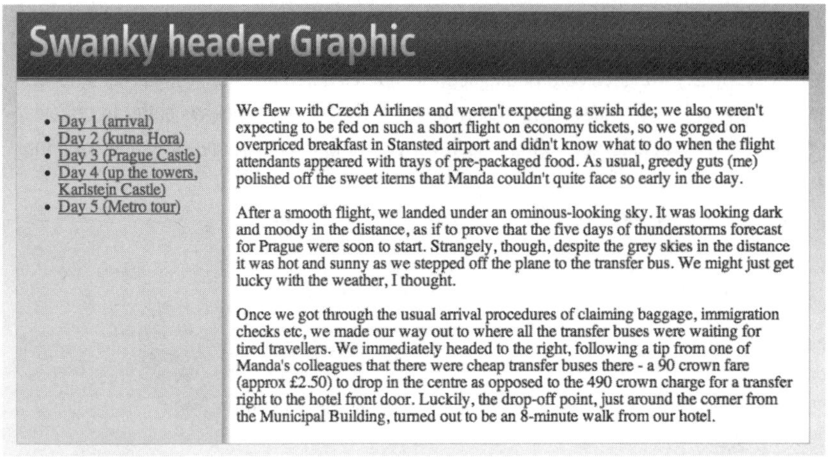

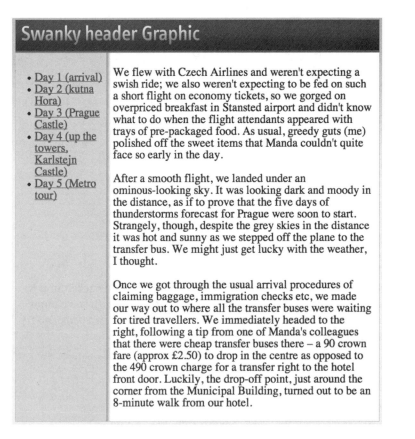

Figure 7-7. *Problem solved!*

If we resize the text somewhat, you'll notice that the page reflows accordingly, as shown in Figure 7-8.

Figure 7-8. *Same page with resized text*

The addition of the footer (admittedly, a footer with no actual content), which is then given the `clear:both;` CSS property/value pairing, solves the problem of the outer element collapsing underneath these floated items—but it's including additional markup for the sake of it, some might argue. There are ways that you can avoid inserting seemingly superfluous markup like this and still manage floated items effectively, something which we cover later in this chapter.

The main issue with this fixed-width layout is still that it won't allow text to resize completely. Eventually you'll run out of horizontal room for the text. So with that in mind, let's look at a more flexible CSS layout.

The Liquid Layout

As its name suggests, a *liquid* layout is one that reflows to fill the available space. Some people swear by this layout as it gives the person viewing your site control ("I want my window this size"). However, this layout has its own dangers:

- If the window is resized to maximum, reading large blocks of text can become difficult; scanning from the end of a line to a new line is not easy.

- If the window is sized down quite a lot, elements of the page may collapse in on each other and overlap in all sorts of weird and not-so-wonderful ways if you don't do your math correctly.

In short, the flexibility that a liquid layout offers may come at a price, depending on how your site visitors set their browsers. But caveat emptor!

Here's the CSS for a liquid layout of the same page design. Rather than set a specific width for the `wrapper` container, we've specified a margin in the `body` element (40 pixels at each side). Because a block-level element will take up 100 percent of the available width by default, the wrapper will stretch to fill whatever size the browser window is; there's no need to specify a width here.

```
body {
  margin:10px 40px;
  padding:0;
  text-align:center;
  background: #f0f0f0 url(body-bg.gif) repeat-x top;
}
#wrapper {
  text-align:left;
  background:#dade75;
  border:1px solid silver;
}
#header {
  background: #272727 url(header-bg.gif) repeat-x bottom left;
  padding:10px 15px 10px 13px;
}
#content-wrapper {
  background:#fff url(nav-to-content-trans.gif) repeat-y left;
  float:right;
  width:75%;
}
#content-inner {
  padding:5px 15px 0 15px;
}
#navigation {
  width:25%;
  float:left;
  padding-top:15px;
}
#footer {
  clear:both;
}
```

See Figure 7.9 for the result, at various widths.

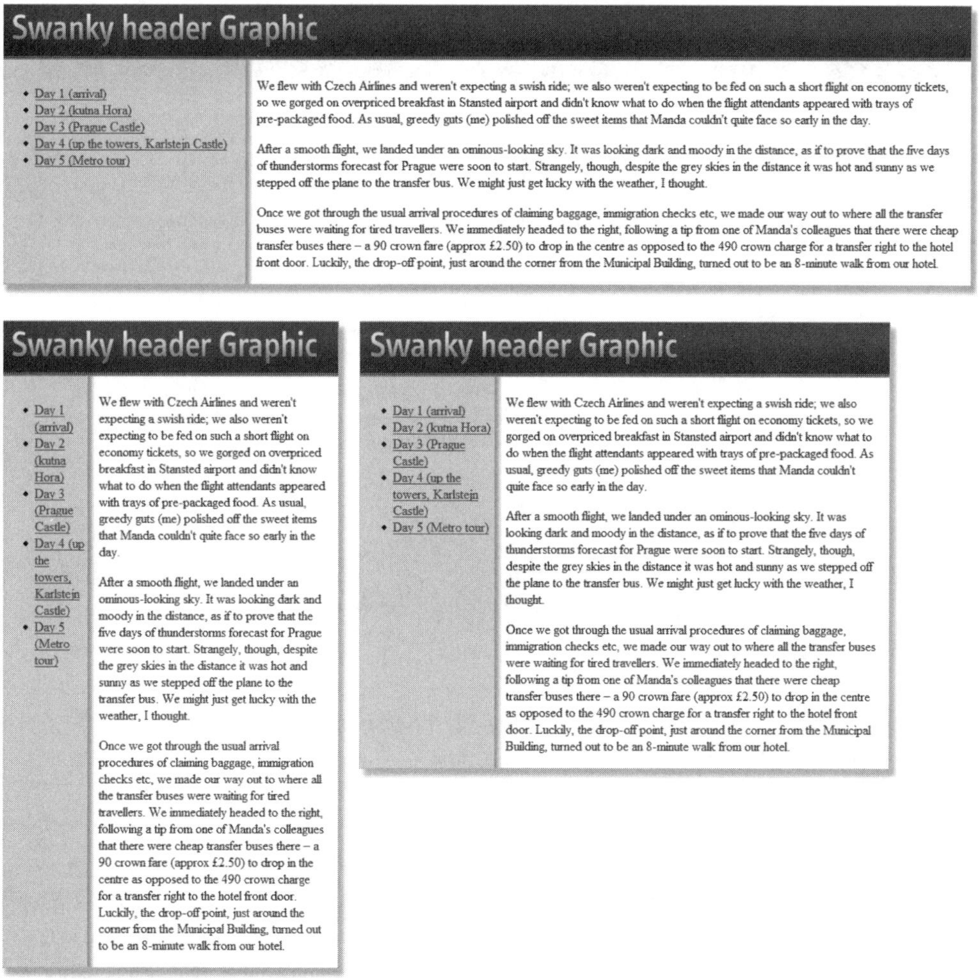

Figure 7-9. *Liquid layout at different sizes*

The width of the navigation and the content add up to 100 percent (75 percent + 25 percent). However, if you were to add a border to either of these elements (even a one-pixel border), you wouldn't have enough room for the two elements to sit side by side, since they are floated. One item would wrap underneath the other (as shown in Figure 7-10). Try not to mix and match in this way or, if you must, shave off the percentage values just a little—perhaps 24% and 74%—and try resizing the screen to see what effect this has.

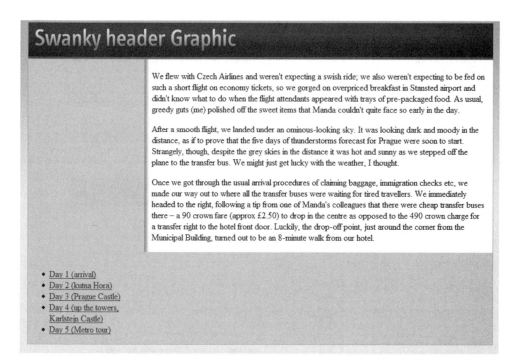

Figure 7-10. *Be careful when adding widths of floated items; if they add up to more than 100 percent, wrapping like this can occur.*

■ Tip You may have wondered why we included both a `content-wrapper` and a `content-inner div`— why not just one container for the content? This is a simple workaround to a problem you'll encounter when calculating widths of elements, especially when using a flexible design. When you're adding padding to an area, such as around the text in the main content, `padding` adds to the widths you've defined and may take the total over 100 percent. It is often much less problematic to use an outer container on which you specify the width, and then apply the padding, border, or margin properties on the inner container. That way, these properties can work independently and won't cause issues with calculating widths. Purists might argue that adding another `div` is a waste of markup, but we feel it is a minor inconvenience to make the CSS work cross-browser. As long as you use sensible `id` attributes for these `div`s, it's a highly practical compromise.

The issue is related to how browsers understand the Box Model, which defines how the width of content in a block-level element is calculated and rendered alongside borders, margins, and padding widths. Earlier versions of IE got the calculation wrong, thus causing untold problems for cross-browser designs. We discuss the Box Model problem—and the hack that solves a lot of the problems associated with it—in Chapter 6 (we also present a hack-less alternative).

Elastic Layouts

As you learned from the previous example, with the liquid layout the browser window is stretched wide and the content becomes difficult to read. What you really want is a page width that works alongside the font size so that the two aspects are linked in some way. If the font size is reduced, the line length—and along with it the page width—comes down accordingly, and vice versa. Thankfully, there is a method for accomplishing this goal: the elastic layout.

In an elastic layout, when you change the font size, other elements scale up or down accordingly. You use em measurements rather than pixels or percentages. An em is directly related to the size of the typeface, so if you specify a width for the wrapper in terms of ems, when you increase the font size the width of the wrapper goes up as well.

The first step is to set a sensible baseline. On most browsers, the default font size is 16 pixels. If you can knock the default down to 10 pixels in the CSS for the body, calculations will be a lot easier from that point on. You can do this by setting font-size in the body to 62.5% (62.5 percent of 16 = 10):

```
body {
  font-size:62.5%;
}
```

Then, knowing that each em represents 10 pixels at the default font size, you can use ems for subsequent measurements. For example:

```
h1 {
  font-size:2em
}
```

would give you level 2 headings of 20 pixels at the default font size, but these headings would scale up if the user prefers.

Let's look at the amended style sheet for the elastic layout. As before, the HTML is unchanged; only the CSS is different. The significant changes are highlighted in bold:

```
body {
  margin:0;
  padding:0;
  text-align:center;
  background: #f0f0f0 url(body-bg.gif) repeat-x top;
  font-size:62.5%;
}
#wrapper {
  font-size:1.4em;
  width:56em;
  margin:10px auto;
  text-align:left;
  background:#dade75;
  border:1px solid silver;
}
#header {
  background: #272727 url(header-bg.gif) repeat-x bottom left;
  padding:10px 15px 10px 13px;
}
#content-wrapper {
  float:right;
  background:#fff url(nav-to-content-trans.gif) repeat-y left;
```

```
    width:40em;
}
#content-inner {
    padding:5px 15px 0 15px;
}
#navigation {
    width:15em;
    float:left;
    padding-top:15px;
}
#footer {
    clear:both;
}
```

The effect is best demonstrated with another comparative screen shot (Figure 7-11). This one shows the page in IE 6/Win set at the five font-size intervals available in the View ➤ Text Size menu.

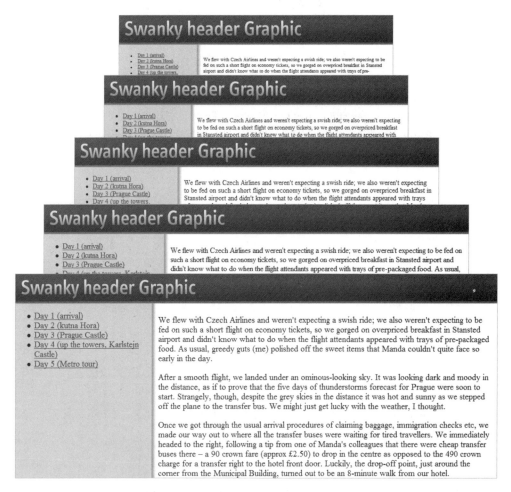

Figure 7-11. *Elastic design in IE at five font sizes*

The two-column widths scale up, as does the text content; the only item that does not scale up is the heading, as this is a fixed-width img element. Given that, you could just as easily use scaling text for that area.

When Elastic Layouts Attack!

Predictably, there's another gotcha to mention now. An elastic layout is perhaps *too* helpful to users. What if they scale things up so much that the page doesn't fit in the browser window? Silly them, you might be tempted to say, but there will be times when you'll want to take back some control. Here's where a hybrid layout comes in.

Elastic Layout: Constrained

In the constrained version—a slight tweak of the previous version—you use ems for sizing the text and the widths of the wrapper, navigation, and content divs. However, you stop them from growing too big by setting a percentage for the max-width property. For the wrapper div, let's tell the browser that the maximum it should go up is 95 percent of the browser viewport. The navigation and content are constrained to 25% and 75%, respectively. Here is the amended CSS:

```
body {
  margin:0;
  padding:0;
  text-align:center;
  background: #f0f0f0 url(body-bg.gif) repeat-x top;
  font-size:62.5%;
}
#wrapper {
  font-size:1.4em;
  width:56em;
  max-width:95%;
  margin:10px auto;
  text-align:left;
  background:#dade75;
  border:1px solid silver;
}
```

```
#header {
  background: #272727 url(header-bg.gif) repeat-x bottom left;
  padding:10px 15px 10px 13px;
}
#content-wrapper {
  float:right;
  background:#fff url(nav-to-content-trans.gif) repeat-y left;
  width:73%;
  max-width:73%;
}
#content-inner {
  padding:5px 15px 0 15px;
}
#navigation {
  width:25%;
  max-width:25%;
  float:left;
  padding-top:15px;
}
#footer{
  clear:both;
}
```

Note Notice that the two widths are 73% and 25% for the content and the navigation, respectively. Choosing 75% and 25% causes IE/Win to show the unsightly wrapping effect demonstrated earlier in this chapter.

For best effect, try this version and compare it to the previous version using a browser such as Firefox, Netscape 7 or 8, or Opera. Internet Explorer? Ah, well, this will only work if you are using IE 7 or above. Earlier versions do not support the max-width CSS property. However, IE 6 and earlier also don't offer limitless scope for scaling fonts up like other browsers do, so you probably don't need to worry about this problem too much. You aren't likely to be able to scale the page design up so that it's bigger than the browser window anyway.

Figure 7-12 shows the web page at the default size, then notched up a bit in the second screen. In the third screen, the width goes no further but the text scales up further within the upper boundaries that have been set.

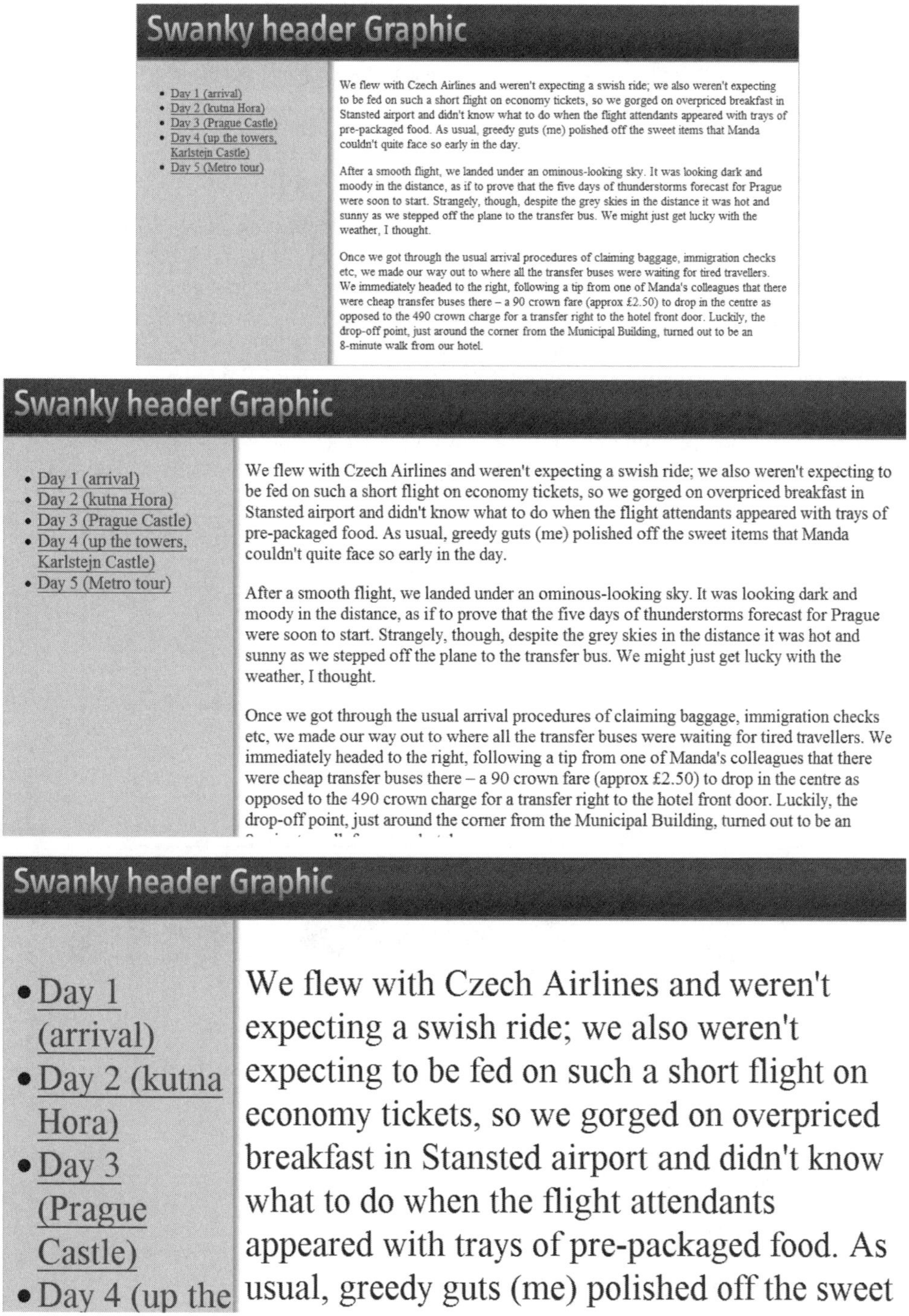

Swanky header Graphic

- Day 1 (arrival)
- Day 2 (kutna Hora)
- Day 3 (Prague Castle)
- Day 4 (up the towers, Karlstejn Castle)
- Day 5 (Metro tour)

We flew with Czech Airlines and weren't expecting a swish ride; we also weren't expecting to be fed on such a short flight on economy tickets, so we gorged on overpriced breakfast in Stansted airport and didn't know what to do when the flight attendants appeared with trays of pre-packaged food. As usual, greedy guts (me) polished off the sweet items that Manda couldn't quite face so early in the day.

After a smooth flight, we landed under an ominous-looking sky. It was looking dark and moody in the distance, as if to prove that the five days of thunderstorms forecast for Prague were soon to start. Strangely, though, despite the grey skies in the distance it was hot and sunny as we stepped off the plane to the transfer bus. We might just get lucky with the weather, I thought.

Once we got through the usual arrival procedures of claiming baggage, immigration checks etc, we made our way out to where all the transfer buses were waiting for tired travellers. We immediately headed to the right, following a tip from one of Manda's colleagues that there were cheap transfer buses there – a 90 crown fare (approx £2.50) to drop in the centre as opposed to the 490 crown charge for a transfer right to the hotel front door. Luckily, the drop-off point, just around the corner from the Municipal Building, turned out to be an 8-minute walk from our hotel.

Swanky header Graphic

- Day 1 (arrival)
- Day 2 (kutna Hora)
- Day 3 (Prague Castle)
- Day 4 (up the towers, Karlstejn Castle)
- Day 5 (Metro tour)

We flew with Czech Airlines and weren't expecting a swish ride; we also weren't expecting to be fed on such a short flight on economy tickets, so we gorged on overpriced breakfast in Stansted airport and didn't know what to do when the flight attendants appeared with trays of pre-packaged food. As usual, greedy guts (me) polished off the sweet items that Manda couldn't quite face so early in the day.

After a smooth flight, we landed under an ominous-looking sky. It was looking dark and moody in the distance, as if to prove that the five days of thunderstorms forecast for Prague were soon to start. Strangely, though, despite the grey skies in the distance it was hot and sunny as we stepped off the plane to the transfer bus. We might just get lucky with the weather, I thought.

Once we got through the usual arrival procedures of claiming baggage, immigration checks etc, we made our way out to where all the transfer buses were waiting for tired travellers. We immediately headed to the right, following a tip from one of Manda's colleagues that there were cheap transfer buses there – a 90 crown fare (approx £2.50) to drop in the centre as opposed to the 490 crown charge for a transfer right to the hotel front door. Luckily, the drop-off point, just around the corner from the Municipal Building, turned out to be an

Swanky header Graphic

- Day 1 (arrival)
- Day 2 (kutna Hora)
- Day 3 (Prague Castle)
- Day 4 (up the

We flew with Czech Airlines and weren't expecting a swish ride; we also weren't expecting to be fed on such a short flight on economy tickets, so we gorged on overpriced breakfast in Stansted airport and didn't know what to do when the flight attendants appeared with trays of pre-packaged food. As usual, greedy guts (me) polished off the sweet

Figure 7-12. *Elastic design with an upper width constraint*

> **Tip** Just as you can use the `max-width` CSS property to set upper width constraints, you can also apply limits the other way using the `min-width` property. Try amending the code and see the effect for yourself.

Resolution-Dependent Layouts

An interesting technique that you might like to employ is the *resolution-dependent* layout. (Actually, that's a bit of a misnomer, as it's not the resolution of your monitor but the size of the window in which you're currently viewing a web site that we're interested in.) With this technique, you display one view of your page as a default (normally a smaller window size) but for users who are viewing the site in a large window, you display an adapted design that maximizes that space available. This layout is not the same as a liquid layout, which resizes continually as you move the browser window's sides around; instead, once a "trigger" point is reached the layout changes and affects the content. You can see a good example of this technique on Simon Collison's web site CollyLogic (`www.collylogic.com/`), as shown in Figure 7-13.

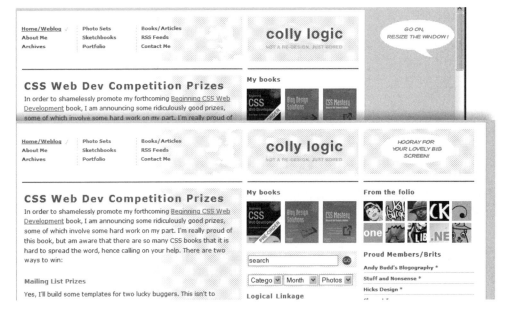

Figure 7-13. *Simon Collison's adaptable page layout on CollyLogic.com*

On his site, Simon uses a combination of

- CSS (for the default styling options)

- JavaScript (to check for window resize events)

- DOM scripting (JavaScript that dynamically changes CSS display property values of the affected elements)

> **Note** It is possible to use floated elements to achieve a similar effect. If the screen is big enough, the extra column floats back up into view, but if not, the column wraps. This is a difficult effect to pull off convincingly without it appearing to be a bug, though!

We won't cover this technique in detail, but Simon explains how it's done here: www.collylogic.com/?/comments/redesign-notes-1-width-based-layout/.

Two Columns or Three?

So far we've seen a simple two-column design at work using various layout methods. What if we want to add in another column or two? In theory it's just a matter of doing your sums correctly and making sure the figures don't add up to more than 100 percent. But as you add more columns to your design you may well run into issues regarding the source order (in other words, the order in which the different sections appear in the HTML source) and the display of those columns. Let's see how adding columns works in an example page.

Say we want to add to the content area a new column for related links. To do this, we'll place the column inside the content's outer container (content-wrapper); then we'll use a float to push the main content over to one side of that content-wrapper. The related links will be floated on the other side. Here's the CSS with relevant parts highlighted in bold:

```
body {
  margin:10px 40px;
  padding:0;
  text-align:center;
  background: #f0f0f0 url(body-bg.gif) repeat-x top;
}
#wrapper {
  text-align:left;
  background:#dade75;
  border:1px solid silver;
}
#header {
  background: #272727 url(header-bg.gif) repeat-x bottom left;
  padding:10px 15px 10px 13px;
}
#content-wrapper {
  float:right;
  background:#fff url(nav-to-content-trans.gif) repeat-y left;
  width:75%;
}
#content-inner {
  width:70%;
  padding-left:15px;
  float:left;
}
```

```
#navigation {
  width:25%;
  float:left;
  padding-top:15px;
}
#related {
  float:right;
  width:25%;
}
#related ul{
  margin:0;
  padding-left:15px;
}
#related h2 {
  font-size:large;
}
#footer {
  clear:both;
}
```

■**Note** We're applying our third column to the liquid layout that we discussed earlier. Also notice that we've added just a smidgen of style to the links in the right column to remove some of the default padding in the list items.

The body of the page has also changed to accommodate the new links in the added column:

```
<body>
  <div id="wrapper">
    <div id="header">
      <img src="swanky-header-graphic.gif" alt="Swanky header graphic"➥
    width="377" height="41" />
    </div>
    <div id="content-wrapper">
      <div id="content-inner">
        <p>We flew with Czech Airlines ... </p>
      </div>
      <div id="related">
        <h2>Related Links</h2>
        <ul>
          <li><a href="/prague/">Prague diary</a></li>
          <li><a href="/sydney/">Sydney diary</a></li>
          <li><a href="/italy/">Italy diary</a></li>
        </ul>
      </div>
    </div>
```

```
    <div id="navigation">
      <ul>
        <li><a href="day1.html">Day 1 (arrival)</a></li>
        <li><a href="day2.html">Day 2 (kutna Hora)</a></li>
        <li><a href="day3.html">Day 3 (Prague Castle)</a></li>
        <li><a href="day4.html">Day 4 (up the towers, Karlstejn Castle)</a></li>
        <li><a href="day5.html">Day 5 (Metro tour)</a></li>
      </ul>
    </div>
    <div id="footer"></div>
  </div>
</body>
```

You can see the result in Figure 7-14.

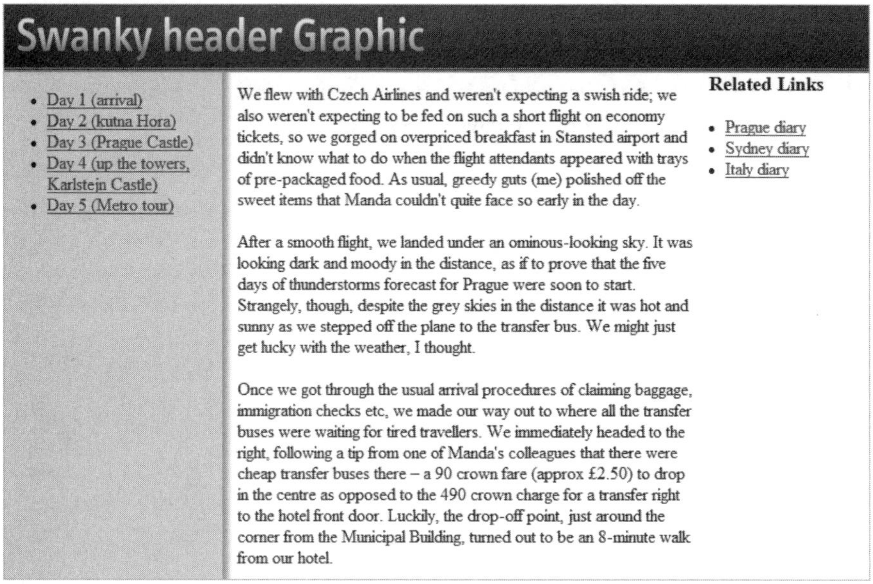

Figure 7-14. *We added the third column to the right of our page.*

Changing Layouts at the Flick of a Switch

People often mention the need for multiple-page templates when dealing with content management systems (CMSs). The pages typically have common themes but can differ significantly in layout, such as the following:

- Pages with navigation on the left

- A page with no left navigation at all

- A three-column layout

- A page with only a header and one large image taking up the entire content area (a splash page)

It is a mistake to assume that each page needs to be built differently. Using CSS, you can create a page structure that contains all the necessary hooks. Think of placeholders in your CMS or editable areas in a template on something like Dreamweaver, but use CSS to display or hide sections depending on what type of page you are in. You specify the page type by using an id or class attribute in the body element, which, through use of contextual selectors in the CSS, affects the rendering of elements further down in the document tree.

Let's look at another example page. A corporate design, this page needs

- A header, for branding and search

- A breadcrumb trail

- Left navigation

- Content

- A third column for related information

- A footer that contains copyright information, back-to-top links, and so forth

This will be the default layout. Let's take a look at how that page could be built before we start switching the layout. Here's the complete page—CSS first:

```
body {
    margin:10px 40px;
    padding:0;
    text-align:center;
    font-family:Tahoma, Verdana, Arial, Helvetica, sans-serif;
    font-size:62.5%;
}
#wrapper {
    text-align:left;
    border:1px solid #033;
    position:relative;
    font-size:1.4em;
}
#header {
    background-color:#033;
    color:#fff;
    padding:10px;
}
h1 {
    padding:0;
    margin:0;
}
#breadcrumb {
    background: #009F9F;
    color:#fff;
    padding:5px 10px;
}
```

```css
#breadcrumb a {
  color:#fff;
}
#content-wrapper {
  padding-left:9em;
  padding-right:11em;
}
#navigation {
  position:absolute;
  top:6.8em;
  left:0;
}
#related {
  position:absolute;
  top:6.8em;
  right:10px;
}
#navigation ul, #related h2 {
  margin-top:0;
  padding-top:0;
}
#related ul {
  margin:0;
  padding-left:15px;
}
#related h2 {
  font-size:large;
}
#footer {
  padding:5px 0 5px 160px;
  clear:both;
  background: #D9FFF8;
  font-size:0.8em;
  color:#030;
}
```

And now the (X)HTML that refers to it:

```html
<!DOCTYPE html PUBLIC "-//W3C//DTD XHTML 1.0 Strict//EN"➥
  "http://www.w3.org/TR/xhtml1/DTD/xhtml1-strict.dtd">
<html xmlns="http://www.w3.org/1999/xhtml">
<head>
<title>Default document layout</title>
<meta http-equiv="Content-Type" content="text/html; charset=iso-8859-1" />
<link href="switcher.css" rel="stylesheet" type="text/css" />
</head>
```

```
<body id="cols3">
  <div id="wrapper">
    <div id="header"><h1>Fictional TravelCo &trade;</h1></div>
    <div id="breadcrumb">
      You are here: <a href="/travel/">Travel</a> &gt;
      <a href="/travel/destinations/">Destinations</a> &gt; Europe
    </div>
    <div id="content-wrapper">
      <div id="content-inner">
        <p>This is the content area for some fictional corporate site.  ... </p>
      </div>
    </div>
    <div id="navigation">
      <ul>
        <li><a href="/linkdest1/">Nav link 1</a></li>
        <li><a href="/linkdest2/">Nav link 2</a></li>
        <li><a href="/linkdest3/">Nav link 3</a></li>
        <li><a href="/linkdest4/">Nav link 4</a></li>
        <li><a href="/linkdest5/">Nav link 5</a></li>
      </ul>
    </div>
    <div id="related">
      <h2>Related Links</h2>
      <ul>
        <li><a href="/related/">Related link</a></li>
        <li><a href="/related/">Another link</a></li>
        <li><a href="/related/">And another</a></li>
      </ul>
    </div>
    <div id="footer">Legal mumbo jumbo goes here</div>
  </div>
</body>
</html>
```

■Note For this layout, we've used absolute positioning on the left and right columns, which we placed using ems rather than floats. We chose this approach because the left and right columns appear after the content in the source order and the main page content will change in size depending on the browser window width. Width calculations are troublesome for floated layouts (because, as mentioned earlier, it's not possible to calculate widths in CSS as 100 percent minus 200 pixels, for example). By using absolute positioning on the left and right navigation elements and setting padding on the body content to match their widths, we can achieve a liquid layout regardless of the HTML source order.

This layout is a hybrid of techniques:

- The overall page container is liquid, so text reflows as you resize the window.

- The left and right columns (the main navigation and the related-links sections, respectively) are positioned absolutely using ems. This gets around the source order problem that can occur with floated layouts; it's as if we've placed the columns over the top of the main content, and that content has been pushed in using padding-left and padding-right properties so that the text does not show underneath those two columns.

Figure 7-15 shows the net result.

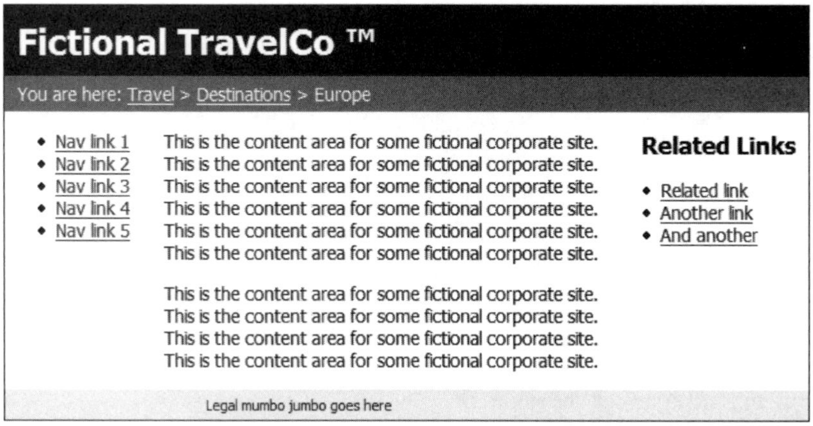

Figure 7-15. *A simple but typical three-column layout*

The main content is significantly larger (in terms of quantity) than the content in the side columns, but the page layout holds together well, even when the window width is stretched wide. As we explained earlier, when you position an element absolutely, you remove it from the document flow and the outer containing element can collapse in underneath if no other content is there to pad it out. If there *were* more content in the absolutely positioned block, the situation in Figure 7-16 could occur.

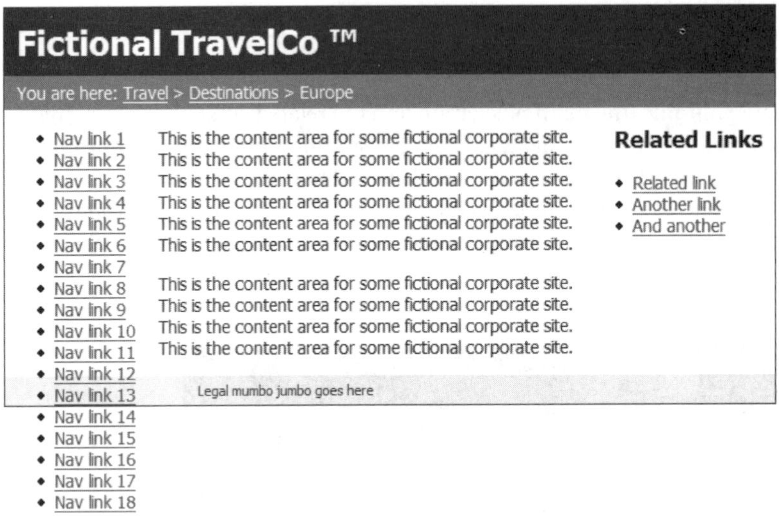

Figure 7-16. *Content pops out of the outer container (absolute positioning).*

Later in this chapter we'll refer you to another layout that gets around this problem. For now, though, we wanted you to at least be aware of this potential hiccup in the layout, as you may well come across it yourself and wonder about the cause.

In the body element for the source code is an id:

```
<body id="cols3">
```
In the CSS, there's currently nothing making use of that, so we'll make some changes:

```
body#cols3 #content-wrapper {
  padding-left:9em;
  padding-right:11em;
}
body#cols3 #navigation {
  position:absolute;
  top:6.8em;
  left:0;
}
body#cols3 #related {
  position:absolute;
  top:6.8em;
  right:10px;
}
```

Now the CSS is telling the browser to lay out the two divs at the sides and add padding to the main content *only* if they are contained in a document with a body id of cols3. If another page calls that style sheet but has a different id in the body (or no id at all), it will ignore those styles and simply present the markup in the order it appears in the source, as shown in Figure 7-17.

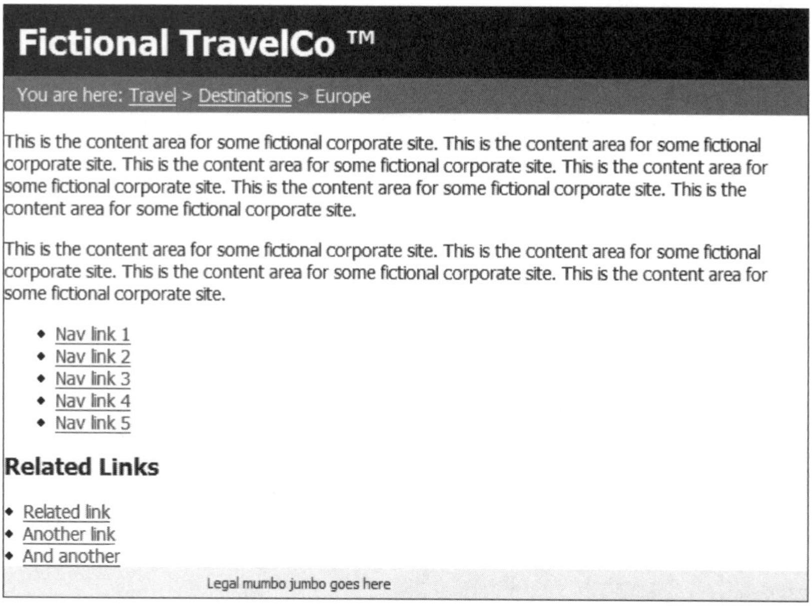

Figure 7-17. *This page has ignored the contextual styles applied to the three content areas.*

So, make sure that you have the correct id in the `<body>` tag (`cols3`) and the browser will know which piece of the CSS it should use to render the web page.

■**Note** We've used `cols3` as the `id` rather than `3cols`—which would be a more appropriate name—because an `id` cannot start with a number, according to the XHTML recommendations defined by the W3C (www.w3.org/TR/html4/types.html#h-6.2).

Switching the Design to a Splash Page

Let's consider another variant of this design: a splash page that doesn't require any left or right navigation (but the header and footer should remain). The first thing we need to do is change the id value in the body element:

```
<body id="splash">
```

Next let's define display rules that will apply only if the page has an id in the body of splash (contextual selectors, as you'll recall):

```
/* Splash page styles */
body#splash #content-wrapper {
  padding-left:1em;
  padding-right:1em;
}
```

```
body#splash #navigation {
  display:none;
}
body#splash #related {
  display:none;
}
body#splash #footer {
  padding:5px 0 5px 1.5em;
}
```

The end result (with a fancy image in the content area instead of paragraphs of text) looks like
Figure 7-18.

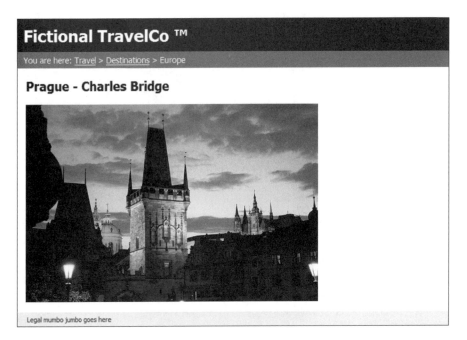

Figure 7-18. *A splash page, switched using CSS*

We've hidden the parts we don't want to see and moved other parts of the page to fill
those spaces vacated. But hang on a minute, what's happened to the navigation and related-
links lists? All we've done is hide them using the CSS display property; it may well be that
unless you've done a bit of pruning, unneeded content will exist in that markup. Ideally, what
you should have is something like this:

```
<body id="splash">
  <div id="wrapper">
    <div id="header"><h1>Fictional TravelCo &trade;</h1></div>
    <div id="breadcrumb">
      You are here: <a href="/travel/">Travel</a> &gt;
      <a href="/travel/destinations/">Destinations</a> &gt; Europe
    </div>
```

```
<div id="content-wrapper">
  <div id="content-inner">
    <h2>Prague - Charles Bridge</h2>
    <p><img src="charles-bridge.jpg" alt="Charles Bridge at night" /></p>
  </div>
</div>
<div id="navigation"></div>
<div id="related"></div>
<div id="footer">Legal mumbo jumbo goes here</div>
</div>
</body>
```

■**Note** The two `divs` that are related to the navigation and related links are still present in the source but they're empty. You could simply remove those elements; however, that would create a different page template, and if you are happy to create many variations of a page by changing the underlying construction, then the style switcher approach is not really relevant. This approach—using CSS attributes to show or hide portions of a page—is most effective and appropriate when you want to have a single-page template that adapts to different circumstances, and you're most likely to use it when implementing in a CMS or using the templating feature in programs like Dreamweaver or GoLive. It's perfectly acceptable to have an empty `div` that doesn't display on screen like this—you'll be adding a few extra bytes to your page, but you'll enjoy the great advantage of maintaining just one page structure across a whole site that can be controlled and switched via CSS rules.

Switching to a Section Entry Page

Let's tweak the design once more to demonstrate the switching technique further. Now we're going to do the following:

- Get rid of the related-links content

- Change the main content so that it takes up 50 percent of the design on the left-hand side

- Move the navigation over to the right and increase the font size on those links substantially

We're also going to change the content that appears in the relevant sections to reflect the type of content we might expect to see in that layout. Remember, though, that the overall page structure—the `divs` that hold everything together—will not change at all. We'll use this page layout as an entry page for a specific section of our site, so we'll give it an `id` of `entry`:

```
<body id="entry">
```

And here are the additions to the CSS file:

```
/* Entry page styles */
body#entry #content-wrapper {
  padding-left:1em;
  padding-right:50%;
}
body#entry #navigation {
  font-size:x-large;
  position:absolute;
  top:4em;
  right:20px;
}
body#entry #related {
  display:none;
}
body#entry #footer {
  padding:5px 0 5px 1.5em;
}
```

Put it all together, and you get the page shown in Figure 7-19.

Figure 7-19. *An entry page to a site section*

We hope you are beginning to see the power of using this technique. You need only create the hooks for areas of a web page that you may or may not need to populate with content and use CSS to decide what gets shown. Wave goodbye to CMS solutions that require different page templates for what may be fairly trivial cosmetic tweaks and let CSS take the strain.

Faux Columns: Using Background Images to Suggest Columns

When we discussed the three-column layout earlier, we fibbed a bit by calling them columns. Why? Because if you look at the layout, there's a "perceived" column—that is, whitespace in the navigation and related links areas *suggests* a column but it's just a block of content floating against a white background. The moment we try to put a background color on that column or apply a border to it, everything goes wrong, as the unsightly foreground and background combination in Figure 7-20 shows:

```
#related {
  position:absolute;
  top:6.8em;
  right:10px;
  background:yellow;
  border-left:2px solid black;
}
```

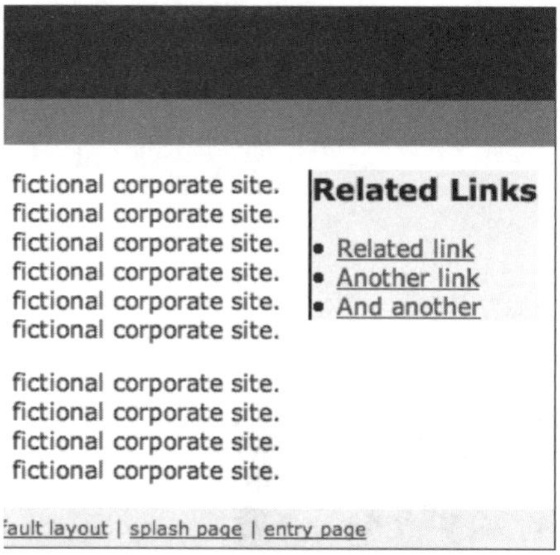

Figure 7-20. *The right column is not really a column at all.*

If you are using floats or absolutely positioned elements in a layout like this, the content will not stretch to fill the available height of the containing element—unless you employ JavaScript to do some clever calculations and resizing. This means you cannot apply background color that fills the entire height—or can you?

Faux Columns to the Rescue

Faux (or fake) columns are the solution. (We snuck in an example of using faux columns earlier when we discussed a fixed-width layout with a fixed height applied to the outer container.) Essentially, this approach involves using a background image, which is tiled along the y-axis. However, this image is applied not to the element that's being floated or positioned but to an element that sits *behind* that (one or more steps up the document tree). By doing this, you avoid the worry of having to know the height of the element in the foreground. This concept is tricky to explain with words alone, so let's look at an example.

First, we need the background image. We'll use one that has solid color and with what appears to be a slightly darker border on the left side. We created the image (Figure 7-21) so that it matches exactly the fixed width of the related-links list that will sit over the top of it.

Figure 7-21. *The background image (which will be tiled)*

In the CSS, we pick an appropriate element to attach it to. An easy one is the outermost wrapper div; everything else sits inside this container and will appear to sit over the top of this background image. The image will be

- Aligned to the right of the container element

- Repeated along the y-axis

Here's the shorthand CSS that achieves this:

```
#wrapper {
  background:#fff url(solid-bg.gif) repeat-y right;
  text-align:left;
  border:1px solid #033;
  position:relative;
  font-size:1.4em;
}
```

With that saved and a quick reload of the page, we see the result shown in Figure 7-22.

Fictional TravelCo ™

You are here: <u>Travel</u> > <u>Destinations</u> > Europe

- <u>Nav link 1</u> This is the content area for some fictional corporate site.   **Related Links**
- <u>Nav link 2</u> This is the content area for some fictional corporate site.
- <u>Nav link 3</u> This is the content area for some fictional corporate site.   • <u>Related link</u>
- <u>Nav link 4</u> This is the content area for some fictional corporate site.   • <u>Another link</u>
- <u>Nav link 5</u> This is the content area for some fictional corporate site.   • <u>And another</u>
  This is the content area for some fictional corporate site.

This is the content area for some fictional corporate site.
This is the content area for some fictional corporate site.
This is the content area for some fictional corporate site.
This is the content area for some fictional corporate site.

Legal mumbo jumbo goes here

Figure 7-22. *The background image appears underneath the absolutely positioned related-links section.*

Hurray! It appears to have done the job, but once again, there's a problem that you need to be aware of.

Scalable Text + Fixed Background Widths = Trouble

If the user resizes the text, the text will grow in length, but the background image is a fixed size, as Figure 7-23 shows.

Figure 7-23. *Fonts scale up but the background does not.*

Tip If you are using Opera, zooming the page will scale the fixed-width background graphic too.

A workaround is to create a much larger image than appears on screen and set its position using a negative em value. Then, as the user scales up the font size, doing so multiplies the negative em value you set, thus pulling the image back along with the enlarged text. However, this technique will not work if the overall page layout is a liquid one. (You need to decide what it is that defines where the image sits—is it the text size or is it the page width?) Next, we'll look at a fixed-width version of the example page that uses ems to set the position of the background image; resizing the browser window no longer has any effect on the page width, so we only need to cater for font resizes.

Fixed-Width Layout: Column Resizes with Font Resize

Here's the CSS for the fixed-width layout but with the background image that adjusts along with the font size (note that we're only showing the parts of the CSS related to this part of the page):

```
#wrapper {
  margin:10px auto 0 auto;
  background:#fff url(solid-bg-big.gif) repeat-y -10.5em;
  width:770px;
  text-align:left;
```

```
  border:1px solid #033;
  position:relative;
  font-size:1.4em;
}
```

The measurement for the left coordinate on that background is –10.5em. We arrived at that measurement somewhat by trial and error:

- We created a background image with a large white background area—bigger than the actual background area it will cover—and a larger background color area for the right column.

- We set the left position to –10.5em after trying various values until the "split" point sat in the right place at the default font size.

- We then scaled the font up and down to see how much the image moved along with the text.

Figure 7-24 illustrates these steps. Note that we've put a solid border around the background image so that you can see its actual size against the white background.

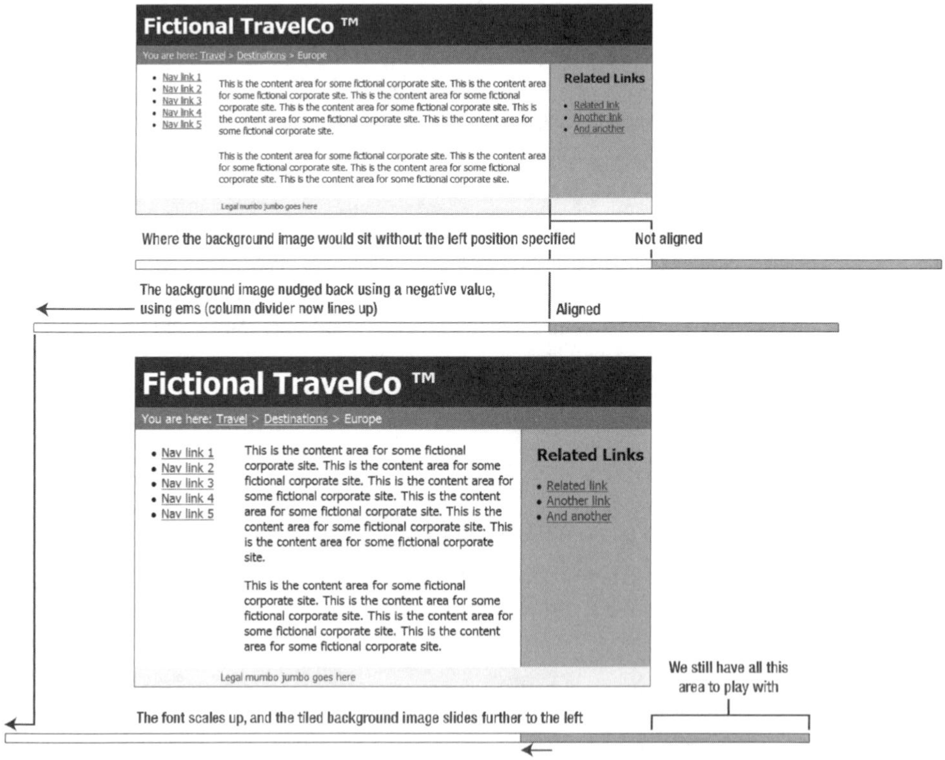

Figure 7-24. *The background image and its relation to the page*

Managing Floats

Earlier in this chapter we mentioned that one of the problems with floating blocks of content in CSS is that the parent container collapses down behind the floated content, as shown in Figure 7-25. What you probably wanted was an effect more like that shown in Figure 7-26.

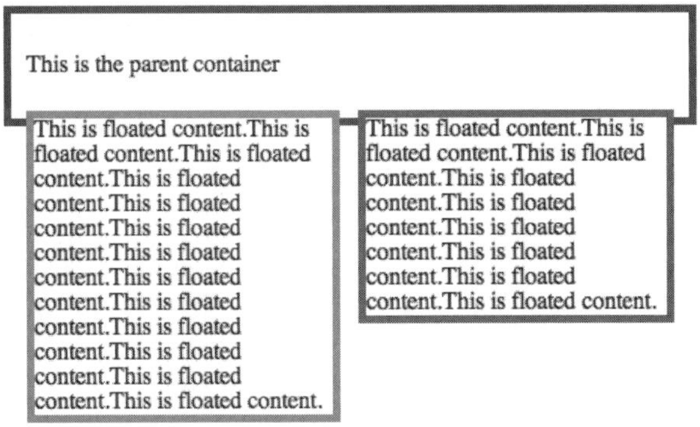

Figure 7-25. *Collapsed float*

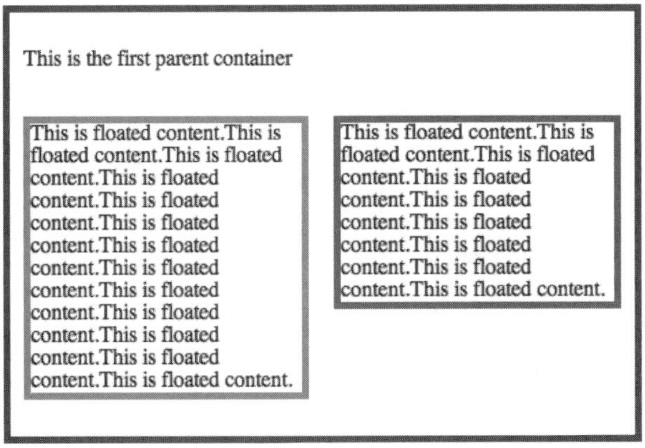

Figure 7-26. *Cleared float*

There are a few ways of dealing with this issue. Earlier we suggested adding some CSS to the footer div (a footer with no content):

```
#footer {
  clear:both;
}
```

When you use the clear property in CSS, you are telling the user agent or browser to no longer honor previous floats at that level. It's like wiping the slate clean and starting fresh. You can specify whether just the elements that are floated to the right or left are affected or, as we've done here, on both sides.

However, markup purists don't like this approach because sometimes it necessitates inserting a div that is not used to contain anything at all—it's simply there as an element that you can "do stuff to" in CSS. Wouldn't it be nice if you could remove this superfluous clearing element and still have the layout you wanted?

Fortunately, there are methods for doing this:

- Floating nearly everything

- Using easy clearing

- Using the overflow property

Floating Nearly Everything

The first method we'll look at involves floating nearly everything on the web page. If you have two floated elements, as in our example, you can float the parent container, which then has the effect of pulling it back around the inner divs. But what happens to that container you've just floated? Figure 7-27 shows the result (we show another parent container to help clarify).

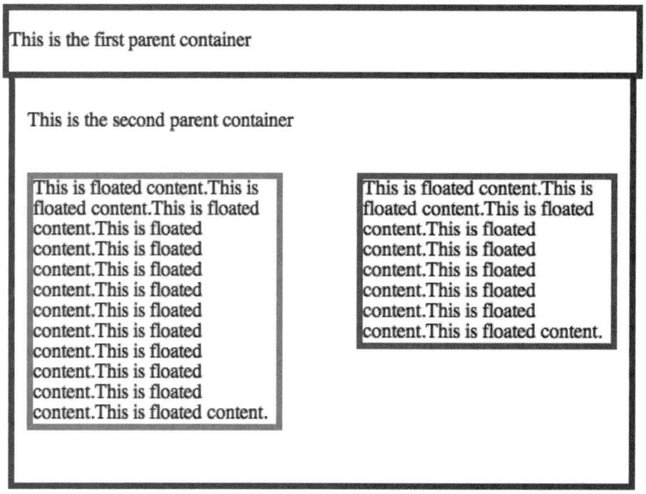

Figure 7-27. *A cleared float inside a collapsed float*

The second parent container has been floated, as have the two blocks inside. However, it appears we have solved one problem while introducing another—the outer parent container has now collapsed in.

Your floated content could be nested many levels down in the document tree, so as you go back up each level floating elements, the secondary effect continues. Eventually you end up having floated nearly everything in the document, as Figure 7-28 shows.

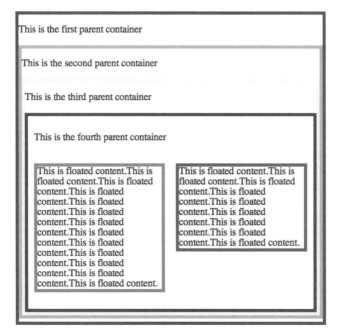

This is the first parent container

This is the second parent container

This is the third parent container

This is the fourth parent container

This is floated content.This is floated content.This is floated content.This is floated content.This is floated content.This is floated content.This is floated content.This is floated content.This is floated content.This is floated content.This is floated content.This is floated content.This is floated content.

This is floated content.This is floated content.This is floated content.This is floated content.This is floated content.This is floated content.This is floated content.This is floated content.

Figure 7-28. *One solution: float everything!*

The float nearly everything method (`http://orderedlist.com/articles/clearing-floats-fne/`) works pretty well, but you may find that it becomes difficult to maintain on pages that have many levels of nesting. A stray clearing element left on the page may cause major page layout malfunctions. Also, if you are part of a group maintaining a site, keep in mind that a great many people don't know about floats (let alone understand why *everything* is floated), and they may "break" your layout unintentionally when they modify the page.

Using Easy Clearing

If you don't want to float everything on the page, another solution is to use the easy float clearing method. There's a full description of the technique at Position Is Everything (`www.positioniseverything.net/easyclearing.html`), but we'll summarize it here.

Earlier we inserted an element inside a parent container but *after* any floated elements in that parent container and then set that newly inserted element to clear the floats. But suppose we don't want that superfluous element. We want to be able to say to the user agent or browser, "You know this container? Yep, the one that's got floated stuff in it. Well, we want this one not to collapse." In webspeak, we want to apply an attribute to that parent container that passes on that message in terms the user agent or browser understands.

This technique is really clever, and approaches the problem by using different browsers' capabilities and foibles. As mentioned in Chapters 2 and 3, there is a way of generating content in CSS using the `after` pseudo-class (to learn more, visit `www.richinstyle.com/guides/generated2.html`), and it's the backbone of this technique. You start with this:

```
.clearfix:after {
  content: ".";
  display: block;
  height: 0;
  clear: both;
  visibility: hidden;
}
```

This code tells the user agent or browser, "For any element that has a class of `clearfix`, add a period after that content; make it a block-level element but then hide it from view by changing the `height` and `visibility`. Oh, and also make it so that this new part of the page clears the floats while you're at it."

We're creating an element, making it perform the clear, and hiding it all in one shot. There's only one problem: this technique doesn't work in IE 6 or earlier. However, we can combine this with another piece of CSS (it uses a hack, so refer to Chapter 6 if you've missed the section on hacks):

```
/* Hides from IE-mac \*/
* html .clearfix {height: 1%;}
/* End hide from IE-mac */
```

This code sorts it out for IE/Win; when you apply a `height` attribute to a container element—1% in this example—IE automatically clears, thus wrapping the container around the floated items. So, some browsers get the generated content fix, and others get the auto-clearing fix. All you need to do is apply the class `clearfix` to any element that you don't want to collapse when it contains floated elements:

```
<!DOCTYPE html PUBLIC "-//W3C//DTD XHTML 1.0 Strict//EN"➥
  "http://www.w3.org/TR/xhtml1/DTD/xhtml1-strict.dtd">
<html xmlns="http://www.w3.org/1999/xhtml">
<head>
<title>Easy Clearing method demonstrated</title>
<meta http-equiv="Content-Type" content="text/html; charset=iso-8859-1" />
<style type="text/css">
  #parent1 {
    border:5px solid purple;
    padding:10px;
  }
  .floatleft {
    border:5px solid red;
    float:left;
    width:200px;
    background:white;
  }
  .floatright {
    border:5px solid green;
    float:right;
    width:200px;
    background:white;
```

```
  }
  .clearfix:after {
    content: ".";
    display: block;
    height: 0;
    clear: both;
    visibility: hidden;
  }
  .clearfix {display: inline-table;}
  /* Hides from IE-mac \*/
  * html .clearfix {height: 1%;}
  .clearfix {display: block;}
  /* End hide from IE-mac */
</style>
</head>
<body>
  <div id="parent1" class="clearfix">
      <p>This is the first parent container</p>
      <p class="floatleft">This is floated content.</p>
      <p class="floatright">This is floated content.</p>
  </div>
</body>
</html>
```

You can see the result in Figure 7-29.

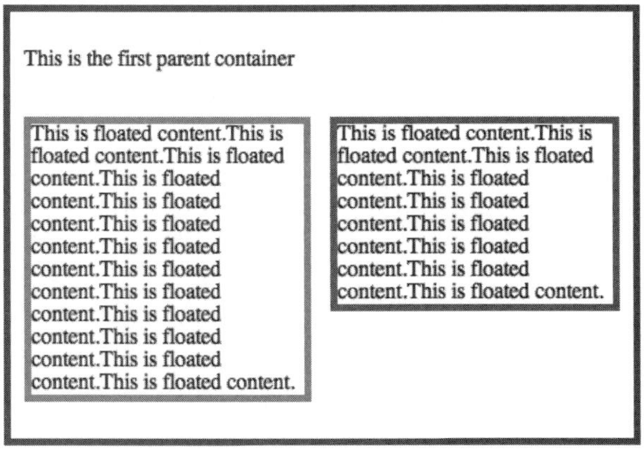

Figure 7-29. *Easy clearing in action*

Using overflow to Control Floats

The final method is so head-slappingly simply that you'll wonder why it took so long to discover (and you can thank one of the folks at SitePoint, www.sitepoint.com/blogs/2005/02/26/simple-clearing-of-floats/, for this idea). We'll highlight the significant parts in the following code:

```
<!DOCTYPE html PUBLIC "-//W3C//DTD XHTML 1.0 Strict//EN"➡
  "http://www.w3.org/TR/xhtml1/DTD/xhtml1-strict.dtd">
<html xmlns="http://www.w3.org/1999/xhtml">
<head>
<title>Overflow auto method demonstrated</title>
<meta http-equiv="Content-Type" content="text/html; charset=iso-8859-1" />
<style type="text/css">
  #parent1 {
    border:5px solid purple;
    padding:10px;
    overflow:auto;
    width:100%;
  }
  .floatleft {
    border:5px solid red;
    float:left;
    width:200px;
    background:white;
  }
  .floatright {
    border:5px solid green;
    float:right;
    width:200px;
    background:white;
  }
</style>
</head>

<body>
  <div id="parent1">
    <p>This is the first parent container</p>
    <p class="floatleft">This is floated content. </p>
    <p class="floatright">This is floated content. </p>
  </div>
</body>
</html>
```

Figure 7-30 shows the result.

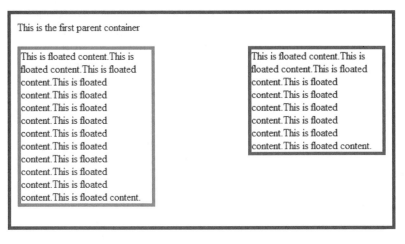

Figure 7-30. *Using* `overflow:auto;` *stops the float collapse problem.*

Note that for this technique to work on IE, you also need to specify a width on the parent container. In the example code, the 100% width combined with the padding and border widths results in a horizontal scrollbar. You can work around this issue with a little planning; check the comments in the SitePoint article if you experience any quirks that you can't get your head around; someone else may have solved the problem.

Negativity Is Good for You

In this chapter you've learned about various positioning schemes and layout types: floated, absolutely positioned, fixed, liquid, and elastic layouts. All of them have their various merits, but they all suffer to some extent from their ability to adapt regardless of the source order of the (X)HTML. It is a well-known fact that search engines like to see content related to search phrases as near to the beginning of the document as possible, which is a good reason to ensure that your basic page source order goes something like this:

- Main page heading
- Content
- Navigation

Note While this order is most beneficial to search engines and people reading your content on small-screen, non-CSS-capable devices, screen reader users may not be so well catered for if they have to search through masses of content to get to the navigation. Some developers favor having navigation up front but with a "skip over navigation to main content" link for users who may not be able to use a mouse and consequently have to tab through the page.

If you have a liquid page design, it's likely that the liquid part will be the content—traditionally the middle section of the page—while navigation areas to the sides remain fixed. That's all well and good, but if you want that source order (heading and content before navigation), either you have to use absolute positioning (which we demonstrated in the fictional travel site earlier) or you can float the content one way and the navigation the other.

Let's suppose you want the navigation to be 200 pixels wide and you want the content to fill the remaining space. You're effectively saying that you want the content to be 100 percent minus 200 pixels. Unfortunately, this complexity of calculation isn't within the capabilities of CSS (although you could use some JavaScript to dynamically work this out, but that method is not exactly tidy).

If you put the navigation first, then float that, the content will wrap around the navigation, giving the visual effect desired. But this exercise is about making sure the content, not the navigation, comes first in the source order.

You can use negative margins to achieve the effect. Let's return to the example page we used at the beginning of this chapter. If you apply a negative margin (right or left) to one of the outer containers, and then apply a positive margin to the same side (right or left) of the first inner container, you can then apply floats to cause the content and navigation sections to slide into position alongside each other. This is all a bit tricky to explain, so an example is called for.

■**Note** Ryan Brill explains the idea behind this approach brilliantly (no pun intended) in his article for A List Apart: http://alistapart.com/articles/negativemargins.

Here is the CSS and (X)HTML that achieves this aim. Note that this time we've used the easy float clearing method to manage the float:

```
<!DOCTYPE html PUBLIC "-//W3C//DTD XHTML 1.0 Strict//EN"➥
"http://www.w3.org/TR/xhtml1/DTD/xhtml1-strict.dtd">
<html xmlns="http://www.w3.org/1999/xhtml">
<head>
<title>Negative Margins example</title>
<meta http-equiv="Content-Type" content-wrapper="text/html; charset=ISO-8859-1" />
<style type="text/css">
  body {
    margin:0;
    padding:0;
    text-align:center;
    background: #f0f0f0 url(body-bg.gif) repeat-x top;
  }
  #wrapper {
    text-align:left;
    width:770px;
    margin:10px auto 0 auto;
    border:1px solid silver;
  }
```

```
  #header {
    background: #272727 url(header-bg.gif) repeat-x bottom left;
    padding:10px 15px 10px 13px;
  }
  #content-wrapper {
    width: 100%;
    background: #fff url(nav-to-content-trans.gif) repeat-y right;
    float: left;
    margin-right: -200px;
  }
  #content-inner {
    margin-right: 200px;
    padding:5px 15px 0 15px;
  }
  #navigation {
    width: 200px;
    float: right;
  }
  .clearfix:after {
    content: ".";
    display: block;
    height: 0;
    clear: both;
    visibility: hidden;
  }
  .clearfix {display: inline-table;}
  /* Hides from IE-mac \*/
  * html .clearfix {height: 1%;}
  .clearfix {display: block;}
  /* End hide from IE-mac */
</style>
</head>
<body>
  <div id="wrapper" class="clearfix">
    <div id="header">
      <img src="swanky-header-graphic.gif" alt="Swanky header graphic" width="377"➥
        height="41" />
    </div>
    <div id="content-wrapper">
      <div id="content-inner">
        <p>We flew with Czech Airlines ... </p>
      </div>
    </div>
    <div id="navigation">
      <ul>
        <li><a href="day1.html">Day 1 (arrival)</a></li>
        <li><a href="day2.html">Day 2 (kutna Hora)</a></li>
```

```
            <li><a href="day3.html">Day 3 (Prague Castle)</a></li>
            <li><a href="day4.html">Day 4 (up the towers, Karlstejn Castle)</a></li>
            <li><a href="day5.html">Day 5 (Metro tour)</a></li>
         </ul>
      </div>
   </div>
</body>
</html>
```

The result (Figure 7-31) resembles the earlier liquid layout of this page; only the underlying structure has changed.

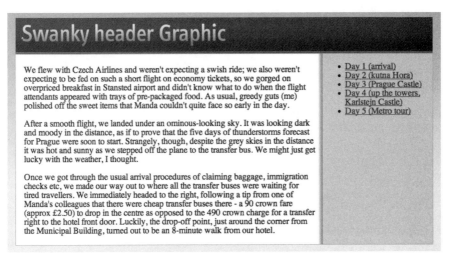

Figure 7-31. *A variation on the two-column layout using negative margins*

Using negative margins can sometimes help you out of a quandary when source order is important and you have to work around it. However, a layout that uses negative margins in many places can be extremely difficult to decipher by anyone other than the author. Therefore, remember to comment your CSS thoroughly, and perhaps include a URL in the comment pointing to an explanatory page.

Flexibility of CSS Layouts

You might be thinking to yourself, "Heck, this is crazy—why should I bother learning all these tricks when a table does the job just fine?" The beauty of setting out your pages in this way is that you are no longer locked into a given layout. If you want to change from one layout to another, you don't need to modify every page on your web site (which may consist of hundreds or even thousands of pages); you can simply switch to a different style sheet. In fact, you can even change the page style using the same style sheet just by changing the id attribute in the body element (as demonstrated earlier in the section "Changing Layouts at the Flick of a Switch").

In case you are thinking, "We redesign once every few years and do a complete rebuild from the ground up each time, so this is not relevant to me," then consider this: suppose you are in the process of building your site and, late in the development stage, the boss comes back from a conference and throws you a curveball that requires a drastic visual rethink. CSS-based layouts would enable you as a developer to react very quickly rather than having to break the underlying structure and start from scratch.

The CSS Zen Garden demonstrates the technique so well that it's worth mentioning that the images shown in Figure 7-32 are of an *identical* document—all that's changed is the CSS.

Figure 7-32. *An inspiration to us all: the many faces of the CSS Zen Garden*

Practical Layout Examples

You may be forgiven for thinking that the CSS Zen Garden examples are not necessarily indicative of the types of pages that you work with—a little *too* pretty, perhaps? Your needs may be far more modest. Perhaps all you need is a framework of a web page to begin with that you can configure in as many different ways as you think you're likely to need. You want some (X)HTML that has been crafted with that level of flexibility in mind. Figure 7-33 shows a great example of such a page: the Layout Gala (which you can learn about at `http://blog.html.it/layoutgala/`).

Figure 7-33. *The Layout Gala: one XHTML document, many possibilities*

At the Layout Gala site, you'll find a vast number of different layout permutations based on the same simple XHTML document, which you can download and try out for yourself. If you're feeling adventurous, you could attempt to merge two style sheets into one and then use the body CSS switcher technique we described earlier to give you different layouts for various page types.

Style Switchers: Giving the User Control

Even if you are not in the habit of having periodical CSS makeovers on your web site, there is still one other benefit to consider: your user might want to have a different design that's best suited to them. In such a case, you can employ a style switcher that the user can control. Perhaps your visitor has impaired vision and wants a higher-contrast version of the page. Or maybe they're using a screen magnification tool to view your page and the layout causes problems because some of the content is easily missed. You can give that control to the user by providing a style switcher tool, a technique that's described in Paul Sowden's article for A List Apart (www.alistapart.com/stories/alternate/). The person using a screen magnification tool would benefit from a "zoom layout," and the best place to learn about that is from accessibility expert Joe Clark (http://joeclark.org/access/webaccess/zoom/). Combing a zoom layout (and other layouts or schemes) with a style switcher lets you capitalize on the flexibility that CSS truly offers.

Summary

Layouts are not the easiest of CSS techniques to learn, but there are many well-documented, well-supported methods that you put into play. And while getting a layout to work across a wide range of browsers consistently can at times seem challenging, the long-term benefits you enjoy in terms of redesign flexibility and adaptability across devices make understanding these techniques far more rewarding than simply using CSS for setting background colors or making fonts look pretty.

In the next chapter we look at creating common page elements, the idea being that, now you've learned how to position the page elements, we can concentrate on the page elements themselves!

CHAPTER 8

■ ■ ■

Creating Common Page Elements

In the previous chapter we showed you several methods for laying out a page using CSS; you now have a multitude of ways to push blocks of content around a page. But once you have the necessary sections in the right places on your web page, you're going to need to put something in those sections, right?

Let's take a moment to consider some of the items you'd find on any given web page:

- Header strip (containing a logo)

- Site search

- Top-level (horizontal) navigation

- Breadcrumb trail/"You are here" indicator

- Secondary navigation (usually left- or right-aligned)

- Main page heading

- Body content and subheadings

- Images and links with hover effects

- Sidebars/callout boxes with rounded corners

This is not an exhaustive list, but it covers most of what you'll likely need on a web page. Some of the items are just smaller examples of a larger topic. For instance, a site search that sits in a page header is probably just a text input and a button and is therefore a form, but is usually treated in a different way (visually) from a "proper" form, as in one that captures a raft of data from a user (forms have their own chapter in this book—see Chapter 11).

So we're focusing on small, specific parts of a web page, but these are things that you'll need to do again and again on different sites that you work on—and you'll need to do them visually different each time. This chapter is all about showing you the ways that you can accomplish this goal in CSS.

Styling a Page Header

When we refer to a *page header*, we're talking about that part of the web page that usually contains things like a company logo, a marketing tagline, a site search, and sometimes other features (links to a site map, "Contact Us," and so on). Page headers are not to be confused with elements inside the <head> tag, nor do we mean headers in the sense of a server's HTTP headers (see "Quick Reference to HTTP Headers," at www.cs.tut.fi/~jkorpela/http.html).

There are as many different ways of approaching header styles as there are colors in the spectrum—basically, each company or individual has its own brand or style and so we cannot look at every possible permutation. We will discuss some techniques you can consider best practices, though.

Using a Small Logo

It may be tempting to put a big logo on your page, but consider that one of the benefits of using CSS is the adaptability of your page layout on different devices. If you view your web page on a device that doesn't support CSS (a mobile device of some kind, most likely) or you've actively disabled CSS display for a given reason, your page layout can adapt; a 600-pixel-wide logo, on the other hand, may not be able to.

If you can keep a logo down to the 200-pixel-wide level, you have a fighting chance of being able to make it fit on a small screen without users having to scroll horizontally to see it.

Mixing and Matching Foreground and Background Images

It is a good idea to separate the essential foreground images (for which you may need to apply an alt attribute, for example, with the company logo) from the purely decorative background images. You shouldn't place anything in background images that conveys essential information; you want to save background images for graphics that are pure decoration and nonessential if switched off. Consider also that if you *do* put something important in as a background image, it's unlikely to be printable as most browser/printing setups by default will ignore background images and color.

Figure 8-1 shows a header design that is typical of the kind of thing that you as a developer might be asked to build. If it looks familiar, pat yourself on the back—it's based on the fictional travel site that we used in the previous chapter to show off the body CSS switcher idea.

Figure 8-1. *A simple header design*

Now you need to put on your special web-building specs and see it for what it is:

- A logo

- A tagline

- A background with a slight gradient fade that is repeated

- A reflection of the logo (let's assume that this is a "trendy" thing the company decided they wanted for the web site but is not their traditional logo)

With that in mind, let's consider the parts we'll need. Figure 8-2 shows what we'll use to make this header.

Figure 8-2. *Our header components*

We'll use CSS to accomplish the following with these components:

- Position the logo and the marketing tagline image precisely where we want them

- Tile the background image

- Place the reflection as a background image

Positioning the Logo and Tagline

In this example, we're using images for the logo and tagline. It might be argued that a heading (h1 or h2 element) might be more appropriate, but you know how marketing departments are about their branding. However, we can place the images inside these elements like so:

```
<h1><img src="01-header/logo.gif" alt="TravelGo.com" /></h1>
 <h2><img src="01-header/getting-you-there.gif"➥
 alt="Getting you there since 1972" /></h2>
```

At least this way we're providing some semantic meaning about the images (or the text that appears in the alt attribute). This could benefit search engines and screen reader users, but it also presents a small layout problem—headings, by default, have a lot of margin space around them. So, we should switch these off like so:

```
#header h1,
#header h2 {
  padding:0;
  margin:0;
}
```

■**Note** We have used contextual selectors here—in other words, we're only affecting h1 and h2 elements that are in the header. If you were to use headings elsewhere, they would not be affected by this CSS.

Now we need to move these images to the correct place in the header. By analyzing the header graphic that was provided in the mock-up (we're trying to make this as real-life as possible here!), we've ascertained that the logo is 8 pixels along and 5 pixels down from the header's top-left corner. The tagline is 193 pixels along and 20 pixels down. We put these in the correct place using absolute positioning:

```
#header {
  background:#033;
  color:#fff;
  height:55px;
  position:relative;
}
#header h1,
#header h2 {
  position:absolute;
  padding:0;
  margin:0;
}
#header h1 {
  top:5px;
  left:8px;
}
#header h2 {
  top:20px;
  left:193px;
}
```

To ensure that they are positioned properly, we've added `position:relative` to the header div, and we also gave it a `height` of 55 pixels to match the original design. Figure 8-3 shows the elements in position.

Figure 8-3. *Our logo and tagline correctly positioned over a solid background color*

Adding the Background Image

Next we need to add the background image. This is a simple process; we use the tiled fade image and repeat it along the x-axis. It needs to be anchored to the bottom of the header div:

```
#header {
  background-color:#033;
  background-image:url(01-header/bg-fade.gif);
  background-repeat:repeat-x;
  background-position:bottom;
  color:#fff;
  height:55px;
  position:relative;
}
```

In fact, we can tidy this up a little by placing all the background property/values in one shorthand declaration that looks like this:

```
#header {
  background:#033 url(01-header/bg-fade.gif) repeat-x bottom;
  color:#fff;
  height:55px;
  position:relative;
}
```

You can see the result in Figure 8-4. The logo and tagline sit cleanly over the background fade.

Figure 8-4. *Now with added gradient!*

Adding in the Reflection Image

The final touch is to add in the reflection. At this point, you might be wondering why it's necessary to do this separately. Why didn't we simply add this in to the logo in one complete piece? As mentioned earlier, the reflection is not part of the company's standard logo—it's a bit of polish that's added for the web site and only makes sense in that context. By separating the reflection from the logo we're going to make it work as a "standard" logo when style sheets are disabled. You'll see in a moment!

The logo image is contained in an h1 element. The obvious place to attach the reflection background image is in that element. However, the logo image is covering up the background, so without a little work you'd never see the reflection. The trick is to make the h1 element tall enough so that the foreground image is visible and the background is showing underneath and below it. The reflection needs to be anchored at the bottom of the containing element:

```
#header h1 {
  top:5px;
  left:8px;
  height:50px;
  background: url(01-header/reflection.gif) no-repeat bottom;
}
```

Figure 8-5 shows the finished effect.

Figure 8-5. *It all comes together!*

Disabling the Style Sheets

If you disable the style sheets on this example (using a tool such as the Web Developer Toolbar for Firefox—see `http://chrispederick.com/work/webdeveloper/`), your images will appear one after the other and will work on a very small screen size, as shown in Figure 8-6.

Figure 8-6. *With the CSS layout disabled, even small screens can display our header successfully.*

Adding Site Search and Sitewide Header Links

Let's consider some other common features you'd expect to see on a web page: a site search and links that appear in the page header. Figure 8-7 shows the image mock-up that our fictional graphic design team has provided for our fictional web site (which you're going to learn how to do for real!).

Figure 8-7. *Sitewide links and site search added*

To approach this task, we could use absolute positioning or we could "float" the features. Either scheme could work here. In fact, we're going to suggest using both techniques:

- *Floating the links section to the right*: By doing this we can set a background image that is bigger than the default area (allowing for font scaling upward), but because of the nature of floats, the containing `div` will close down and use only the amount of room it needs. Oh, and it will also position it on the right as we would like—perfect!

- *Absolutely positioning the search area*: If we floated this item, it would float next to the links section. Not what we want. By positioning it to the top and right, but setting the top measurement far enough down so that it appears underneath the links, we should be just fine.

The XHTML for this is as follows:

```
<div id="header">
 <h1><img src="logo.gif" alt="TravelGo.com" /></h1>
 <h2><img src="getting-you-there.gif" alt="Getting you there since 1972" /></h2>
 <div id="headerlinks"><a href="/contact/">Contact Us</a> | <a
href="/sitemap/">Site Map</a> | <a href="/finder/">Store Locator</a></div>
 <div id="headersearch"><form><input type="text" name="txtSearch" id="txtSearch" />
 <input type="image" src="searchbutton.gif" alt="Search" /></form></div>
 </div>
```

Unstyled, these sections would appear on the left of the header section (underneath the logo, in fact, as we have already positioned them absolutely). Time to get CSS on the case.

Floating the Links into Place

Starting with the links section (headerlinks), we need to float that block to the right:

```
#headerlinks {
  float:right;
}
```

The text is pretty small in the graphical mock-up, so we'll bump that down somewhat in the CSS to match:

```
#headerlinks {
  float:right;
  font-size:0.8em;
}
```

Now we need to apply the background image. Figure 8-8 shows what the background looks like (and the area that we want to be visible by default).

Figure 8-8. *The links background image*

A larger background image is used so that if the user scales text up, the background image reflows accordingly. To make sure this happens, we need to specify that the image is anchored to the bottom left of the container:

```
#headerlinks {
  float:right;
  font-size:0.8em;
  background: url(links-bg.gif) no-repeat left bottom;
}
```

Finally, the text needs a bit of padding to move it away from the edges:

```
#headerlinks {
  float:right;
  font-size:0.8em;
  background: url(links-bg.gif) no-repeat left bottom;
  padding:6px 6px 8px 10px;
}
```

You can see the final result in Figure 8-9.

Figure 8-9. *Links are floated right with a background image.*

Positioning the Search Box

It's a good idea to remove padding and margins from forms before trying to position or align form elements, so that's the first thing we'll do. As with the headings inside the page header area, we're suggesting using contextual selectors to ensure that this change on the form style only affects the one in the header:

```
#headersearch form {
  padding:0;
  margin:0;
}
```

With that done, we can position the search area like so:

```
#headersearch {
  position:absolute;
  top:2em;
  right:5px;
}
```

We've chosen to use ems for the top measurement. That way, if font sizes are scaled up and the header links grow, the search box will move down as well.

The form consists of just two input elements. One is a text input, and the other is an image, which is used as a submit button. We could have used a styled form button instead (styling of form elements is covered in Chapter 11). We want these to align nicely, so we use the vertical-align property in CSS (which is used to align inline elements horizontally to the top, bottom, or center of the containing element), and once again, it's a good idea to reset any margin or padding values that these elements might have by default:

```
#headersearch form input {
  padding:0;
  margin:0;
  vertical-align:middle;
}
```

■**Note** Unfortunately, `vertical-align` does not work for block-level elements, something that bothers a great many web developers, this author included!

In the original design mockup provided, the text input has a black border, but by default, form inputs on most browsers have a slightly beveled border on them. You can override this in CSS, though, and you can also affect the height so that it matches exactly the height of the search button and the width so that it fits nicely underneath the links:

```
#txtSearch {
  height:17px;
  width:115px;
  border:1px solid black;
}
```

The complete CSS for the search box looks like this:

```
#headersearch form {
  padding:0;
  margin:0;
}
#headersearch {
  position:absolute;
  top:2em;
  right:5px;
}
#headersearch form input {
  padding:0;
  margin:0;
  vertical-align:middle;
}
#txtSearch {
  height:17px;
  width:115px;
  border:1px solid black;
}
```

The final result of all these CSS touches can be seen in Figure 8-10.

Figure 8-10. *The finished CSS-styled header*

Creating CSS-Based Tabbed Navigation

On most web sites, somewhere in the header (or shortly after), you're likely to find some kind of "tabbed" navigation facility. In this design, it sits directly above the breadcrumb trail.

Normally, this type of navigation can be a styled unordered list. That technique actually warrants a chapter in its own right (and indeed it gets one—see Chapter 12), so rather than rush through a styled list here, we're going to show how you can style a series of divs. The list approach is certainly preferable, but you may find that in some circumstances you are not able to do this (perhaps your content management system, or CMS, is limited in what it can spit out or you're styling legacy markup that cannot easily be changed). Whatever the reason, be aware that a styled list would be preferable.

So, we've handed you the loaded gun and told you that you shouldn't really pull the trigger. But here's how we get the firing mechanism to work, folks!

Creating the Markup

Going back to our design, we can see five top-level links. In the markup, it would look like this if you were using div elements:

```
<div id="tablinks">
   <div><a href="/">Home</a></div>
   <div><a href="/travel/">Travel</a></div>
   <div><a href="/flights/">Flights</a></div>
   <div><a href="/hotels/">Hotels</a></div>
   <div><a href="/late-deals/">Late Deals</a></div>
</div>
```

Positioning the Links

By default, the divs would appear one after the other in a vertical stack, but we can transform them in the CSS to line up side by side by using floats:

```
#tablinks div {
  float:left;
}
```

Note Reminder about floated elements: you need to clear the floats afterward! (See the methods for managing floats in the previous chapter.) In this example we'll use the "easy clearing" method.

This code gets them in the right position, but there's plenty of work left to do, as Figure 8-11 proves.

Figure 8-11. *Our links are in the right place, but they need more work.*

Styling the Links

We need to do the following to get this looking the way we want:

- Apply a background image to the entire horizontal strip

- Give each one of the links a bit of padding

- Add some borders between the links

- Create a background image that can be used to identify the current location in the site

Applying a Background

This is a straightforward job. We simply tile a background image to the strip, repeating it along the x-axis. In the design, there is a slight fade from the top strip, so we need to anchor it at the top:

```
#tablinks {
  background:#336868 url(tab-bg.gif) repeat-x top;
}
```

Padding Out the Links and Adding Borders

Where we've floated the div elements that contain the links, the widths have all collapsed down. We can add padding in—all around, as it happens—because these are block elements that we're dealing with and as such they honor padding and border attributes that we set. We'll set the border at the div level but we'll set the padding to the link inside. Why? Because we want to apply a different background to the link on hovers and on the current page, so we want the link to stretch all the way out to the container rather than be pushed in by padding that's applied to the div element.

In order to add padding to the link (an inline element) inside the floated div element (a block-level element), we need to convert the link to a block-level element. This is easily done!

```
#tablinks div {
  float:left;
  border-right:1px solid #094747;
}
#tablinks a {
  display:block;
  padding:5px 10px;
}
```

■**Note** To achieve this visual effect, you don't actually even need to wrap each link in a div element—by "promoting" the inline a element to a block element, you could float them, apply padding and margins and so on to get the same effect. However, if you have total control over the HTML for these navigation blocks, you would be wise to put them in an unordered list, as previously noted.

Setting the Link Color and Background Image for the Current Tab

We have just a couple of small tasks left to do—set the font color for the links and set a background that is going to be used for the current page:

```
#tablinks a:link,
#tablinks a:visited,
#tablinks a:hover,
#tablinks a:active {
  color:white;
  text-decoration:none;
}
#tablinks a.current {
  background:#047070 url(tab-bg-hover.gif) repeat-x top;
}
```

Remember to set the class of current to the appropriate link (applied to the a element, not the containing div):

```
<div><a href="/travel/" class="current">Travel</a></div>
```

The final result is shown in Figure 8-12.

Figure 8-12. *The finished product: styled divs in a tab-like style*

■**Note** In the previous example it would be up to you to manually or programmatically write in the current class for the section you're in. There is a smarter way of achieving this using CSS contextual selectors that takes the effort out of this; see Chapter 12.

Breadcrumb Trails

A *breadcrumb trail* is an often-used technique on web sites for letting visitors know exactly where they are within the site hierarchy. It's a great way to allow people to jump several levels back up the site, and it's also invaluable for orienting visitors who arrive at the site from a search engine result.

Unfortunately, it's nearly always the case that when you see these breadcrumbs, the markup used for it is something like this:

```
<div class="breadcrumb">You are in: <a href="/preferences/">
preferences</a> &rarr; <a href="/preferences/page-style/">page style</a> &rarr;
</div>
```

Showing the Hierarchy of the Breadcrumb Trail

In the previous example, the links look fine and the XHTML is all valid, so what's the problem? If you think about it, a breadcrumb is a reflection of a site hierarchy (imagine navigating through folders on your own computer—it's effectively the same as the process the server does when trawling through the file system). What you really want is something that hints at that hierarchy, and nested lists can give you just that. Let's look at the travel site example; this is how the breadcrumb trail appears on the page:

> *You are in Travel > Destinations > Europe*

This could be better expressed in the XHTML like this:

```
<div id="breadcrumb">
You are here:
<ul>
 <li><a href="/travel/">Travel</a>
  <ul>
   <li><a href="/travel/destinations/">Destinations</a>
    <ul>
     <li>Europe</li>
    </ul>
   </li>
  </ul>
 </li>
</ul>
</div>
```

■**Note** At this point, some people may claim that this is a case of semantics gone mad—that all you really need is a straight line of text links with an appropriate separator between them. That might do the job visually, but it's good to think about the relationship that elements have with one another, and that's partly why we've gone for this technique rather than a flat piece of text.

Styling the Hierarchical Order

Now the aim is to flatten that list so that it renders in one line but retains the semantic meaning that it has in a nested list. You can use `display:inline` to make each of the list items appear one after the other. Here's a first stab at it:

```
#breadcrumb ul,
#breadcrumb li {
  display:inline;
  padding:0;
  margin:0;
}
```

The effect is almost what we want, as Figure 8-13 shows.

Figure 8-13. *The breadcrumb list, flattened with CSS*

What we really want, though, is some kind of separator between the links, as we had in the non-CSS version. You can use one of two techniques to achieve this:

- Generated content (using the `:after` pseudo-class)

- An image placed in the background of the list items

The second option is the better supported of the two, so this is what we'll use. Because we've set the `li` elements in the header to `display:inline`, we can no longer do things that we could if they were block-level elements, such as apply `height` or `padding` at the top and bottom (not that we want to, for that matter), but we *can* specify `padding` on the left and right on inline elements. This is key, because we need to nudge the content of those `li` elements across so that the background image is clearly visible:

```
#breadcrumb li {
  padding-left:14px;
  background: url(arrow.gif) no-repeat left center;
}
```

You can see the effect in Figure 8-14.

Figure 8-14. *An arrow character separates the breadcrumb trail items.*

Just one last thing to clean up: we don't want the first list item to be preceded by an arrow but just the subsequent ones. You can use specificity (which you learned about in Chapter 3) to control this:

```
#breadcrumb ul li {
  padding-left:0;
}
#breadcrumb ul li ul li {
  padding-left:14px;
  background: url(arrow.gif) no-repeat left center;
}
```

Essentially, the rule only applies to `li` items after one level of nesting; the first level gets no special treatment, as Figure 8-15 shows.

Figure 8-15. *The final styled breadcrumb navigation*

■**Note** Secondary navigation (aka left nav and right nav) is perhaps the most common feature of any web page, but we're going to skip over it in this chapter. The method we suggest for navigation of this type is to use unordered lists styled in CSS, and this is covered in full in Chapter 12. In addition, page headings and body copy are common features on web pages, but we're going to skip them here and simply refer you to another chapter that deals with them in greater detail—the next chapter, in fact, which is all about typography.

Images and Hover Effects

In the bad old days of early web development, fancy image effects (such as hovering over an item and the image changing) were the realm of JavaScript, and some of these scripts were far more complicated than they needed to be. Although JavaScript has its place—and indeed some argue that a visual effect such as a change on hover is a "behavioral" feature and *should* be controlled with JavaScript—CSS lets you create a number of image effects quite simply. So throw out your old JavaScript functions, get rid of your `onclick` and `onmouseover` inline event handlers, and use some CSS instead.

The Simple Image Swap

Let's start at the beginning. You may have used this kind of thing in the past:

```
onmouseover="this.src='house-renovated.gif';"
onmouseout="this.src='house.gif';" />
```

The problem with this approach is that it requires you to change any effect like this right there in the source code. Imagine if this were a common navigation element that had some kind of hover effect, was repeated several times on any web page, and was present on *hundreds* of web pages—that's a lot of changes to make! CSS lets you centralize this type of effect; all you need to do is specify a class in the markup where you want the effect to apply and specify the image swap in the CSS. Here's how it's done:

```
.ex1 {
  display:block;
  width:200px;
  padding:10px;
  border:1px solid black;
  margin:0 0 10px 0;
  text-decoration:none;
  text-align:center;
  background:#fff url(stars-dim.gif) no-repeat center center;
}
.ex1:hover {
  border:1px dotted red;
  background:#fff url(stars.gif) no-repeat center center;
}
...
<div><a href="nowhere.html" class="ex1">Hover over me</a></div>
<div><a href="nowhere.html" class="ex1">Hover over me</a></div>
```

There is a selection of other styles that we've applied in the previous example, but the key part is highlighted in bold. Figure 8-16 shows a screen shot of the default state and the hover state.

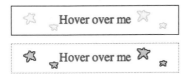

Figure 8-16. *The background image changes on hover; we set this using CSS.*

Avoiding "Divitis"

Using a div in this way does the job perfectly well, but it can be improved a little. If the previous technique were applied to a navigation area, or some other section where the technique is used over and over again, using so many class attributes would be overkill. We can tidy this up by wrapping all of the links in a containing div and then using a contextual selector to achieve the same effect. Here's an amended version:

```
div.ex2 a {
  display:block;
  width:200px;
  padding:10px;
  border:1px solid black;
```

```
  margin:0 0 10px 0;
  text-decoration:none;
  text-align:center;
  background:#fff url(stars-dim.gif) no-repeat center center;
}
div.ex2 a:hover {
  border:1px dotted red;
  background:#fff url(stars.gif) no-repeat center center;
}
...
<div class="ex2">
  <div><a href="nowhere.html">Hover over me</a></div>
  <div><a href="nowhere.html">Hover over me</a></div>
</div>
```

Sprites: Using One Image for All States

In the techniques we discussed so far, we have a different image for the default background and the hover background. When the visitor hovers over the link, only then will the server retrieve the new image and display it. On a fast connection and with a small image, this should be OK, but if you were to use this effect in less favorable circumstances, there might be a time lag.

A simple technique to get around this issue is to have both image states compiled into one single image. Then, you display just one portion of that image to the visitor (imagine trying to admire a work of art through a mailbox—that's the general idea). When the user hovers over the link that acts as the trigger, the image is nudged along by however many pixels are required to reveal the hover state. In Figure 8-17, you can see two stars: the dimmed default version and the bright hover version. The image is 34 pixels wide and 15 pixels high. We'll set the container element to be just 17 pixels wide, so only the first half of the image will show.

Figure 8-17. *The single image with the default and hover state included*

The CSS required for this follows:

```
.ex3 {
  background:#fff url(all-stars.gif) no-repeat 0 0;
  display:block;
  height:15px;
  width:17px;
}
.ex3:hover {
  background:#fff url(all-stars.gif) no-repeat -17px 0;
}
...
<a href="nowhere.html" class="ex3"></a>
```

As you can see from the CSS, in the hover state the background image is slid 17 pixels to the left, thus revealing the different portion of the image.

Because the image has already been downloaded for the default state, there is no need to call a new image off the server, so we have effectively preloaded all the images we need.

Remote Image Swaps

Perhaps you're thinking. "Ah, that's all well and good if I want the image underneath the mouse pointer to change on hover, but my JavaScript changes an image *elsewhere* on the page. CSS can't do that, can it?"

Actually, it can . . . but not in all cases. Let's look at an example. The following CSS works by placing an empty span element inside the link that triggers the hover effect, and applying a unique id to that link:

```
<ul>
  <li><a href="nowhere.html" id="ex4">Link one<span></span></a></li>
  <li><a href="nowhere.html" id="ex5">Link two<span></span></a></li>
  <li><a href="nowhere.html" id="ex6">Link three<span></span></a></li>
</ul>
```

When the mouse hovers on that link, we can set the span element to display as a block-level element somewhere else on the page (using absolute positioning) and with whatever background image we want. Because that span element is empty, we'll also need to specify height and width, as illustrated in Figure 8-18; otherwise, it won't show up on the page.

Figure 8-18. *An empty span, positioned absolutely and set to display as a block-level element and given a fixed height and width (border shown for demonstration purposes only)*

And here's the CSS that achieves the aims stated in the preceding section—the positioning aspects are highlighted in bold:

```
#ex4:hover span {
  background: url(metro.jpg);
  background-repeat: no-repeat;
  display:block;
  width:100px;
  height:100px;
  position:absolute;
  top:450px;
  left:300px;
}
#ex5:hover span {
  background-image: url(tower.jpg);
```

```
  background-repeat: no-repeat;
  display:block;
  width:100px;
  height:100px;
  position:absolute;
  top:450px;
  left:400px;
}
#ex6:hover span {
  background-image: url(clock.jpg);
  background-repeat: no-repeat;
  display:block;
  width:100px;
  height:100px;
  position:absolute;
  top:450px;
  left:500px;
}
...
```

You can see the effect in Figure 8-19 (the mouse cursor does not show in the screen shots, but you can see from the link styles which one is being hovered over).

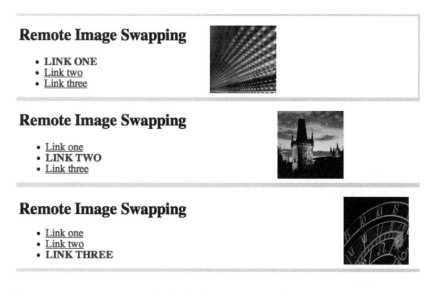

Figure 8-19. *Hovering over links displays an image elsewhere on the page.*

Remote Image Swapping and Sprites Combined

The previous example showed that it's possible to make an image appear elsewhere on the page, not just underneath your mouse pointer. The problem with this technique, once again, is the issue of preloading. These images may be quite large in file size and you don't want to have a time delay. So, you can use the sprites technique (placing all the images in one image and revealing only what's needed), but that could make matters worse as when the visitor to your site hovers over the link, the server needs to fetch one large image only to display a portion of it. Madness? No, because we can preload by placing an element on the page (a span) and apply the background image to that element. However, because the span element is empty, the preloaded background image will not show but when the visitor hovers over the link: bingo! The image is already downloaded there on the computer's hard drive. Whichever link we hover over, we know the image is there ready and waiting to be used.

```css
#imagepreload {
  background-image: url(prague-big.jpg);
}
#ex7:hover span {
  background-image: url(prague-big.jpg);
  background-repeat: no-repeat;
  display:block;
  width:100px;
  height:100px;
  position:absolute;
  top:550px;
  left:300px;
}
#ex8:hover span {
  background-image: url(prague-big.jpg);
  background-repeat: no-repeat;
  background-position: -100px 0;
  display:block;
  width:100px;
  height:100px;
  position:absolute;
  top:550px;
  left:400px;
}
#ex9:hover span {
  background-image: url(prague-big.jpg);
  background-repeat: no-repeat;
  background-position: -200px 0;
  display:block;
  width:100px;
  height:100px;
  position:absolute;
  top:550px;
  left:500px;
}
...
<span id="imagepreload"></span>
```

```
<ul>
  <li><a href="nowhere.html" id="ex7">Link one<span></span></a></li>
  <li><a href="nowhere.html" id="ex8">Link two<span></span></a></li>
  <li><a href="nowhere.html" id="ex9">Link three<span></span></a></li>
</ul>
```

These techniques show that it is possible to do dynamic image swapping using CSS. Naturally, you can adapt these ideas to your own needs, but there is one limitation that we haven't mentioned that you may have wondered about. In all the examples, we attached the hover behavior to a link (an a element). What if you don't have a link on the web page where you want the effect to happen? Unfortunately, it's not possible to do this on Microsoft Internet Explorer 6 or earlier, but for most other browsers, including IE 7, you can use the hover pseudo-class on any element. However, Microsoft is offering IE 7 as part of its Windows Update web site and will automatically be downloaded for people who have opted in to the Automatic Updates service. So it's hoped (at least by web developers who love web standards!) that the numbers of IE 6 users and earlier should go into something of a decline.

Rounded-Corner Boxes

With border styles and padding at your disposal, it's all too easy to create blocks of content that look, well, boxy! Wouldn't it be nice if we could create rounded corners and smooth off some of those hard edges?

To achieve rounded corners, you need to make prodigious use of background images combined with a suitable solid background color (in case images are disabled in the browser or are slow to download).

Creating a Fixed-Width Rounded Box

Figure 8-20 shows a background with rounded edges that is split into three. The top and bottom sections will be used as background images, while the middle section is solid background color. Note that the bottom image has a slight gradient effect applied.

Figure 8-20. *A rounded corner box, "exploded" view*

In the sample web page, we'll apply this to the related links section. Because this will be constructed from a background image that is exactly 200 pixels wide, we need to make sure that the containing div is also set to that amount (and, for that matter, the right margin for the main page content):

```
body#cols3 #content-wrapper {
  padding-left:9em;
  padding-right:220px;
}
...
#related {
  width: 200px;
}
```

The top image is set as a background for the related links heading (an h2 element), with an appropriate amount of padding applied so that the text has some breathing space:

```
#related h2 {
  margin: 0;
  padding: 10px;
  font-size: large;
  background: url(top.gif) no-repeat;
}
```

The bottom part of the image is set on the outer container—the div with an id of related—and anchored to the bottom. The heading stays at the top while the bottom part moves up and down, accordion-style, depending on the amount of content inside:

```
#related {
  width: 200px;
  background:#013433 url(example1/bottom.gif) no-repeat bottom;
}
```

One minor cosmetic touch is still required—the text color needs to be white against the dark teal:

```
#related,
#related a {
  color:white;
}
```

By applying the background images in this way, you can achieve a rounded-corner box, as shown in Figure 8-21.

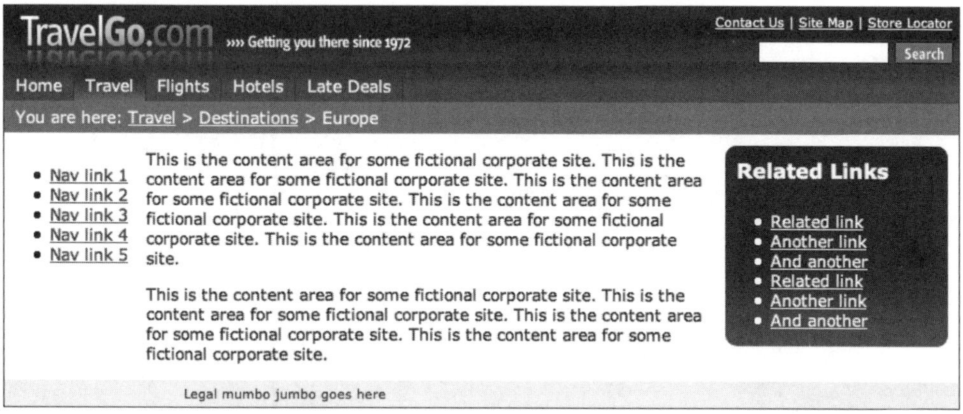

Figure 8-21. *The related links section with rounded corners*

Creating a Rounded Box That Scales

Making a box with rounded corners is pretty straightforward—you only need two pieces that move up and down. Creating a box that can be scaled up so that its width and heights change and still retaining the rounded-corner effect takes a bit more work.

In the past, an effect like this would have been achieved using a table with three columns and three rows and a separate image piece in each corner table cell. With CSS it is possible to do this using just two images by carefully revealing different parts of those images underneath clean, semantic XHTML. You can see this ingenious technique, devised by Ethan Marcotte (www.sideshOw.com/), on the BrowseHappy (www.browsehappy.com/) web site.

Making the Background Images

The trick to making a rounded box that scales is to create background images that are much wider and taller than you believe they are going to need to be. As with techniques described earlier in this chapter, we'll only show as much of those images as is needed (see Figure 8-22).

Figure 8-22. *Two background images,* left.gif *and* right.gif

---

■**Note** Although these images are large in terms of dimensions, they are still very small in file size because of the limited color palette and the continuous nature of the colors.

The outer container—the div with the id of related—has the larger right image applied, anchored to the top right, as demonstrated in the following CSS and in Figure 8-23:

```
#related {
  background: #013433 url(example2/right.gif) no-repeat right top;
}
```

Related Links

- Related link
- Another link
- And another
- Related link
- Another link
- And another

Figure 8-23. *The first image is applied to the outer container.*

Next, we apply the left image to the h2 heading, anchoring it to the top left. Because the left image is only a few pixels wide, it does not obscure the border previously applied—the join is essentially seamless, as shown in Figure 8-24.

```
#related h2 {
  margin: 0;
  padding: 10px;
  font-size: large;
  background: url(example2/left.gif) no-repeat left top;
}
```

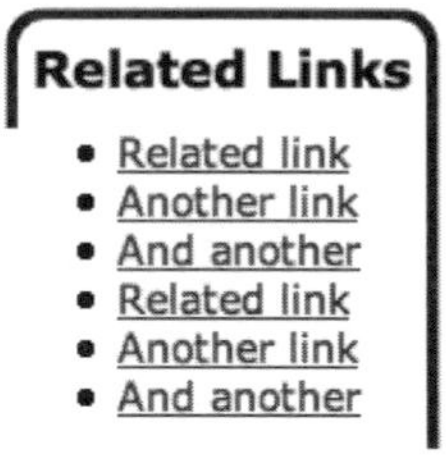

Figure 8-24. *Corner applied to the heading*

The next element to be treated is the unordered list (ul). We've already taken care of the top-left corner (applying an image to the h2) and the top and right edges (applied to the #related div), and now we're going to add in another piece to this jigsaw on the left side. This image will be anchored to the bottom left of the ul element.

■**Note** It's necessary to remove margins from the unordered list so that there is no gap between the heading and the list (otherwise, the border effect would be broken).

The following CSS does the trick (Figure 8-25 is the proof):

```
#related ul {
  margin:0;
  padding-bottom:10px;
  background: url(example2/left.gif) no-repeat left bottom;
}
```

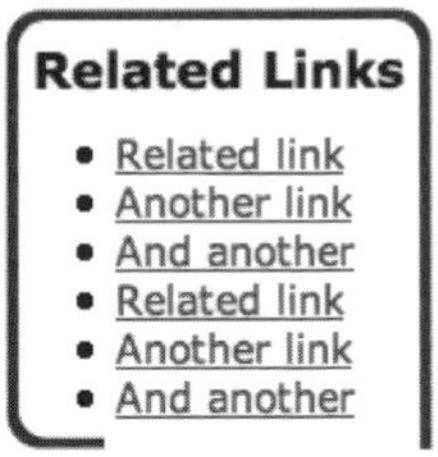

Related Links

- Related link
- Another link
- And another
- Related link
- Another link
- And another

Figure 8-25. *The jigsaw is nearly complete.*

Keeping with the jigsaw analogy, isn't it annoying when you get to the end of putting the puzzle together only to find there's a piece missing? We have a similar predicament here—there is no element for us to attach the final piece to, so we have to create an element simply for the purpose of hanging the background image on. It needs to be in between the outer container div and the unordered list. Here's the markup with the new div added in:

```
<div id="related">
  <h2>Related Links</h2>
  <div>
    <ul>
      <li><a href="/related/">Related link</a></li>
      <li><a href="/related/">Another link</a></li>
      <li><a href="/related/">And another</a></li>
      <li><a href="/related/">Related link</a></li>
      <li><a href="/related/">Another link</a></li>
      <li><a href="/related/">And another</a></li>
    </ul>
  </div>
</div>
```

The CSS to attach the final piece to the bottom-right edge follows. Figure 8-26 shows the end result at various different font sizes to demonstrate the scaling ability.

```
#related div {
  background-: url(example2/right.gif  no-repeat  right bottom;
}
```

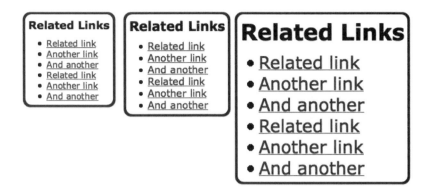

Figure 8-26. *Scaling the box up does not break the rounded-corner effect.*

The addition of a seemingly superfluous div to finish the technique is not ideal, but with a bit of planning you may not need to do this—in our example, it would be possible to apply a class to the last list item and add the background image there.

Conclusion

JavaScript is a powerful tool in the right hands but is not always required for visual effects on a web page, and HTML need not be overtly complex to achieve certain stylish touches. The aim of this chapter was to show that most, if not all, of what you may have used in the past—for example, JavaScript—to create common page elements can be done with CSS. Even better, though, you can usually do it more simply, with more semantic and meaningful markup and in ways that offer you great flexibility for change later on. And for those common features on a page that have not been covered here, we hope the examples we provided can give you enough hints about how to tackle the problem for yourself.

So with that out of the way, we'll borrow some techniques from print design, and turn to typography in our next chapter. We'll explore how some simple typographic techniques can really improve the look of our web page text.

CHAPTER 9

■■■

Typography

With all the attention given to multimedia on the Web, it sometimes seems strange that text still is the content king. Type and the written word has been with us much longer than photos, videos, audio recordings, and the like, and quite an art has developed around it. Typography is the art of setting type. This art exists to honor the content it sets—to enhance legibility and embody the character of the words within. All too often, web designers think that typography means "picking a cool font." They believe it's simply not possible to achieve quality typography on the Web, or they reduce the art to a set of mundane rules like "Always use sans serif fonts on the Web." In reality, attention to typography is one of the hallmarks of well-designed sites that differentiate them from their amateurish counterparts.

CSS was designed with typography at the forefront, and today it is possible to properly set type in a manner that might even make Gutenberg proud. This is what we'll explore in this chapter. Specifically, we'll look at

- Understanding the various typeface classifications

- Selecting typefaces with CSS

- Assigning font weights

- Sizing type

- Choosing font styles

- Transforming text

- Understanding font variants

- Setting blocks of text

- Styling headings and subheads

■Note Although today the words *typeface* and *font* are sometimes used interchangeably, they don't mean the same thing. A typeface is a particular design of type (Baskerville, Caslon, Helvetica, etc.). A font, in the digital age, is the particular file on your computer that holds an entire set of glyphs, or characters, for a particular typeface. Traditionally, a font was a collection of wood or metal characters for a particular typeface. So, Helvetica is a typeface. There are several different fonts of that typeface, some of which are digital and some of which are physical, and each of which has its own inconsistencies and quirks. There are also other typefaces based on Helvetica, such as Helvetica Neue. Helvetica Neue is rightfully a typeface of its own, and not just a font of Helvetica, because it is not exactly the same design—it's only *based on* the original Helvetica. Helvetica Bold and Helvetica Condensed are fonts within the typeface known as Helvetica.

Typeface Classification

Classifying type is a complex science if you want to get specific about it. For a great read on type classification, and typography in general, check out Robert Bringhurst's *The Elements of Typographic Style*, 2nd edition (Hartley & Marks Publishers, 2002). For the purposes of this book, though, you only need to understand the five font classifications defined by CSS (termed *generic font families*).

Serif (font-family: serif;)

Characters in a serif font have a proportional width and have serifs. A font is proportional when its characters do not all have the same width. Most type we read is proportional (including the paragraph typeface for this book). Typically, the uppercase M is the widest character in a proportional font. A lowercase i or an exclamation point may be the slimmest. Serifs are small strokes added to the beginning or end of a letter's main stroke or strokes. Serifs are not merely decoration—they were designed to enhance legibility, and it is for this reason that you'll find most books and newspapers set the majority of their text in serif typefaces. Examples of common serif typefaces include Times New Roman, Georgia, and Garamond.

Serif type is sometimes seen as classical, formal, and traditional in nature (although modern serif typefaces certainly exist). Serif is often used in print and other media for body text—extended passages of paragraphs and the like—and is less commonly used for headers and subheads.

An archaic usability principle states that serif fonts should not be used on the Web. The rationale that led to this belief was that computer screens are relatively low resolution and they don't have the capacity to display complex characters, such as those including serifs, with the detail they need. This may have been true at one time, but today, computer display resolutions have increased (but are still much lower than the typical printed page), and most operating systems now offer built-in antialiasing, a process in which the edges are blurred slightly to mask the inherent pixel grid of the screen. This has led to much better on-screen type rendering and a resurgence of serif type on the Web. Figure 9-1 shows an example of a serif typeface.

The quick brown fox jumps over a lazy dog.

Figure 9-1. *Adobe Caslon, a popular font of the Caslon typeface, designed by William Caslon*

Sans Serif (font-family: sans-serif;)

Characters in a sans serif font have a proportional width and do not have serifs. Examples of sans serif fonts include Helvetica, Verdana, Arial, and Univers.

In classical typography, sans serif fonts were sometimes classified as grotesque. This reflects the fact that they were once seen as unsightly and not practical for setting long bodies of text. In the past hundred years or so, this attitude has changed, and sans serif type is a lot more common on the Web than serif (no doubt due in part to the relic usability rule stated earlier). Even as sans serif has become more acceptable for body text, it is still used most often for headers and subheads. Figure 9-2 shows an example of a sans serif typeface.

The quick brown fox jumps over a lazy dog.

Figure 9-2. *Gill Sans, the classic sans serif typeface by Eric Gill*

Monospace (font-family: monospace;)

Characters in a monospace font are not proportional. Instead, each character has a uniform width. Monospace type may or may not have serifs. Examples of monospace fonts include Courier and Monaco.

Monospace type is generally used to indicate typed text, such as code. It may also be used to emulate older technology, such as typewriters or early computer screens. Figure 9-3 shows a monospaced font.

The quick brown fox jumps over a lazy dog.

Figure 9-3. *Consolas, the monospace font included in Microsoft's upcoming Windows Vista operating system*

Cursive (font-family: cursive;)

CSS considers any typeface that attempts to emulate human handwriting *cursive*. Examples of cursive fonts include Comic Sans, Zapf Chancery, and Zapfino.

These typefaces are usually less readable than their serif and sans serif counterparts, and are not generally appropriate for body text. See Figure 9-4 for an example of a cursive typeface.

The quick brown fox jumps over a lazy dog.

Figure 9-4. *ITC Zapf Chancery, a cursive typeface designed by Hermann Zapf*

Fantasy (font-family: fantasy;)

CSS defines a sort of "catchall" classification called fantasy that is defined as consisting of fonts that are primarily decorative while still containing representations of characters (as opposed to Pi or Picture fonts, which do not represent characters). Some examples include Desdemona, Playbill, and Herculanum.

This type classification is rarely practical for web use. See Figure 9-5 for a fantasy font example.

THE QUICK BROWN FOX JUMPS OVER A LAZY DOG.

Figure 9-5. *Herculanum, a fantasy typeface included wih Mac OS X*

Typeface Selection with CSS

CSS provides two ways to select typefaces for an element: generic font families and specific typeface families.

Using Generic Font Families

Using a generic font family in your (X)HTML document is a simple matter of assigning its associate value to the font-family attribute:

```
p {
  font-family: serif;
}
```

The user agent will choose a serif typeface and apply it to the selection (in this case, the paragraph element).

Using a Specific Typeface

Most often, designers will want a bit more control than generic font families offer. The same font-family property can also be used to specify a particular typeface, like so:

```
h1 {
  font-family: Arial;
}
h2 {
  font-family: 'Times New Roman';
}
```

The user agent will then display all h1 elements in Arial and all h2 elements in Times New Roman, if they are available to the user agent.

Note that typeface names that contain one or more spaces (such Times New Roman or Trebuchet MS) should be enclosed in quotation marks (single or double—both are acceptable), as should any font that contains symbols (such as % or #) in its name.

If the specified typeface is not available, the user agent will resort to using its default font (which can often be adjusted by the user in the agent's preferences or settings area).

The designer can also provide a comma-separated list of typefaces in the order of preference. The user agent will use the first one available to it. Here's an example:

```
code {
  font-family: Monaco, 'Courier New', Courier;
}
```

In this instance, the user agent will look through the list of monospaced typefaces one by one, and use the first one it finds. Since Monaco is commonplace on Macs, Mac users will likely see code elements displayed in Monaco. Windows users are likely to see Courier New. If the user agent finds neither Monaco nor Courier New, it will search for Courier. If none are found, the user agent will resort to its default font—which may or may not be monospaced.

For this reason, it is a best practice to always end any font-family declaration with a generic font family name. This way, even if none of your specific fonts are found, the user agent will at least display the selected text in a face of the same classification:

```
code {
  font-family: Monaco, 'Courier New', Courier, monospace;
}
```

The Typeface Problem on the Web

A limitation of web design that frustrates designers more than any other is the lack of selection in typefaces. Because (X)HTML content is rendered and displayed on the viewer's end, designers must ensure their sites work properly with only the fonts installed on the viewer's computer (or other device).

Because of this limitation, it has been a common practice to use only those typefaces that are preinstalled on both Windows and Mac computers. Sadly, the list of typefaces a designer can reliably count on to be installed on most computers is quite short. See Figures 9-6 through 9-14 for examples of these font names and classifications.

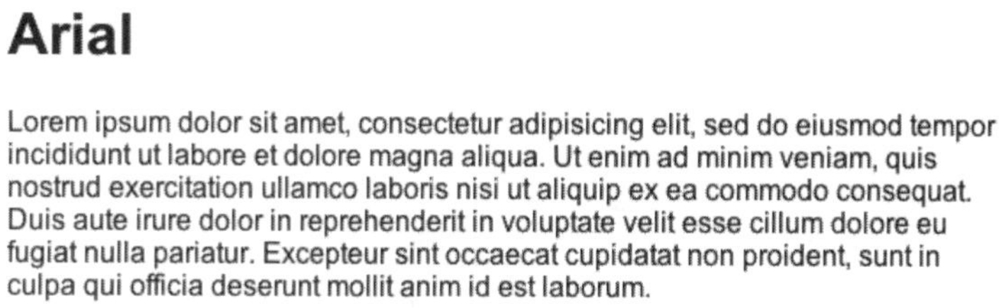

Arial

Lorem ipsum dolor sit amet, consectetur adipisicing elit, sed do eiusmod tempor incididunt ut labore et dolore magna aliqua. Ut enim ad minim veniam, quis nostrud exercitation ullamco laboris nisi ut aliquip ex ea commodo consequat. Duis aute irure dolor in reprehenderit in voluptate velit esse cillum dolore eu fugiat nulla pariatur. Excepteur sint occaecat cupidatat non proident, sunt in culpa qui officia deserunt mollit anim id est laborum.

Figure 9-6. *Arial (sans serif)*

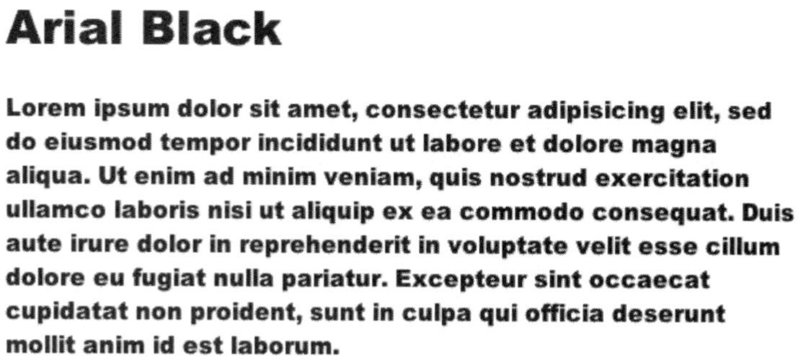

Arial Black

Lorem ipsum dolor sit amet, consectetur adipisicing elit, sed do eiusmod tempor incididunt ut labore et dolore magna aliqua. Ut enim ad minim veniam, quis nostrud exercitation ullamco laboris nisi ut aliquip ex ea commodo consequat. Duis aute irure dolor in reprehenderit in voluptate velit esse cillum dolore eu fugiat nulla pariatur. Excepteur sint occaecat cupidatat non proident, sunt in culpa qui officia deserunt mollit anim id est laborum.

Figure 9-7. *Arial Black (sans serif)*

Verdana

Lorem ipsum dolor sit amet, consectetur adipisicing elit, sed do eiusmod tempor incididunt ut labore et dolore magna aliqua. Ut enim ad minim veniam, quis nostrud exercitation ullamco laboris nisi ut aliquip ex ea commodo consequat. Duis aute irure dolor in reprehenderit in voluptate velit esse cillum dolore eu fugiat nulla pariatur. Excepteur sint occaecat cupidatat non proident, sunt in culpa qui officia deserunt mollit anim id est laborum.

Figure 9-8. *Verdana (sans serif)*

Trebuchet MS

Lorem ipsum dolor sit amet, consectetur adipisicing elit, sed do eiusmod tempor incididunt ut labore et dolore magna aliqua. Ut enim ad minim veniam, quis nostrud exercitation ullamco laboris nisi ut aliquip ex ea commodo consequat. Duis aute irure dolor in reprehenderit in voluptate velit esse cillum dolore eu fugiat nulla pariatur. Excepteur sint occaecat cupidatat non proident, sunt in culpa qui officia deserunt mollit anim id est laborum.

Figure 9-9. *Trebuchet MS (sans serif)*

Times New Roman

Lorem ipsum dolor sit amet, consectetur adipisicing elit, sed do eiusmod tempor incididunt ut labore et dolore magna aliqua. Ut enim ad minim veniam, quis nostrud exercitation ullamco laboris nisi ut aliquip ex ea commodo consequat. Duis aute irure dolor in reprehenderit in voluptate velit esse cillum dolore eu fugiat nulla pariatur. Excepteur sint occaecat cupidatat non proident, sunt in culpa qui officia deserunt mollit anim id est laborum.

Figure 9-10. *Times New Roman (serif)*

Georgia

Lorem ipsum dolor sit amet, consectetur adipisicing elit, sed do eiusmod tempor incididunt ut labore et dolore magna aliqua. Ut enim ad minim veniam, quis nostrud exercitation ullamco laboris nisi ut aliquip ex ea commodo consequat. Duis aute irure dolor in reprehenderit in voluptate velit esse cillum dolore eu fugiat nulla pariatur. Excepteur sint occaecat cupidatat non proident, sunt in culpa qui officia deserunt mollit anim id est laborum.

Figure 9-11. *Georgia (serif)*

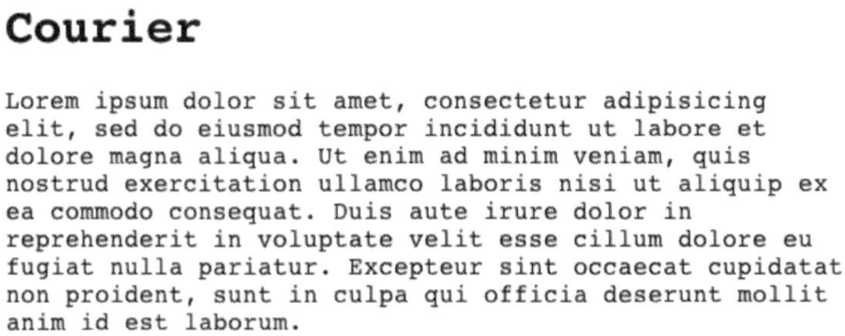

Courier

Lorem ipsum dolor sit amet, consectetur adipisicing
elit, sed do eiusmod tempor incididunt ut labore et
dolore magna aliqua. Ut enim ad minim veniam, quis
nostrud exercitation ullamco laboris nisi ut aliquip ex
ea commodo consequat. Duis aute irure dolor in
reprehenderit in voluptate velit esse cillum dolore eu
fugiat nulla pariatur. Excepteur sint occaecat cupidatat
non proident, sunt in culpa qui officia deserunt mollit
anim id est laborum.

Figure 9-12. *Courier (monospace)*

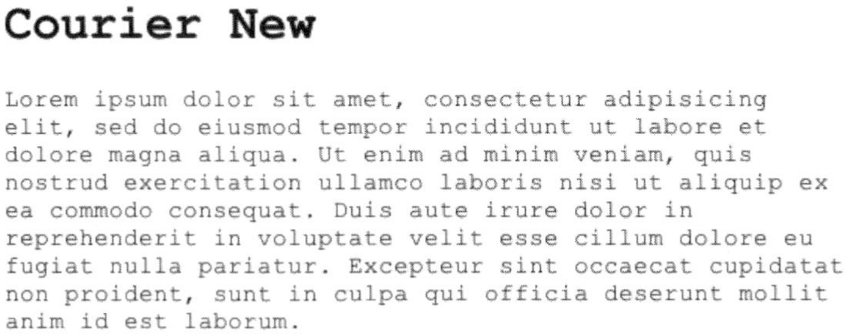

Courier New

Lorem ipsum dolor sit amet, consectetur adipisicing
elit, sed do eiusmod tempor incididunt ut labore et
dolore magna aliqua. Ut enim ad minim veniam, quis
nostrud exercitation ullamco laboris nisi ut aliquip ex
ea commodo consequat. Duis aute irure dolor in
reprehenderit in voluptate velit esse cillum dolore eu
fugiat nulla pariatur. Excepteur sint occaecat cupidatat
non proident, sunt in culpa qui officia deserunt mollit
anim id est laborum.

Figure 9-13. *Courier New (monospace)*

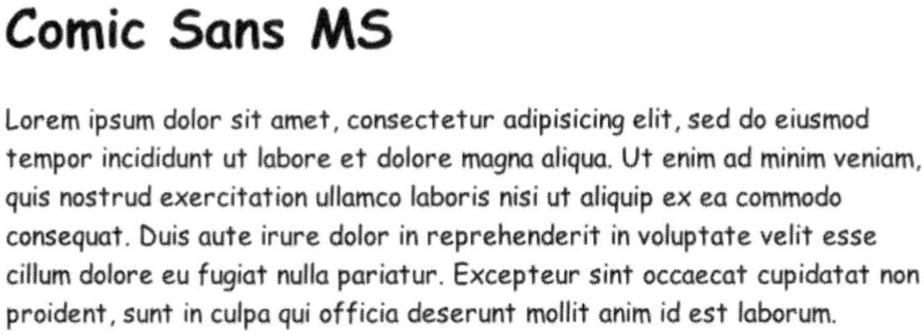

Comic Sans MS

Lorem ipsum dolor sit amet, consectetur adipisicing elit, sed do eiusmod
tempor incididunt ut labore et dolore magna aliqua. Ut enim ad minim veniam,
quis nostrud exercitation ullamco laboris nisi ut aliquip ex ea commodo
consequat. Duis aute irure dolor in reprehenderit in voluptate velit esse
cillum dolore eu fugiat nulla pariatur. Excepteur sint occaecat cupidatat non
proident, sunt in culpa qui officia deserunt mollit anim id est laborum.

Figure 9-14. *Comic Sans MS (cursive)*

These typefaces are found on 95 percent of Macs and Windows-based computers, according to a survey by VisiBone (`www.visibone.com/font/FontResults.html`). Still, it's important to understand there is no font you can count on to be there 100 percent of the time, especially when you factor in additional operating systems like Linux and other devices like PDAs and cell phones. Some portion of your audience will always see your site in a typeface you didn't expect.

Designers, especially those who come from print media and are used to having thousands of typefaces at their disposal, often wonder why it's not possible to embed fonts into a web page. CSS 2 did define mechanisms for downloadable fonts, but they weren't implemented by most web browsers, partially due to concerns of font manufacturers (called *foundries*), who felt it would enable piracy of their fonts.

In short, it is simply impossible (without using some additional technology such as images or Flash) to force a particular font upon a user of your web site. You can string together a long set of preferred typefaces in hopes that your reader may have one of them, but there are no guarantees. The small selection and relatively low quality of typefaces we can count on to be installed on most computers compounds this problem and frustrates many designers. We can use CSS to make the fonts we do have available look as good as possible, though, and there is at least some hope that quality typefaces that we can use well online will become available in the near future.

The Microsoft Vista Fonts

There is some small amount of relief on the horizon, though. Microsoft's Windows Vista operating system and other upcoming products will bundle a set of six typefaces optimized for on-screen use that are of higher quality and that are more flexible than what we can use today. These faces have been designed by renowned designers, including Lucas de Groot and Jeremy Tankard. It remains to be seen whether these fonts will make their way to users of older versions of Windows and users of other operating systems, such as Mac OS X (although Apple has previously licensed fonts from Microsoft, so it's certainly possible they'll do so again). This new set should provide designers with an exciting new core for typographic exploration. The so-called "Vista Fonts" appear in Figures 9-15 through 9-20.

Calibri

Lorem ipsum dolor sit amet, consectetur adipisicing elit, sed do eiusmod tempor incididunt ut labore et dolore magna aliqua. Ut enim ad minim veniam, quis nostrud exercitation ullamco laboris nisi ut aliquip ex ea commodo consequat. Duis aute irure dolor in reprehenderit in voluptate velit esse cillum dolore eu fugiat nulla pariatur. Excepteur sint occaecat cupidatat non proident, sunt in culpa qui officia deserunt mollit anim id est laborum.

Figure 9-15. *Calibri (sans serif)*

Candara

Lorem ipsum dolor sit amet, consectetur adipisicing elit, sed do eiusmod tempor incididunt ut labore et dolore magna aliqua. Ut enim ad minim veniam, quis nostrud exercitation ullamco laboris nisi ut aliquip ex ea commodo consequat. Duis aute irure dolor in reprehenderit in voluptate velit esse cillum dolore eu fugiat nulla pariatur. Excepteur sint occaecat cupidatat non proident, sunt in culpa qui officia deserunt mollit anim id est laborum.

Figure 9-16. *Candara (sans serif)*

Corbel

Lorem ipsum dolor sit amet, consectetur adipisicing elit, sed do eiusmod tempor incididunt ut labore et dolore magna aliqua. Ut enim ad minim veniam, quis nostrud exercitation ullamco laboris nisi ut aliquip ex ea commodo consequat. Duis aute irure dolor in reprehenderit in voluptate velit esse cillum dolore eu fugiat nulla pariatur. Excepteur sint occaecat cupidatat non proident, sunt in culpa qui officia deserunt mollit anim id est laborum.

Figure 9-17. *Corbel (sans serif)*

Cambria

Lorem ipsum dolor sit amet, consectetur adipisicing elit, sed do eiusmod tempor incididunt ut labore et dolore magna aliqua. Ut enim ad minim veniam, quis nostrud exercitation ullamco laboris nisi ut aliquip ex ea commodo consequat. Duis aute irure dolor in reprehenderit in voluptate velit esse cillum dolore eu fugiat nulla pariatur. Excepteur sint occaecat cupidatat non proident, sunt in culpa qui officia deserunt mollit anim id est laborum.

Figure 9-18. *Cambria (serif)*

Constantia

Lorem ipsum dolor sit amet, consectetur adipisicing elit, sed do eiusmod tempor incididunt ut labore et dolore magna aliqua. Ut enim ad minim veniam, quis nostrud exercitation ullamco laboris nisi ut aliquip ex ea commodo consequat. Duis aute irure dolor in reprehenderit in voluptate velit esse cillum dolore eu fugiat nulla pariatur. Excepteur sint occaecat cupidatat non proident, sunt in culpa qui officia deserunt mollit anim id est laborum.

Figure 9-19. *Constantia (serif)*

Consolas

```
Lorem ipsum dolor sit amet, consectetur adipisicing elit, sed
do eiusmod tempor incididunt ut labore et dolore magna aliqua.
Ut enim ad minim veniam, quis nostrud exercitation ullamco
laboris nisi ut aliquip ex ea commodo consequat. Duis aute
irure dolor in reprehenderit in voluptate velit esse cillum
dolore eu fugiat nulla pariatur. Excepteur sint occaecat
cupidatat non proident, sunt in culpa qui officia deserunt
mollit anim id est laborum.
```

Figure 9-20. *Consolas (monospace)*

Font Weights

You might assume that choosing the weight of your font—such as boldfaced or not—is a simple matter in CSS. You'd be both right and wrong. CSS uses the `font-weight` property for this, and allows for two types of attribute values: keywords and numeric.

Assigning font-weight with Keywords

You can use one of four possible keyword values to indicate the weight of your type. They are `normal`, `bold`, `bolder`, and `lighter`. As you might expect, `normal` indicates the standard weight of the font and `bold` indicates a boldfaced version. You can use these like so:

```
h1 {
  font-weight: bold;
}
p {
  font-weight: normal;
}
```

That's the simple part, and it covers most real-world use cases.

Assigning font-weight with Numerical Values

However, many typefaces include not just a normal and bold weight but several other weights as well. For example, the typeface Myriad Pro includes light, normal, semibold, bold and black variations. The OpenType font file format provides for up to nine weights of the same typeface. To account for this, CSS also allows you to specify weight in a numeric notation, with the possible values 100, 200, 300, 400, 500, 600, 700, 800, and 900. If a font has nine weights, each of them corresponds directly to a weight, with 100 being the lightest and 900 being the heaviest.

However, if a typeface doesn't have all nine weights, the user agent is required to go through a complex set of steps to map the weights that do exist within the font to a particular numeric value. Those steps are as follows:

1. If a weight is labeled by the font as Normal, Regular, Roman, or Book, it is assigned to the numeric value 400 (which corresponds with the keyword `normal`).

2. If a weight labeled Medium is found in the font, it is given the value 500. However, if Medium is the only weight available, it is assigned the value 400 instead of 500.

3. If the value 500 is still unassigned, it is assigned to the same weight that was assigned the numeric value 400.

4. If 300 is unassigned, it is assigned to the next lighter font weight than that assigned to 400, if a lighter one exists. If a lighter weight does not exist, it is assigned to the same weight that was assigned the value 400. The same method is applied for 200 and 100.

5. If 600 is unassigned, it is assigned to the next heavier font weight than that assigned to the value 400, if a heavier one exists. If a heavier weight does not exist, it is assigned to the same weight that was assigned the value 500. This method is also used for 700, 800, and 900.

The long and short of this is that in any font that has fewer than nine weights (which is most of them), several numeric values will result in the typeface being rendered in the same weight. For example, if a font has just two weights, Normal and Bold, the values 100, 200, 300, 400, and 500 will all return the Normal weight (as will the normal keyword, which is equivalent to 400), and the values 600, 700, 800, and 900 (as well as the bold keyword) will result in the bold weight of the font. This scale varies for every font based on both the number of weights available and the label those weights are given within the font file itself.

Given that you already can't determine what typeface will be displayed on a user's screen, it's almost impossible to know how many weights are available to you. As such, your best bet in most situations is to stick with the keyword values. And speaking of keyword values, there's two more we haven't discussed yet: bolder and lighter.

bolder and lighter

The values bolder and lighter increase or decrease the weight of the type based on the weight of the parent. Sounds simple, right? We're afraid not.

In order for the user agent to render type bolder or lighter, it must first determine the numeric value of the weight of the parent. This is somewhat problematic, though, as the actual rendered font weight can evaluate to multiple numeric values—Myriad Regular may be both 400 and 500, for example. In these instances, the user agent chooses the lowest applicable numeric value—400, in our hypothetical Myriad Regular example. bolder then evaluates to 500—which turns out to also be Myriad Regular in our example, not Myriad Bold as you probably intended. And remember, all this is true only if the user has Myriad installed—if not, all these evaluations are taking place on a different font, which likely has a different scale than Myriad.

The Final Word on Font Weights

For practical purposes, it's usually best to simply stick to using the normal and bold keywords. If you need more fine-grained control over font weight, go ahead and use the numeric values, but don't expect them to work reliably across your entire user base, because you can't predict exactly which fonts they'll be seeing your type in. You'll just have to accept that not everyone is going see the type exactly as you intended it, and ensure your designs still work well in these situations.

Sizing Type

Before we can discuss sizing type with CSS, we need to understand how type is sized in general. A key unit of measurement in typography is called an *em* (pronounced like the letter m). This unit is specific to a particular font and is specified in the font file itself by the font's designer. Ems are usually thought of as a square unit—a box, called an em square or em box. A single em refers to the size of the space between baselines (the invisible line on which uppercase characters sit) when the typeface is *set solid*—or without leading (more on leading later in this chapter). The em unit does not in any way define the size of individual characters within a font. Many fonts have characters that are either larger or smaller (in height and/or width) than a single em. This is the key point to understand. When we refer to the size of type, as specified by the font-size CSS property, we are talking about the size of its *em square* (whether or not we actually use the em unit to define it), or the size of a box that is one em tall and one em wide. We are not referring to the size (height or width) of any individual characters within the font.

Also keep in mind that user agents provide default sizes for type (which is typically alterable by the user via the preferences or settings area of the browser). It is typical (but not absolutely universal) for a desktop computer web browser to set its default type size to 16 pixels. In other words, most of your visitors will be using a browser that default to an em square that is 16 pixels by 16 pixels in size.

Absolute-Size Keywords

CSS establishes seven absolute-size keywords for the `font-size` property: `xx-small`, `x-small`, `small`, `medium`, `large`, `x-large`, and `xx-large`.

```
p {
  font-size: large;
}
```

The keywords provide relative font sizes to one another based on a scaling factor of the user agent. This scaling factor is somewhat of a moving target, as different user agents may provide different scaling factors. Even the CSS specification changed its recommendation between versions 1 and 2. (CSS 1 specified a scaling factor of 1.5 going up and .66 going down, but changed to a more vague "between 1.0 and 1.2" in the CSS 2 specification.)

Because of this, the exact pixel sizes of rendered type vary from browser to browser when size is specified using absolute-size keywords. If we assume a default (`medium`) em square size of 16 pixels (like most desktop browsers give us out of the box), we end up with the following translations to pixel sizes for scaling factors of 1.5 and 1.2:

Keyword	Scaling 1.5	Scaling 1.2
xx-small	5 px	9 px
x-small	7 px	11 px
small	11 px	13 px
medium	16 px	16 px
large	24 px	19 px
x-large	36 px	23 px
xx-large	54 px	28 px

■**Note** Internet Explorer versions 5.5 and lower assigned the "default" font size (usually 16 pixels) to `small`, whereas most other browsers assigned it to `medium`. IE 6 solved this issue in its standards compliance mode (see Chapter 4 for more information on standards compliance mode and `DOCTYPE` switching), but still displays improperly when in quirks mode.

Relative-Size Keywords

In addition to the absolute-size keywords, CSS allows for larger and smaller values, which do pretty much what you'd expect: they cause the type size of the selected element to be scaled up or down based on the same scaling factor the user agent uses in the absolute-size keywords. These keyword sizes are relative to the computed font-size value of their parent element.

```
* {
  font-size: medium;
}
strong {
  font-size: larger;
} /* evaluates to the same size as the large keyword /*
```

One interesting note about relative-size keywords is that they don't have the same limits as absolute-size keywords. The following is possible:

```
* {
  font-size: xx-large;
}
strong {
  font-size: larger;
} /* evaluates to the size of xx-large times the scaling factor /*
```

In this case, the size of the strong element's text is still scaled by the user agent's scaling factor, resulting in larger text than the inherited xx-large.

Using Pixels to Size Text

The font sizing we've done so far has been relative to the user agent's default font size. However, it is possible to specify the font-size property explicitly in pixels, overriding any inherited size (either from the user agent's defaults or from parent element[s]). For example:

```
p {
  font-size: 12px;
}
```

In this case, the size of the em square for the paragraph element would be 12 pixels by 12 pixels regardless of what size may have been inherited.

Although this is extremely useful, it is often not considered a best practice among web developers for two reasons. First, Internet Explorer 6 and lower do not allow the user to resize fonts whose sizes are specified in pixels. This poses accessibility problems for those visitors who simply must increase the size of type in order to accommodate for low vision. Additionally, most web designers feel it's important to acknowledge a user's default browser setting (which the user may have adjusted). By setting type in keywords, ems, or percentages, you allow users to decide that all type should be scaled based on whatever default they have chosen, instead of one you have chosen as the designer.

Using Percentages and Ems to Size Text

It is also common to size text using percentages or ems as the unit of measurement specified in your CSS. This approach works in a similar fashion as relative-size keywords in that it's based on the inherited `font-size` value of the parent element. Consider the following example:

```
p {
  font-size: 120%;
}
```

If we assume a default size of 16 pixels, this creates an em square of 19.2 pixels (note that some browsers may round these values to the nearest whole number).

Similarly, you can use the em CSS unit for sizing fonts relative to the inherited value. CSS defines that 1 em is equivalent to 100 percent when sizing fonts. Because of this, the following would result in the same 19.2-pixel rendered size as our 120 percent example earlier:

```
p {
  font-size: 1.2em;
}
```

This method is a favorite among standards-oriented web developers, and part of the reason is the so-called "62.5 percent hack."

Richard Rutter's 62.5 Percent Hack

Richard Rutter, proprietor of the popular web design blog Clagnut (`www.clagnut.com/`), wrote a seminal piece in web typography back in May 2004. Titled "How to size text using ems," Rutter's blog post (`www.clagnut.com/blog/348/`) outlined a simple method that allows for the inheritance and resizability of percentages and keywords (even in Internet Explorer), and the precision of pixels.

The key to Richard's method is one simple line of CSS:

```
body {
  font-size:62.5%;
}
```

Why 62.5 percent? Recall that nearly all modern web browsers default their text size to 16 pixels. Because 62.5 percent of 16 pixels is 10 pixels, any element that is a sibling of the body element has now been reset to display type based on a 10-pixel em square. Now, remember that 100 percent is equal to 1 em. Now that 1 em is 10 pixels, our math becomes very easy: 1 em is 10 pixels, .8 em is 8 pixels, 1.4 em is 14 pixels, and so on.

This is probably the single most popular type sizing method among standards-oriented designers today, and can definitely be described as a best practice.

Font Styles

CSS provides the `font-style` property for choosing between `normal`, `italic`, and `oblique` text. It is as simple as naming the appropriate keyword:

```
p {
  font-style: normal;
}
em {
  font-style: italic;
}
```

Those of you not schooled in typography may not be familiar with the concept of "oblique" text. Whereas italicized text contains unique characters separate from the normal, or roman, version of the typeface, oblique text is simply a slanted version of the normal (roman) font. Few typefaces contain both oblique and italic variants in their fonts, so user agents are instructed to obey a set of rules when italic or oblique font styles are requested via CSS:

1. If there is both an italic and oblique version of the face, use the requested version.

2. If there is an oblique face but not an italic face, the oblique may be substituted for the missing italic. However, the opposite is not true. A user agent may not substitute an italic font for a missing oblique.

3. If neither is found, the user agent may generate an oblique version simply by slanting the normal, or roman, version of the font.

The practical uses for oblique type are rare—in fact, it's usually considered in bad typographic form to substitute an oblique for a proper italic. For this reason, the oblique keyword is rarely used. If it's italic you want, then it's italic you should specify.

Transforming Text

Oftentimes, a designer will elect to display a passage of type (especially headers or other short bursts) in all-caps, all-lowercase, or initial caps (in which the first letter of each word is capitalized). The text-transform CSS property accommodates these cases. Using only CSS, you can render text using any of these casing techniques regardless of the case in which the content appears in the (X)HTML source.

- `h1 { text-transform: uppercase; } /* creates all caps */`

- `h2 { text-transform: capitalize; } /* creates initial caps */`

- `h3 { text-transform: lowercase; } /* creates all lowercase */`

Font Variants

Some fonts also offer variants. CSS offers support for one of these—small caps—via the font-variant property. For example:

```
h3 {
  font-variant: small-caps;
}
```

If the font being used provides a small-caps variant, it will be used. If not, the browser may generate a small-caps face by scaling uppercase letters. This is not ideal, but it's better than nothing.

Note Internet Explorer 5.5 and lower display text in all caps rather than small caps.

Setting Blocks of Text

Let's face it: reading long passages of text on a screen is hard on the eyes. But, by following some basic rules of typography and learning how to apply them with CSS, you can make it a whole lot easier on your visitors.

Line Length

Typographers call the length of a single line of text the *measure*. Choosing an appropriate measure is a key component of readability. In CSS, the line length is defined by setting the width property of the element (or a parent element). Although you can use any CSS measurement unit, width of text blocks (like paragraphs) is usually best handled by the em unit, which is based on the size of the font in use.

```
p { width: 45em; }
```

A general rule of thumb is that lines should be 45–75 characters long for optimal readability. Lines that are either too long or too short can become difficult to read. We can approximate that the average character is about two-thirds of an em long (wider characters are longer, thin ones are shorter). Based on this, somewhere between 30 and 50 ems can be seen as an ideal line length. However, this is just a rule of thumb, and your mileage may vary.

The CSS properties min-width and max-width are extremely helpful for line length, especially in liquid (or fluid) layouts that scale when the browser window is resized and in cases where widths of some elements are set in pixels. Consider a div element that is 75 percent wide—taking up three-fourths of the browser window. If the browser window is very large, the line lengths of paragraphs within this div will become very long, severely limiting readability. Using min-width and max-width, you can set the line lengths to be flexible but have constraints so they never become too long or too short.

```
div#content {
  width: 75%;
}
div#content p {
  min-width: 30em;
  max-width: 50em;
}
```

Similarly, you may have a div with a larger pixel width, but not want text within to stretch that entire width (the result is shown in Figure 9-21):

```
div#content {
  width: 600px;
}
div#content p {
  max-width: 450px;
}
```

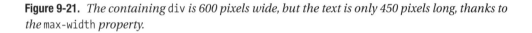

Lorem ipsum dolor sit amet, consectetur adipisicing elit, sed do
eiusmod tempor incididunt ut labore et dolore magna aliqua.
Ut enim ad minim veniam, quis nostrud exercitation ullamco
laboris nisi ut aliquip ex ea commodo consequat. Duis aute
irure dolor in reprehenderit in voluptate velit esse cillum dolore
eu fugiat nulla pariatur. Excepteur sint occaecat cupidatat non
proident, sunt in culpa qui officia deserunt mollit anim id est
laborum.

Figure 9-21. *The containing* div *is 600 pixels wide, but the text is only 450 pixels long, thanks to the* max-width *property.*

Note Internet Explorer 6 and lower do not properly support mix-width and max-width. When these properties are used, IE will interpret them as the width property.

Leading (or line-height)

Leading (rhymes with "bedding") refers to the amount of space between lines of type. The name comes from traditional letterpress-style typesetting, in which strips of lead or other metal are used to separate one line of text from the next.

In CSS, this space is defined using the line-height property. For example:

```
p {
  font-size: 10px;
  line-height: 14px;
}
```

In this case, the type's em square will be 10 pixels tall, but 2 pixels of extra space (or leading) will be added above and below each line. Typographers refers to this as text being set *10 over 14*, or *10/14*. Note that you can also have negative leading:

```
p {
  font-size: 10px;
  line-height: 8px;
}
```

Here, the text is set 10/8. Depending on the nature of the typeface, this may cause characters to overlap one another vertically. Negative leading is sometimes used in short bursts of text such as ad copy or headers, but is rarely useful in blocks of text. Adding positive leading is one of the single most effective ways to increase readability of your site's body text. Although any unit can be used, the `line-height` property is unique in that it can be specified without a unit. When this is done, the value is taken as a scaling factor based on the font size of the element (whether inherited or stated explicitly). For example:

```
p {
  font-size: 10px;
  line-height: 1.4; /* evaluates to 14px /*
}
p {
  font-size: 10px;
  line-height: .8; /* evaluates to 8px /*
}
```

A few basic leading rules go like this:

- Blocks of text almost always require positive leading. Text rarely reads well in blocks set solid (i.e., no leading) and almost never reads well in blocks set with negative leading.

- Darker (or heavier) faces need more lead than light ones. If you are using boldfaced text, or you are simply using a heavy typeface (such as Arial Black or Impact), you will likely need more leading than when you use lighter typefaces.

- Sans serif typefaces often require more lead than serif typefaces.

- Longer measures require more leading. Shorter measures require less leading.

Kerning

In typography, kerning is the process of adjusting the space between certain combinations of letters so that a "limb" of one projects over or under the body of another. This is common in certain letter combinations, such as "To" or "VA." Kerning at this level is not possible via CSS (and usually unnecessary anyway, as common kerning pairs are generally built into most modern fonts). However, CSS does provide a `letter-spacing` property that adjusts the spacing between all characters. Positive values will cause letters to be further apart and negative values will cause letters to be closer together. For example:

```
p {
  letter-spacing: -.05em;
}
```

Although this property can occasionally be used effectively in setting headers and other short bursts of text, it's not often useful for blocks of body text.

Text Alignment and Justification

The CSS property `text-align` handles horizontal alignment of text. Possible values include `left`, `right`, `center`, and `justify`. If `left` or `right` is specified, the text will be set flush to that size, producing a "ragged" edge on the opposite side. To set text "ragged right," use `text-align: left`. If you want text to be centered, use the `center` value. For example:

```
h1 {
  text-align: center;
}
p {
  text-align: left;
}
```

These styles will produce centered headers and left-aligned (or "ragged right") paragraphs.

`text-align` also offers the ability to "justify" text, in which case the space between words is adjusted so that the text creates a clean edge on both the left and right sides:

```
p {
  text-align: justify;
}
```

This is a common effect in printed type, and can be seen in most newspapers. The downside to justified text is the inconsistent spacing between words, which can sometimes lead to unsightly "rivers" of whitespace flowing vertically down the page and decreasing readability. What typically prevents this effect in print is hyphenation. By breaking up words via hyphenation, the full width of the measure can be put to use and the word spacing becomes more consistent. However, web browsers (and CSS) do not currently offer automatic hyphenation. As such, justified text is uncommon on the Web. If you elect to use it, be sure to choose your line length wisely, or you're likely to see large white holes in your lines of text. Justified text tends to work better with longer measures.

Block Paragraphs vs. Traditional Paragraphs

By default, web browsers display block paragraphs—that is, paragraphs are separated by a line break. However, traditional typography, like that you'll find in most books, magazines, and newspapers, does not provide a line break in between paragraphs. Web browsers create this line break with the CSS `margin` property. Generally, a margin of 1 em is applied above and below each paragraph, like so:

```
p {
  margin: 1em 0;
}
```

In order to remove the line break, you simply need to override this default style with a zero margin:

```
p {
  margin: 0;
}
```

Indicating New Paragraphs

If you choose to remove the line break, though, you will need to find some other visual device for separating one paragraph from the next. The most common technique used is indenting. Indenting in CSS is done via the `text-indent` property. As with many of the text-related properties in CSS, `text-indent` can accept any unit of measurement, but em is often used due to its relationship to the current text size. For example:

```
p {
  text-indent: 2em;
}
```

This moves the beginning of the first line of a paragraph over to the right by two em squares. Although less common, it's also possible to outdent text by using a negative value on the text-indent property:

```
p {
  text-indent: -2em;
}
```

As you would expect, this moves the start of the first line two em squares to the left.

Typographers generally set opening paragraphs (those that start a story or chapter, and those that follow a header or other break in the text) without an indent, and then indent the paragraphs that follow. This can be accomplished using CSS's adjacent sibling selectors:

```
p {
  text-indent:  0;
}
p + p {
  text-indent:  1.5em;
}
```

This will indent only paragraphs that occur directly after another paragraph. Opening paragraphs (those that follow any element other than a paragraph) will not be indented.

■**Note** Internet Explorer 6 and lower does not support adjacent sibling selectors and will simply ignore rules that contain them.

In addition to the typical indent, there are other techniques for indicating new paragraphs. Some typographers use ornamentation to set off a paragraph. This can be accomplished using CSS's content generation module to place an ornament before the paragraph element:

```
p + p:before {
  content: "\2767";
  margin-right: 0.5em;
}
```

This CSS will place a floral ornament (Unicode character 2767) before paragraphs that follow other paragraphs. A right margin has been added as well to separate the ornament from the text of the paragraph.

Another option is to display paragraphs as a continuous string of text separated by ornaments (commonly used is the *pilcrow* paragraph character). To accomplish this, we must change the paragraph display value from *block* to *inline*:

```
p {
  display: inline
}
p + p:before {
  content: "\2761";
  margin: 0 .5em;
}
```

Note Internet Explorer 7 and lower does not support CSS content generation. Most other modern browsers, including Safari, Firefox, and Opera, do.

Setting Quotations

It is common practice in typography to set block quotations in italics, and this happens to be the default styling for the `blockquote` (X)HTML element in most browsers. Still, we recommend that you explicitly state this preference to ensure it is set:

```
blockquote {
  font-style: italic;
}
```

Additionally, block quotes are sometimes set with a margin on both sides. This can be accomplished using CSS as follows:

```
blockquote {
  font-style: italic;
  margin: 1em 3em;
}
```

Headings and Subheads

Setting headings and subheads is where web designers often find themselves especially frustrated with the lack of typeface selection available on the Web. For this reason, it has become common to use CSS (and sometimes JavaScript or other scripting as well) to "replace" heading text with images or even Flash files.

Header Margins

As with paragraphs, headers are given a default vertical margin of 1 em in most web browsers. Many times, though, designers prefer headers to have less of a bottom margin—or maybe no bottom margin at all—so that they sit directly atop the text to which they relate. Achieving this is relatively simple:

```
h1, h2, h3, h4, h5, h6 {
  margin-bottom: .2em;
}
```

Image Replacement

If you want complete typographic control over the appearance of your headers, there is no substitute for type embedded in an image (usually created with a graphics package such as Adobe Photoshop or Adobe Illustrator). However, using img elements in (X)HTML source instead of semantic elements like h1 and h2 that properly indicate what the text is would be ill advised. Doing so makes your page less accessible, as those who cannot see images (either because they're browsing with images turned off in their browser or because they are vision-impaired and visiting your site with a screen-reading device) will not be able to read your headers. It also hinders your search engine results, as search engine crawlers place greater importance on keywords found in header tags than in other elements or attributes.

So, back in 2003, a clever fellow by the name of Todd Fahrner developed a way to use CSS to effectively replace text in a header element (or technically, any element, although this is most commonly applied to headers) with an image (which typically contains the same text). Fahrner's original technique, which came to be known as Fahrner Image Replacement (FIR), is no longer recommended for use, but it spawned other creative minds to develop similar techniques that are now widely use.

Leahy/Langridge Image Replacement (LIR)

At similar times but independent from each another, Stuart Langridge (www.kryogenix.org/code/browser/lir/) and Seamus Leahy (www.moronicbajebus.com/playground/cssplay/image-replacement/) developed a technique for image replacement that remains quite popular today. It works by taking a heading with an id like this:

```
<h1 id="replaced">This text will be replaced with our image</h1>
```

and applying some CSS to it as follows:

```
h1#replaced {
  padding-top: 55px; /* height of the replacement image */
  height: 0;
  overflow: hidden;
  background-image: url("replacement_image.jpg");
  background-repeat: no-repeat;
}
```

What this does is set the height of our header to 0, but with a top padding the same size as the image we intend to use for the header. Then, we set the background image of the header element to our replacement image and tell it to not repeat. Because of the top padding, the (X)HTML/CSS text is displayed below the image—actually outside the dimensions of the header element's box. By setting the overflow property to hidden, we instruct the user agent not to show anything outside the element's box, leaving us with only our background image showing.

The beauty of this method is that the (X)HTML is semantic, accessible, and clean. This holds to the philosophy of keeping images that are of a decorative nature in CSS (those that are of a contextual nature can still be in the (X)HTML, of course).

Rundle Image Replacement

Web designer Mike Rundle (http://phark.typepad.com/phark/2003/08/accessible_imag.html) developed yet another technique, and it may be the simplest of all. Mike simply shifts the textual content of the header element out of the visible area of the browser window by using an extremely large negative `text-indent` value, like so:

```
h1#replaced {
  height: 55px; /* height of the replacement image */
  text-indent: -20000em;
  background-image: url("replacement_image.jpg");
  background-repeat: no-repeat;
}
```

The text is technically still there, but it's shifted so far to the left that it will not be seen in any imaginable browser window. But since it is still there, search engine crawlers and screen readers will still read it.

Complete Example

To demonstrate several of the techniques discussed in this chapter, we've put together a simple page containing headers, paragraphs, and a block quotation. Using three colors (red, almost-black, and a lighter gray), two font groupings (one serif, one sans), a bit of CSS, and absolutely no graphics, we crafted an elegantly styled page very quickly. It goes to show that the art of typography is alive and well on the Web.

The code for the example page follows, starting with the markup. For brevity, we have left all the text content out. For the full markup, see the `web_typography.html` file in the code download for this chapter.

```
<!DOCTYPE html PUBLIC "-//W3C//DTD XHTML 1.0 Strict//EN"\➥
"http://www.w3.org/TR/xhtml1/DTD/xhtml1-strict.dtd">
<html xmlns="http://www.w3.org/1999/xhtml" xml:lang="en" lang="en">
<head>
  <meta http-equiv="Content-Type" content="text/html; charset=utf-8"/>
  <title>Web Typography Example</title>
  <link rel="stylesheet" media="screen" type="text/css" href="typography.css" />
</head>
<body>
  <div id="content">
    <h1>Lorem ipsum</h1>
    <p class="intro">
      ...content goes here...
    </p>
    <h2>dolor sit amet</h2>
    <p>
      ...content goes here...
    </p>
    <blockquote>
      <p>
        ...content goes here...
      </p>
    </blockquote>
```

```
      <h2>consectetur adipisicing elit</h2>
      <p>
        ...content goes here...
      </p>
      <h3>sed do eiusmod</h3>
      <p>
        ...content goes here...
      </p>
      <p>
        ...content goes here...
      </p>
      <h3>tempor incididunt ut</h3>
      <p>
        ...content goes here...
      </p>
      <p>
      ...content goes here...
      </p>
    </div>
  </body>
</html>
```

Now the CSS—we included comments for each style applied, to explain what's doing what:

```
/* In the body element, we set our base font size
   to 62.5% and set up our initial font. */
body {
  font-family: Constantia, Georgia, "Times New Roman", serif;
  font-size: 62.5%;
  color: #1a1a1a;
}


/* div#content contains all of our text. here, we set
   the mix and max width so that our line lengths
   never get too long or too short. */
div#content {
  min-width: 20em;
  max-width: 40em;
  font-size: 1.4em;
  width: 75%;
  margin: 6em auto;
}


/* Some base styles for our headers. Note the
   smaller bottom margin, capitalization, and
   kerning (letter-spacing ) */
```

```css
h1, h2, h3 {
  margin:  1em 0 .25em 0;
  font-family:  Calibri, Helvetica, Arial, sans-serif;
  text-transform:  capitalize;
  letter-spacing:  -.05em;
}

/* Specific styles for h1 and h2 */
h1 { font-size:  2em; }
h2 { font-size:  1.66em; color:  #666; }

/* Let's put a decorative flueron before h2s */
h2:before {
  content: "\2767";
  margin-right: 0.5em;
  margin-left:  -1.25em;
}

/* For h3, we'll use a different color and font, all uppercase,
   and without the tighter letter-spacing */
h3 {
  font-size:  1em;
  font-family: Constantia, Georgia, "Times New Roman", serif;
  font-weight:  normal;
  text-transform:  uppercase;
  letter-spacing:  0;
  color:  #cc0000;
}

/* Base styles for paragraphs. We'll remove the margins
   and increase the leading (line-height) */
p {
  margin:  0;
  line-height:  1.4;
}

/* Paragraphs after other paragraphs should be indented. */
p + p { text-indent:  1.5em; }

/* Make our intro paragraph a little bigger and with small-caps
   on the first line. Also, justify the text. */
p.intro {
  text-align:  justify;
  font-size:  1.33em;
  line-height:  1.2;
}
```

```css
p.intro:first-line { font-variant:  small-caps; }

/* Make the first letter of our intro be a drop cap.
   We'll use a much larger font-size and float the letter
   to the left to acomplish this. */
p.intro:first-letter {
  float:  left;
  font-size:  3.5em;
  line-height:  1;
  color:  #cc0000;
  margin:  0 .1em 0 0;
}

/* Give our blockquotes some margin, and make them italic. */
blockquote {
  font-style:  italic;
  margin: 2em 5em;
}

/* Paragraphs within blockquotes will get our sans-serif font
   and be a lighter gray */
blockquote p {
  text-indent:  -.4em;
  color:  #666;
  font-family:  Calibri, Helvetica, Arial, sans-serif;
}

/* Make CSS generate and include quotation marks before and after
   the paragraph. */
blockquote p:before {
  content:  "\201C";
  text-indent:  -.5em;
}
blockquote p:after {
  content:  "\201D";
}
```

Although the exact display will vary depending on the browser and fonts installed, this page renders as shown in Figure 9-22.

Lorem Ipsum

S ED DO EIUSMOD TEMPOR INCIDIDUNT UT LABORE ET DOLORE MAGNA aliqua. Ut enim ad minim veniam, quis nostrud exercitation ullamco laboris nisi ut aliquip ex ea commodo consequat. Duis aute irure dolor in reprehenderit in voluptate velit esse cillum dolore eu fugiat nulla pariatur. Excepteur sint occaecat cupidatat non proident, sunt in culpa qui officia deserunt mollit anim id est laborum.

❧ Dolor Sit Amet

Sed ut perspiciatis unde omnis iste natus error sit voluptatem accusantium doloremque laudantium, totam rem aperiam, eaque ipsa quae ab illo inventore veritatis et quasi architecto beatae vitae dicta sunt explicabo. Nemo enim ipsam voluptatem quia voluptas sit aspernatur aut odit aut fugit, sed quia consequuntur magni dolores eos qui ratione voluptatem sequi nesciunt. Neque porro quisquam est, qui dolorem ipsum quia dolor sit amet, consectetur, adipisci velit, sed quia non numquam eius modi tempora incidunt ut labore et dolore magnam aliquam quaerat voluptatem. Ut enim ad minima veniam, quis nostrum exercitationem ullam corporis suscipit laboriosam, nisi ut aliquid ex ea commodi consequatur? Quis autem vel eum iure reprehenderit qui in ea voluptate velit esse quam nihil molestiae consequatur, vel illum qui dolorem eum fugiat quo voluptas nulla pariatur?

> *"Fusce enim. Nam nisl est, rhoncus vitae, dapibus sed, accumsan sed, eros.*
> *Suspendisse eu leo in metus porttitor feugiat. Vivamus sollicitudin*
> *malesuada neque. Ut turpis est, dictum dapibus, porta non, volutpat nec,*
> *lorem. Morbi dolor dolor, viverra eu, convallis ut, congue id, tortor. Ut*
> *semper mi at erat. Cras lectus nisi, nonummy sagittis, tempor eget, tempor*
> *vitae, quam. Praesent pretium urna eget urna. Nunc vel dolor. Quisque*
> *mollis nibh ut massa. Nullam cursus lacus id sem tincidunt iaculis. Morbi*
> *enim tellus, euismod eget, euismod in, sodales vitae, lacus. Morbi eget*
> *nibh. Proin bibendum. Proin mi nibh, egestas vitae, dignissim a, malesuada*
> *et, purus. Aliquam ut purus et lorem dictum tristique. Pellentesque quis nisi*
> *eget odio porttitor rhoncus. Maecenas molestie pellentesque dui. "*

❧ Consectetur Adipisicing Elit

Nunc dapibus tellus. In hac habitasse platea dictumst. Vivamus at quam ut mauris congue mollis. Suspendisse ut odio ut nibh laoreet elementum. Ut lorem ante, euismod pharetra, aliquet eget, placerat sit amet, tortor. Maecenas cursus vulputate mauris. Nunc at velit. Donec ornare. Morbi enim sem, ultricies sit amet, mollis non, mollis eu, nibh. Suspendisse diam velit, vestibulum id, pellentesque a, interdum at, tortor. In non velit. Aliquam in massa eu sem scelerisque euismod. Mauris ut dolor. Donec quis mauris. Duis dictum orci ut metus elementum facilisis. Praesent eu libero. Cras suscipit. Phasellus rutrum ipsum ac massa.

SED DO EIUSMOD

Fusce interdum volutpat mi. Quisque venenatis, nisl vitae congue tincidunt, erat arcu luctus dui, eu mattis elit arcu in elit. Phasellus et nisi. Vestibulum tincidunt. Cras cursus, turpis eu venenatis tempor, massa elit lacinia nisl, at sagittis mauris nulla non arcu. Aenean eleifend lacus sit amet tellus. Mauris congue elit id lorem. Integer sagittis scelerisque odio. Etiam diam ipsum, porttitor vitae, faucibus sed, fringilla at, sem. Nulla ultricies fringilla eros. Nunc interdum odio non ante. Vestibulum et leo consectetuer diam blandit suscipit. Fusce placerat, tellus vitae mollis congue, eros sem euismod diam, sed mattis purus arcu vel tellus. Etiam laoreet, lorem ac scelerisque auctor, metus dolor pharetra purus, vitae egestas tellus nunc sit amet quam. Duis nulla urna, rhoncus id, hendrerit quis, dictum non, nunc. Maecenas posuere porta dui. Nunc a tortor.

Sed ut perspiciatis unde omnis iste natus error sit voluptatem accusantium doloremque laudantium, totam rem aperiam, eaque ipsa quae ab illo inventore veritatis et quasi architecto beatae vitae dicta sunt explicabo. Nemo enim ipsam voluptatem quia voluptas sit aspernatur aut odit aut fugit, sed quia consequuntur magni dolores eos qui ratione voluptatem sequi nesciunt. Neque porro quisquam est, qui dolorem ipsum quia dolor sit amet, consectetur, adipisci velit, sed quia non numquam eius modi tempora incidunt ut labore et dolore magnam aliquam quaerat voluptatem. Ut enim ad minima veniam, quis nostrum exercitationem ullam corporis suscipit laboriosam, nisi ut aliquid ex ea commodi consequatur? Quis autem vel eum iure reprehenderit qui in ea voluptate velit esse quam nihil molestiae consequatur, vel illum qui dolorem eum?

TEMPOR INCIDIDUNT UT

In bibendum varius libero. Morbi lacus. Pellentesque ante sem, molestie sit amet, placerat ut, egestas eget, mi. Donec mauris. Praesent elementum placerat sem. Morbi malesuada, odio nec accumsan ornare, neque leo scelerisque sem, id molestie dui augue eu nunc. Nulla tempor nonummy purus. Suspendisse eleifend adipiscing augue. Vestibulum lobortis metus vitae augue. Aenean gravida mollis orci. Sed pharetra nisl at erat. Vivamus suscipit quam ullamcorper velit. Cras interdum lectus at velit. Lorem ipsum dolor sit amet, consectetuer adipiscing elit. Donec quam.

Suspendisse nec nulla ac felis condimentum laoreet. Nullam diam. Cras lacinia ante in sapien. In orci eros, dictum a, aliquet ac, egestas non, nisl. Praesent et neque eget neque ultricies accumsan. Nulla fringilla, leo eu euismod vestibulum, urna leo laoreet risus, a tempor elit risus sit amet magna. Aenean felis. Nullam viverra porta metus. Donec accumsan augue at magna. Ut malesuada tellus eu enim. Sed vehicula, sem euismod viverra faucibus, urna tellus gravida massa, eget tempus enim augue tincidunt nunc. Suspendisse nec diam. Morbi malesuada magna non felis.

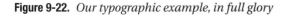

Figure 9-22. *Our typographic example, in full glory*

Summary

Typography on the Web not yet to the advanced state designers in print and other media have come to know and love. However, CSS does provide us with enough core functionality to create relatively beautiful type on the Web—if the designer is willing to give text the attention it deserves. The primary action people perform on the Internet is still reading—remember that, and treat your text accordingly.

With a solid understanding of CSS typographical techniques, let's move on to Chapter 10 and see how we can apply this knowledge to (X)HTML tables.

■ ■ ■

Styling Tables

While the most familiar use of (X)HTML tables—the layout grid—is considered a no-no in web standards–based development (as it is a *presentational* use of (X)HTML rather than a *semantic* one), the humble `table` element does still provide an essential function, for which it was intended when it was created all those many years ago: displaying tabular data.

Tabular data could be defined as two-dimensional information that benefits from being laid out with rows and columns. Examples of this sort of information include charts, spreadsheets, poll results, and file listings.

None of these things *have* to be laid out in rows and columns, but they make sense in rows and columns, and this sort of display conveys the relationships between the various data attributes. Anytime you have that sort of data, you have a candidate for a data table.

In this chapter we'll discuss how to use CSS to enhance the visual presentation of tables.

Table Markup

Before we get into CSS styling of tables, let's talk a bit about marking up tabular data with (X)HTML. It turns out there are several more table-related elements available to us than most web developers realize. Taking advantage of these provides several benefits, including enhanced accessibility, greater semantic meaning, and more "hooks" upon which to hang your styling information.

If you've used tables in the past—for data or for layout—you're probably familiar with the (X)HTML elements for rows (`tr`) and cells (`td`). You've probably seen tables that look something like this:

```
<table>
  <tr>
    <td>Name</td>
    <td>Affiliation</td>
    <td>Website URL</td>
  </tr>
  <tr>
    <td>Jeff Croft</td>
    <td>World Online</td>
    <td>http://jeffcroft.com</td>
  </tr>
```

```
  <tr>
    <td>Ian Lloyd</td>
    <td>Accessify</td>
    <td>http://accessify.com</td>
  </tr>
  <tr>
    <td>Dan Rubin</td>
    <td>Webgraph</td>
    <td>http://superfluousbanter.org/</td>
  </tr>
</table>
```

This code results in a table that looks like the one in Figure 10-1.

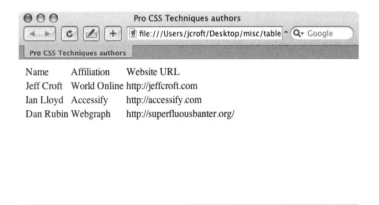

Figure 10-1. *Basic, unstyled table using almost exclusivey* tr *and* td *elements*

As you may have noticed, the (X)HTML for this table is almost exclusively tr and td elements. These are the building blocks of most (X)HTML tables, but they are only the beginning of the host of table-related elements and attributes (X)HTML provides. Now we'll explore all the other exciting table-related elements you have at your disposal.

The caption Element

By adding a caption element immediately after the opening <table> tag, you can provide a name or short description of your table. While this is not required, it's a good practice that adds extra context and meaning to your table. A caption element for our example table would look like this:

```
<table>
  <caption>Pro CSS Techniques authors</caption>
```

Note that while the caption element belongs at the top of your table, it does not have to be displayed there. CSS offers a property for placement of the caption, which we'll discuss later in the chapter.

The th Element

The th element is used to hold header information. Like td, th defines a table cell, but it indicates a special cell that is the header of a row or column (typically across the top or down the left of a table—but not necessarily). In our table, the first row, consisting of "Name, "Affiliation," and "Website URL," contains headers. As such, these should all be marked up with th elements, like so:

```
<tr>
  <th>Name</th>
  <th>Affiliation</th>
  <th>Website URL</th>
</tr>
<tr>
  <td>Jeff Croft</td>
  <td>World Online</td>
  <td>http://jeffcroft.com</td>
</tr>
```

Most browsers, by default, will display th elements in bold and centered in the table cell—but keep in mind you'll be able to style them however you like using CSS.

th is a key element for both usability and accessibility. A visual indication of a particular row or column in the header makes tables much easier to scan and parse quickly, and the element also allows assistive technology such as screen readers to handle the data differently than other data cells. For example, some screen readers may read a row in this table as follows: "Name: Jeff Croft, Affiliation: World Online, Website URL: http://jeffcroft.com." Bear this in mind when designing your tables.

The abbr Attribute

The abbr attribute is a great addition to table cells (whether they are td or th elements). It allows you to provide an alternate (usually shorter) description for the data in the cell. Rendering devices, especially screen readers and other assistive technology, use these abbreviated versions to enhance usability of the table. In our example table, we may wish to provide a shortened version of one of our headers:

```
<tr>
  <td>Name</th>
  <td>Affiliation</th>
  <td abbr="URL">Website URL</th>
</tr>
```

Now, when a screen reader reads a row, it might say, "Name: Jeff Croft, Affiliation: World Online, URL: http://jeffcroft.com."

The scope Attribute

The scope attribute associates a particular header with the appropriate data cells. It can be added to either th or td elements (although it's most commonly used on th), and expects one of four possible values: col, row, colgroup, or rowgroup. Adding this attribute helps the user agent understand which cells are related to one another. Again, this is especially helpful to screen readers and other assistive technology. It helps them read or display tables more logically.

Our example table, with the scope attribute added, might look something like this:

```
<table>
  <tr>
    <th scope="col">Name</th>
    <th scope="col">Affiliation</th>
    <th scope="col" abbr="URL">Website URL</th>
  </tr>
  <tr>
    <td scope="row">Jeff Croft</td>
    <td>World Online</td>
    <td>http://jeffcroft.com</td>
  </tr>
  <tr>
    <td scope="row">Ian Lloyd</td>
    <td>Accessify</td>
    <td>http://accessify.com</td>
  </tr>
  <tr>
    <td scope="row">Dan Rubin</td>
    <td>Webgraph</td>
    <td>http://superfluousbanter.org/</td>
  </tr>
</table>
```

Note that the element containing the names of individuals is marked up as a td, not a th, but is still assigned the scope attribute. Because our names are data values in this table and not simply generic labels, they should be table data cell elements rather than table header elements. However, they still provide context for the rest of the information in the row, so the addition of the scope attribute is appropriate.

Assigning scope in Complex Tables

As your tables become more complex, you may find cases where the header information for a particular data cell is not the same row or column as that cell, or where three or more headers apply to a single data cell. In these cases, scope breaks down and you'll need to use the headers attribute on your cells. By assigning a unique id to your headers, you can then reference them as the context for a data cell. Our example is simple enough that scope works fine, but here's an example of how it looks using headers instead:

```
<table>
  <tr>
    <th id="name">Name</th>
    <th id="affiliation">Affiliation</th>
    <th id="url" abbr="URL">Website URL</th>
  </tr>
  <tr>
```

```
    <td id="jeff_croft">Jeff Croft</td>
    <td headers="jeff_croft affiliation">World Online</td>
    <td headers="jeff_croft url">http://jeffcroft.com</td>
  </tr>
  <tr>
    <td id="ian_lloyd">Ian Lloyd</td>
    <td headers="ian_lloyd affiliation">Accessify</td>
    <td headers="ian_lloyd url">http://accessify.com</td>
  </tr>
  <tr>
    <td id="dan_rubin">Dan Rubin</td>
    <td headers="dan_rubin affiliation">Webgraph</td>
    <td headers="dan_rubin url">http://superfluousbanter.org/</td>
  </tr>
</table>
```

As this markup is far more complex than using the scope attribute, it's always best to use scope where possible—and it works great for most cases. Only quite complex tables require the use of the headers attribute.

The thead, tfoot, and tbody Elements

Rows within a table can be optionally grouped in a table head, table foot, and one or more table body sections, using the thead, tfoot, and tbody elements, respectively. Typically, the thead element is used to contain the header rows of the table, the tbody element is used to hold the main content, and the tfoot element is used to collect any totals and similar "closing" information. By including these divisions in your markup, you provide the "hooks" necessary to create common and often desirable presentational effects, and also allow the user agent to do logical things, such as including the same header and footer on each page of a printed version of your table. It is worth remembering that both the thead and tfoot elements should appear above any tbody elements in your markup. The browser will still display the tfoot element at the bottom of the table where it belongs.

Our example table doesn't have data appropriate for multiple tbody elements or a tfoot element, but as it gets a bit more complex, it may. Consider the following:

```
<table summary="A small table displaying the names, ➥
affiliations, web addresses, and roles of the ➥
authors and editors of Pro CSS Techniques.">
  <caption>Pro CSS Techniques authors and editors</caption>
  <thead>
    <tr>
      <th scope="col">Name</th>
      <th scope="col">Affiliation</th>
      <th scope="col" abbr="URL">Website URL</th>
      <th scope="col">Role</th>
    </tr>
  </thead>
  <tbody id="authors">
```

```
        <tr>
          <td scope="row">Jeff Croft</td>
          <td>World Online</td>
          <td>http://jeffcroft.com</td>
          <td>Author</td>
        </tr>
        <tr>
          <td scope="row">Ian Lloyd</td>
          <td>Accessify</td>
          <td>http://accessify.com</td>
          <td>Author</td>
        </tr>
        <tr>
          <td scope="row">Dan Rubin</td>
          <td>Webgraph</td>
          <td>http://superfluousbanter.org/</td>
          <td>Author</td>
        </tr>
      </tbody>
      <tbody id="editors">
        <tr>
          <td scope="row">Chris Mills</td>
          <td>Apress/friends of ED</td>
          <td>http://www.friendsofed.com/bloggED</td>
          <td>Editor</td>
        </tr>
        <tr>
          <td scope="row">Wilson Miner</td>
          <td>Apple Computer</td>
          <td>http://wilsonminer.com</td>
          <td>Technical Editor</td>
        </tr>
      </tbody>
    </table>
```

Here, we've wrapped our first row in the thead element, and also added a second tbody section for the book's editors. We haven't used the tfoot element, as this set of data doesn't have any information appropriate for it. A case where you may use tfoot may be for the totals at the bottom of a spreadsheet or invoice. You're probably already envisioning ways these markup additions could be exploited with CSS styles—we'll get to that later in the chapter.

Columns

Tables have always contained the tr element to designate table rows, but only more recently did columns earn their way into the (X)HTML specifications. However, no current browser supports using CSS to style columns, so their current benefits are purely semantic and "future proofing." If you define columns now, you won't have to when browsers begin supporting the styling of them; therefore, we've decided to cover them here.

The `colgroup` element provides a way to define a set of columns for your table. Individual columns are then defined using the `col` element. To define proper columns for our table, we would add the following code:

```
<colgroup>
  <col id="name" />
  <col id="affiliation" />
  <col id="url" />
  <col id="role" />
</colgroup>
```

The summary Attribute

Data tables can take an optional summary attribute whose purpose is to provide a description of the table's purpose and structure. The `summary` attribute, by default, doesn't display on the page (although by using CSS attribute selectors, you could make it display). The `summary` attribute is especially helpful to nonvisual viewers of your content. When writing a table summary, consider explaining any nonobvious relationships between rows and columns, as well as defining the relationship between the table and the context of the document that contains it.

Although our example table is very simple and may not require a summary, one could be added like so:

```
<table summary="A small table displaying the names, affiliations, and web➡
  addresses of the authors of Pro CSS Techniques.">
```

All Marked Up

So, our fully marked-up, semantic table code looks like this:

```
<table summary="A small table displaying the names, ➡
affiliations, web addresses, and roles of the ➡
authors and editors of Pro CSS Techniques.">
  <caption>Pro CSS Techniques authors and editors</caption>
  <colgroup>
    <col id="name" />
    <col id="affiliation" />
    <col id="url" />
    <col id="role" />
  </colgroup>
  <thead>
    <tr>
      <th scope="col">Name</th>
      <th scope="col">Affiliation</th>
      <th scope="col" abbr="URL">Website URL</th>
      <th scope="col">Role</th>
    </tr>
  </thead>
  <tbody id="authors">
```

```
      <tr>
        <td scope="row">Jeff Croft</td>
        <td>World Online</td>
        <td>http://jeffcroft.com</td>
        <td>Author</td>
      </tr>
      <tr>
        <td scope="row">Ian Lloyd</td>
        <td>Accessify</td>
        <td>http://accessify.com</td>
        <td>Author</td>
      </tr>
      <tr>
        <td scope="row">Dan Rubin</td>
        <td>Webgraph</td>
        <td>http://superfluousbanter.org/</td>
        <td>Author</td>
      </tr>
    </tbody>
    <tbody id="editors">
      <tr>
        <td scope="row">Chris Mills</td>
        <td>Apress/friends of ED</td>
        <td>http://www.friendsofed.com/bloggED</td>
        <td>Editor</td>
      </tr>
      <tr>
        <td scope="row">Wilson Miner</td>
        <td>Apple Computer</td>
        <td>http://wilsonminer.com</td>
        <td>Technical Editor</td>
      </tr>
    </tbody>
</table>
```

With the addition of a handful of useful elements and attributes, we've added a great deal of meaning, usability, and accessibility to even this simple table. But perhaps more importantly (at least in the context of this book), we've added a plethora of hooks within the table we can attach CSS styles to.

Adding Style

Data tables may seem like boring spreadsheets of mind-numbing information—and often they are. But that is, if anything, a really good reason to give them special attention when it comes to visual and information design. With a bit of CSS work, we can take the mundane, ordinary table and transform it into a fascinating resource that is a pleasure to browse. In this section, we'll cover some of the common styles and features you can add to your table to increase readability, findability, and aesthetic value.

First, take a look at Figure 10-2, which shows our finished example table as it appears in a browser with no CSS styling.

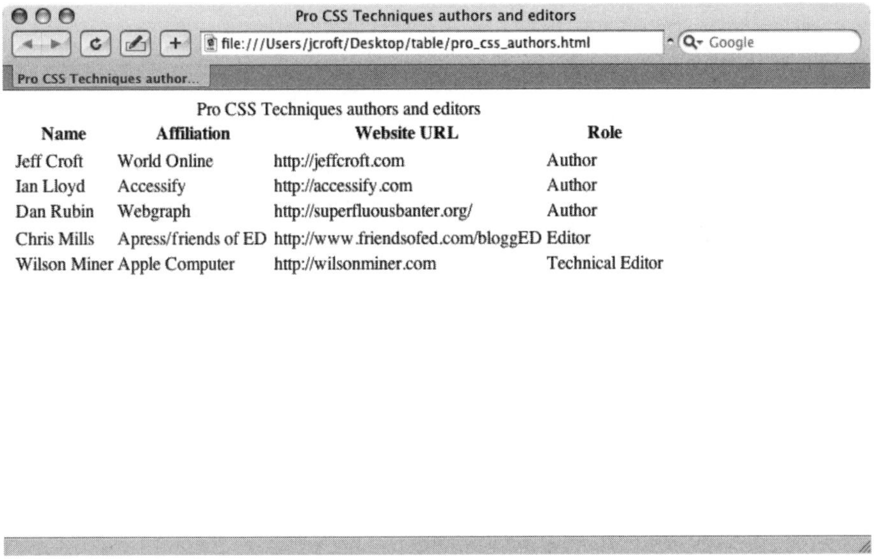

Figure 10-2. *Our sample table, completely unstyled*

Most folks will agree this isn't ideal. Let's add some basic table styles, as well as some type styling (see the previous chapter), to enhance its presentation. We'll start with this CSS:

```
table {
  width: 90%;
  margin: 0 auto;
  font-family: "Lucida Grande", Verdana, Helvetica, Arial, sans-serif;
  font-size: .9em;
  line-height: 1.4em;
}
```

By simply making the table 90 percent wide, centering it on the page (by giving it auto left and right margins), and tweaking the type a bit, we get a good start toward a cleaner presentation, as shown in Figure 10-3.

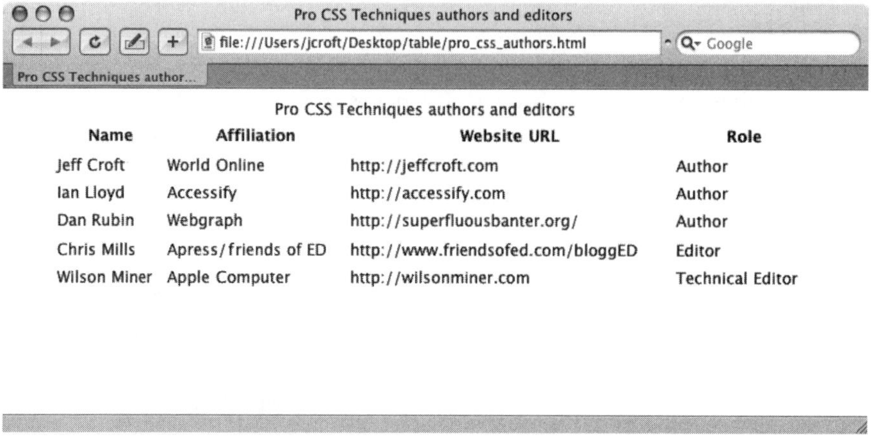

Figure 10-3. *Some basic tweaks have already improved our table to no end!*

Now, what about those headers? We'd rather see them left-aligned, and perhaps a border under them would help delineate them from the data cells:

```
th {
  text-align: left;
  border-bottom: 1px solid #000;
}
```

Let's also adjust the color of the text in the data cells while we're at it:

```
td {
  color: #333;
}
```

Our table now looks like Figure 10-4.

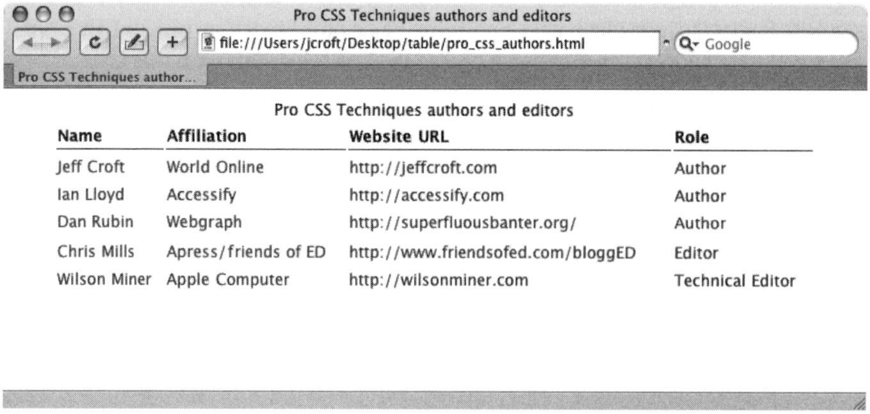

Figure 10-4. *Basic delineation of headers and body using color and a border*

Getting better already! But nothing we've done so far is table specific. We've simply styled some type and added some borders, just as we can do on any element with CSS.

Table Borders

CSS defines two separate models for table borders: collapsed and separate. The default rendering mode for most browsers is the separate model, in which borders around cells are kept separate from one another. For example, adding a one-pixel border to our example table in separate mode produces the results shown in Figure 10-5.

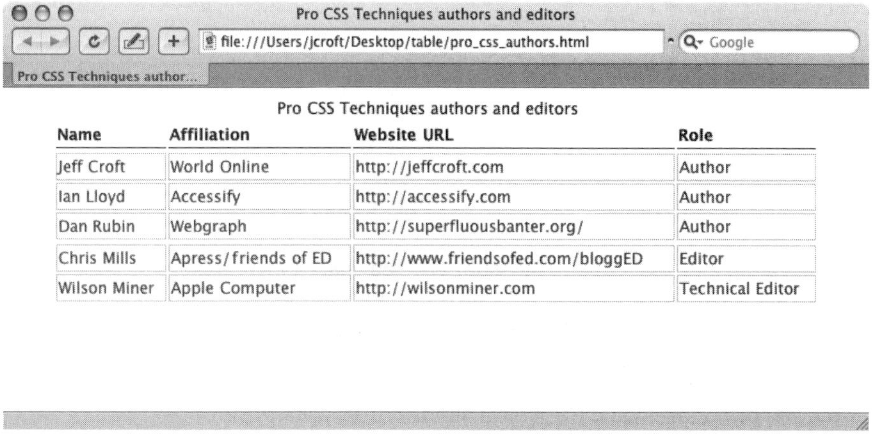

Figure 10-5. *Table borders in the separate model*

You'll note there is some space between each cell, and each cell receives its own, nonconnecting border. Let's change the border model to collapsing before we add our border, like so:

```
table {
  width: 90%;
  margin: 0 auto;
  font-family: Lucida Grande, Verdana, Helvetica, Arial, sans-serif;
  font-size: .9em;
  line-height: 1.4em;
  border-collapse: collapse;
}

th {
  text-align: left;
  border-bottom: 1px solid #000;
}

td {
  color: #333;
  border: 1px solid #ccc;
}
```

As you can see in Figure 10-6, the result is quite different.

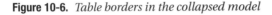

Figure 10-6. *Table borders in the collapsed model*

The borders have "collapsed" into one another and the space between cells has been removed. For most purposes, this collapsed model is more useful than it's separate counterpart. The rules that control the collapsed model are quite specific:

- The `table` element itself cannot have padding (although it can have margins). This means there is never any space between a table's border and its outermost cells.

- In addition to the `table` element, cells, rows, columns, row groups, and column groups can all have borders.

- There is never any space between cell borders. Borders themselves collapse into one another so that only one is actually drawn. So, if two cells each have a one-pixel-wide border, rather than two adjacent one-pixel-wide borders (for a total width of two pixels), you will see only one border line with a one-pixel weight.

- If two cells collapsing into one another have differing `border-style` attributes, the style with the greater priority will be displayed. The priority, from most preferred to least preferred, is as follows: `hidden`, `double`, `solid`, `dashed`, `dotted`, `ridge`, `outset`, `groove`, `inset`, `none`. If the two collapsing cells have the same `border-style` attribute, that value will be used.

- If two cells collapsing into one another have borders of the same style and width but different color, the displayed color is taken from the element with the greater priority. The priority, from most preferred to least preferred, is as follows: cell, row, row group, column, column group, table. If the two elements are of the same type, then no behavior is defined, and each user agent or browser is left to its own devices when choosing which color to display.

With that in mind, let's experiment with some different border styles for our example table:

```
table {
  width: 90%;
  margin: 0 auto;
  font-family: Lucida Grande, Verdana, Helvetica, Arial, sans-serif;
  font-size: .9em;
  line-height: 1.4em;
  border-collapse: collapse;
}

tr {
  border: 1px solid #666;
}

th {
  text-align: left;
  border-left: 1px solid #333;
  border-right: 1px solid #333;
  border-bottom: 3px double #333;
  padding: 0 .5em;
}

td {
  color: #333;
  border: 1px dotted #666;
  padding: 0 .5em;
}
```

Adding these styles to our CSS gives us the result shown in Figure 10-7.

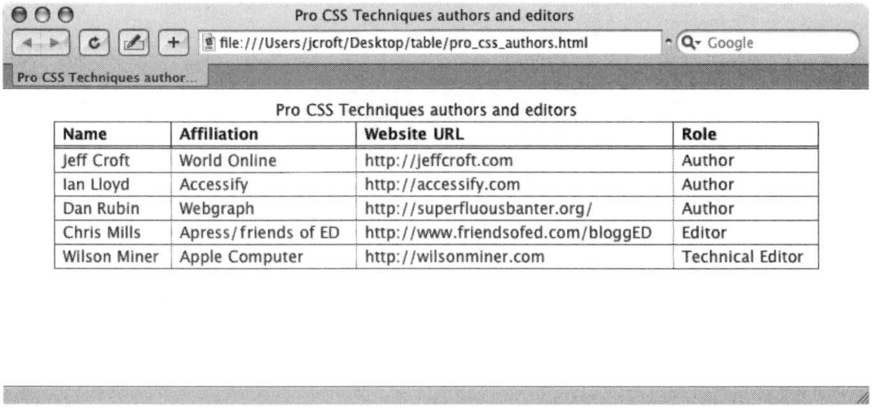

Name	Affiliation	Website URL	Role
Jeff Croft	World Online	http://jeffcroft.com	Author
Ian Lloyd	Accessify	http://accessify.com	Author
Dan Rubin	Webgraph	http://superfluousbanter.org/	Author
Chris Mills	Apress/friends of ED	http://www.friendsofed.com/bloggED	Editor
Wilson Miner	Apple Computer	http://wilsonminer.com	Technical Editor

Figure 10-7. *Adding some basic border styles to our sample table*

As you can see, there are countless ways to use borders with tables. Throughout the chapter, the examples will use different borders to show more possibilities.

Zebra Tables

A common interface idiom with any kind of table is to display alternating rows or columns with subtly different background colors. Doing so aids in reading, and it helps keep readers on top of which column or row they are currently reading.

Most major browsers do not currently support styling the col element. As such, this approach is only practical for rows. (You could achieve the effect on columns, but it would require adding a class to a lot of cells. This may be OK for very small tables but usually proves to be impractical for tables of any size.) However, future versions of browsers should let you apply the same approach to columns as well.

To do this in today's browser environment, you'll need to add a class to every other row in your table. A common practice is to add class="odd" to each of the odd numbered-rows. However, this isn't a practical thing to do manually, especially on large tables. Besides needing to manually put the class on every row, you also have to go back and rework the entire table when you add a single row to the middle of the table somewhere. As such, web developers often use DOM scripting or server-side template languages to add the class automatically. (For an example of such a DOM scripting trick, check out David F. Miller's article at http://alistapart.com/articles/zebratables.) No matter how you add the class to your document, it's simple to style the table accordingly once it's there:

```
tr.odd {
  background-color: #dfdfdf;
}
```

Check out the result in Figure 10-8.

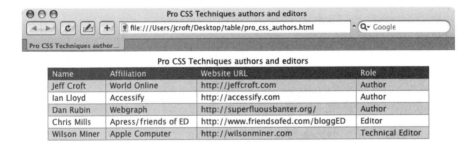

Figure 10-8. *Making our table into a zebra!*

Note CSS 3 provides a selector that allows for this sort of thing. However, no major browser currently supports it:

```
tr:nth-child(odd) {
  background-color: #dfdfdf
}
```

Styling the Caption

Early in the chapter, we added the caption element to our table. By default, it will appear above your table. However, CSS offers a property, caption-side, which positions the caption on the top, bottom, left, or right of the table. Let's position our caption at the bottom of the table, and give it some additional style as well:

```
caption {
  caption-side: bottom;
  line-height: 4em;
  font-family: Georgia, "Times New Roman", serif;
  font-size: .85em;
  font-style: italic;
}
```

This gives us the result shown in Figure 10-9.

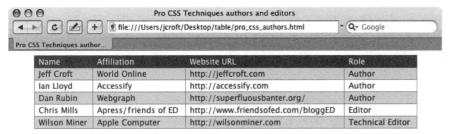

Figure 10-9. *Styling our table caption effectively*

Ideas for Going Further

You can find many examples of deliciously styled tables online. Beyond the basic examples shown here, you can consider using the `background-image` property on the tables, individual rows, or heads to achieve great effects. Veerle Pieters does this very well in her example at `http://veerle.duoh.com/index.php/blog/comments/a_css_styled_table/`, as well as her CSS-styled calendar at `http://veerle.duoh.com/index.php/blog/comments/a_css_styled_calendar/`. Nathan Smith also uses a calendar as a demonstration of some beautiful table design at `http://sonspring.com/journal/scoping-things-out`.

Using your creativity and CSS's power, you should be able to make tables that not only look brilliant but are accessible, readable, and usable to boot.

Summary

CSS allows you to present data tables in virtually limitless ways. Although the examples here are relatively simple, they illustrate the kind of things you can do—and your creativity can take it from here. A real key to creating tables that are useful, readable, and interesting to look at is the (X)HTML markup you use to provide those additional styling "hooks." By taking advantage of some of the newer and more semantic elements, you can create tables that both look great and work effectively for users visiting your site with assistive technology and other alternate devices.

Now that you're familiar with styling tabular data, let's move on to laying out another common web page component: forms.

CHAPTER 11

■■■

Styling Forms

Using the power of CSS, forms can be styled in many interesting and creative ways to enhance not only their aesthetics, but also their usability. However, forms are also the single area where default styling and differences in CSS support are the most inconsistent across browsers. There are two main components to forms and CSS: laying out entire forms and styling individual form widgets. Let's start with the latter.

Styling Form Widgets

The degree to which individual form widgets can be styled varies greatly from browser to browser. For example, Safari does not allow for CSS borders or backgrounds on input elements (although this may be changing in the near future), but Firefox does. Web designers often find this frustrating. However, there are two schools of thought on whether browsers *should* let CSS authors modify the appearance of form widgets. Whereas smart designers can use CSS's widget styling to create usable forms that better integrate with the overall design of a site, less savvy CSS authors may abuse the power to the point where a form is rendered unusable. Also, users come to expect their default form widgets and can be confused by controls that appear unusual to them.

Either way, the important thing to understand when styling form elements is that it's very likely users of some browsers will see the standard, default form widgets supplied by their operating system and/or browser instead of your custom-styled versions. You should ensure that your design works well with or without the custom styles you are applying.

It's also important to understand that the default styles of button, text fields, radio buttons, check boxes, and other form element vary drastically from one browser and platform to the next. Where a select box may be 16 pixels tall in one browser, it could be 20 pixels tall in another. Again, your design should accommodate these inconsistencies.

Web professional Roger Johansson created what may be the world's most authoritative source on both the default styles of form elements and which CSS properties can and cannot be applied to them in various browsers across multiple platforms. In a blog post titled "Styling even more form controls," (www.456bereastreet.com/archive/200410/styling_even_more_form_controls/), Roger provides screen shots and comparisons of tests he ran across the board. It's an invaluable resource.

The conclusion Roger reaches may be disheartening, but it's accurate: "Very little styling is applied the same way in every browser," he says, "Trying to style form controls to look the same across platforms is often a waste of time."

In short, the best practice is probably to leave most form controls alone, or to style them only lightly, using basic properties such as those for font color, size, and style, borders, and background colors—and to do so with the expectation that these styles will often go unseen by your visitors.

Laying Out Forms

As we've said, the default styling of form elements is notoriously inconsistent between browsers. Sadly, this applies not only to the individual field widgets, but to the overall style of the whole form. To demonstrate how this affects web designers looking to create usable and attractive forms on the Web, let's first look at the same basic form in both Safari and Firefox on Mac OS X (see Figures 11-1 and 11-2).

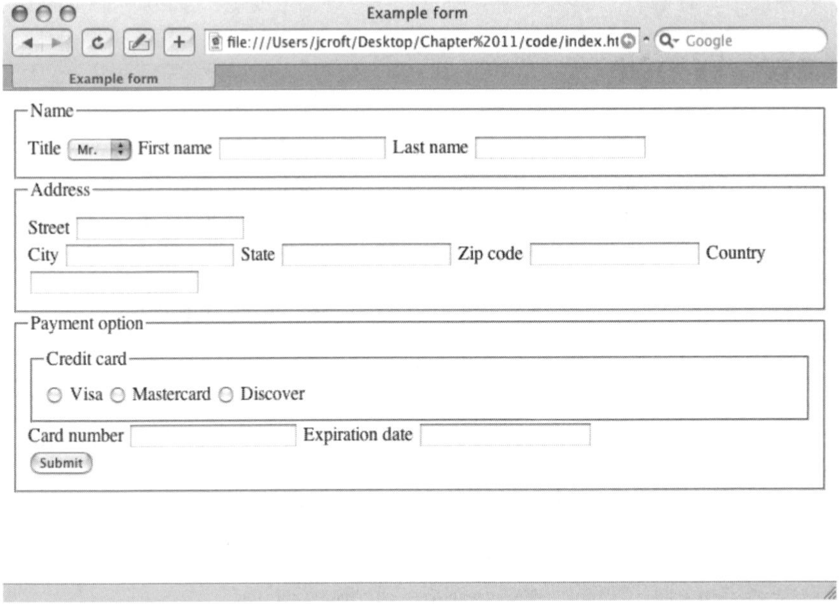

Figure 11-1. *Basic unstyled form as seen in Safari*

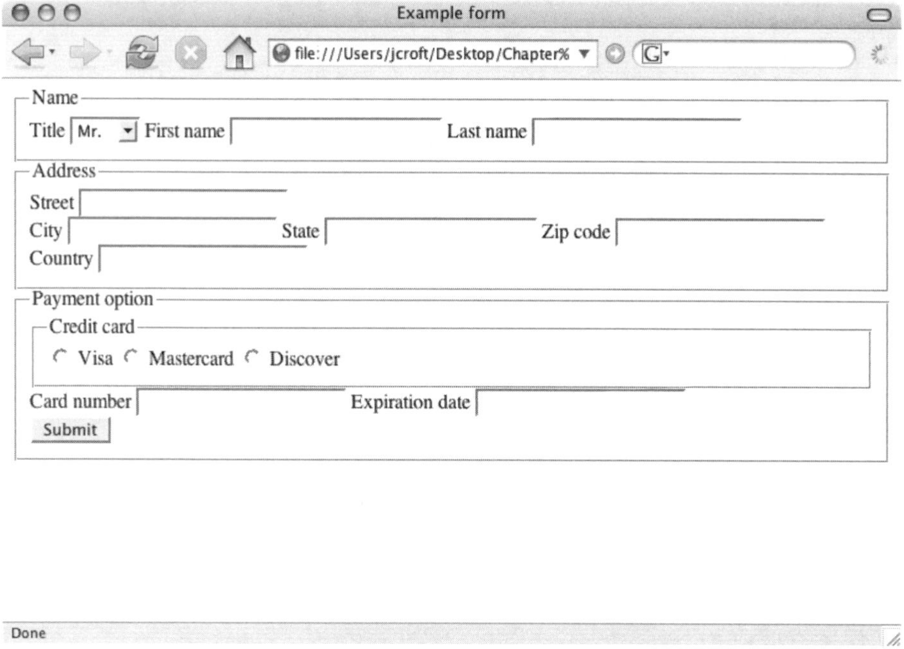

Figure 11-2. *Basic unstyled form as seen in Firefox*

Although the two may appear similar at first glance, closer inspection shows considerable differences in margins, spacing, and font size—and that's beyond the obvious differences in widgets for select boxes, radio buttons, and submit buttons.

For this reason, it becomes more essential than ever to use some kind of mass reset style sheet (as described in Chapter 5) to start with as level a playing field as possible. Applying the mass reset style sheet provided in the Yahoo! User Interface library to our form results in the comparison shown in Figures 11-3 and 11-4.

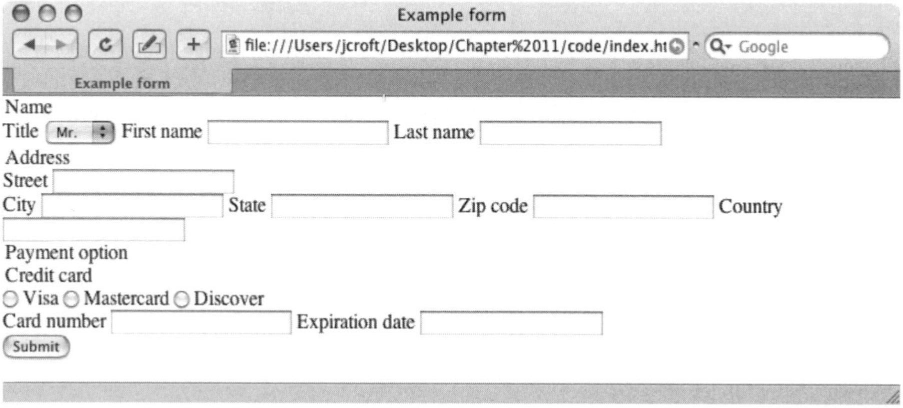

Figure 11-3. *Basic unstyled form in Safari, after applying a mass reset*

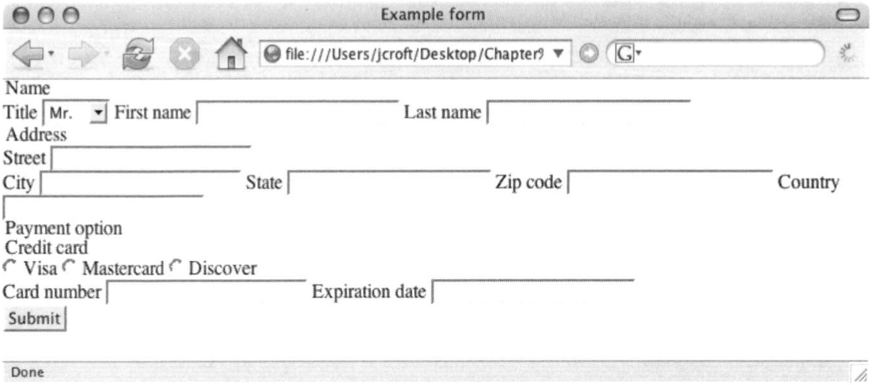

Figure 11-4. *Basic unstyled form in Firefox, after applying a mass reset*

While this is certainly less attractive, it's at least much closer to being the same across both browsers. It may not be a clean slate, but it's a lot cleaner than it was before. Now let's start looking at the (X)HTML behind well-designed forms.

Semantic (X)HTML for Forms

As has been noted throughout this book, CSS styling works best and most consistently when it is applied to pages that are built with clean, semantic (X)HTML. (X)HTML provides a few helpful yet underused elements for forms that not only add structure and meaning to your document but also provide significant form usability improvements and copious hooks on which to hang CSS styles.

The fieldset and legend Elements

The fieldset element is used for grouping form elements. In the example screen shots earlier, three fieldset elements are shown. You can detect them in the unstyled version by their default styling, which is typically a thin dark border (note that this border is turned off by our mass reset style sheet, and thus is not visible in those screen shots).

Within fieldset elements, the page author can optionally provide a legend element, which serves as a title for the grouping of form elements the fieldset contains. In the screen shots, you'll find legends containing the fieldset titles "Name," "Address," and "Payment option."

The label Element

As you may guess from its name, the label element serves to give a label to each widget in your form. More than anything, the label element serves important usability and accessibility functions. In most user agents, clicking on a field's label will bring the keyboard focus to that field. label elements also help assistive technology like screen readers understand the relationship between a textual label and a form field. The label element can be used one of two ways in (X)HTML. It can be wrapped around the field it is associated with, like so:

```
<label>Street <input id="street" name="street" type="text" value="Street" /></label>
```

In this method, the relationship is implicit; because the input field with the id attribute value street is nested within the label element, the label is related to that field. The relationship can also be defined explicitly:

```
<label for="street">Street</label>
<input id="street" name="street" type="text" value="Street" />
```

Here, the input element is not nested, so the relationship is defined explicitly by using the label element's for attribute—it is set to the id value of the related form element. When defining relationship explicitly, the label element doesn't need to be near the form element to which it relates in the (X)HTML source. Once in a while, this proves advantageous, but most of the time, it really doesn't matter which way you choose to use the label element.

Our Example Form

For the rest of the examples in this chapter, we'll be using this example form:

```
<!DOCTYPE html PUBLIC "-//W3C//DTD XHTML 1.0 Strict//EN" ➥
 "http://www.w3.org/TR/xhtml1/DTD/xhtml1-strict.dtd">
<html xmlns="http://www.w3.org/1999/xhtml" xml:lang="en" lang="en">

  <head>
    <meta http-equiv="Content-Type" content="text/html; charset=utf-8"/>
    <title>Example form</title>
    <link rel="stylesheet" href="reset-min.css" type="text/css" media="screen" />
    <link rel="stylesheet" href="basic.css" type="text/css" media="screen" />
    <link rel="stylesheet" href="intermediate.css" type="text/css" media="screen" />
  </head>

  <body>
    <form id="payment_form" action="/path/to/action" method="post">

      <fieldset id="name">
        <legend>Name</legend>
        <label>Title
          <select id="title1" name="title1">
            <option selected="selected">Mr.</option>
            <option>Mrs.</option>
            <option>Ms.</option>
          </select>
```

```
      </label>
      <label>First name
        <input id="first-name" name="first-name" type="text" />
      </label>
      <label>Last name
        <input id="last-name" name="last-name" type="text" />
      </label>
      <br />
  </fieldset>

  <fieldset id="address">
    <legend>Address</legend>
    <label>Street
      <input id="street" name="street" type="text" />
    </label>
    <br />
    <label>City
      <input id="city" name="city" type="text" />
    </label>
    <label>State
      <input id="state" name="state" type="text" />
    </label>
    <label>Zip code
      <input id="zip" name="zip" type="text" />
    </label>
    <br />
    <label>Country
      <input id="country" name="country" type="text" />
    </label>
    <br />
  </fieldset>

  <fieldset id="payment">
    <legend>Payment option</legend>
      <fieldset id="credit_card">
        <legend>Credit card</legend>
        <label><input id="visa" name="visa" type="radio" /> Visa</label>
        <label><input id="mastercard" name="mastercard" ➡
          type="radio" /> Mastercard</label>
        <label><input id="discover" name="discover" ➡
          type="radio" /> Discover</label>
```

```
          <br />
        </fieldset>
      <label>Card number
        <input id="card_number" name="card_number" type="text" />
      </label>
      <label>Expiration date
        <input id="expiration" name="expiration" type="text" />
      </label>
      <br />
      <input class="submit" type="submit" value="Submit" />
      <br />
    </fieldset>

  </form>
 </body>

</html>
```

Applying Basic Styling to the Form

To start with, let's apply some basic, simple styles to the form. First, we'll set the form to be 75 percent wide and to be centered horizontally with a 3em vertical margin:

```
form {
  margin:  3em auto;
  width:  75%;
}
```

We'll also shape up our `fieldset` elements a bit, giving them a background color, a border, and some margin and padding:

```
fieldset {
  background-color:  #dfdfdf;
  border:  1px solid #ccc;
  margin:  2em 0;
  padding:  1em;
}
```

This yields the result shown in Figure 11-5.

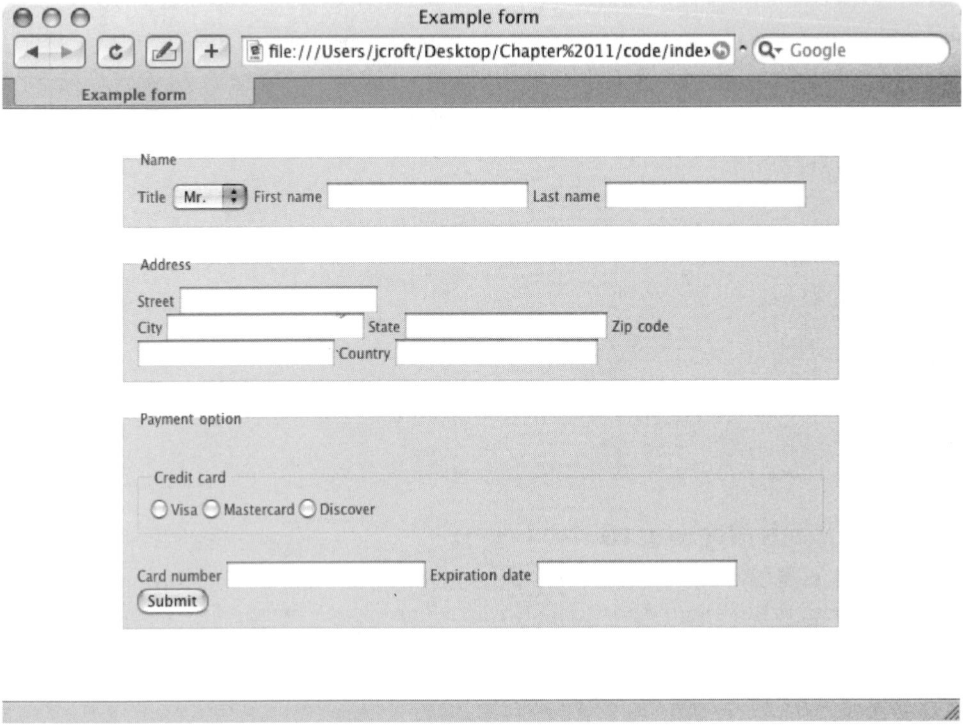

Figure 11-5. *Some very basic styles have been added to our example form.*

OK! Already we're seeing a significant improvement. Now, let's turn our attention to the input elements and their labels.

In order to create a line break after each label/control pair, we can set the label elements to display: block;. While we're at it, let's set the font-weight for labels to bold and put a bottom margin on the input elements to make the form a bit more readable:

```
label {
  display:  block;
  font-weight:  bold;
}

input {
  margin:  0 0 .5em 0;
}
```

Now we've got the display shown in Figure 11-6.

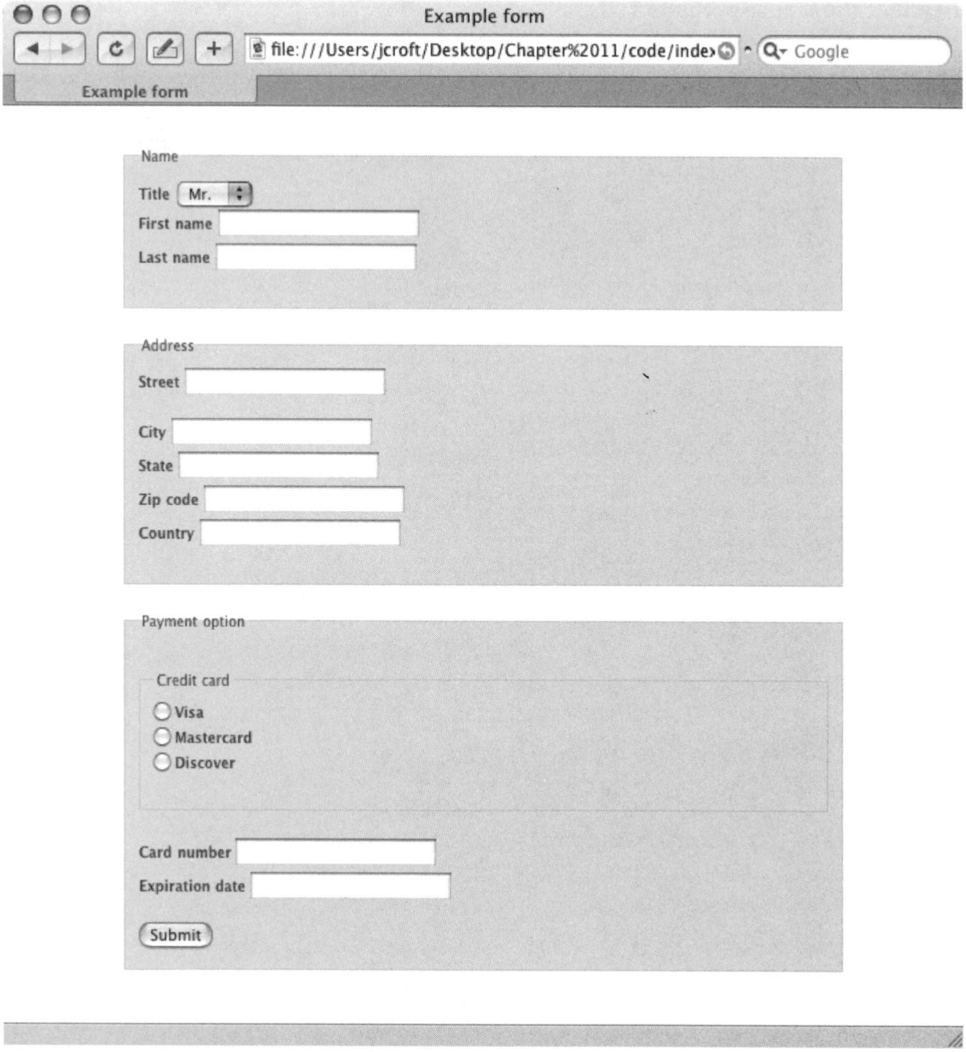

Figure 11-6. *Thanks to* `display: block;` *being set on* `label` *elements, our label/form element pairs now each exist on a line of their own.*

Not bad at all! But it would be even better if we made those `legend` elements look a little better. Let's make them bigger and bold, and move them up and outside of the `fieldset` boxes:

```
legend {
  font-size:  1.4em;
  font-weight:  bold;
  position:  relative;
  top:  -.4em;
}
```

You can see the change in Figure 11-7.

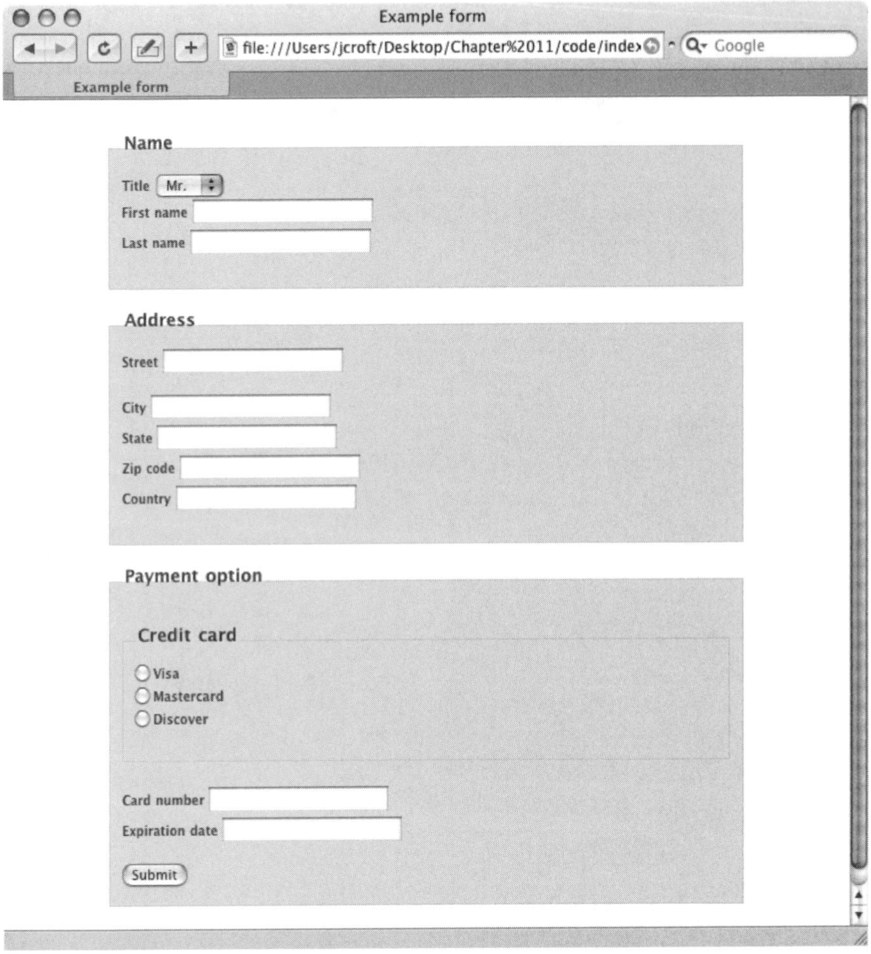

Figure 11-7. *The* legend *elements in our example form have been styled and positioned.*

That helps a lot. But notice our styles for fieldset and legend were applied not only to our three main fieldset elements, but also to the "Credit card" fieldset that is nested within the "Payment option" fieldset. If we want to style that one separately, we could target it by its id attribute (which is credit_card, so we'd use a selector like fieldset#credit_card in CSS). However, in this case it may be wiser to style any fieldset elements nested within a fieldset. We only have one now, but if the form expands as we continue to develop our site, we'll be able to kill more than one bird with the same stone.

```
fieldset fieldset {
  background-color:  #efefef;
  margin:  1em 0;
}
```

```
fieldset fieldset legend {
  font-size:  1.2em;
}
```

Here, we've adjusted the margin on nested `fieldset` elements, given them a different background color, and also made their labels a bit smaller (Figure 11-8).

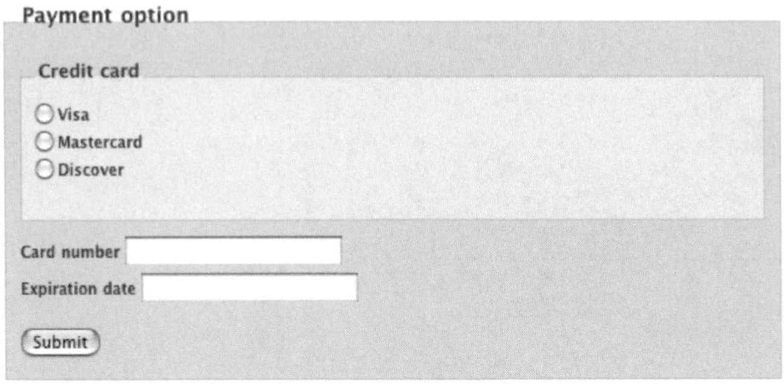

Figure 11-8. *By using the descendant selector* `fieldset fieldset`, *we are able to style* `fieldset` *elements that are nested inside other* `fieldsets`.

We've now created a good, basic form that is readable, accessible, and usable. But let's keep taking this a bit further.

Intermediate Form Styling

Our current form takes up a lot of vertical space. Perhaps we can reduce its length by displaying some of the label/form pairs on the same line. We can do this using CSS's float model. You may have noticed a few `<br />` tags in the (X)HTML for the form—we'll use them as the "clearing" elements, creating line breaks in the right places.

Let's start by setting our `input` elements to a consistent width and floating the `label` elements (which contain our `input` fields) to the left:

```
input {
  width:  12em;
}

label {
  float:  left;
  margin-right:  1em;
}
```

We've also given our `label` elements a small right margin in order to separate one field from the next, as Figure 11-9 shows.

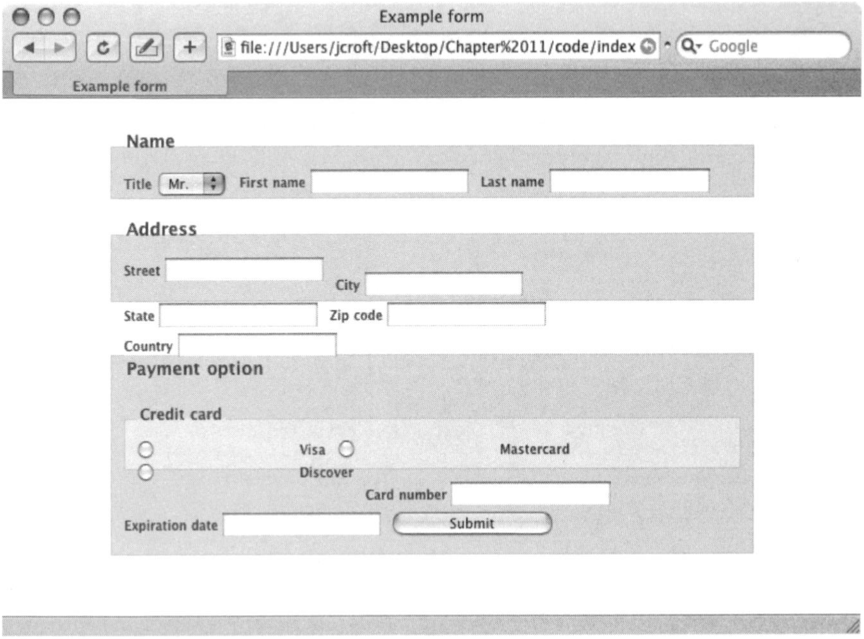

Figure 11-9. *After floating* label *elements, some parts of our form seem to spill out of their containing* fieldset.

Whoops! That's not right. Some of the form controls are not contained within their associated fieldset. The reason for this is our decision to float the label elements to the left. Floating an element takes it out of the normal flow of the document, causing the fieldset elements to not expand and contain them. One way to work around this behavior is to have an element at the end of the fieldset "clear" the floats. Doing so will cause the parent fieldset element to stretch vertically and contain the form controls. We've strategically placed br elements at the end of each fieldset for exactly this reason. Ideally, you'd place the clear on an element that already exists, but since no such element exists, the br element is a semantically sound one to add.

```
br {
  clear:  both;
}
```

This code works like a charm, as you can see in Figure 11-10.

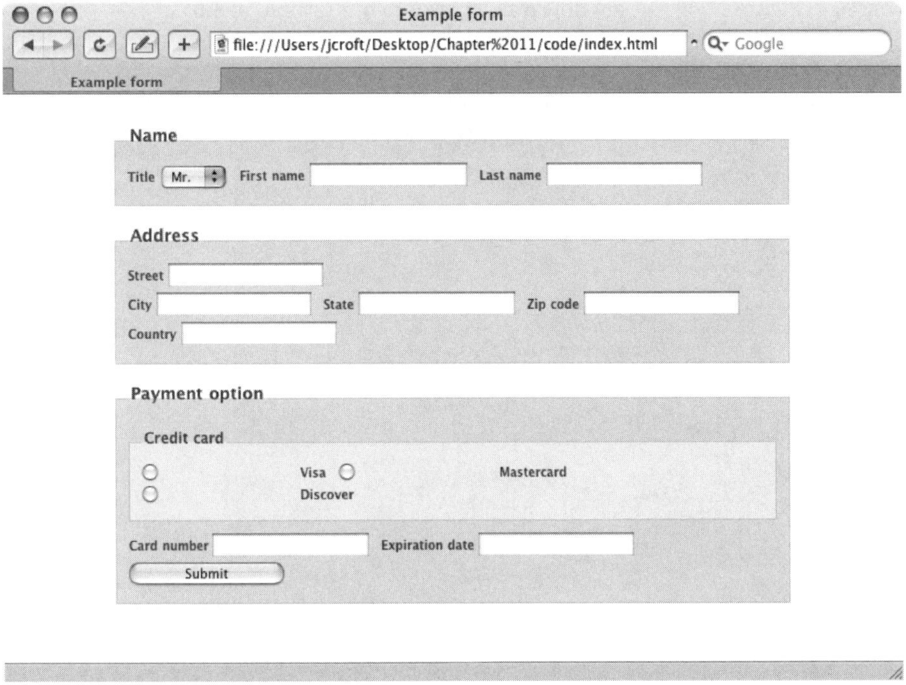

Figure 11-10. *The* clear *property in CSS helps us ensure all elements are visually contained by their parent* fieldset.

There are a few things that don't work quite right here, though. First, our "State," "Zip code," "Card number," and "Expiration date" fields are unnecessarily long. Since we can predict how many characters will go into those fields, it makes sense to set their width accordingly. Using the em unit, we can size the input fields pretty close to their ideal width. Keeping in mind that a single em is the size of the widest character in the alphabet (usually a capital "M"), we'll set the widths to the same number of ems as the number of characters they should contain:

```
input#state {
  width:  2em;
}
input#zip {
  width: 5em;
}
input#card_number {
  width:  16em;
}
input#expiration {
    width:  4em;
}
```

As you can see in Figure 11-11, we are now much closer to our desired result.

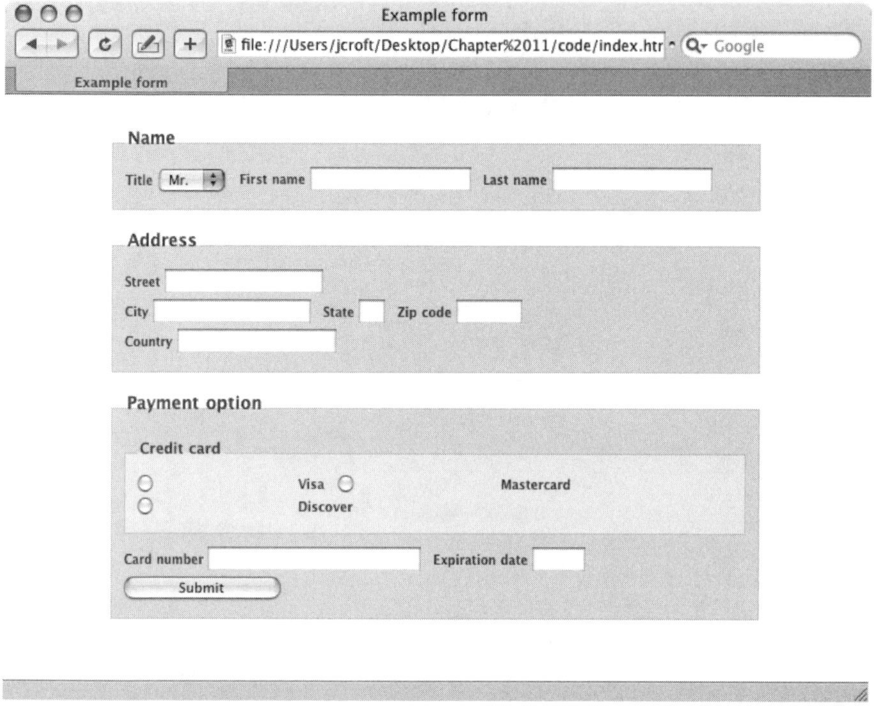

Figure 11-11. *Form fields with a predictable width have been individually styled.*

However, we still have something strange going on in our "Credit card" `fieldset`. We set the width of input elements to `12em`, and that is getting applied to our radio button inputs and submit button as well. This can be solved using the CSS attribute selector:

```
input[type=radio],
input[type=submit],
input[type=checkbox] {
  width:  auto;
}
```

Here, we are saying that any `input` element whose `type` attribute is set to `radio`, `submit`, or `checkbox` should have its width set automatically, overriding our previous specification of `12em`. Figure 11-12 shows the result.

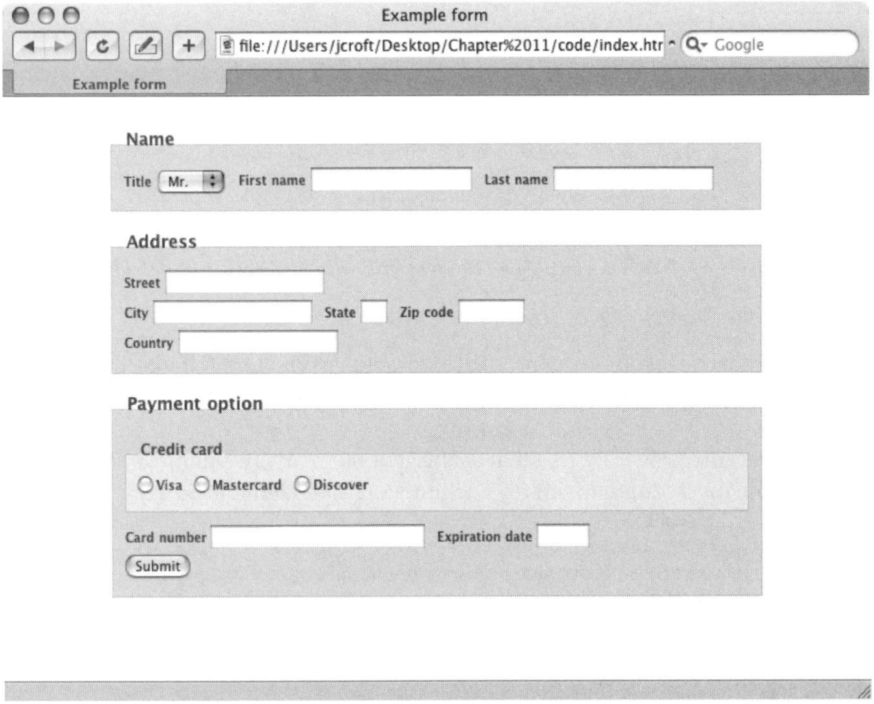

Figure 11-12. *By setting the* width *property for radio buttons and submit buttons to* auto, *we've corrected the oversized elements we had previously.*

Although we don't have any in this form, it's a good idea to set this for checkboxes anyway—it "future-proofs" our form, so that if we add checkboxes, we needn't come back and style them.

■**Note** Internet Explorer 6 and lower does not support attribute selectors. As such, a more practical way to handle this may be to place a class attribute of radio on each radio button and then include a CSS rule like input.radio { width: auto; } in your style sheet.

We've managed to create a nice, clean form using a handful of CSS rules and semantic (X)HTML markup. Now, let's try something a little different.

Aligning Labels and Their Fields in the Middle

One popular form layout style is have each label/field pair broken by lines, with the label on the left but right-aligned, creating a nice column down the middle where the labels meet the input areas. This layout style is shown in Figure 11-13.

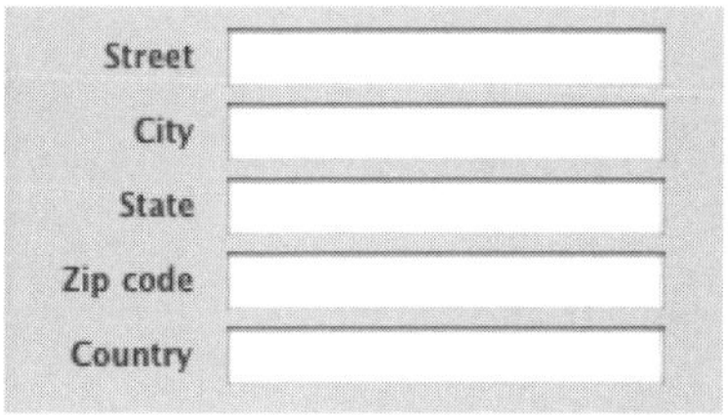

Figure 11-13. *Form labels to the left of their input fields, but with text right-aligned, creating a clean center line*

Many developers have used nonsemantic `table` elements to create this look—but it's not necessary. Instead, we can take advantage of the fact that `input` elements need not be nested within their label.

We've modified our form's (X)HTML so that each `input` element is a sibling of, rather than a child of, its label (note the addition of the `for` attribute on `label` elements to explicitly state the relationship):

```
<form id="payment_form" action="/path/to/action" method="post">

  <fieldset id="name">
    <legend>Name</legend>
    <label for="title">Title</label>
      <select id="title1" name="title1">
        <option selected="selected">Mr.</option>
        <option>Mrs.</option>
        <option>Ms.</option>
      </select>
    <label for="first-name">First name</label>
      <input id="first-name" name="first-name" type="text" />
    <label for="last-name">Last name</label>
      <input id="last-name" name="last-name" type="text" />
    <br />
  </fieldset>

  <fieldset id="address">
    <legend>Address</legend>
    <label for="street">Street</label>
    <input id="street" name="street" type="text" />
    <br />
    <label for="city">City</label>
    <input id="city" name="city" type="text" />
    <label for="state">State</label>
    <input id="state" name="state" type="text" />
    <label for="zip">Zip code</label>
    <input id="zip" name="zip" type="text" />
    <br />
    <label for="country">Country</label>
```

```
      <input id="country" name="country" type="text" />
    <br />
  </fieldset>

  <fieldset id="payment">
    <legend>Payment option</legend>
      <fieldset id="credit_card">
        <legend>Credit card</legend>
        <label for="visa">Visa</label>
        <input id="visa" name="visa" type="radio" />
        <label for="mastercard">Mastercard</label>
        <input id="mastercard" name="mastercard" type="radio" />
        <label for="discover">Discover</label>
        <input id="discover" name="discover" type="radio" />
        <br />
      </fieldset>
    <label for="card_number">Card number</label>
    <input id="card_number" name="card_number" type="text" />
    <label for="expiration">Expiration date</label>
    <input id="expiration" name="expiration" type="text" />
    <br />
    <input class="submit" type="submit" value="Submit" />
    <br />
  </fieldset>

  </form>
```

Although the difference is small, it is significant in our styling. Now, when we position a label element, it won't also move the associated input element. With that in mind, let's apply the following CSS:

```
label {
  display:  block;
  float:  left;
  clear:  left;
  width:  9em;
  padding-right:  1em;
  text-align:  right;
  line-height:  1.8em;
}

input {
  display:  block;
  float:  left;
}

br {
  clear:  both;
}
```

Here, we're floating both input and label elements to the left so that they are now butted up against one another. To achieve the line break each time, we have a new label/field pair: we apply clear: left to labels. We set the label element's width to 9em (plus a padding of 1em on the right, for a total width of 10em) and aligned the text to the right. Finally, we set the line-height attribute to 1.8em, approximately the same as the default height of our input boxes. (Note that because every browser's input box height is slightly different and there's no consistent way to make it the same, this is nonexact. It is, however, quite close.)

Since we're again floating elements within our fieldset, we'll want the br { clear: both; } in our style sheet.

The result is almost exactly what we'd hoped for (see Figure 11-14).

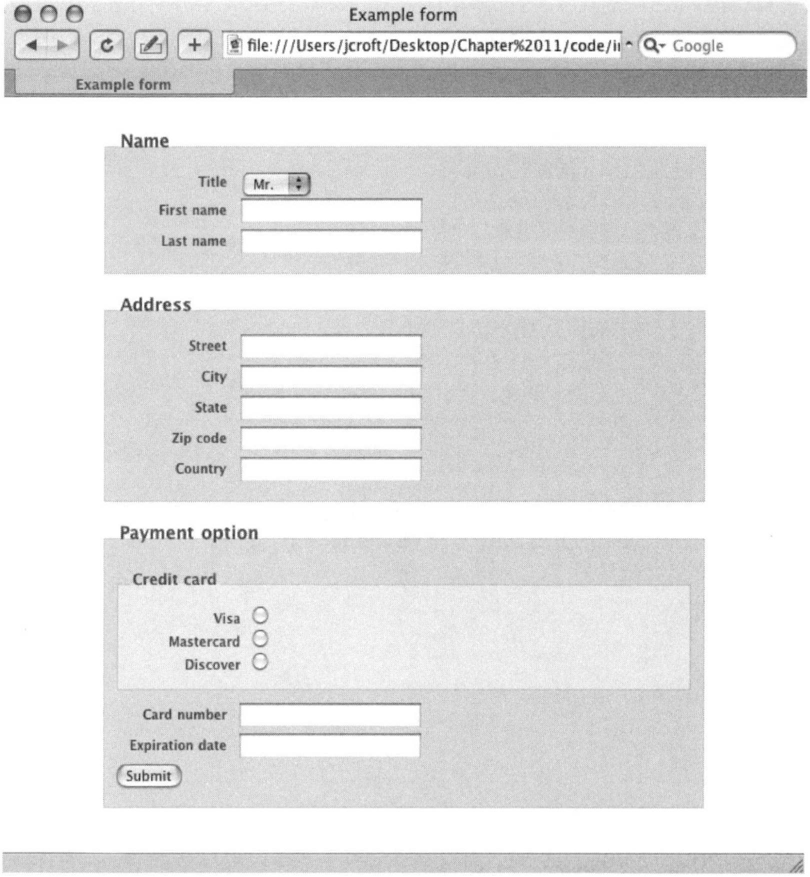

Figure 11-14. *Example form after styling for the clean middle line*

The one notable quirk here is that our credit card type labels don't quite align with their radio boxes. This is because our line-height setting of 1.8em was chosen to duplicate the height of the input text boxes, but radio buttons are shorter. A line-height of 1.2em seems to achieve the desired effect:

```
fieldset#credit_card label {
  line-height:  1.2em;
}
```

See Figure 11-15—much better!

Figure 11-15. *We've corrected our radio button label alignment by properly setting the* line-height *property.*

Summary

There's no doubt that form styling on the Web is less consistent from browser to browser than most other (X)HTML elements. However, using semantic (X)HTML and CSS it is possible to achieve clear, clean, concise forms that are at once usable, accessible, and attractive. As with the previous chapter on table styling, your creativity is the only limit. Try using background images and other CSS properties within forms to achieve even more fabulous looks.

Now that you're comfortable with styling the forms in your web pages, let's move on to another very common page element: lists.

CHAPTER 12

■■■

Styling Lists

Back in the dim distant past (well, Chapter 8 actually, but it feels like a while back now), we committed something of a sin—we demonstrated a CSS technique that took a series of links inside div elements and styled them so that they ranged across the page horizontally to form header navigation. As we admitted at the time, that approach is not the best way to accomplish our goal; we were merely doing it that way to show that it's possible. For some people, styling a div could be the only choice they have, due to restrictions of a CMS or HTML that's output by some other process. However, even with that disclaimer firmly stated, we still had a dirty feeling about it. Here's where we ask for absolution.

The truth is, the header links that we were demonstrating were, at their heart, a list of links. You may not have thought so at the time, given that their design—one link after another horizontally—doesn't look the same as a "standard" list. But the whole point of CSS is that the presentation (horizontal, gradient background, whatever) is separate from the underlying semantics (it's a list of links, or a logical grouping).

With that in mind, let's revisit the header that we built in Chapter 8, break apart the offending markup, and start from scratch. Afterward, we'll look at some of the many ways lists can be presented depending on their purpose or position on the page.

The Basic List

So, we're getting rid of the <div> tags and instead opting for list items. Here's how the XHTML for the navigation looks:

```
<div id="tablinks" class="clearfix">
  <ul>
    <li><a href="/">Home</a></li>
    <li><a href="/travel/" class="current">Travel</a></li>
    <li><a href="/flights/">Flights</a></li>
    <li><a href="/hotels/">Hotels</a></li>
    <li><a href="/late-deals/">Late Deals</a></li>
  </ul>
</div>
```

Note We've kept the unordered list inside the same outer containing `div` with an `id` of `tablinks`, as we did in the previous layout in Chapter 8. It's not always necessary to wrap the list in a containing `div`—you could simply give the `ul` an `id` and manipulate that. We've also left `class="current"` on one of the links for the purposes of getting the styling right, but we'll show you a smarter way of indicating what page you are on later in this chapter.

The previous code would result in a dull-looking and entirely inappropriate list, as shown in Figure 12-1.

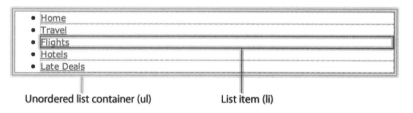

Figure 12-1. *The unstyled list: it needs a bit of work to become a navigation bar, doesn't it?*

Removing Browser Default Styling

There's a process that we need to go through to get this list of links looking the way we want. The first step is to reset some of the default styling that each browser applies to the list—for example, the bullet points and the padding and margins. To see where these different parts of the list item are located, take a look at Figure 12-2, which shows the block-level elements that make up this list.

Unordered list container (ul)   List item (li)

Figure 12-2. *The list's structure revealed*

You can see in Figure 12-2 that the unordered list, the `ul` element, has padding on the left side; the individual list items have no margins, but the bullet icon sits outside of the list items. At least, this is how the list items are understood by Firefox—other browsers may treat the default styling of lists differently or to varying degrees, so the safest way to begin is to reset all of it. The following CSS shows how you can do this (but only for lists that are in the `div` with an `id` of `tablinks`):

```
#tablinks ul,#tablinks li {
  padding:0;
  margin:0;
  list-style:none;
}
```

Figure 12-3 demonstrates the effect of removing padding and margins. Remember, the borders in this image are for demonstration purposes only so that you can see the effect of removing the margins and padding. If you were to copy the CSS *exactly*, the borders would not display as they do in Figure 12-3.

Figure 12-3. *The list with all padding and margin attributes reset*

Flattening the List

Just as it's possible to set a series of divs out so they line up side by side, you can do the same with list items. You have a couple of options, each with its own pros and cons:

- Set the li elements to display:inline. By doing this, you convert the block-level list item to an inline one and thus lose the ability to style it in certain ways, such as setting heights, vertical padding, and so on. You can still specify right and left padding, but this may not be enough to achieve the design you want. That said, you avoid a problem that's associated with the other method: floating each li element.

- Float each li element with float:left. This keeps the list item as a block-level element, giving you greater control over styling with CSS, but at the same time it causes another issue to rear its not-so-attractive head once more: you have to deal with the sometimes tricky task of containing floats.

As you've already learned about the various ways of managing floats (check out "Managing Floats" in Chapter 7), it's safer to use the second method and retain the styling capabilities that block-level elements can offer.

■Note When you float a block-level element, it will only take up as much space horizontally as it needs. Unlike the list items shown in the previous images in this chapter, a floated list item won't stretch across the page and take up 100 percent of the container element.

Here's some amended CSS and XHTML to flatten our list. The clearfix class applied to the containing div ensures that we don't run into problems with the floated elements.

```
#tablinks ul,#tablinks li {
  padding:0;
  margin:0;
  list-style:none;
}
#tablinks li {
  float:left;
}
...
<div id="tablinks" class="clearfix">
  <ul>
    <li><a href="/">Home</a></li>
    <li><a href="/travel/" class="current">Travel</a></li>
    <li><a href="/flights/">Flights</a></li>
    <li><a href="/hotels/">Hotels</a></li>
    <li><a href="/late-deals/">Late Deals</a></li>
  </ul>
</div>
```

The result doesn't look all that great yet—it's still basic in appearance, as Figure 12-4 shows, but the orientation is correct and the padding has been reset.

Figure 12-4. *The flattened list of links—all ready for a lick of paint!*

Now that we've removed all the nasty browser defaults, we're once again on a level playing field and we can look at applying a few cosmetic touches. The CSS that follows is almost exactly the same as the CSS in Chapter 8 that we applied to the div elements. We'll apply a background image, a border to the right of each list item, and some padding (which is applied to the anchors inside the list items):

```
#tablinks ul,#tablinks li {
  padding:0;
  margin:0;
  list-style:none;
}
#tablinks li {
  float:left;
}
#tablinks {
  background:#336868 url(tab-bg.gif) repeat-x top;
}
#tablinks li {
  float:left;
  border-right:1px solid #094747;
}
```

```
#tablinks a {
  display:block;
  padding:5px 10px;
}
#tablinks a:link,
#tablinks a:visited,
#tablinks a:hover,
#tablinks a:active {
  color:white;
  text-decoration:none;
}
#tablinks a.current {
  background:#047070 url(tab-bg-hover.gif) repeat-x top;
}
```

The final result is shown in Figure 12-5.

Figure 12-5. *The CSS-styled list is complete.*

In this example we've demonstrated a specific application of CSS and list items, but one that you're likely to use often (and, indeed, one that you might have approached using another method, such as the div layout or, heaven forbid, a table layout). There are so many other things you can do with a list in CSS, as we will demonstrate next.

Custom Bullets

The browser's default styling for lists is not entirely inspiring. Figure 12-6 shows a nested list in IE 6 for Windows by way of example with different symbols displaying at the various nesting levels.

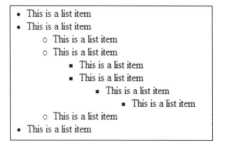

Figure 12-6. *A nested list showing the browser default bullet styles*

You can override the default style using the list-style-type CSS property. There are many values that can be applied, theoretically (such as Japanese ideographs), but you're most likely to stick with just a handful:

- circle

- disc

- square

There's little point in a screen shot at this juncture—those values will apply the bullet styles shown in Figure 12-6 earlier (in the order disc, circle, and square for the first three nesting levels, respectively), but at least you now have control over the default style (you could specify that all levels of list items be set to use the square symbol, for example).

Styled Ordered Lists

A useful feature of lists in CSS is the ability to create sequential lists that go beyond the browser default of numbering 1, 2, 3, and so on. Figure 12-7 shows an unstyled ordered list on the left and, on the right, some other ordering options.

```
1.  This is a list item          1.  This is a list item
2.  This is a list item          2.  This is a list item
     1.  This is a list item            A.  This is a list item
     2.  This is a list item            B.  This is a list item
          1.  This is a list item              a.  This is a list item
          2.  This is a list item              b.  This is a list item
               1.  This is a list item               I.  This is a list item
               2.  This is a list item              II.  This is a list item
               3.  This is a list item             III.  This is a list item
                    1.  This is a list item                i.  This is a list item
                    2.  This is a list item               ii.  This is a list item
                    3.  This is a list item              iii.  This is a list item
```

Figure 12-7. *Ordered list styles*

The CSS to achieve the numbering shown in the list on the right in Figure 12-7 is

```
ol li ol li {
  list-style-type:upper-alpha;
}
ol li ol li ol li {
  list-style-type:lower-alpha;
}
ol li ol li ol li ol li {
  list-style-type:upper-roman;
}
ol li ol li ol li ol li ol li {
  list-style-type:lower-roman;
}
```

Of course, you don't have to apply these different styles to these levels—you could apply any one of those styles, for example lower-alpha, to *all* of the list items (even *unordered* list items will accept this sequential presentation, although that's not the proper underlying markup for the job).

Custom Bullets with Background Images

You are not limited to using only the characters and symbols we've discussed, which is a good thing, because unlike with text, you have little control over the presentation of the bullet beyond the shape. What if you want a bigger bullet or one that is in a different color from the text it sits next to? To do this, you can specify a custom symbol using the `list-style-image` property:

```
li {
  list-style-image:url(bullet.gif);
}
```

Figure 12-8 shows the effect of applying a bullet image (literally—ah, the irony of it) in this way, but it's not exactly a perfect solution.

Figure 12-8. *Custom bullet point image—a bullet, no less!*

The screen shot was taken on IE 6 for Windows. In Firefox the bullets lined up perfectly, so getting the image lined up properly in IE (perhaps by adding space directly to the image itself) would then cause it to go out of line in other browsers. So, although a property exists that's designed specifically for using custom bullet images, we recommend a different approach: hide the default bullet symbol and instead place *as a background image* the image you want to use as a bullet. By doing this, you gain greater control over placement. The visual effect is improved and you're not affecting the underlying markup in any way—you're still dealing with a list. Because you're no longer simply swapping the browser's default bullet image with a similar-sized replacement, you'll need to change some other CSS properties, namely the padding on the left of the list item (otherwise, the text will sit directly over the background image). You'll also probably need to tinker with the default indenting of the list items. Here's some CSS that achieves this aim:

```
ul, li {
  padding:0;
  margin:0;
}
ul#list2 li {
  list-style:none;
  background: url(bullet.gif) no-repeat left center;
  padding-left:20px;
}
```

The visual effect is much the same—actually, make that better in IE's case. A glance at Figure 12-9 shows that the alignment issues have been sorted out quite nicely by using the background-image approach.

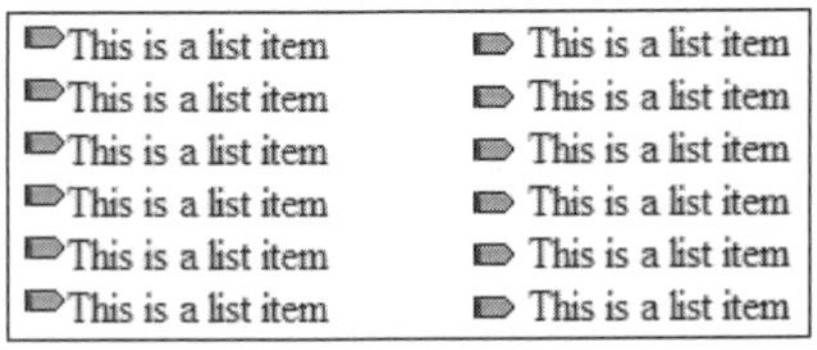

Figure 12-9. *This side-by-side comparsion in IE shows that the background-image approach (on the right) offers more fine-tuned control over positioning and alignment than using list-style-image (on the left).*

Right-Aligned Bullets

You can file this section under "curiosity" or "experimental." A list item's symbol will, by default, appear on the left. What if, for some crazy reason, you wanted the bullet to appear on the right and have text right-aligned? Well, it's not possible to change the position of a real bullet point symbol, but the background-image approach allows you to do that with this code:

```
ul li {
  list-style:none;
  background: url(bullet-reversed.gif) no-repeat right center;
  padding-right:20px;
  text-align:right;
}
```

The result is shown in Figure 12-10.

Figure 12-10. *Right-aligned bullets? Whatever next?*

Why you'd want to do this is another matter, but we put this in to emphasize that while the list-style-image property is there for the taking, you'll probably get better mileage out of the background approach.

Vertical Navigation Links

At the beginning of this chapter, we showed how a list containing links could be "flattened" to make horizontal header links, but you're just as likely—if not more likely—to want to treat a vertical list of links in a similar way. Remember in Chapter 8 when we were working through common page elements? The fictional travel web site was almost completed, but not quite— the links on the left and right sides in Figure 12-11 leave a bit to be desired.

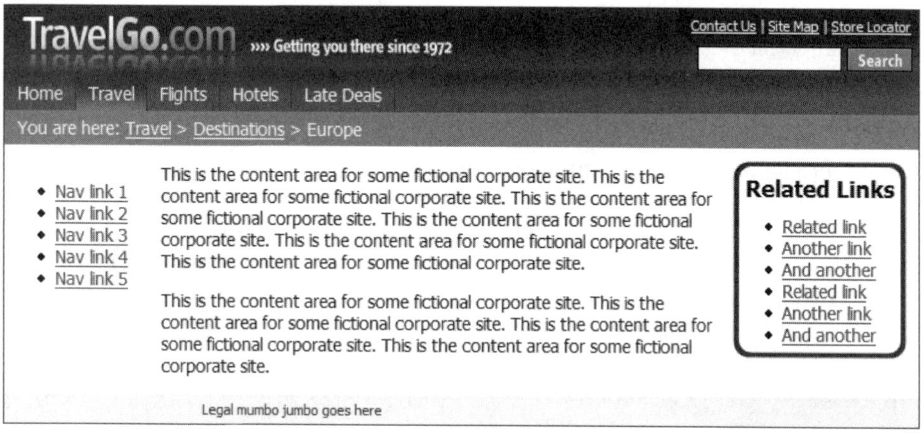

Figure 12-11. *The not-quite-completed travel site*

The first thing to do is to reset the browser's built-in styles, just as we did with the horizontal links:

```
#navigation ul,
#related ul,
#navigation li,
#related li {
  padding:0;
  margin:0;
  list-style:none;
}
```

■**Note** We've focused on the lists *only* in the `navigation` and `related` sections using contextual selectors; otherwise, we may affect other lists that could appear in the body text or even undo work in the header area.

This code does cause an unsightly effect on the right side of the page. The links are now sitting over the top of the rounded border that was applied previously, as shown in Figure 12-12.

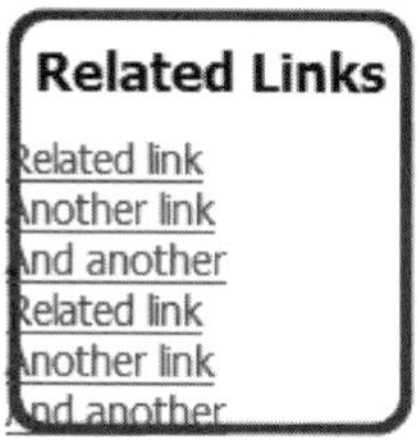

Figure 12-12. *Resetting the margins has affected this set of links.*

Don't worry, though, we'll sort this problem out soon. You just need to start with these items all reset and then push them into the correct positions.

Padding Out the Links

A link is an inline element and thus cannot have heights or top and bottom padding values set—or at least it can't unless we "promote" it to a block-level element using `display:block`. And that's precisely what we recommend with any link that you have inside a list item. The link will stretch to fill the available area and you can then apply background colors, borders, and padding to your heart's content. We'll use that technique on the navigation that sits on the left of the screen. In the CSS that follows, we've also applied a small margin to the left of each of the list items to push them away from the left edge of the page, and we've set a width to match the container it sits in (using ems, as this is an elastic page layout).

```
#navigation li {
  margin:0 0 0 10px;
  width:8em;
}
#navigation li a {
  display:block;
  border-bottom:1px solid #033;
  text-decoration:none;
  padding:2px 2px 2px 5px;
}
```

■Note Notice that the `text-decoration` property is set to none? You may hear people say that all links should be underlined or, conversely, that nothing should be underlined unless it's a link. In body text, this is certainly true, but in a navigation list, often the underline of the text is at odds with the width of the navigation block. The underline only applies to the wording, and each link is going to be slightly different. In short, it can look a little ugly and staggered, especially if the link is inside a button-like container. For this type of link, it's perfectly acceptable to switch off the underline—people using your web site will know it's a navigation link without the underline.

The link is given some padding to take the text away from the edges. But how do you know where the edges are? A hint is provided by a border that sits underneath the link. Because the link is now a block-level element, it stretches to fill all the available space, as shown in Figure 12-13.

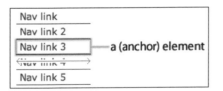

Figure 12-13. *The link fills the available space once it's converted to a block-level element.*

Link Hover Behavior

The mere position and presentation of the links should be enough to convince anyone browsing the site that these are indeed links that can be clicked on. However, you can always reinforce this behavior by providing a hover style (using the :hover pseudo-class). For this block of navigation, we could invert the color scheme so that the background darkens and the text turns white. Because the border is applied to the link, you can also affect that aspect of the design. But let's not stop there—let's throw in another trick we introduced earlier in this chapter: the background image. We could use the same arrow image that's used in the breadcrumb trail in the header and make it appear on hover. Here's the CSS that achieves all of these aims:

```
#navigation li {
  margin:0 0 0 10px;
  width:8em;
}
#navigation li a {
  display:block;
  border-bottom:1px solid #033;
  text-decoration:none;
  padding:2px 2px 2px 5px;
}
#navigation li a:hover {
  background:#009f9f url(arrow.gif) no-repeat 2px center;
  color:#fff;
  border-bottom:1px solid #000;
  padding:2px 2px 2px 14px;
}
```

You can see the final result in Figure 12-14, which shows how a link looks when the mouse hovers over it (the mouse cursor does not appear in the screen shot, but it was there a-hoverin'!).

Figure 12-14. *The styled navigation list*

We'll take a shortcut now and get straight to a solution for the right-hand navigation list. It's similar to the previous example, but because the links are contained in the rounded-corner box, we'll go a little easier on the styling. The bottom border can go, but we'll place the arrow background image next to each of the links in their "static" state as well as hover:

```
#related ul {
  padding-bottom:15px;
}
#related li {
  margin:0 0 0 10px;
  width:8em;
}
#related li a {
  display:block;
  text-decoration:none;
  background:#fff url(arrow.gif) no-repeat 2px center;
  padding:2px 2px 2px 20px;
}
#related li a:hover {
  background:#009f9f url(arrow.gif) no-repeat 2px center;
  color:#fff;
  padding:2px 2px 2px 14px;
}
```

The finished Related Links list is shown in Figure 12-15.

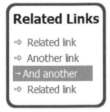

Figure 12-15. *The styled Related Links list*

The Complete Page

Little by little, we've built the fictional travel web site and styled it entirely with CSS. With these navigation changes, the page is now complete. So, how does it look? Check out Figure 12-16 for the answer; it shows both the styled page and the unstyled (CSS disabled) version.

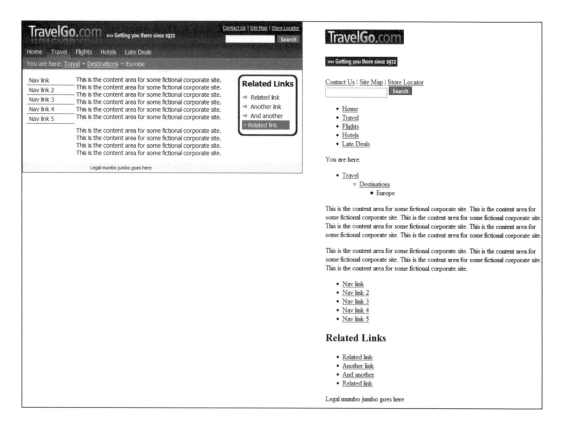

Figure 12-16. *Styled and unstyled versions of the same page*

■**Note** A tool is available that takes much of the pain out of creating both horizontal and vertical CSS-styled navigation bars. Written by Ian Lloyd, one of the authors of this book, it's called List-o-Matic, and you can find it on Accessify.com at `http://accessify.com/tools-and-wizards/developer-tools/list-o-matic/`. In addition, you can download List-o-Rama, a Dreamweaver plug-in based on this web-based tool, for free at `www.dmxzone.com/ShowDetail.asp?NewsId=5618`.

Titling and Hiding Groups of Links

If you wanted to view the sample site using a non-CSS supporting browser (a simple handheld device perhaps), you would have no trouble working out what the various groups of links do—the site would appear similar to the unstyled document as previously shown in Figure 12-16. However, you could add some extra help in the form of a heading or two but use CSS to hide those extra headings for browsers that *do* understand CSS:

```
.hide {
  display:none;
    }
```

That's all you need to do to hide the content from display. Now what parts of the page do you want to hide? They appear in bold in the following code. Note that the related links already have a visible heading—there's no need to hide that particular heading.

```
<div id="wrapper">
  <div id="header">
  <h1><img src="logo.gif" alt="TravelGo.com" /></h1>
  <h2><img src="getting-you-there.gif" alt="Getting you there since 1972" /></h2>
  <div id="headerlinks"><a href="/contact/">Contact Us</a> | <a
href="/sitemap/">Site
  Map</a> | <a href="/finder/">Store Locator</a></div>
  <div id="headersearch">
  <form>
  <input type="text" name="txtSearch" id="txtSearch" />
  <input type="image" src="searchbutton.gif" alt="Search" />
  </form>
  </div>
  </div>
  <h3 class="hide">Primary navigation</h3>
  <div id="tablinks" class="clearfix">
  <ul>
    <li><a href="/">Home</a></li>
    <li><a href="/travel/" class="current">Travel</a></li>
    <li><a href="/flights/">Flights</a></li>
    <li><a href="/hotels/">Hotels</a></li>
    <li><a href="/late-deals/">Late Deals</a></li>
  </ul>
  </div>
```

```
<div id="breadcrumb">
  You are here:
  <ul>
  <li><a href="/travel/">Travel</a>
    <ul>
      <li><a href="/travel/destinations/">Destinations</a>
        <ul>
          <li>Europe</li>
        </ul>
      </li>
    </ul>
  </li>
</ul>
</div>
<div id="content-wrapper">
  <div id="content-inner">
  <p>This is the content area  ... </p>
  </div>
</div>
<h3 class="hide">Navigation for this section</h3>
<div id="navigation">
  <ul>
    <li><a href="/linkdest1/">Nav link </a></li>
    <li><a href="/linkdest2/">Nav link 2</a></li>
    <li><a href="/linkdest3/">Nav link 3</a></li>
    <li><a href="/linkdest4/">Nav link 4</a></li>
    <li><a href="/linkdest5/">Nav link 5</a></li>
  </ul>
</div>
<div id="related">
  <h2>Related Links</h2>
  <div>
    <ul>
      <li><a href="/related/">Related link</a></li>
      <li><a href="/related/">Another link</a></li>
      <li><a href="/related/">And another</a></li>
      <li><a href="/related/">Related link</a></li>
    </ul>
  </div>
<div id="footer">Legal mumbo jumbo goes here</div>
</div>
```

The headings won't display on a CSS-capable browser but may be useful when viewed on lesser user agents, as Figure 12-17 shows.

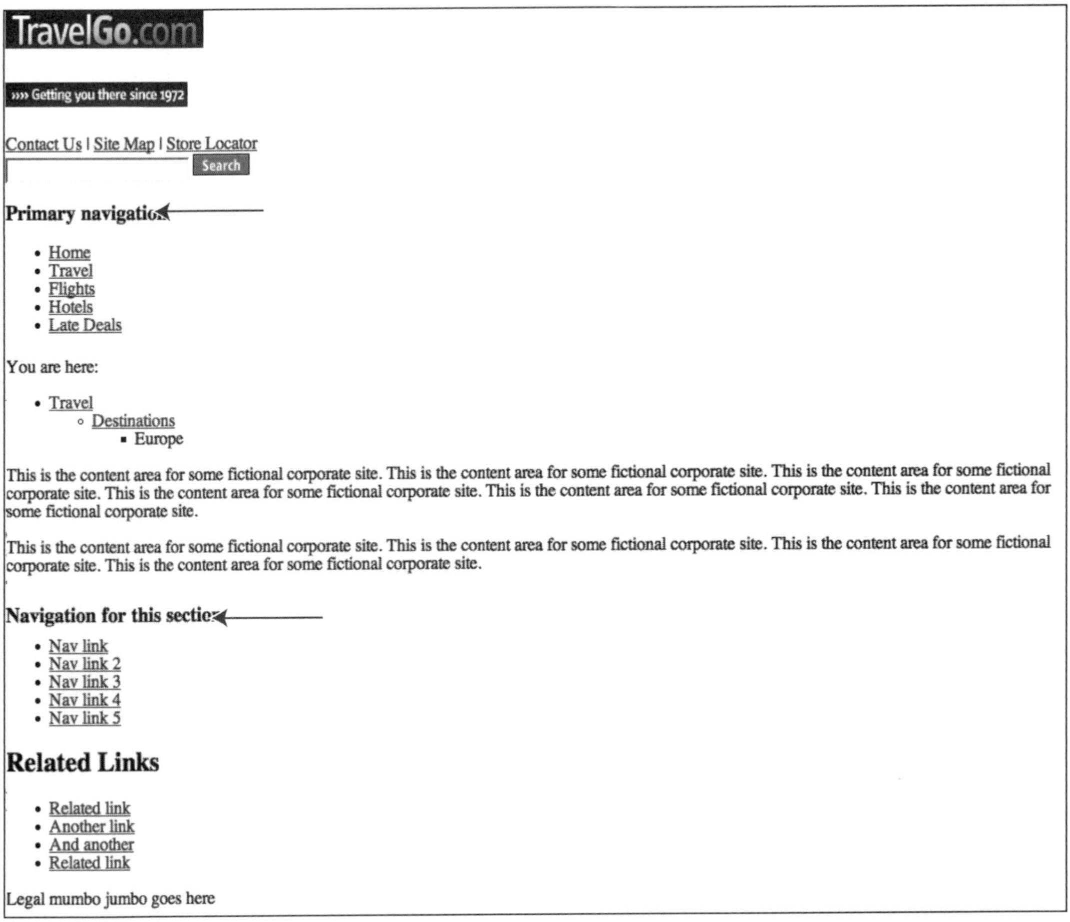

Figure 12-17. *Headings are revealed in non-CSS-capable browsers.*

■**Tip** Applying headings before blocks of content can be extremely useful for nonvisual browsing, too, and by that we mean screen reader users. It is possible—and very convenient—to navigate through a page by jumping from heading to heading, and providing a heading prior to key navigation areas can help immensely. However, there is a small problem: screen readers ignore content that is set to `display:none`. An alternative approach that will work for screen readers is to position the headings absolutely (thus removing them from the document flow) and then using a massive negative text indent to shift the text content off screen, like so: `.hiddenHeading {position:absolute;text-indent:-10000px;font-size:1px;}`.

Using Contextual Selectors to Show Location

In the header design for the fictional travel site, we've used a class of current to show the location in the site. If this were a site that was manually maintained, it would soon be a pain to update new pages. If it were programmatically generated, maintenance would be less of an issue, but there's a cunning way you can manage this with CSS (and this technique is closely related to the one demonstrated in Chapter 8 for changing a page layout by switching a body id attribute).

First, you need to add a class to each of the header links. The class name should be obviously related to the link destination, like so:

```
<div id="tablinks" class="clearfix">
  <ul>
    <li><a class="home" href="/">Home</a></li>
    <li><a class="travel" href="/travel/">Travel</a></li>
    <li><a class="flights" href="/flights/">Flights</a></li>
    <li><a class="hotels" href="/hotels/">Hotels</a></li>
    <li><a class="late-deals" href="/late-deals/">Late Deals</a></li>
  </ul>
</div>
```

In the body you add a class attribute that matches the page you are currently on. Assuming that it's a page in the travel section, you'd have

```
<body id="cols3" class="travel">
```

■Note You could use an id instead of a class, but we've already used that for the purpose of defining the page layout.

Now what we need is some CSS that makes the connection between the class attribute in the body and the class attribute in the links. And here's the very CSS required (which we can apply to five contextual selectors in one go by comma-separating them):

```
body.home a.home,
body.travel a.travel,
body.flights a.flights,
body.hotels a.hotels,
body.late-deals a.late-deals {
  background:#047070 url(tab-bg-hover.gif) repeat-x top;
}
```

Taking the first line, it translates to "If the body element has a class of home, set links with a class of home with this background image." Of course, you need to be sure that you don't apply the class of home, travel, or whatever your terms are to just any link—reserve them for the header, or whichever navigation mechanism you intend to apply this technique to.

Note In case you're thinking "Hang on, you've replaced one CSS selector of current with five different contextual selectors . . . and you *still* need to update the body element. What's the benefit?" Agreed, on a small, simple site there may not be a massive benefit to doing this. But like the body style switching technique, this approach could be used to change a number of different parts of the page, thanks to inheritance, which would negate the need for making multiple changes in the document. One change higher up the document tree can affect multiple child elements. It's a good way to start thinking about things, and this is a great—and simple—practical example to start off with.

Styling Definition Lists

So far, we've focused on unordered and ordered lists. They are great mechanisms for suggesting hierarchy and collecting together groups of related things, such as a collection of links used in a header or a simple to-do list. However, these are not the only kinds of lists available to you in XHTML. There is another, oft-misunderstood list that can be incredibly useful for suggesting relationships between items: the definition list. You can also do quite a lot with it in CSS—and after all, isn't that the purpose of this book?

The basic markup required for a definition list is as follows:

```
<dl>
  <dt>SLR</dt>
  <dd>Abbreviation of Single Lens Reflex</dd>
  <dd>A specific type of camera - one that uses a mirror to display the
  <em>exact</em> image to be captured through the viewfinder</dd>
  <dd>SLR cameras are usually used by professional, semi-professional and
  hobbyists as they offer greater creative control than a point-and-shoot
camera</dd>
</dl>
```

The building blocks are

- dl—for definition list

- dt—for definition term

- dd—for definition description

The premise behind the definition list is that a relationship exists between two parts: the dt contains the item you are referring to, while the content of the dd provides further information about or related to that dt element. You can also have multiple dd elements, as our example shows, and you can even include other block-level elements inside the dd element (in fact, you could place an unordered list inside the dd). Unfortunately, you cannot place block-level elements inside the dt element, as much as you might be tempted to. That said, definition lists have a number of possible practical uses, including

- Schedules for events

- Critiques of goods, hotels, services, etc.

- Descriptions of geographic locations

In fact, the list could go on for pages, but we would rather cut to the chase and look at some of the styling choices you might make.

Note Some people propose using definition lists for marking up dialogue. Actually, "some people" is the W3C in this case: "Another application of DL, for example, is for marking up dialogues, with each DT naming a speaker, and each DD containing his or her words" (www.w3.org/TR/html4/struct/lists.html#h-10.3). However, despite this sanctioned use, many web standards evangelists think this is *not* an appropriate use for the definition list, that in fact the W3C is wrong to suggest this use. Who's right and who's wrong? This is a proverbial can of worms that we won't open up—it'll just get messy.

Example 1: Schedule of Events

Take this sample XHTML:

```
<dl class="schedule">
  <dt>20th August</dt>
  <dd>Beachbuggin - VW meet at Southsea Seafront (all day schedule)</dd>
  <dd>VW Festival Leeds</dd>
  <dt>3rd September</dt>
  <dd>VW Action - Herts County Showground</dd>
  <dt>9th September</dt>
  <dd>Vanfest - Three Counties Showground, Malvern</dd>
</dl>
```

This (as yet) unstyled definition list would appear as shown in Figure 12-18.

Figure 12-18. *An unstyled definition list*

In the sample code, we've used relative positioning to move the dt where we want it (we could have chosen a float but that would require the usual float-clearing workarounds). Because the dd content will take up more vertical space, we'll apply a border to their left edge rather than a border to the right edge of the dt element. This helps to separate the two parts quite effectively:

```
.schedule dt {
  position: relative;
  left: 0;
  top: 1em;
```

```
    width: 14em;
    font-weight: bold;
}
.schedule dd {
    border-left: 1px solid silver;
    margin: 0 0 0 7em;
    padding: 0 0 .5em .5em;
}
```

This simple transformation can be seen in Figure 12-19.

20th August	Beachbuggin - VW meet at Southsea Seafront (all day schedule)
	VW Festival Leeds
3rd September	VW Action - Herts County Showground
9th September	Vanfest - Three Counties Showground, Malvern

Figure 12-19. *A definition list, styled using positioned* dt *elements*

Example 2: A Critique of Goods

Let's consider another example: a product critique of some kind. It includes an image and some text in the dt, with the actual comments in the dd where they should be. Here's the basic HTML for this:

```
<dl class="critique">
  <dt><img src="chair.jpg" alt="" />Union Jack Chair</dt>
  <dd>
    <p>What can I say? This is the perfect tool for sitting on ... </p>
  </dd>
</dl>
```

The default layout of the definition list isn't ideal for this, and the image could benefit from some treatment. Here's the CSS we need, which includes some simple background images that are applied to the dt and dd elements, respectively:

```
.critique dt {
  font-size:2em;
  font-family:Arial, Helvetica, sans-serif;
  clear:left;
  border-bottom:1px solid red;
  background: url(dt-bg.jpg) repeat-x bottom;
}
```

```
.critique dt img {
  display:block;
  border:2px solid black;
  float:left;
  margin:0 10px 10px 0;
}
.critique dd {
  margin:10px 0 60px 0;
  border-bottom:2px solid silver;
  background: url(dd-bg.jpg) repeat-x bottom;
}
```

Figure 12-20 shows the effect. Does it look like a definition list now?

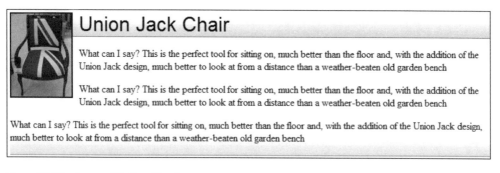

Figure 12-20. *A more "defined" style*

If you've determined that the markup you are after for a given purpose is a definition list, you would do well to check out Russ Weakley's tutorial on Maxdesign.com (`www.maxdesign.com.au/presentation/definition/index.htm`), which includes a gallery of styling options.

Summary

With the humble ordered, unordered, and definition lists, you can create a raft of features on a web page and style it in CSS to suit almost any whim. It's no longer a technique that's exclusive to just a handful of in-the-know web standards snobs with their shiny, up-to-the-minute browsers—it's something that enjoys excellent support across current browsers. There is no excuse for not using lists where a list is the perfect candidate for the job. Simple markup combined with some clever CSS and some nice graphical touches—it's a winner every time. And with that, it's time to look at the oft-uncharted territory of styling for print and other media.

■ ■ ■

CHAPTER 13

Styling for Print and Other Media

It may come as something of a revelation to people that CSS is not just about presentation of a web page on a computer screen—that there are ways of controlling layout, colors, and even the sound of certain parts of your web page for other media. These other uses for CSS may not be so well known for a few reasons, perhaps reasons that you can identify with:

- The boss (or client) has never requested a media-specific design from you.

- It's been "on the radar" but has never been investigated because you've heard that browser support is a bit flaky.

- There aren't enough hours in the day to worry about other media—it's a challenge just to get the screen display working cross-browser.

If any of these ring true, then we hope that after reading this chapter you'll realize that there are enough goodies to be found in this area to justify spending just a little extra time on style sheets for other media types. First things first, then: how do you tell the browser, or *user agent*, what style sheets to pay attention to and which ones to ignore?

Note In most cases, when dealing with CSS you'll hear people referring to the browser, but a web browser is just one type of *user agent*, defined as the piece of software that's used to access the web page. Because we're dealing with other media types, you may encounter this slightly less user-friendly term in this chapter.

Introducing Media Types

There are many different media types that you can apply to CSS, some of which are more useful than others, and they let you specify the look, feel, or sound of the web page that is linked to the CSS files. In this section, we'll look at the various media types that are available (as gleaned from the official source, namely the W3C: www.w3.org/TR/REC-CSS2/media.html#q1). However, rather than list them all and suggest wonderfully practical ways to use them, we'll break the list down into two categories: useful and not-so-useful (read: which ones you're likely to use on a day-to-day basis in the foreseeable future and those that you won't touch in a month of Sundays).

The Useful Media Types

This list includes the media types that you will truly find a use for on regular occasions:

- *screen*—For color computer screens

- *print*—For printed versions of the document

- *projection*—For presentation or kiosk versions of the document (where toolbars are removed, and the display renders completely full screen)

- *all*—For styles that are suitable for all devices

■**Note** *Kiosk mode* (as mentioned above in the projection media type) is where a computer runs the software full screen while preventing users from accessing system functions—for example, by hiding the Taskbar in Windows or file menus.

We'll be using (or covering briefly) these media types in this chapter's examples.

The Not-So-Useful Media Types

Remember what we were saying about those media types that you'd never use in a month of Sundays? Well, here they are, listed for your soon-to-be-ignored pleasure:

- *aural*—For use with speech synthesizers or talking browsers

- *braille*—For Braille-tactile feedback devices

- *embossed*—For paged Braille printers

- *handheld*—For handheld devices (for example, small-screen PDAs and cell phones)

- *tty*—For media using a fixed-pitch character grid, such as Teletypes, terminals, or portable devices with limited display capabilities

- *tv*—For television-type devices

■**Note** A Braille-tactile feedback device translates alphabetical characters on screen into the Braille equivalent through a series of "pins" that are raised on the fly. Visually impaired users would normally pass their fingertips over a page of characters and feel the characters, but in one of these devices, the raised pins scroll past underneath the user's fingertips.

We won't focus on these types because, while the reasoning behind them is good, support for their usage may be nonexistent. However, we'll expand on the aural and handheld types in the section "Style Sheets for Other Media Types" later in this chapter.

Specifying the Media Type

Next, let's look at how you can tell the user agent which medium (or media) the styles you are asking it to render should apply to.

Adding a media Attribute to the link Element

Arguably, the simplest method for linking to a style sheet is to use the `link` element, like so:

```
<link rel="stylesheet" href="css/mainstylesheet.css" />
```

This code tells the user agent that the link is to a style sheet and where it can find the link (`css/mainstylesheet.css`). The user agent will then deal with the link however it sees fit. You can, however, "scope" the use of the CSS contained in that style sheet with the `media` attribute:

```
<link rel="stylesheet" href="css/mainstylesheet.css" media="screen" />
```

In this example, only devices that will be displaying the content on a large screen will do anything with that style sheet. And where `screen` is concerned, that pretty much means a PC (Windows, Mac, Linux, etc.) and a web browser (Firefox, IE, and so on).

Adding a media Attribute to the @import Statement

If you are using the `@import` method for linking to a style sheet (perhaps to throw older, non-standards-friendly browsers like Netscape 4 off the scent), you could use the following syntax:

```
<style type="text/css">
@import url("css/printstylesheet.css") print;
</style>
```

There is a small problem with this approach, however: IE versions 6 and earlier won't deal with this syntax (at the time of this writing, IE 7 didn't understand this construct either), so you're probably going to have to use the previous method for linking wholesale to a CSS file.

■Note You can place the `@import` statement in a style block as shown in the example, or you can embed that `@import` statement in another style sheet that is already linked to the document, but the `@import` statement must be at the beginning of that style sheet, not after any other CSS selectors.

Adding the Media to Specific Selectors within a Style Sheet

Finally, you can embed some media-specific styles within another style sheet like so:

```
<style type="text/css">
body {font-size:62.5%;
h1 {
  color:red;
}
h2 {
```

```
  color:blue;
}
@media print {
  h1 {
    color:black;
  }
  h2 {
    color:gray;
  }
}
</style>
```

Creating a Print Style Sheet

In our experience, the greatest use you'll have for different media types is with printed output. There are a few quirks to be aware of (and we'll cover those), but it's very well supported in general and can be put to great use.

We've mentioned the various techniques that you can use to link to a style sheet with different media. Our preference is to do the following:

- Create a basic CSS file that contains generic visual styles that are understood by most browsers. Avoid CSS layout and anything that could be considered intermediate-to-advanced CSS. This CSS file is attached to the document using a link element but without specifying any media type whatsoever.

- Create a second style sheet that is used for more advanced screen styles and use the @import statement embedded in the basic.css file to attach it. Netscape 4 won't see this advanced file, but other newer browsers will.

- Create a print-only style sheet and attach it using the link element with media="print".

Note You should declare the print style sheet last (link to it even after any <style></style> block inside the HTML page). If you declare the print style sheet first, you could undo any values set there in the subsequent generic style sheets if they are not scoped for screen or some other medium.

Translating that English into markup, we get this in the document:

```
<!DOCTYPE html PUBLIC "-//W3C//DTD XHTML 1.0 Transitional//EN"
"http://www.w3.org/TR/xhtml1/DTD/xhtml1-transitional.dtd">
<html xmlns="http://www.w3.org/1999/xhtml">
<head>
<title>Simple print test</title>
<meta http-equiv="Content-Type" content="text/html; charset=iso-8859-1" />
<link rel="stylesheet" href="css/basic.css" />
<link rel="stylesheet" href="css/print.css" media="print"  />
</head>
```

and in the basic CSS file:

```
@import url("advanced.css");
```

What Do You Put in a Print CSS File?

There are not any real hard-and-fast rules about what should or shouldn't go into a print CSS file. However, let's take a moment to consider some of the characteristics of the printed format. Keep in mind that in print you *can't* do the following:

- Click on navigation items to take you to another piece of paper
- Conduct a search or carry out a calculation
- Zoom in or out on a map or resize text using a text widget of some kind
- "E-mail this story to a friend"
- Scroll the page
- Send feedback

What you *can* do with print CSS is almost the reverse of the previous list:

- Hide all navigation elements that are no longer any use
- Hide search facilities or other interactive form elements
- Hide controls that affect on-screen display
- Hide links that spawn some browser or application functionality

In fact, anything that you can click on or interact with on screen may need some kind of alternative treatment for print. Examples include hiding the element entirely or removing some display attribute that no longer works in the printed format (for example, removing underlines in body text links).

Note In most browsers, you do not need to be too concerned about dealing with background images that appear on screen; they are usually set *not* to print by default and, as such, are unlikely to need any special print-only treatment. One exception is Opera, which *will* print backgrounds out by default (or at least it does in versions 8 and 9 that we tested), but this can easily be unset in the File ➤ Print Options menu. If you have a sufficient number of Opera users, you might want to override background images for given elements, for example, body {background-image:none;}, so that users do not have to specify this for themselves—but it's not a major consideration that you need to worry about.

Resetting Layout

One of the first things you should consider with a print layout is resetting any layout mechanisms you've used for the screen view. This involves removing floats, absolute positioning, padding, and margins. You may want to go through each element and create a print alternative for each, but that may take time. We suggest using the old "sledgehammer-to-crack-a-nut" approach: apply several styles to several different elements in one go, and then deal with the exceptions.

Our travel web site is a good example that we can now prep for print. First things first; let's link to the necessary CSS files:

```
<!DOCTYPE html PUBLIC "-//W3C//DTD XHTML 1.0 Strict//EN"➡
"http://www.w3.org/TR/xhtml1/DTD/xhtml1-strict.dtd">
<html xmlns="http://www.w3.org/1999/xhtml">
<head>
  <title>TravelGo.com - Getting you there since 1972</title>
  <meta http-equiv="Content-Type" content="text/html; charset=iso-8859-1" />
  <link href="basic.css" rel="stylesheet" type="text/css" />
  <!-- which imports the advanced.css file -->
  <link href="print.css" rel="stylesheet" type="text/css" media="print" />
</head>
```

Here's the first part of the print CSS for this site. As you can see, we list all the elements that have been manipulated in one way or another and then reset the CSS back to basics:

```
body, div, img, h1, h2, h3, ul, ol, li, a, form {
  position:static;
  float:none;
  padding:0;
  margin:0;
}
```

This won't fix all the problems for the print view, mainly because of specificity reasons (remember reading about that as far back as Chapter 3?). Some of the rules in the main style sheet have a higher specificity and so, despite our redefinitions in the print CSS, the generic styles previously declared are more specific. So, we'll need to add some selectors to target those elements and they must have the same (or greater) specificity (see the additions in bold):

```
body, div, img, h1, h2, h3, ul, ol, li, a, form,
div#breadcrumb,
div#header,
body#cols3 #content-wrapper {
  position:static;
  float:none;
  padding:0;
  margin:0;
}
```

■**Note** We are resetting some, but not all, values that were specified in the advanced style sheet. That advanced style sheet was imported but had no media type specified. The style sheet will therefore automatically apply to any medium, and what we're doing here is overriding some styles for print.

Another approach is to create two `link` elements in the document head: one that links to a screen CSS file with the `media="screen"`, and the second file to the print CSS file. The problem with this approach is that the print view is starting from scratch as it sees none of the styles applied for screen. You end up having to come up with new styles. In our experience, it's easier to take the main style sheet (by not applying a media type) and then reset the layout aspects for print as required.

Hiding Navigation and Other Interactive Elements

The next step is to identify what parts of the page can be removed entirely from print. In the travel site, it would be the parts shown in Figure 13-1.

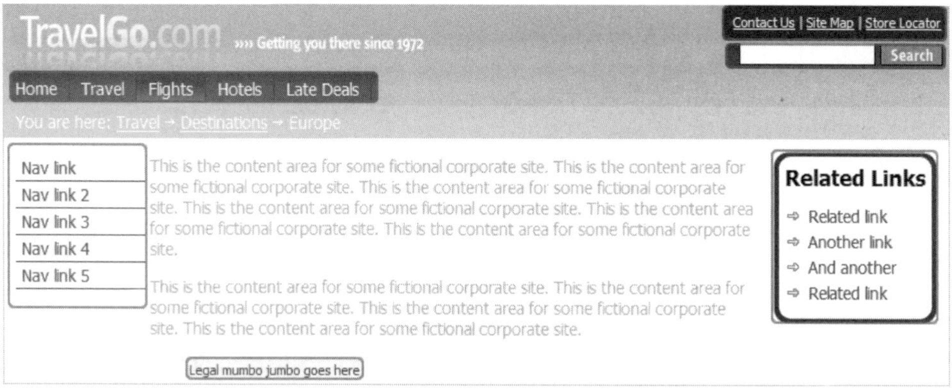

Figure 13-1. *Navigation areas that have little use for print*

If we hide these elements, we'll be left with just the page logo, the breadcrumb trail (which we suggest be left in for print as it is an orientation device as much as it is a navigation device), and the page content. It would have been easier, of course, to hide the header area as a whole, but that would also cause the site branding to disappear. Therefore, we've suggested picking out specific elements to hide and ones that should remain in the printout. To hide these chosen elements, we can simply apply one rule as follows:

```
#headerlinks, #headersearch, #tablinks, #navigation, #related, #footer {
  display:none;
}
```

With the layout aspects reset and all superfluous navigation items hidden, we end up with the results shown in Figure 13-2 (which shows a print preview in Firefox). The print preview facility is not always a perfect rendering of how it will appear on the printed page (there can be some quirky bugs), but it's a great way of testing your printed page without wasting reams and reams of paper before you get it just right. Internet Explorer on Windows also offers a preview that you can access from the File menu.

Figure 13-2. *A simpler document for print, but still some issues to correct*

Correcting Minor Issues Inherited from the Screen Style Sheet

A closer look at Figure 13-2 reveals some slight issues. These issues result from our decision to apply generic rules to a wide range of elements and our expectation that everything will work out of the box—which does not always happen. In the example, a height applied to the h1—which was there solely for the purpose of creating space for the reflected background image underneath the logo text—is adding unnecessary whitespace; the breadcrumb trail items could also benefit from additional space between them. A couple of tweaks added to the print CSS file will correct these issues:

```
h1 {
  background:none !important;
  height:33px !important;
}
#breadcrumb ul li ul li {
  padding-left:14px !important;
}
```

Note In general, for print CSS files you should specify measurements using cm, mm, or em rather than px (pixels are for screen display), particularly where fonts, margins, and padding are concerned. However, we've specified pixels in our tweaks as they relate directly to images that are also expressed in terms of pixels.

So, how are we doing with the print-only makeover? Figure 13-3 shows the progress so far, but as with many things in life there's still room for further refinements if you make the effort.

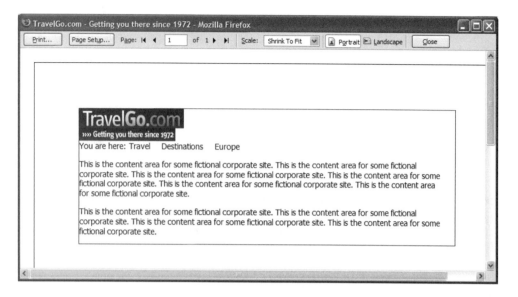

Figure 13-3. *The final result? There's always more to do!*

Tips for Even Better Printed Pages

Our previous example showed a simple printout that you can achieve by resetting certain CSS properties and redefining others. There is more that you can do to improve matters, though:

- Use serif fonts. Because of the low resolution that monitors provide, and the fact that a large number of users do not have something like ClearType (www.microsoft.com/typography/cleartype/tuner/Step1.aspx) enabled, small-sized serif fonts often look poor on screen—there simply aren't enough pixels available to render all the little flourishes (or serifs) at the ends of letters. It's no mistake that a large number of web sites use sans-serif fonts (such as Verdana, Arial, and Helvetica) on screen; the lack of serifs makes them easier to render and thus easier to read. *On screen*. For the *printed* version, though, you can quite easily use a serif font, such as Georgia or Times New Roman. Serif fonts provide extra shape to the letters and can often help distinguish among similar-looking characters; the serifs also create an implied horizontal line that's supposed to aid readability.

- If you've lost background images for print, you might be able to work around this by including an inline image that is hidden in the main style sheet (give it a unique id so that you can reference it) with a display:none but is made visible in your print CSS file using display:block or display:inline. The downside is that you are including an image that, for the vast majority of users, will not be seen but will still get downloaded to the client. If that's something that concerns you (and it probably depends on how big the image is), you could use CSS-generated content to dynamically write in the image—for example, in the print style sheet, div.offer:after {content: "<img src='printimage.gif' alt="Special offer" />"}. But remember that IE 7 and earlier won't pay any attention to that code. Certainly, the former technique enjoys better support.

- Bullet points missing? In the previous chapter, we suggested that applying background images was the best method for creating custom list item symbols. When you print them, though, the images won't show. For that reason you should redefine the display for print so that the image is attached using `list-style-image` (or simply remove the custom bullet styles altogether and go with the basic styles that the browser would apply).

- Provide special offers for printouts. While the browser will, by default, print information such as the date, URL, and page number, you can add custom information for the printed version. As an example, if on our travel site you found the perfect vacation and printed out the details, you could include a print-only section on how to make a booking. This section might include a telephone number and a reference number, while the screen view would instead display a link to the e-commerce section of the site to make an online booking.

This is just a small selection of ideas that you can almost certainly expand on depending on the nature of the web site that you run or maintain. Once again, A List Apart has some excellent ideas about the topic in the articles "CSS Design: Going to Print" (`http://alistapart.textdrive.com/articles/goingtoprint`) and "Designing for Context with CSS" (`http://alistapart.textdrive.com/articles/designingforcontext`).

Things to Watch Out For

With a little care and attention, you can create web pages that perfectly suit the printed medium. Yet be aware that there are some things you need to take into account.

Checking Your Page Width

If you have defined a width for your page using pixels, you will need to redefine that for print using a real-world measurement such as centimeters, millimeters, or inches. Be sure to allow for the fact that the printer your site visitor is using may not be able to print right up to the edges. If you take a US letter or A4 sized piece of paper, measure its width, then take off a couple of centimeters or a quarter inch from either side, that should give you a printable page width.

Printing Errors with CSS Positioning

If you have reset all the positioning properties as suggested earlier in this chapter, you will probably not run into difficulties. However, be sure to try printing a web page with a lot of content—a page that you would expect to run into several printed pages—to make sure that the entire web page prints. Using floats and absolute position can affect the printout, resulting in only the first page getting printed. If this happens, double-check the CSS for the container of the content that is being "clipped" and ensure that you have set `float:none` and `position:static`.

Note In case you're wondering "What's that `static` value? And why haven't we heard about it before?" it's because that's the browser's default positioning model. You would not normally need to set this yourself—we only have to do this to get around a known printing problem.

Getting Feedback About Your "Funny Printouts"

Despite all your hard work, someone is bound to ask, "Why does your page not print out properly?" Many users expect that what they see on screen will be replicated in the printout. Remember that you can use print CSS itself to address the issue (e.g., perhaps a block of text that reads "This page has been crafted for perfect printing..." that is hidden on screen but set as `display:block` for the printed version).

An alternative method is to use generated content using the `:after` pseudo-attribute, which is covered in Chapter 3 and Appendix A. However, as previously mentioned, the support for this is still not there (keep in mind that IE 7 and earlier do not support this feature).

Advanced Print CSS Techniques

Hiding and showing or restyling content dependent on the medium is fairly straightforward stuff once you've grasped the basics. In this section, we'll examine some more advanced features that introduce some extra dynamics into the usually static world of print. This is where browser support can get a little flakier, though, so be sure to treat these as "nice-to-haves" rather than as essential features that must be available to all browsers.

Inserting URLS in Printed Pages

The great thing about reading a web page with links is that when you see an underlined phrase you can click on that link and immediately investigate another avenue. With that page printed out, you have no way of following that link, so you have a couple of choices:

- Suppress the underline (or any other link styling, such as bold text) for print so that it doesn't get in the way needlessly; there's no point signifying a link that can't be followed.

- Choose the opposite route—instead of hiding the link styling, expand on it and dynamically create a printed version of the web address (whatever is in that link's `href` attribute).

The latter is definitely doable, but it requires some slightly advanced CSS (not supported by IE 7 or earlier) or a JavaScript solution.

Using Generated Content to Write Out the URL

Here is the basic CSS that does the job of writing out links on the page (be sure to add this *only* to the print CSS file):

```
a:after {
content: " (" attr(href) ") ";
}
```

This code tells the browser to get the value of an attribute (the `href` attribute, as detailed in the parentheses) and then place that value in a string that begins and ends with parentheses. If you are familiar with JavaScript, it's equivalent to

```
" (" + this.getAttribute('href') + ")"
```

but there is no concatenation symbol such as + or &. In this example HTML:

```
<h3>
  <a href="/book/bookDisplay.html?bID=10079">
    Building Flickr Applications with PHP
  </a>
</h3>
```

it would render on the printed version like so:

```
Building Flickr Applications with PHP
(http://www.apress.com/book/bookDisplay.html?bID=10079)
```

Tip You probably wouldn't want every link on the page to get this treatment, so you may want to scope it by using a contextual selector, for example #bodycontent a:after {content: " (" attr(href) ") ";}.

Using JavaScript and the DOM to Write Out the URL

Because of the flaky support for this, you can turn to JavaScript and the Document Object Model (DOM) to do the same thing. The following script accomplishes these goals:

- Looks through the document and finds all links

- Gets the href attribute from each link and adds it to a new span element that is created on the fly

- Adds the new span into the link

```
<script type="text/javascript">
function findLinks()
{
var el = document.getElementsByTagName("a");
for (i=0;i<el.length;i++)
  {
    href = el[i].getAttribute("href");
    var newEl = document.createElement("span");
    var newElText = document.createTextNode(" (" + href + ")");
    newEl.appendChild(newElText);
    el[i].appendChild(newEl);
  }
}
window.onload=findLinks;
</script>
```

Without a bit of further intervention, this will render on screen as well as print, so you will need to do a little more work on the CSS to prevent this:

```
<style type="text/css">
#bodycontent a span {
  display:none;
}
@media print {
  #bodycontent a span {
    display:inline;
  }
}
</style>
```

You can see the result in Figure 13-4.

Write out link hrefs for print

This is lloydi's blog. What a shameful plug for a such a lousy web page. You might find his flickr photos of more interest to be honest.

Write out link hrefs for print

This is lloydi's blog (http://lloydi.com/blog/). What a shameful plug for a such a lousy web page. You might find his flickr photos (http://www.flickr.com/photos/ianlloyd/) of more interest to be honest.

Figure 13-4. *The top part shows the screen rendering; the bottom shows the content revealed for the printout.*

This is a fairly simple script to address the issue, but it works. However, you can do a lot better than this. When looking at a block of content, a long URL directly after the text can make it a little difficult to read, regardless of the benefit offered by having the reference there. Wouldn't it be great if you could simply create a footnote from each link and just place a number after the link that references the footnote link? Well, you can thank Aaron Gustafson for devising a JavaScript technique that does just that, all ready for you to download and implement (`http://alistapart.textdrive.com/articles/improvingprint`).

Selective Printing Using the DOM and CSS

One final advanced technique that you might like to consider is mixing together DOM scripting and CSS to create specific printable areas of a page. An example of how this works is a FAQ page that contains many blocks of content. You might want to print only one section of that page; by using JavaScript you can dynamically toggle display attributes of different sections so that only the part you want printed is shown—but without affecting the screen view.

This is a fairly involved technique, which is covered thoroughly (a chapter in its own right!) in *Web Standards Creativity* by Cameron Adams et al. (friends of ED, February 2007), although you can also read about the technique online on my personal blog (`http://lloydi.com/blog/2006/03/21/how-to-print-selective-sections-of-a-web-page-using-css-and-dom-scripting-2/`).

Style Sheets for Other Media Types

As we mentioned at the beginning of this chapter, the support for other media types is very spotty indeed, and what you can do with it is severely limited. Because this book is all about providing practical advice that works in the real world, we won't explore all the various CSS property values that you can use with audio style sheets (it's highly unlikely that such a discussion would be of use to most readers), but we'll look at a few media types.

The Projection Media Type

Another media type that does have a modicum of support is projection. As far back as version 4, Opera has supported this type, but what does it do? Projection is intended for use with presentation versions of a web page; all browser toolbars and the like are removed, and the information is presented in full screen. A good example is S5 (http://meyerweb.com/eric/tools/s5/), a web page–based presentation format that CSS guru Eric Meyer devised and which is used by many web standards advocates throughout the world. In Opera you trigger the Projection mode by choosing View ➤ Full Screen. The example HTML that follows shows how you might create content that appears only when viewed in this full-screen mode:

```
<!DOCTYPE HTML PUBLIC "-//W3C//DTD HTML 4.01 Transitional//EN"
"http://www.w3.org/TR/html4/loose.dtd">
<html>
<head>
<title>Projection test</title>
<meta http-equiv="Content-Type" content="text/html; charset=iso-8859-1">
<style type="text/css">
.projection-only {
  display:none;
}
@media projection {
  .projection-only {
    display:block;
  }
}
</style>
</head>
<body>
  <h1>Can you see anything below?</h1>
  <p class="projection-only">Well howdi y'all!</p>
</body>
</html>
```

If you have a copy of Opera, try it out—it works! But you will probably find it an interesting idea for all of a few seconds. Firefox and IE will not render the projection content when viewed in full-screen mode, so you have to ask yourself: What benefit can you get from using this?

The Aural Media Type

With the aural CSS properties, you should be able to control the pitch, speed, tone, and other attributes for speech-synthesized versions of the web page to great effect, but support for this is very much lacking. To date, we've only seen (or rather heard) one good application of this: a plug-in for Firefox called Firevox, which is definitely worth downloading (`http://firevox.mozdev.org/installation.html`) and checking out to see what *should* be possible with this technology. You can find out more about the various CSS aural properties and values at the W3C (`www.w3.org/TR/REC-CSS2/aural.html`), or for a simpler example try the W3Schools introduction to this topic (`www.w3schools.com/css/css_ref_aural.asp`).

The Handheld Media Type

Another example of "great in theory, but almost useless in practice," the handheld media type is perfect for specifying styles that can be used for a cell phone–based browser, Blackberry, or similar device. However, the mobile market (phones in particular) are almost a law unto themselves and have devised various strategies for rendering web pages in the struggle to gain a competitive edge. At `http://css-discuss.incutio.com/?page=HandheldStylesheets` you'll find a quote that pretty much sums up the sorry state of handheld support:

> *Some current phones apply "screen" styles as well as "handheld" styles, others ignore both, and in some cases the phone carrier runs pages through a proxy that strips styles out even if the phone could recognize them, so it's a crapshoot figuring out what will get applied.*

So, all bets are off! It's good to be aware that the media type exists and what its intended use is, but, seriously, don't waste effort in trying to design a slick interface for a given handheld device and expect it to honor only your handheld styles and ignore the screen styles—and certainly don't expect the next handheld to do the same!

The All Media Type

The all media type is pretty much superfluous. If you want a style sheet to be rendered on all devices, you may just as well not set a media type at all and let the device, browser, or user agent work it out for itself.

Summary

The ability to create specific style sheets for different media seems, on the face of it, to be a very powerful tool. However, in practice you are limited in what you can do. It seems a shame to end on a sour note, but we hope the things that you can do with the print medium more than make up for the rest. Now, if only the mobile market could decide on a standard and stick with it, we could do great things with those devices just as we can with the printed medium. Well, we can hope—and a good place to start is with Blue Flavor's presentation on mobile web design, which can be found at `www.blueflavor.com/presentations/DesigningforMobile.pdf`.

We've covered a lot of ground in the preceding chapters. You may well have mastered nearly everything there is to know about CSS except, perhaps, for one thing: what happens when things don't go as planned? In the next chapter we'll look at techniques for identifying where and why things go wrong and, more importantly, what you can do to put things right again.

■ ■ ■

CHAPTER 14

Everything Falls Apart

Knowing all the tips, tricks, hacks, browser quirks, optimizations, and the 347,982 methods of combining them to form a layout doesn't offer much solace if your site appears mangled when viewed in a popular browser. As important as all the advanced CSS techniques we've covered are, the ability to troubleshoot and diagnose problems is equally important, and that's what this chapter is all about. We're going to look at ways to narrow down the source of a problem (especially vexing when everything looks right in your code but not in the browser), examine common mistakes made when working with CSS (and how to avoid them), revisit some of the more common browser bugs we covered solutions for in Chapter 6, and then walk through a CSS layout from creation, to testing, to finding problems and fixing them.

What to Do When You Don't Know What Went Wrong

It's usually easy to solve problems when there's an obvious answer, say, if the background color of your page is blue when you meant it to be green (check the `background-color` declaration on the `body` element), or your sidebar is on the right when you wanted it on the left (you probably used the wrong float direction). However, when developing with CSS, problems and their solutions are often much less obvious (for instance, when a `background-image` is set on your `body` element but no image displays in the browser, or your floated sidebar is appearing below your content in IE 6), and require a combination of a few handy tools and some logical thinking. The steps to follow are usually along these lines:

- Validate markup and styles
- Disable styles in chunks
- Disable hacks
- Create minimal test cases

If you use the utilities and browser extensions described in this section and follow these steps (which we'll cover in detail later in this chapter), you should be able to catch any error during your development process.

Useful Browser Add-ons and Utilities

Sometimes it's not enough just to use your detective skills to solve strange CSS problems. Luckily, there are a few browser extensions and tools out there that can help in your search for the root of a CSS problem.

Web Developer Extension (Firefox)

The big papa of them all (if you develop using Firefox) is Chris Pederick's Web Developer Extension (www.chrispederick.com/work/webdeveloper). The extension adds a toolbar of goodies that fits in nicely with the browser's UI (Figure 14-1), and hidden within its menus are a bevy of beautiful functions to help make your day more pleasant, including the ability to disable CSS, replace images with the contents of their alt attribute, show detailed information about elements on the page (Figure 14-2), and almost everything else you can think of. It's a perfect extension to the best browser for web developers.

Figure 14-1. *The Web Developer Extension adds an über toolbar to Firefox.*

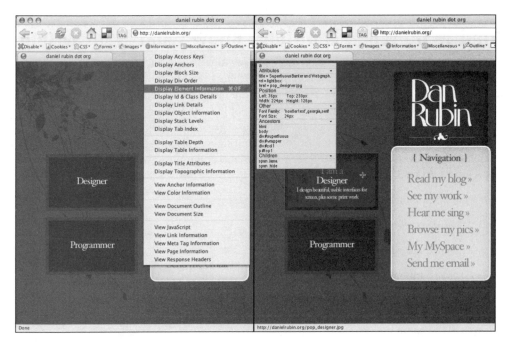

Figure 14-2. *Simply place your cursor over the element you wish to examine to get all the juicy details.*

Note The next version of Safari will include a new feature, Web Inspector, that provides similar functionality to the Web Developer Extension for Firefox. For those of you who prefer to do your developing in Safari, this will be a welcome addition to the toolbox. If you can't wait for the final version when it ships with OS X Leopard, visit `http://nightly.webkit.org/builds/` and download the latest WebKit nightly.

Firebug Extension (Firefox)

Another great add-on for Firefox is Joe Hewitt's Firebug (`www.joehewitt.com/software/firebug/`). Much like the Web Developer Extension's Display Element Information option (Figure 14-2), Firebug features an Inspector that shows you all elements in the document tree, their styles, layout/positioning specifics, and more (Figure 14-3).

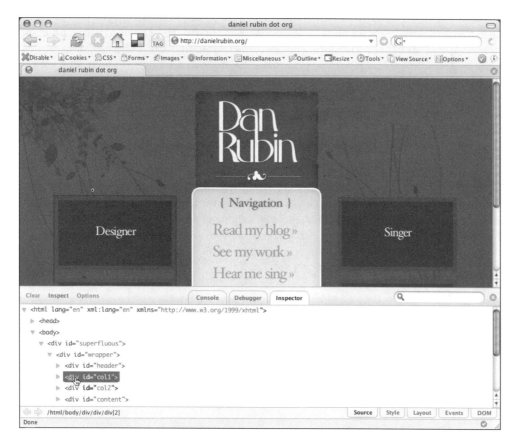

Figure 14-3. *Hovering or clicking on an element in Firebug's Inspector outlines that element in the browser.*

As a bonus, Firebug places a small icon at the bottom of the browser window at all times. Clicking the icon activates the Firebug interface, but the icon also alerts you to any JavaScript errors on the page (and the extension has extra features specific to debugging JavaScript, the DOM, and Ajax/XMLHttpRequest), allowing you to see at a glance if there's something you need to check out (Figure 14-4).

Figure 14-4. *Firebug's icon lets you know if everything's hunky-dory with your JavaScript.*

Web Developer Toolbar (Internet Explorer)

Like it or not, at some point we must all test our sites in IE/Win. This can be a painful process thanks to its various bugs and rendering inconsistencies, but thankfully Microsoft makes a browser addition that can, if nothing else, make the process of debugging and testing your site a little easier in IE.

The Web Developer Toolbar (visit www.microsoft.com/downloads/ and search for "web developer toolbar") works much like Firefox's Web Developer Extension, offering similar options to aid in the testing and bug-fixing process. If you develop sites that *must* work in IE, this add-on will help you retain some sanity during the testing process.

Safari Tidy

If you develop on OS X and prefer Safari, this little plug-in from Kasper Nauwelaerts can save you the trouble of running your code through the W3C validators (www.zappatic.net/safaritidy/). While this plug-in is a one-trick pony, its browser window icons (similar to Firebug's) make it downright impossible to miss validation errors (Figure 14-5).

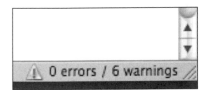

Figure 14-5. *Safari Tidy's browser window notes give you the skinny on validation issues.*

Other Utilities

Many tools are available online and as applications, and it could take years to sift through all of them, so here are a few of our favorite helpers for OS X and Windows XP:

- Xyle scope (OS X; `www.culturedcode.com/xyle/`)

- TextMate (OS X; `http://macromates.com/`)

- xScope (OS X; `http://iconfactory.com/software/xscope/`)

- Style Master (OS X/Win XP; `www.westciv.com/style_master/`)

- Dreamweaver (OS X/Win XP; `www.adobe.com/products/dreamweaver/`)

Validate Markup and Styles

Nothing is more frustrating than spending hours trying to fix a problem only to discover that it was a minor mistake that *you* made and that you could have easily avoided. Luckily for you (and the rest of us), the W3C maintains two online tools that can help check your markup (`http://validator.w3.org/`) and styles (`http://jigsaw.w3.org/css-validator/`). Validating helps you eliminate a lot of human errors from your code: unclosed elements, improperly formed tags and attributes, incorrect properties/values, and more can be quickly located and corrected with the help of the validators. And by running your page through the validators as you fix the problems they report, it's easy to tell when you still have errors (Figure 14-6) and when you've caught them all (Figure 14-7).

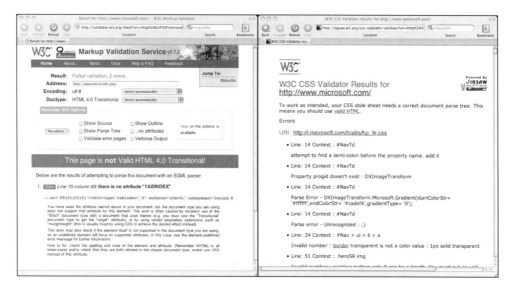

Figure 14-6. *After we validate markup (left) and styles (right), we see Microsoft.com has some problems (though there are only two errors, so be gentle).*

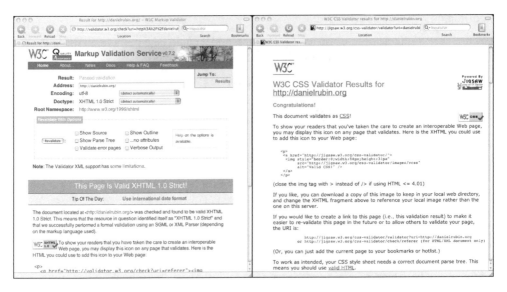

Figure 14-7. *The no-hack layout from Chapter 6 is strictly valid, baby!*

Disable Styles in Chunks

Once you've determined that obvious human error is not contributing to your plight (which isn't to say mistakes aren't hiding in your style sheet—it just means you've caught the blatant ones with the validator), the next step is to narrow your list of suspects. If your problems involve major layout or positioning issues, the easiest way to do this is by completely removing large portions of your style sheet and seeing if the problem still remains. Start by temporarily deleting the part of your style sheet that logically relates to the problem you are seeing, then save and reload your page. You can easily tell if the problem still exists, and if it doesn't, it's a fair bet that your culprit lies elsewhere within your style sheet. Continue narrowing the field by using the same process on each block of likely suspects until you've found the culprit. If the source of your problem is proving difficult to track down, you can cast a wider net by deleting *half* of your style sheet and following the same process to narrow the list of offending styles.

Though styles and markup can also be commented out, you might run into problems mass-commenting blocks of your document or style sheet due to existing (X)HTML or CSS comments you've already used. It's better (and safer) to create a backup of your files and delete blocks of code rather than comment them out.

Disabling styles isn't a surefire way to determine every possible problem, due in large part to the cascade (covered in Chapter 3), since rules at one end of a style sheet can affect rules at the other end. If this method doesn't help, try creating a minimal test case, as shown later in this chapter.

■**Tip** Delete the most likely blocks of styles first—this is where logic comes into play. For instance, if you are having a problem with an unordered list, then delete the rule(s) that target that `ul`; if your problem disappears, slowly add the deleted styles back one by one until the problem reappears.

Disable Hacks

Hacks, while usually very focused (especially those discussed in Chapter 6 and throughout this book), are still capable of causing some problems, especially in the browsers they target (typically IE/Win, but not always). If you are having problems with a browser that is targeted by some of your hacks, disable them and see if your troubles remain (yet another reason to keep your hacks in separate style sheets; commenting out or temporarily deleting a `<link>` or `@import` is much easier than removing hacks from your main style sheet).

Create Minimal Test Cases to Simplify Problems

If a problem is proving to be considerably vexing, creating a simplified version of the markup and styles (known as a reduction or "minimal test case") allows you to confirm whether you are running into a browser bug or an error in your (X)HTML/CSS.

The cascading nature of CSS often results in compound problems, unwanted effects resulting from more than one rule or declaration combining in unexpected ways. Simplifying the associated markup and styles helps rule out possible causes, similar to disabling styles as we discussed earlier.

There is no simple example to give, because by definition something that needs to be reduced to its most simple form must be complex to begin with, and would be impractical to display on these pages. And there is usually no pattern to the problems that require reduction (once you've solved a complex problem, you can recognize it more easily the next time you encounter it).

Like the method of disabling styles, creating a minimal test case is all about *logical simplification* of the affected elements (both markup and styles). For instance, if you think items in a list are being affected by combined styles, create a test document containing only the list and its related styles and see if the problem remains. If it does, your error is within the reduction—solve it and update your main styles and markup; if things look as intended, slowly add the surrounding markup (and styles), testing with each addition until the problem resurfaces, at which point you can begin to narrow down the possibilities.

This approach can be time consuming, but the more complex your styles and markup become, so too does the process of debugging them.

Common CSS Mistakes

We've all been there at some point: that long night of testing, spending hours trying to squash a bug in your layout, having no success with anything, only to discover (finally) that it was a simple error. *On your part.* Nothing feels quite like that moment of discovery and realization that those wasted hours could have been avoided if only you hadn't made the mistake to begin with. We've done it, you've done it, and we can pretty much guarantee that it'll happen to each of us many more times over our lifetime.

Now, while we'd love to explain to you how to never make a mistake again *ever*, reality has other plans, so instead we'll shoot for a few of the more (or less) obvious examples of human error that frequently trip up developers.

■Note Layout issues frequently arise due to improper *source order* of elements in your markup. Source order describes the actual order in which elements appear in your markup, and certain methods of positioning behave differently depending on the order of the elements being positioned. For more information on source order and how to avoid its related issues, see Chapter 7.

Specificity Problems

A long time ago, in a chapter far, far away—Chapter 3 to be exact—we looked into the core of CSS, and the rules of specificity that are governed by the cascade. As it happens, improper use of these rules (due to a lack of understanding) often causes much dismay, strife, and general frustration among developers.

Take, for example, this code (taken from ch14_example_specificity.html in the example files for this book in the Source Code/Download section at the Apress web site):

Markup

```
<div id="wrapper">
  <div id="main">
    <div id="content">
      <div class="item">
        <ul>
          <li>Lorem <a class="readmore" href="nextpage.html">ipsum</a>.</li>
        </ul>
      </div>
    </div>
  </div>
</div>
```

Styles

```
#main #content .item a.readmore {
  color:red;
  background-color:yellow;
}

#wrapper #main #content a {
  color:green;
}

#main #content .item ul li a {
  color:blue;
  font-weight:bold;
  background-color:transparent;
}
```

Which is the most specific selector? Frequently, the third (#main #content .item ul li a) will be assumed, since it targets only a elements within list items in unordered lists, contained by the #main and #content elements, plus it's the last in the style sheet. However, the first selector is more specific (because it has an extra class) and the second selector is the most specific of the bunch thanks to the extra ID. The result is a bold, green link with a yellow background (as seen in Figure 14-8, though the colors aren't visible in the screen shot). Because location within the style sheet doesn't affect selectors with different levels of specificity, you can see how rules scattered throughout a long style sheet can combine to cause trouble. Knowing the rules of specificity (and playing by them) can save you from having to deal with the effects.

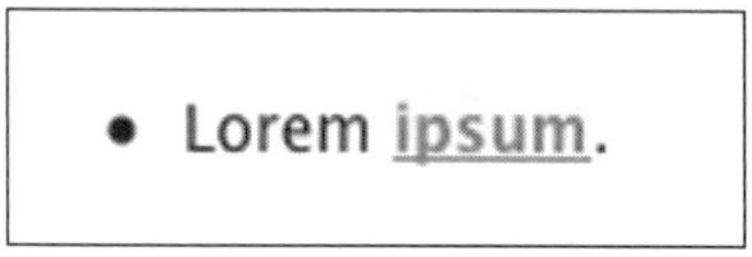

Figure 14-8. *Specificity turned this link into an ugly green monster with jaundice.*

Image Paths

Wondering why your background image isn't displaying? The first thing to check is the path in your style sheet—image paths are relative to the location of the style sheet, unless an absolute URL (http://mydomain.com/images/my_repeating_texture.jpg) or a root-relative path (/images/my_repeating_texture.jpg) is used. This means that if your style sheet's location (relative to the root directory) is /css/main.css, and your background image is /images/my_repeating_texture.jpg, the following variations will *not* work:

```
#header {
  background:url(my_repeating_texture.jpg);
}
```

```
#header {
  background:url(images/my_repeating_texture.jpg);
}
```

Instead, you should use one of the following:

```
#header {
  background:url(../images/my_repeating_texture.jpg);
}
```

```
#header {
  background:url(/images/my_repeating_texture.jpg);
}
```

Notice the last example is root-relative. This will work no matter where the style sheet is located within your directory structure, since the root of your site doesn't change (but it will not work for local testing when opening documents using the file system), as opposed to the first example (../images/), which tells the browser to look for the images directory one level up within the directory structure.

Link Order (LoVe/HAte)

Though covered in Chapter 3, it's worth mentioning again: if your link styles aren't working properly, check to make sure your rules are properly ordered within your style sheet:

```
a:link {
  color:blue;
}
a:visited {
  color:purple;
}
a:hover {
  background-color:black;color:white;text-decoration:none;
}
a:active {
  background-color:red;color:white;text-decoration:none;
}
```

Clear All Floats

Floats are cool, as we all know, and they allow us to create all sorts of nice layouts. But forgetting to clear a float can wreak all kinds of havoc. Always make sure all floated elements are cleared, either using the easy float clearing method described in Chapter 6, or by inserting a clearing div immediately following the floated element, or clearing the next element that appears in the document (see Chapter 7 for some additional clearing methods). You'll save a ton on headache medicine, and have more time to focus on the real bugs in your layout.

Common CSS Bugs (in IE)

So you know how to avoid problems during development, but that doesn't exempt you from running into browser bugs during testing, and as you should be familiar with by this point, the usual troublemaker is IE 6/Win.

Back in Chapter 6, we discussed some popular hacks that solve problems developers run into with IE. Now we'll put those hacks to good use in order to squash the most common bugs you'll encounter when testing your layouts in IE 6. It's worth noting that, as of this writing, these bugs no longer exist in IE 7!

■**Tip** Remember to keep any hacks in a separate style sheet, and serve them to IE 6 and earlier using conditional comments, as described in Chapter 6.

Doubled Float-Margin Bug

The first of these creepy crawlies is one you've probably encountered if you've ever used floats to position, well, almost anything. If you apply a margin to the same side of an element as its floated direction (e.g., `margin-right` on a box assigned `float:right`), and that margin comes in direct contact with the side of the float's container element, IE 6 will take it upon itself to double that margin's declared width (and the bug only occurs on the first floated element in a row).

Let's take the following example:

Markup

```
<div id="float">
  <p>floated div</p>
</div>
<div class="clear"><!-- clears the float above --></div>
```

Styles

```
#float {
  float:left;
  margin-left:100px;
  width:200px;
  height:150px;
  background:#ddd;
  text-align:center;
}

.clear {
  clear:both;
}
```

The empty clearing `div` has been included for clarity, though the same effect would be achieved by using the easy float clearing method from Chapter 6.

Although there should only be a 100px left margin between the float and the left border of the page (non-IE browsers get this right), IE 6 inexplicably doubles the margin to 200px (Figure 14-9). This odd behavior could definitely make your life miserable for a while, but thankfully there's a fix, and it's dead simple: declare `display:inline` on the floated box, and the margin returns to normal. Why does this work? Who knows, really? With IE bugs, sometimes just knowing how to solve it is enough (you can find an expanded write-up at www.positioniseverything.net/explorer/doubled-margin.html).

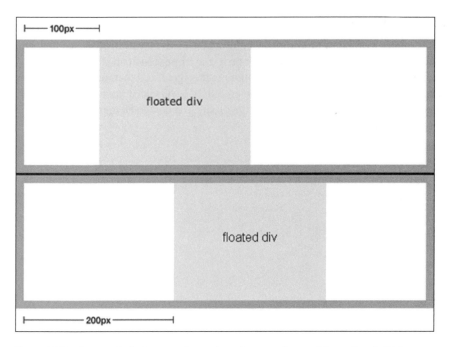

Figure 14-9. *On top, Safari correctly renders the margin, and then there's IE 6...*

Three-Pixel Jog

Next up is an even weirder bug that affects elements adjacent to floats. This one's often difficult to catch, because its effects are so seemingly minor, and in certain layouts may be easily over-looked. For some unknown reason, IE 6 adds three pixels to any inline elements next to a float, even if those elements are contained by a block element. The results range from a simple cosmetic flaw in the positioning of text (see Figure 14-10 for a before/after view), to complete and utter chaos with pixel-precise layouts (an extra three pixels is enough to wreak all sorts of havoc).

For our example, let's float a div next to another div containing some text (we've shortened the dummy text here; you'll need enough text to extend beyond the bottom of the floated element to see the effects):

```
<div id="floated">
  floated div
</div>

<div id="notfloated">
  Lorem ipsum dolor sit amet, consectetur adipisicing elit, sed do eiusmod➡
  tempor incididunt ut labore et dolore magna aliqua...
</div>
```

Next, we'll add some basic styles:

```
#floated {
  float:left;
  width:300px;
```

```
  height:50px;
  background:#ccc;
}

#notfloated {
  margin-left:300px;
  background:#eee;
}
```

At this point, everything will look right in Firefox and Safari, but not IE 6 (see Figure 14-10).

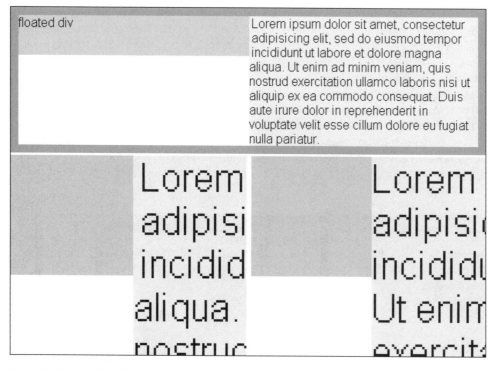

Figure 14-10. *The "jog" isn't very noticable (top), but it's definitely there (zoomed on left); on the right, the fix has been applied.*

However, we can fix that by applying the Holly hack to the nonfloated box and reducing its left margin by three pixels, then declaring a negative three-pixel margin on the floated box (be sure to drop these in your hack style sheet so they don't affect other browsers):

```
#floated {
  margin-right:-3px;
}
#notfloated {
  height:1%;
  margin-left:297px;
}
```

Again, as with the doubled float-margin bug, it's not entirely known why this works, though there is extended information available at (yet again) www.positioniseverything.net/explorer/threepxtest.html.

Absolute Positioning in a Relative Container

Just in case you're growing tired of the whole "we haven't a single clue why IE is doing this" routine, here's a bug that makes a *little* more sense, even though IE's behavior is completely incorrect.

By default, an element assigned position:absolute should be positioned relative to the edges of the browser window (as long as the element doesn't have any ancestors that have been assigned any position value other than static, which is the default). To allow more control, an absolutely positioned element contained within a box with something other than the default position declared should be positioned relative to that container rather than the browser window. The usual trick employed by designers is to declare position:relative on a container and then position:absolute on a particular element within (this technique was made incredibly popular by Doug Bowman in his article "Making the Absolute, Relative," www.stopdesign.com/articles/absolute/). This is incredibly handy when, for instance, you need to anchor an element to the *bottom* of its containing box.

It's that particular position which causes IE 6 grief: if the containing element (position:relative) does not have an assigned height, IE positions the absolute box relative to the page borders, not the containing element as it should (Figure 14-11). This is the only reason why this bug is somewhat understandable: at least IE is using some form of logic, however twisted and incorrect it may be.

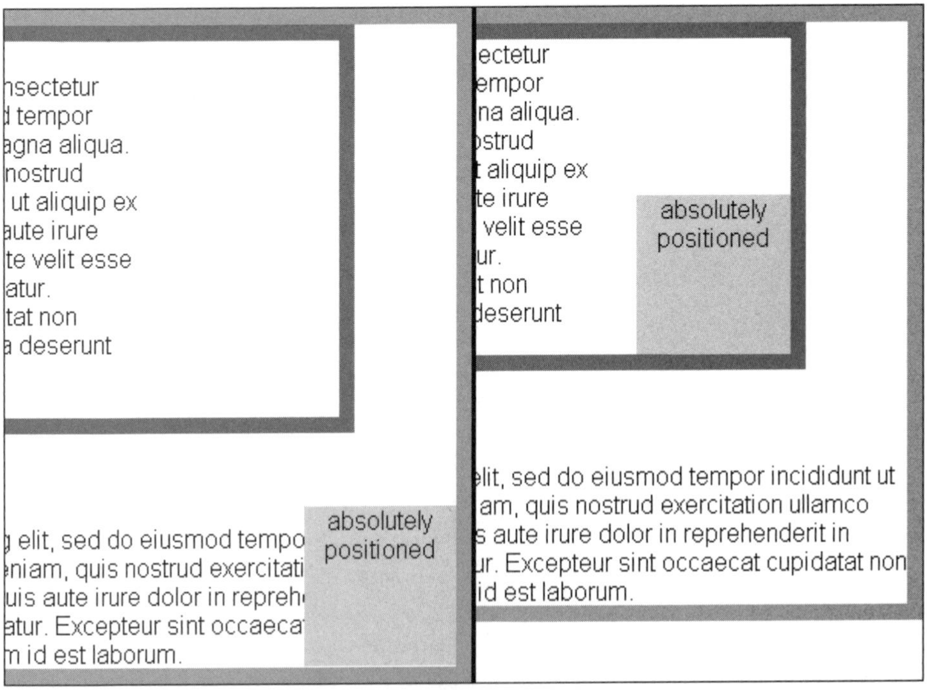

Figure 14-11. *On the left, IE 6 positions the absolute box at the bottom of the window; all is well after applying the Holly hack to the container* div *(right).*

Riding to our rescue once again is the Holly hack, the jack-of-almost-all-trades when it comes to correcting IE/Win rendering bugs. By assigning `height:1%` to the container element, we ensure that IE is able to properly calculate the correct position for our absolute box, while at the same time *incorrectly* ignoring the 1% height and expanding the container to fit its contents. (Other positioning oddities can occur, such as slight rounding errors; you can see one of these issues in Figure 14-11, where the incorrectly positioned box doesn't completely touch the bottom border. Luckily these are all fixed by our lovely hack.)

Live examples and some more esoteric details can be found at Position Is Everything's "Absolutely Buggy II" (`www.positioniseverything.net/abs_relbugs.html`).

Whitespace Bug

It's not uncommon to use an unordered list (`ul`) for site navigation elements, so it's likely you've seen this final IE bug before. Once again, for reasons known only to its programmers (and possibly not even to them), IE will sometimes react to whitespace in your markup, leading to unexpected and most certainly undesired results.

While other browsers ignore the whitespace, IE gives it life, usually ruining your layout in the process. For example, let's say you're using an unordered list to create a 200-pixel wide vertical navbar, with `display:block` declared on each a so the links fill the entire width:

Markup

```
<ul>
  <li><a href="page.html">Link</a></li>
  <li><a href="page.html">Link</a></li>
  <li><a href="page.html">Link</a></li>
  <li><a href="page.html">Link</a></li>
  <li><a href="page.html">Link</a></li>
  <li><a href="page.html">Link</a></li>
</ul>
```

Styles

```
ul {
  list-style:none;
  background:#999;
  width:200px;
  margin:0;padding:0;
}

ul a {
  display:block;
  background:#ddd;
  padding:.5em;
  border-bottom:1px solid #fff;
}
```

IE insists on displaying the whitespace between each `li` when it renders the list. Although this can be countered by removing the whitespace from your markup, it's not very friendly if you need to edit it later:

```
<ul><li><a href="page.html">Link</a></li><li><a href="page.html">Link</a></li>➡
<li><a href="page.html">Link</a></li><li><a href="page.html">Link</a></li><li>➡
<a href="page.html">Link</a></li><li><a href="page.html">Link</a></li></ul>
```

Thankfully an easier solution is available, and guess what? Yup, the Holly hack saves the day, once again. Just drop the following rule into your IE 6 hack style sheet, and everything returns to normal (see Figure 14-12):

```
ul li a {
  height:1%;
}
```

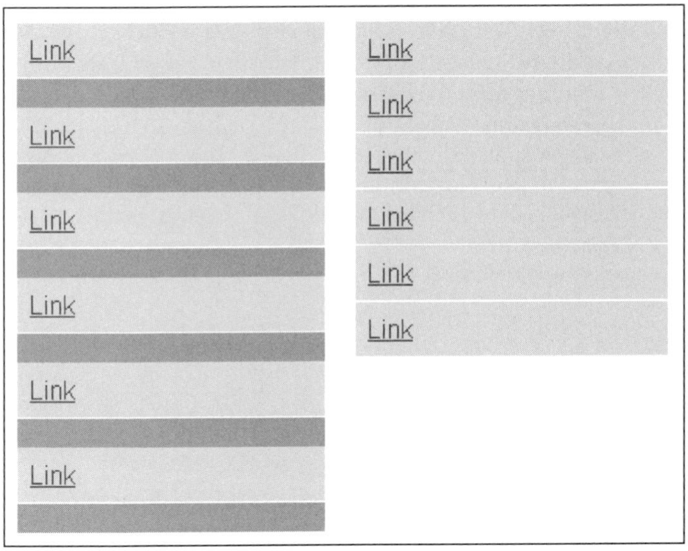

Figure 14-12. *A gray background color on the* ul *shows that IE is adding space under each* li, *where it doesn't belong.*

Solving Problems in the Real World: A Walkthrough

Descriptions of individual bugs are helpful (knowing how to recognize the more common problems helps narrow down the root causes much more quickly), but nothing beats seeing how they might arise in an actual layout. We're going to create a fairly common layout (header, navbar, subnav, three columns, and a footer, all fluid), then test for problems, apply fixes, and test again, repeating as needed until everything looks hunky-dory, even in IE 6 (see Figure 14-13 for the final layout).

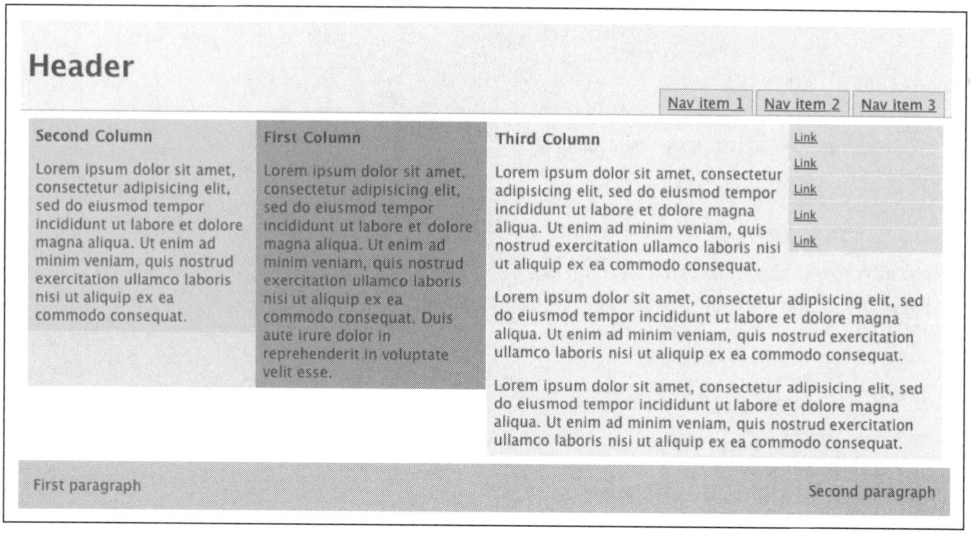

Figure 14-13. *It should look like this when we're done.*

Creating the Layout

For this example, we're going to borrow a three-column layout method from Position Is Everything that allows the center column's content to come first in our markup, with the left column second, and the right content third (see www.positioniseverything.net/ordered-floats.html for how and why it works). Assuming the most important content is in the center column, this is great for search engines, and also when viewed on alternate devices or with older browser versions. We also want a small margin between the columns and the header and footer, and the left and right columns should be indented slightly.

Our markup is fairly straightforward and properly structured, though we're going to omit the subnav within the third column for now, and add that in later (the dummy text seen in the screen shots throughout this example has been trimmed from the printed markup to save space and a few trees—open ch14_example_walkthrough_broken.html from the book's example files in a text editor to get the full source, including styles, before any fixes have been applied):

```
<div id="header">
  <h1>Header</h1>
  <ul id="nav">
    <li><a href="somepage.html">Nav item 1</a></li>
    <li><a href="somepage.html">Nav item 2</a></li>
    <li><a href="somepage.html">Nav item 3</a></li>
  </ul>
</div>
```

```
<div class="float-wrapper">

  <div class="first-col">
    <p><strong>First Column</strong></p>
    <p>Lorem ipsum dolor sit amet...</p>
  </div>

  <div class="second-col">
    <p><strong>Second Column</strong></p>
    <p>Lorem ipsum dolor sit amet...</p>
  </div>

</div>

<div class="third-col">
  <p><strong>Third Column</strong></p>
  <p>Lorem ipsum dolor sit amet...</p>
  <p>Lorem ipsum dolor sit amet...</p>
  <p>Lorem ipsum dolor sit amet...</p>
</div>

<div id="footer">
  <p class="first-para">First paragraph</p>
  <p class="second-para">Second paragraph</p>
</div>
```

Our CSS sets some defaults, styles the ul elements as a horizontal navbar (and positions it at the bottom of the header using position:absolute), positions the columns with floats and margins, and makes sure our footer clears the floated columns above:

```
body {
  padding:.5em;
  color:#333;
  font-family:'lucida grande', sans-serif;
}

p {
  padding:.5em;
}

#header {
  margin:0 0 .5em;
  padding:.5em;
  background-color:#eee;
  border-bottom:1px solid #999;
  position:relative;
}
```

```css
ul#nav {
  list-style:none;
  margin:0;padding:0 .5em 0 0;
  position:absolute;
  right:0;
  bottom:0;
}
ul#nav li {
  float:left;
  margin:0 0 0 .25em;
  background-color:#ddd;
  border-width:1px 1px 0;
  border-style:solid;
  border-color:#999;
}
ul#nav a {
  float:left;
  padding:.25em .5em;
}
ul#nav a:hover {
  background:#ccc;
}

.float-wrapper {
  float:left;
  width:49%;
  margin-left:1%;
  background-color:#ddd;
}

.first-col {
  float:right;
  width:50%;
  background-color:#999;
}

.second-col {
  margin-right:50%;
  background-color:#ccc;
}

.third-col {
  margin-left:50%;
  margin-right:1%;
  background-color:#eee;
}
```

```
#footer {
  clear:both;
  margin:.5em 0 0;
  padding:.5em;
  background-color:#bbb;
}

.first-para {
  float:left;
}

.second-para {
  float:right;
}
```

Having written the code knowing how it *should* look when rendered, let's now test it in Firefox and see how close we are (Figure 14-14).

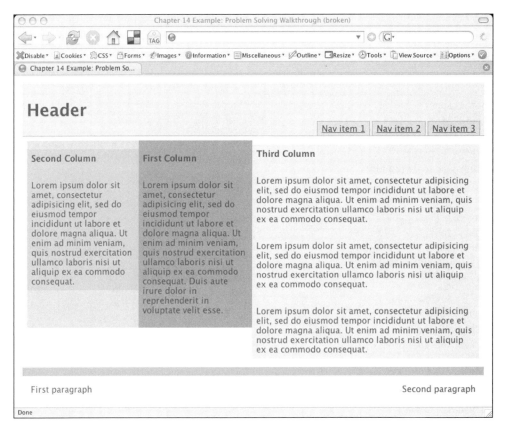

Figure 14-14. *The first test in Firefox looks pretty good, but not quite perfect just yet.*

Getting It Right in Firefox

Remember, we want everything to look "right" in Firefox before we check IE, so there are a few small things to take care of before we move on. There is some uneven spacing at the top of each column, and our footer isn't surrounding the text it contains.

After we run through our checklist, the footer jumps out as an easy fix: though the #footer element itself is cleared (because of the floated columns above), the floats *within* the footer have not been cleared. The fix is a simple matter of adding the easy float clearing rules from Chapter 6 to our style sheet and making one small addition to the markup to provide the hook:

```
<div id="footer" class="clearfix">
```

Solving the spacing issue in the columns is a matter of logic and observation, with a dash of experience. Looking at the paragraphs of text, the spacing seems a bit extreme, so our first guess is that the problem is related to margins on the p elements. Lucky for us, declaring margin:0 for paragraphs takes care of the issue:

```
p {
  margin:0;
  padding:.5em;
}
```

Tip The trial-and-error process is your friend; follow your instincts, make a change, and see what happens. You can always undo or go back to your backup code.

After these small tweaks, our layout is looking nice and crisp, except for the margin between our columns and footer (Figure 14-15).

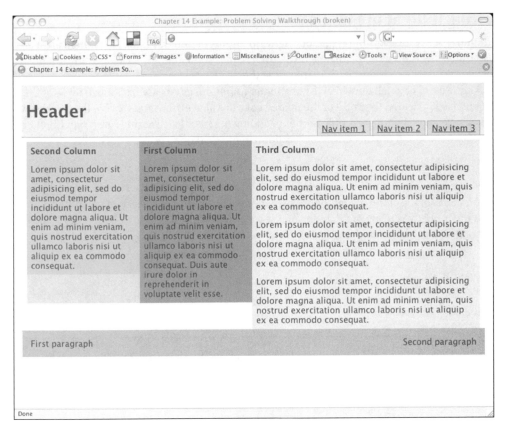

Figure 14-15. *Almost there...*

Removing the margins from our paragraphs has brought the footer right up to the bottom of our longest column (experiment with different amounts of content in each column—the result is the same on all three). It takes only a few seconds to discover that adding margin-top to the #footer rule doesn't change anything, so instead we'll add margin-bottom:.5em to the wrapper div surrounding columns one and two, and to column three (.third-col), which puts some distance between the columns and the footer (Figure 14-16).

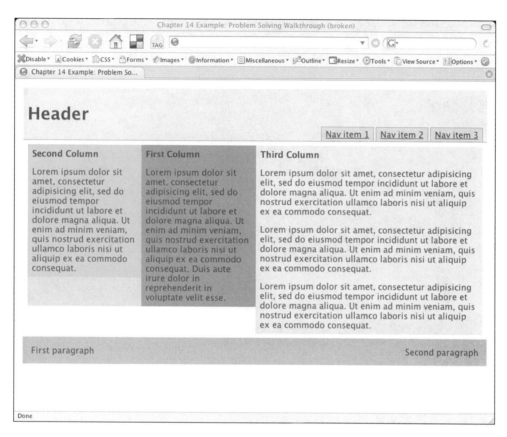

Figure 14-16. *Looking good in Firefox!*

Now it's time to fire up IE 6 and find out how much work is ahead of us.

Woe Is IE

Truth be told, it could be worse, but we still have some problems to solve after our first test in IE (Figure 14-17):

- The left margin is too wide on our second column (probably IE's doubled float-margin bug at work).

- The three-pixel jog bug is at work in our third column (due to either the `.float-wrapper` or the floated `.first-col`).

- Our navbar is nowhere near the header (smells like a problem with absolute positioning).

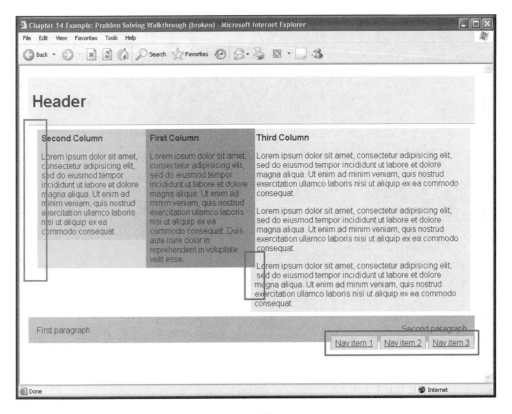

Figure 14-17. *First look in IE 6: a few issues to tackle*

Since we're going to need some hacks to work around these problems, the first step is creating the conditional comment that will hide our hack style sheet from browsers other than IE 6 and earlier:

```
<!--[if lte IE 6]>
  <link rel="stylesheet" href="iehacks.css" type="text/css" />
<![endif]-->
```

All the IE-specific rules will be placed in `iehacks.css` and kept separate from our main styles. Let's tackle the bugs one by one.

Fixing the Doubled Float-Margin Bug

Since we've recognized the doubled float-margin bug, it's easy to apply the fix (with a CSS comment so the purpose of the hack is clear to anyone who reads it). Knowing how the bug works also lets us target the right element without any further testing (since the bug only appears when a margin is applied in the same direction as the float, so it can only be .float-wrapper):

```
/* fix doubled float margin bug */
.float-wrapper { display:inline; }
```

There, that was easy, wasn't it?

Squashing the Three-Pixel Jog

As with the doubled float-margin bug, it's easy to deduce which elements are the likely culprits with the three-pixel jog. Again, using trial and error, stepping through each likely solution one by one is the best way to solve the problem. In this case, we'll start with .float-wrapper (as the outermost float coming in contact with our third column). As luck would have it, applying the fix to that element (along with the third column) does the trick:

```
/* fix three pixel jog bug */
.float-wrapper { margin-right:-3px; }
.third-col { height:1%;margin-left:0; }
```

Two down, one to go.

Repositioning the Navbar

It's a fair assumption (based on what we know of IE's problems with positioning absolute elements within relative containers) that our navbar is positioned incorrectly because our #header doesn't have a specified height. Once again, our hunch pays off, and one more line is added to our special style sheet:

```
/* fix absolute/relative positioning bug */
#header { height:1%; }
```

This puts the navbar where it belongs, but for some reason the position of the <h1> title changes slightly. To get it back in line with Firefox, we just have to add an extra line to our fix:

```
#header h1 { padding-top: .75em; }
```

With all three bugs now taken care of, our layout is identical in Firefox and IE (Figure 14-18).

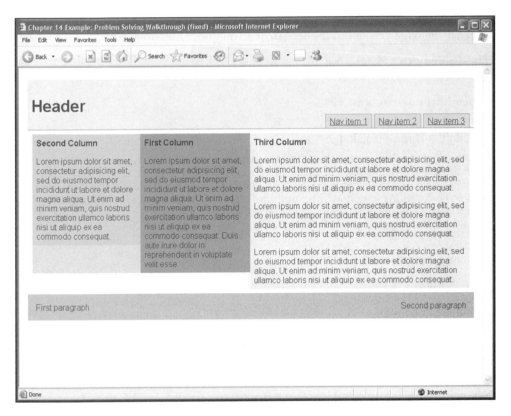

Figure 14-18. *IE 6 plays nice after a few quick hacks.*

Adding the Subnav

The last thing our layout needs is a list of links within the third column. The markup (another unordered list) goes at the top of the third column in the source:

```
<div class="third-col">
  <ul class="subnav">
    <li><a href="somepage.html">Link</a></li>
    <li><a href="somepage.html">Link</a></li>
    <li><a href="somepage.html">Link</a></li>
    <li><a href="somepage.html">Link</a></li>
    <li><a href="somepage.html">Link</a></li>
  </ul>
...
</div>
```

Then we add a few rules to our main style sheet:

```
ul.subnav {
  float:right;
  list-style:none;
  width:150px;
```

```
   margin:0 0 .5em .5em;
   padding:0;
   font-size:80%;
}
ul.subnav a {
   display:block;
   background:#ddd;
   margin-bottom:1px;
   padding:.5em;
}
ul.subnav a:hover {
   background:#ccc;
   margin-bottom:1px;
}
```

After viewing our changes in Firefox, everything looks perfect (Figure 14-19), but when we take a look in IE 6, we find the whitespace bug has struck (Figure 14-20).

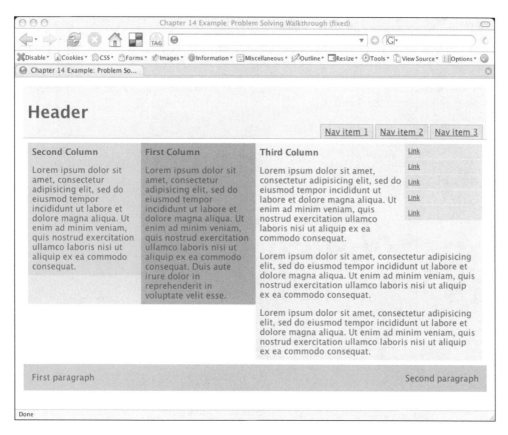

Figure 14-19. *Firefox displays the subnav correctly on the first try.*

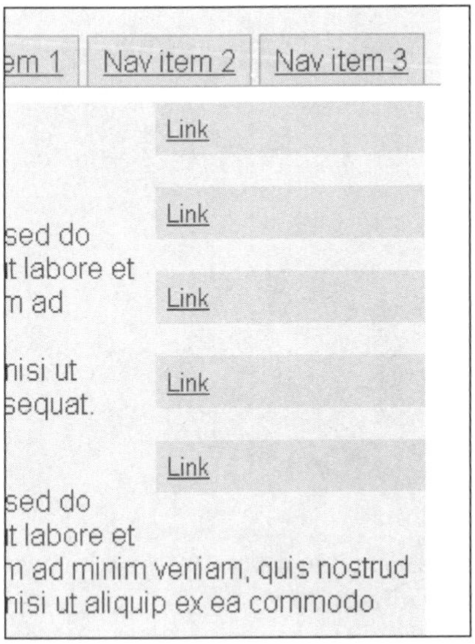

Figure 14-20. *IE's whitespace bug is no doubt the culprit.*

Thankfully, it's another quick fix for us to add to the hack style sheet:

```
/* fix whitespace bug */
ul.subnav a { height:1%; }
```

And with that, IE is right as rain (Figure 14-21).

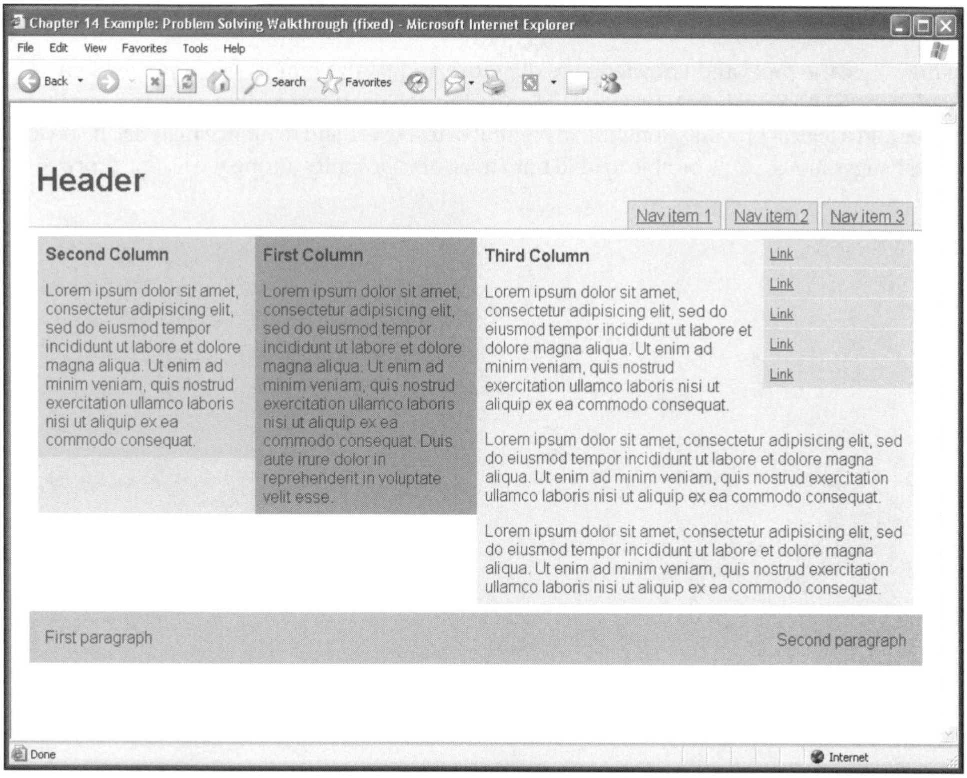

Figure 14-21. *Our layout looks almost as pretty in IE as it does in Firefox.*

Why You Shouldn't Group Your Hacks

Even though three of the fixes for these bugs all use the exact same hack (the Holly hack), and thus their rules could be grouped, it is better to leave them separate and commented so it is clear what purpose they serve. That way, when it comes time for you or anyone else to edit the hack style sheet in the future, it won't be a mystery.

Summary

You now have the tools and knowledge to diagnose and fix the major issues you're likely to encounter developing with (X)HTML and CSS. No CSS problem is impossible to solve; it just takes patience and a logical process, along with a handful of resources and reference material. If you follow these suggestions, you'll be able to hold onto most of your sanity during the testing process.

APPENDIX A

■ ■ ■

CSS Reference

Appendix A serves as a full reference to all CSS 2.1 properties, including basic browser support information for the four most commonly used desktop browsers: Firefox, Safari, Opera, and Internet Explorer.

CSS Units, Keywords, and Other Property Values

CSS includes a fixed set of units and keywords as values for several of its properties. The first section of this appendix covers these property values. Later in the appendix, when we cover individual properties you'll find references to these predefined values.

Factors and Integers

Numeric values in CSS can be either factors (decimal numbers) or integers (whole numbers). In most cases, negative versions of both are allowed.

Colors

CSS colors can be specified as a red, green, and blue (RGB) value, a hexadecimal value, or one of 17 predefined color name keywords. Few web designers use RGB values. Hexadecimal is the most common method used, followed by color keywords.

Hexadecimal Value

A hexadecimal value is the hash symbol, or pound sign (#), followed by pairs of hexadecimal digits specifying red, green, and blue components of the intended color. Hexadecimal digits are numbers or letters in the range 0–9 or a–f. Three-digits shortcuts in the form #rgb can be substituted for #rrggbb.

Examples: #50017c, #d0cecf, #dfdfdf, #f80, #9c0

Color Name

The available color names are aqua, black, blue, fuchsia, gray, green, lime, maroon, navy, olive, orange, purple, red, silver, teal, white, and yellow.

RGB Value

Red, green, and blue components are specified as either percentages or integers in the range 0–255.
    Examples: rgb(100%, 50%, 0%), rgb(255, 128, 0)

Fonts

The different font families and system font keywords are listed here.

Generic Font Families

First, here are the generic font families:

- Sans-serif
- Serif
- Monospace
- Cursive
- Fantasy

System Font Keywords

There are six possible system font keywords: caption, icon, menu, message-box, small-caption, and status-bar.
    These are not intended to be used by CSS designers, but rather are used by the browsers themselves. They're included here for the sake of completeness, but you, as the CSS author, needn't concern yourself with them that much.

Length

CSS lengths are indicated as a decimal number followed by an absolute or relative unit. All CSS length values must include a unit, unless that value is 0. Also, note that the line-height property can accept a number without a unit, but this is actually a scaling factor, not a length.

Absolute Units

Absolute units that can accompany length values include the following:

- mm (millimeter)
- cm (centimeter)
- in (inch)
- pt (point)
- pc (pica)

Relative Units

Relative units that can accompany length values include the following:

- em (size of em square in current font)

- ex (size of x-height in current font)

- px (pixel)

Percentages

Several CSS properties allow for percentages as values. A percentage in CSS is indicated as a decimal number in the range 0–100 followed by a percent symbol (%).

Position Keywords

Five position keywords as available as values for several properties: `left`, `right`, `center`, `top`, and `bottom`.

URLs

Some properties can take a URL to a file (often an image) as a value. In these cases, the possible syntaxes are as follows:

```
url(protocol://server/pathname)
url(pathname)
```

Properties That Accept Multiple Instances

The following properties can be used to set the associated individual top, right, bottom, and left properties: `margin`, `padding`, `border-width`, `border-style`, and `border-color`.

When multiple instances of a property are used, the following ordering applies: top, right, bottom, left (clockwise around the element).

Examples include

- `margin: 1em; /* all margins set to 1em */`

- `margin: 1em 2em; /* top and bottom margin set to 1em, left and right margin set to 2em */`

- `margin: 1em 2em 3em; /* top margin set to 1em, left and right margin set to 2em, bottom margin set to 3em */`

- `margin: 1em 2em 3em 4em; /* top, right, bottom, left, respectively */`

Inherit

The keyword `inherit` is a valid value for all CSS properties. Anytime `inherit` is stated, the associated property will be set to the same value as the parent of the selected element or elements. Most properties inherit naturally, so many times you will not need to specify it explicitly, but it is available if you need it.

CSS Properties

The following is a reference to all CS properties. In the Value component of each, the pipe character (|) indicates the word "or." In the "Supported by" component, Firefox refers to Firefox 1.5, Safari refers to Safari 2.0, Opera refers to Opera 9, and Internet Explorer refers to Internet Explorer 6 (the current versions of these browsers at the time of this writing).

Typefaces, Text Color, Text Size, and Similar Properties

The following properties control the appearance of text on your page.

color

Indicates the text color. Note that the value of the `color` property is also applied for text decorations (such as underlines) and as an initial value for border colors (but it's overridden if a border color is explicitly specified).

Value: `<rgb value>` | `<hexadecimal value>` | `<color name>`

Initial value: Determined by user agent

Inherited: Yes

Applies to: All elements

Supported by: Firefox, Safari, Opera, Internet Explorer

font

A shorthand property for specifying all font properties as well as line height.

Value: `font-style font-variant font-weight font-size/line-height font-family` | `<system font keyword>`

Initial value: See individual properties

Inherited: Yes

Applies to: All elements

Supported by: Firefox, Safari, Opera, Internet Explorer

■**Note** `line-height` is optional. `font-style`, `font-variant`, and `font-weight` are optional and may appear in any order.

---

font-family

Indicates the font family (typeface) to be used. The first listed font family (whether specific or generic) found to be available to the user agent will be used.

Value: A comma-separated list of `<specific font families>` | `<generic font families>`

Initial value: Determined by user agent

Inherited: yes

Applies to: all elements (except replaced elements)

Supported by: Firefox, Safari, Opera, Internet Explorer

font-size

Indicates the size of the type. Note that sizes refer to the size of the font's em square, not the size of any particular character within the font.

Value: `<length>` | `<percentage>` | `<absolute size>` | `<relative size>` | `xx-small` | `x-small` | `small` | `medium` | `large` | `x-large` | `xx-large` | `smaller` | `larger`

Initial value: `medium`

Inherited: Yes

Applies to: All elements

Supported by: Firefox, Safari, Opera, Internet Explorer

font-style

Used to specify an oblique or italic style within the current font family.

Value: `normal` | `italic` | `oblique`

Initial value: `normal`

Inherited: Yes

Applies to: All elements

Supported by: Firefox, Safari, Opera, Internet Explorer

font-variant

Used to specify a small-caps style within the current font family.

Value: `normal` | `small-caps`

Initial value: `normal`

Inherited: Yes

Applies to: All elements

Supported by: Firefox, Safari, Opera, Internet Explorer

font-weight

Used to specify the weight of the current font.

> Value: `normal` | `bold` | `bolder` | `lighter` | `100` | `200` | `300` | `400` | `500` | `600` | `800` | `800` | `900`
>
> Initial value: `normal`
>
> Inherited: Yes
>
> Applies to: All elements
>
> Supported by: Firefox, Safari, Opera, Internet Explorer

text-decoration

Used to specify underlining, overlining, strikeout, and blinking effects.

> Value: `none` | any combination of: `underline`, `overline`, `line-through`, `blink`
>
> Initial value: `none`
>
> Inherited: No
>
> Applies to: All elements
>
> Supported by: Firefox, Safari, Opera, Internet Explorer

text-transform

Used to specify the case of text.

> Value: `capitalize` | `uppercase` | `lowercase` | `none`
>
> Initial value: `none`
>
> Inherited: Yes
>
> Applies to: All elements
>
> Supported by: Firefox, Safari, Opera, Internet Explorer

Type Spacing and Alignment

CSS offer several properties related to the spacing and alignment of type.

white-space

Used to specify how tabs, line breaks, and extra whitespace in an element's content are handled.

> Value: `normal` | `pre` | `nowrap` | `pre-wrap` | `pre-line`
>
> Initial value: `normal`
>
> Inherited: Yes
>
> Applies to: Block-level elements
>
> Supported by: Firefox, Safari, Opera, Internet Explorer (see note)

Note No major browser supports `pre-wrap` and `pre-line`.

text-align
Used to specify the horizontal alignment of text.

Value: `left` | `right` | `center` | `justify`

Initial value: Determined by user agent

Inherited: Yes

Applies to: Block-level elements

Supported by: Firefox, Safari, Opera, Internet Explorer

text-indent
Used to specify the indention of the first line of text.

Value: `<length>` | `<percentage>`

Initial value: `0`

Inherited: Yes

Applies to: Block-level elements

Supported by: Firefox, Safari, Opera, Internet Explorer

line-height
Used to specify the distance between baselines of lines of text.

Value: `<factor>` | `<length>` | `<percentage>`

Initial value: Determined by user agent

Inherited: Yes

Applies to: All elements

Supported by: Firefox, Safari, Opera, Internet Explorer

word-spacing
Used to specify an additional amount of space to be added between words in text. Negative lengths can be used to reduce space between words.

Value: `normal` | `<length>`

Initial value: `normal`

Inherited: Yes

Applies to: All elements

Supported by: Firefox, Safari, Opera, Internet Explorer

letter-spacing

Used to specify an additional amount of space to be added between letters in text. Negative lengths can be used to reduce space between letters.

> Value: `normal` | `<length>`
>
> Initial value: `normal`
>
> Inherited: Yes
>
> Applies to: All elements
>
> Supported by: Firefox, Safari, Opera, Internet Explorer

vertical-align

Used to raise or lower letters and images above or below the baseline of text.

> Value: `<percentage>` | `<length>` | `sub` | `super` | `top` | `text-top` | `middle` | `bottom` | `text-bottom`
>
> Initial value: `baseline`
>
> Inherited: no
>
> Applies to: Inline elements and table cells
>
> Supported by: Firefox, Safari, Opera, Internet Explorer

direction

Used to specify the writing direction, the direction of table column layout, the direction of horizontal overflow, and the position of incomplete last lines of text.

> Value: `ltr` | `trl`
>
> Initial value: ltr
>
> Inherited: Yes
>
> Applies to: All elements
>
> Supported by: Firefox, Safari, Opera, Internet Explorer

unicode-bidi

Controls the Unicode standard bidirectional rendering algorithm.

> Value: `normal` | `embed` | `bidi-override`
>
> Initial value: `normal`
>
> Inherited: No
>
> Applies to: All elements
>
> Supported by: Firefox, Opera, Internet Explorer

Box Model

Next we look at the various properties that can be used to control the box model of your page elements.

margin

A shorthand property used to specify all four individual margin properties in one step.

> Value: Multiple instances of `<length>` | `<percentage>` | `auto`
>
> Initial value: `0`
>
> Inherited: No
>
> Applies to: All elements
>
> Supported by: Firefox, Safari, Opera, Internet Explorer

margin-top, margin-right, margin-bottom, margin-left

Used to specify the space between the element's bounding box and the bounding boxes of adjacent elements.

> Value: `<length>` | `<percentage>` | `auto`
>
> Initial value: Determined by user agent, and different for different elements
>
> Inherited: No
>
> Applies to: All elements
>
> Supported by: Firefox, Safari, Opera, Internet Explorer (see note)

Note In Internet Explorer 6 and lower, several margin-related bugs are exhibited. Among them: margins may double when element is floated, percentages may refer to the incorrect parent element, and `auto` may act in an unexpected manner when elements are absolutely positioned. The Position Is Everything web site (`www.positioniseverything.net/`) covers all IE 6 bugs in exhaustive detail.

---

padding

Used to specify all four individual padding properties in one step.

> Value: Multiple instances of `<length>` | `<percentage>`
>
> Initial value: `0`
>
> Inherited: No
>
> Applies to: All elements
>
> Supported by: Firefox, Safari, Opera, Internet Explorer

padding-top, padding-right, padding-bottom, padding-left

Used to specify how much space to insert between the contents of an element and its margin or border (if they exist).

Value: `<length>` | `<percentage>`

Initial value: `0`

Inherited: No

Applies to: All elements

Supported by: Firefox, Safari, Opera, Internet Explorer

border, border-top, border-right, border-bottom, border-left

Used to specify the width, color, and style of the element's borders.

Value: `border-width border-style border-color`

Initial value: See individual properties

Inherited: No

Applies to: All elements

Supported by: Firefox, Safari, Opera, Internet Explorer

Note Individual values are optional and may appear in any order. `1px solid black`, `1em dotted`, and `red` are all valid border property values.

---

border-width

Used to specify the border's thickness.

Value: Multiple instances of `<length>` `thin` | `medium` | `thick`

Initial value: `medium`

Inherited: No

Applies to: All elements

Supported by: Firefox, Safari, Opera, Internet Explorer

border-top-width, border-right-width, border-bottom-width, border-left-width

Used to specify the border's thickness for one side of the element.

Value: `<length>` `thin` | `medium` | `thick`

Initial value: `medium`

Inherited: no

Applies to: All elements

Supported by: Firefox, Safari, Opera, Internet Explorer

border-style

Used to specify all individual border styles in one step.

Value: Multiple instances of: `none` | `dotted` | `dashed` | `solid` | `double` | `groove` |
     `ridge` | `inset` | `outset` | `hidden`

Initial value: `none`

Inherited: No

Applies to: All elements

Supported by: Firefox, Safari, Opera, Internet Explorer (see note)

■**Note** In Internet Explorer 6 and lower, `border-style` is not implemented for row groups and the `dotted` value is not supported when the `border-width` is `1px` (`dashed` is displayed instead).

---

border-top-style, border-right-style, border-bottom-style, border-left-style

Used to specify the style of the border for one side of the element.

Value: `none` | `dotted` | `dashed` | `solid` | `double` | `groove` | `ridge` | `inset` | `outset` |
     `hidden`

Initial value: `none`

Inherited: No

Applies to: All elements

Supported by: Firefox, Safari, Opera, Internet Explorer (see note)

Note In Internet Explorer 6 and lower, `border-style` is not implemented for row groups and the `dotted` value is not supported when the `border-width` is `1px` (`dashed` is displayed instead).

border-color

Used to specify all border colors in one step.

Value: Multiple instances of `<rgb value>` | `<hexadecimal value>` | `<color name>` | `transparent`

Initial value: Set to the value of the `color` property of the element

Inherited: No

Applies to: All elements

Supported by: Firefox, Safari, Opera, Internet Explorer (see note)

Note In Internet Explorer 6 and lower, `border-color` is not implemented for row groups (indicated by the `thead`, `tbody`, and `tfoot` elements) and the `transparent` value is not supported (the initial value is displayed instead).

border-top-color, border-right-color, border-bottom-color, border-left-color

Used to specify the color of the border for individual sides of the element.

Value: `<rgb value>` | `<hexadecimal value>` | `<color name>` | `transparent`

Initial value: set to the value of the color property of the element

Inherited: No

Applies to: All elements

Supported by: Firefox, Safari, Opera, Internet Explorer (see note)

Note In Internet Explorer 6 and lower, `border-color` is not implemented for row groups and the `transparent` value is not supported (the initial value is displayed instead).

outline

A shorthand property used for setting all three individual outline properties. Outlines are drawn around the element but don't take up space. Therefore, they may overlap adjacent elements. This is in contrast to borders, which do take up space within the document.

Value: `outline-width outline-style outline-color`

Initial value: See individual properties

Inherited: No

Applies to: All elements

Supported by: Firefox, Safari, Opera

■**Note** Individual values are optional and may appear in any order.

---

outline-width

Used to specify the width of an outline.

Value: `<length>` | `thin` | `medium` | `thick`

Initial value: `medium`

Inherited: No

Applies to: All elements

Supported by: Firefox, Safari, Opera

outline-style

Used to specify the style of an outline.

Value: `none` | `dotted` | `dashed` | `solid` | `double` | `groove` | `ridge` | `inset` | `outset` | `hidden`

Initial value: `none`

Inherited: No

Applies to: All elements

Supported by: Firefox, Safari, Opera

outline-color

Used to specify the color of the outline.

Value: Either `invert` or one of the color values.

Initial value: `invert`

Inherited: No

Applies to: All elements

Supported by: Firefox, Safari, Opera

width

Used to specify the width of an element's content area.

Value: `<length>` | `<percentage>` | `auto`

Initial value: `auto`

Inherited: No

Applies to: Block-level and replaced elements

Supported by: Firefox, Safari, Opera, Internet Explorer (see note)

Note In Internet Explorer 6 and lower, several width-related bugs may occur. Among them: the box's width may increase to valid overflow, the width may use the wrong parent block, and percentages may be computed incorrectly. In all browsers, when applied to the table element, width percentages refer to the parent element's width.

---

min-width

Used to specify the minimum width of a "flexible" element (such as a box whose width has been set with a percentage).

Value: `<length>` | `<percentage>`

Initial value: `0`

Inherited: No

Applies to: All elements except nonreplaced inline elements and table elements

Supported by: Firefox, Safari, Opera

max-width

Used to specify the maximum width of a "flexible" element (such as a box whose width has been set with a percentage).

Value: `<length>` | `<percentage>` | `none`

Initial value: `none`

Inherited: No

Applies to: All elements except nonreplaced inline elements and table elements

Supported by: Firefox, Safari, Opera

height

Used to specify the height of an element's content area.

Value: <length> | auto

Initial value: auto

Inherited: No

Applies to: Block-level and replaced elements

Supported by: Firefox, Safari, Opera, Internet Explorer (see note)

Note In Internet Explorer 6 and lower, several height-related bugs may occur. Among them: the box's height may increase to valid overflow, the height may use the wrong parent block, and percentages may be computed incorrectly.

---

min-height

Used to specify the minimum height of a "flexible" element (such as a box whose height has been set with a percentage).

Value: <length> | <percentage>

Initial value: 0

Inherited: No

Applies to: All elements except nonreplaced inline elements and table elements

Supported by: Firefox, Safari, Opera

max-height

Used to specify the maximum height of a "flexible" element (such as a box whose height has been set with a percentage).

Value: <length> | <percentage> | none

Initial value: none

Inherited: No

Applies to: All elements except nonreplaced inline elements and table elements

Supported by: Firefox, Safari, Opera

overflow

Determines the display of child elements that do not fit within the content area of the element.

Value: `visible` | `hidden` | `scroll` | `auto`

Initial value: `visible`

Inherited: No

Applies to: Block-level and replaced elements

Supported by: Firefox, Safari, Opera, Internet Explorer

clip

Used to clip the visible portion of an element to a specified rectangle.

Value: `rect(<length>, <length>, <length>, <length>)` | `auto`

Initial value: `auto`

Inherited: No

Applies to: Absolutely positioned elements

Supported by: Firefox, Safari, Opera, Internet Explorer

Positioning

The following properties relate to positioning your containers on the page.

display

Determines the method in which an element is displayed.

Value: `none` | `inline` | `block` | `list-item` | `run-in` | `inline-block` | `inline-table` |
`table-row-group` | `table-header-group` | `table-footer-group` | `table-row` |
`table-column-group` | `table-column` | `table-cell` | `table-caption`

Initial value: `inline`

Inherited: No

Applies to: All elements

Supported by: Firefox, Safari, Opera, Internet Explorer (see note)

Note In Internet Explorer 6 and lower, `run-in`, `inline-table`, `table-row-group`, `table-header-group`, `table-footer-group`, `table-row`, `table-column-group`, `table-column`, `table-cell`, and `table-caption` are not available. Also, `inline-block` is supported only for inline elements.

---

position

Used to specify the method by which the position of the element's box is determined. Note that the values `absolute` and `fixed` imply that the element's `display` value must be `block`. The `display` property is ignored in this case. Elements that do not use static positioning make use of the properties `top`, `right`, `bottom`, and `left`.

Value: `static` | `relative` | `absolute` | `fixed`

Initial value: `static`

Inherited: No

Applies to: All elements

Supported by: Firefox, Safari, Opera, Internet Explorer (see note)

■**Note** In Internet Explorer 6 and lower, `fixed` is not supported. Also, `absolute` may cause problems with margin calculation.

---

top, right, bottom, left

Used to specify the position of elements whose `position` property is set to `fixed`, `absolute`, or `relative`.

Value: `<length>` | `<percentage>` | `auto`

Initial value: `auto`

Inherited: No

Applies to: Elements with position other than `static`

Supported by: Firefox, Safari, Opera, Internet Explorer

float

Used to specify whether an element is floated, and if so, to which direction.

Value: `left` | `right` | `none`

Initial value: `none`

Inherited: No

Applies to: All elements

Supported by: Firefox, Safari, Opera, Internet Explorer

clear

Defines the sides of an element on which no floating elements may appear.

Value: none | left | right | both

Initial value: none

Inherited: No

Applies to: All elements

Supported by: Firefox, Safari, Opera, Internet Explorer

z-index

Used to specify the order in which overlapping elements are stacked on top of each other. If z-index is not specified, elements that come later in the source document will be displayed on top of earlier elements.

Value: auto | <integer>

Initial value: auto

Inherited: No

Applies to: Positioned elements

Supported by: Firefox, Safari, Opera, Internet Explorer

visibility

Used to make an element completely transparent without removing it from the document flow.

Value: visible | hidden | collapse

Initial value: visible

Inherited: Yes

Applies to: All elements

Supported by: Firefox, Safari, Opera, Internet Explorer

Background Colors, Images, and Similar Properties

Backgrounds are controlled using the following properties.

background

A shorthand property for setting all five background properties in one step.

Value: `background-attachment background-color background-image`
        `background-position background-repeat`

Initial value: See individual properties

Inherited: No

Applies to: All elements

Supported by: Firefox, Safari, Opera, Internet Explorer

■Note Individual values can be specified in any order. If values are omitted, the initial values of the respective properties are assumed.

---

background-attachment

Determines whether a background image should be fixed or movable when the element is scrolled.

Value: `scroll | fixed`

Initial value: `scroll`

Inherited: No

Applies to: All elements

Supported by: Firefox, Safari, Opera, Internet Explorer (see note)

■Note In Internet Explorer 6 and lower, `fixed` is not supported on any element other than `body`.

---

background-color

Used to specify the background color of the element's content and padding areas.

Value: `<rgb value> | <hexadecimal value> | <color name> | transparent`

Initial value: `transparent`

Inherited: No

Applies to: All elements

Supported by: Firefox, Safari, Opera, Internet Explorer

background-image

Used to specify a background image at a specified URL as the background for an element.

Value: `<url>` | `none`

Initial value: `none`

Inherited: No

Applies to: All elements

Supported by: Firefox, Safari, Opera, Internet Explorer

background-position

Used to specify the initial position of a background image.

Value: A horizontal position value followed by a vertical position value. Both are specified by: `<length>` | `<percentage>` | `<position keyword>`

Initial value: `0 0`

Inherited: No

Applies to: All elements

Supported by: Firefox, Safari, Opera, Internet Explorer

Note Percentages are used to determine points both in the element and the background image. The image is placed so that both points match. For example, a value of `50% 50%` would result in a background image whose center is lined up with the center of the element's box.

---

background-repeat

Determines whether the background image is repeated in the element, and if so, how.

Value: `repeat` | `repeat-x` | `repeat-y` | `no-repeat`

Initial value: `repeat`

Inherited: No

Applies to: All elements

Supported by: Firefox, Safari, Opera, Internet Explorer

Lists

The following properties can be used to style lists.

list-style

A shorthand property for specifying individual list-style properties in one step.

Value: `list-style-type list-style-position list-style-image`

Initial value: See individual properties

Inherited: Yes

Applies to: List items and elements with a `display` value of `list-item`

Supported by: Firefox, Safari, Opera, Internet Explorer

■Note Individual values are optional and can appear in any order.

---

list-style-type

Used to specify the style of list item markers.

Value: `none | disc | circle | square | decimal | decimal-leading-zero | lower-roman | upper-roman | lower-alpha | upper-alpha | lower-latin | upper-latin | lower-greek | Armenian | georgian`

Initial value: `disc`

Inherited: Yes

Applies to: Elements with a `display` value of `list-item`

Supported by: Firefox, Safari, Opera, Internet Explorer (see note)

■Note In Internet Explorer 6 and lower, `decimal-leading-zero`, `lower-greek`, `armenian`, and `georgian` are not supported.

---

list-style-position

Determines whether the list item marker is placed inside or outside the `list-item` element's box.

Value: `inside | outside`

Initial value: `outside`

Inherited: Yes

Applies to: List items and elements with a `display` value of `list-item`

Supported by: Firefox, Safari, Opera, Internet Explorer

list-style-image

Used to specify an image (via URL) to be used as the list item marker.

Value: `<url>` | `none`

Initial value: `none`

Inherited: Yes

Applies to: Elements with a `display` value of `list-item`

Supported by: Firefox, Safari, Opera, Internet Explorer

Tables

The following properties can be used to style tables.

border-collapse

Determines whether table cells have separate borders or share borders with adjacent cells, groups of rows and columns, or the table itself.

Value: `collapse` | `separate`

Initial value: `separate`

Inherited: Yes

Applies to: Tables and inline tables

Supported by: Firefox, Safari, Opera, Internet Explorer

border-spacing

Determines the space between pairs of table, group, or cell borders.

Value: Either one or two instances of a length. If two values are present, the first one determines horizontal and the second vertical distance.

Initial value: `0`

Inherited: Yes

Applies to: Table and inline tables with separate borders

Supported by: Firefox, Safari, Opera

empty-cells

Used to hide borders for empty table cells.

Value: Either show | hide

Initial value: show

Inherited: Yes

Applies to: Table cells with separate borders

Supported by: Firefox, Safari, Opera

table-layout

Used to specify the layout mode for tables. If table-layout is set to fixed, then the width of the table columns are computed after the first row. Explicit values for width on column elements are honored.

Value: auto | fixed

Initial value: auto

Inherited: No

Applies to: Tables and inline tables whose width property is not set to auto

Supported by: Firefox, Safari, Opera, Internet Explorer

caption-side

Determines whether the caption is placed above or below the table.

Value: top | bottom

Initial value: top

Inherited: Yes

Applies to: table-caption elements

Supported by: Firefox, Safari, Opera

Generated Content

The properties that follow can be used to generate content.

content

Used to specify text to be inserted as the content of pseudo-elements that were introduced using :before or :after pseudo-element selectors.

Value: One of more of: a text string, a counter, counters, or the keywords `normal` |
`open-quote` | `close-quote` | `no-open-quote` | `no-close-quote`

Initial value: `normal`

Inherited: No

Applies to: `:before` and `:after` pseudo-elements

Supported by: Firefox, Safari, Opera

quotes

Used to specify the actual quote marks to be used when open-quote or close-quote values are specified for the content property.

Value: Either `none` or any number of text string pairs. Each pair of strings defines open- and close-quote marks for increasingly nested levels of quotations.

Initial value: Determined by the user agent

Inherited: Yes

Applies to: All elements

Supported by: Firefox, Opera

counter-increment

Increments the specified counters.

Value: `none` | `<counter name>`

Initial value: `none`

Inherited: No

Applies to: All elements

Supported by: Firefox, Opera

counter-reset

Resets the specified counters.

Value: `none` | `<counter name>`

Initial value: `none`

Inherited: No

Applies to: All elements

Supported by: Firefox, Opera

cursor

Determines the cursor the user agent will display when an element is "moused over."

Value: `<url>` | `auto` | `default` | `pointer` | `text` | `help` | `wait` | `progress` |
`crosshair` | `move` | `e-resize` | `ne-resize` | `n-resize` | `nw-resize` |
`w-resize` | `sw-resize` | `s-resize` | `se-resize`

Initial value: `auto`

Inherited: Yes

Applies to: All elements

Supported by: Firefox, Safari, Opera, Internet Explorer (see note)

Note In Firefox, Safari, and Opera, the `url` value is not supported.

Printing

These properties determine how a page should be handled when printed.

page-break-before

Determines how page breaks before an element should be handled. The values `left` and `right` indicate that a page break should occur, and that the element should be placed on the left or right page, respectively. For example, when printing books it is common for all chapters to start on the right page. This can be achieved by applying `page-break-before: right` to each chapter title.

Value: `auto` | `always` | `avoid` | `left` | `right`

Initial value: `auto`

Inherited: No

Applies to: Block-level elements

Supported by: Firefox, Safari, Opera, Internet Explorer (see note)

Note In Opera and Internet Explorer, `left` and `right` behave normally. In Firefox, `left` and `right` are not supported. In Safari, only `auto` and `always` are supported.

page-break-after

Determines how page breaks after an element should be handled. The values left and right indicate that a page break should occur, and that the next element should be placed on the left or right page, respectively. For example, page-break-after: avoid can be used to prevent page breaks after headings.

Value: auto | always | avoid | left | right

Initial value: auto

Inherited: No

Applies to: Block-level elements

Supported by: Firefox, Safari, Opera, Internet Explorer (see note)

■Note In Opera and Internet Explorer, left and right behave normally. In Firefox, left and right are not supported. In Safari, only auto and always are supported.

---

page-break-after

Determines how page breaks after an element should be handled. The values left and right indicate that a page break should occur, and that the next element should be placed on the left or right page, respectively. For example, page-break-after: avoid can be used to prevent page breaks after headings.

Value: auto | always | avoid | left | right

Initial value: auto

Inherited: No

Applies to: Block-level elements

Supported by: Firefox, Safari, Opera, Internet Explorer (see note)

■Note In Opera and Internet Explorer, left and right behave normally. In Firefox, left and right are not supported. In Safari, only auto and always are supported.

---

page-break-inside

Indicates whether a page break inside an element should or should not occur. For example, `page-break-inside: avoid` could be used on list elements like `ul`, `ol`, and `dl` to prevent list items from appearing on different pages.

Value: `auto` | `avoid`

Initial value: `auto`

Inherited: Yes

Applies to: Block-level elements

Supported by: Opera

widows

If a paragraph is broken across two pages, some of its lines appear at the top of the next page and the others remain at the bottom of the page. These are referred to as "widows" and "orphans," respectively. This property defines the minimum number of widows.

Value: `<integer>`

Initial value: 2

Inherited: Yes

Applies to: Block-level elements

Supported by: Opera

orphans

If a paragraph is broken across two pages, some of its lines appear at the top of the next page and the others remain at the bottom of the page. These are referred to as "widows" and "orphans," respectively. This property defines the minimum number of orphans.

Value: `<integer>`

Initial value: 2

Inherited: Yes

Applies to: Block-level elements

Supported by: Opera

■ ■ ■

CSS Specificity Chart

Knowing how to calculate specificity is key to mastering CSS, so to that end, we've created this chart as a quick reference to turn to whenever you need to polish up on your calculations. Bear in mind that while we're only using three columns in this chart, the fourth column to the left still exists for any properties labeled !important, and that the *universal selector* (*) is equal to 0 in all columns (see Chapter 3 for details).

The columns in this chart list an example selector, its specificity score, and then a description of which element(s) the selector targets in plain English.

Element Selectors

Selector	# of IDs	# of Classes	# of Elements	In English
h1	0,	0,	1	The contents of any h1 element
strong	0,	0,	1	The contents of any strong element
p.note	0,	1,	1	The contents of any p element with a class of note
body#contact	1,	0,	1	The contents of the body element with the ID of contact
li#nav-portfolio. current	1,	1,	1	The contents of any li element with the ID of nav-portfolio and a class of current

Descendant, Child, and Adjacent Sibling Selectors

Selector	# of IDs	# of Classes	# of Elements	In English
h1 em	0,	0,	2	Any em contained within any h1
p > img	0,	0,	2	Any img that is the child of a p
div#sidebar h3 + p	1,	0,	3	Any p that immediately follows an h3 contained within a div with the ID of sidebar
div#header ul#nav li.current a	2,	1,	4	Any anchor (a) contained within an li with a class of current, which is a descendant of a ul with the ID of nav, contained within a div with the ID of header

Attribute Selectors

Attribute selectors are considered classes in the specificity calculation, even when the targeted attribute is an ID.

Selector	# of IDs	# of Classes	# of Elements	In English
input[type=text]	0,	1,	1	The contents of any input with a value of text in the type attribute
a[href~=".org"]	0,	1,	1	The contents of any a with an href value that includes .org
dl#address dd h3[title]	1,	0,	3	The contents of any h3 that has any value set in its title attribute, and that is contained within a dd that is a descendant of a dl with the ID of address

Pseudo-Class Selectors

Pseudo-classes are considered classes in the specificity calculation.

Selector	# of IDs	# of Classes	# of Elements	In English
div#content p:first-child	1,	1,	2	The contents of the p that is the first child of a div with the ID of content
a:visited em	0,	1,	2	The contents of any em contained within an a that is in the visited state
div#sidebar p:hover	1,	1,	2	The contents of any p in the hover state that is contained within a div with the ID of sidebar
input:focus	0,	1,	1	The contents of any input field when it has the focus of the browser

Pseudo-Elements

Pseudo-elements are considered elements in the specificity calculation.

Selector	# of IDs	# of Classes	# of Elements	In English
dl.wines dd:first-line	0,	1,	3	The first line of any dd contained within a dl with a class of wines
ul li#description p:first-letter	1,	0,	4	The first letter of any p contained within an li with the ID of description, contained within a ul
ol#priority li:before	1,	0,	3	Inserts content before any li contained within an ol with the ID of priority
div#main p. item-footer:after	1,	1,	3	Inserts content after any p with a class of item-footer contained within a div with the ID of main

■ ■ ■

Browser Grading Chart

To help you avoid browser support problems and troubleshoot your style sheets, we've compiled this simple chart of the majority of CSS 2.1 properties, leaving out properties that don't work properly in any modern browser. The browsers listed make up the vast majority in use as of this writing (with the exception of IE 7, which is included now that its CSS support has been declared feature complete), and are as follows:

- Firefox (Linux/OS X/Windows, version 1.5)

- Safari (OS X, version 2)

- Internet Explorer (Windows, versions 6 and 7)

Note Netscape 8 uses the same rendering engine as Firefox, so you may use the Firefox column for compatibility with that browser.

The chart uses the following system: Y means the property is supported by the browser, N means it isn't. We've split the properties into groups based on usage, following the order and grouping used in Appendix A of Simon Collison's *Beginning CSS Web Development: From Novice to Professional* (Apress, 2006), which makes this chart the perfect companion to Simon's property index.

Background

Property	Firefox	Safari	IE 6	IE 7
background	Y	Y	Y	Y
background-attachment	Y	Y	Y*	Y
background-color	Y	Y	Y	Y
background-image	Y	Y	Y	Y
background-position	Y	Y	Y	Y
background-repeat	Y	Y	Y	Y

* background-attachment:fixed *is supported on all elements in IE 7, but only the* body *element is supported in IE 6.*

Border

Property	Firefox	Safari	IE 6	IE 7
border	Y	Y	Y	Y
border-bottom	Y	Y	Y	Y
border-bottom-color	Y	Y	Y	Y
border-bottom-style	Y	Y	Y	Y
border-bottom-width	Y	Y	Y	Y
border-color	Y	Y	Y	Y
border-left	Y	Y	Y	Y
border-left-color	Y	Y	Y	Y
border-left-style	Y	Y	Y	Y
border-left-width	Y	Y	Y	Y
border-right	Y	Y	Y	Y
border-right-color	Y	Y	Y	Y
border-right-style	Y	Y	Y	Y
border-right-width	Y	Y	Y	Y
border-style	Y	Y	Y	Y
border-top	Y	Y	Y	Y
border-top-color	Y	Y	Y	Y
border-top-style	Y	Y	Y	Y
border-top-width	Y	Y	Y	Y
border-width	Y	Y	Y	Y

Margin

Property	Firefox	Safari	IE 6	IE 7
margin	Y	Y	Y	Y
margin-bottom	Y	Y	Y	Y
margin-left	Y	Y	Y	Y
margin-right	Y	Y	Y	Y
margin-top	Y	Y	Y	Y

Padding

Property	Firefox	Safari	IE 6	IE 7
padding	Y	Y	Y	Y
padding-bottom	Y	Y	Y	Y
padding-left	Y	Y	Y	Y
padding-right	Y	Y	Y	Y
padding-top	Y	Y	Y	Y

Dimension

Property	Firefox	Safari	IE 6	IE 7
height	Y	Y	Y	Y
max-height	Y	Y	N	Y
max-width	Y	Y	N	Y
min-height	Y	Y	N	Y
min-width	Y	Y	N*	Y
width	Y	Y	Y	Y

* Though IE 6 doesn't support min-width, it incorrectly treats width the way other browsers treat min-width, expanding the box beyond the specified dimension to enclose the content.

Text

Property	Firefox	Safari	IE 6	IE 7
color	Y	Y	Y	Y
direction	Y	Y	Y*	Y
letter-spacing	Y	Y	Y	Y
line-height	Y	Y	Y	Y
text-align	Y	Y	Y	Y
text-decoration	Y	Y	Y	Y
text-intent	Y	Y	Y	Y
text-shadow	N	Y	N	N
text-transform	Y	Y	Y	Y
white-space	Y	Y	Y	Y
word-spacing	Y	Y	Y	Y

*direction *is supported in IE 6, but can result in unexpected behavior when used with floated elements.*

Font

Property	Firefox	Safari	IE 6	IE 7
font	Y	Y	Y	Y
font-family	Y	Y	Y	Y
font-size	Y	Y	Y	Y
font-style	Y	Y	Y	Y
font-variant	Y	Y	Y	Y
font-weight	Y	Y	Y	Y

List and Marker

Property	Firefox	Safari	IE 6	IE 7
list-style	Y	Y	Y	Y
list-style-image	Y	Y	Y	Y
list-style-position	Y	Y	Y	Y
list-style-type	Y	Y	Y	Y

Positioning

Property	Firefox	Safari	IE 6	IE 7
bottom	Y	Y	Y	Y
clip	Y	Y	Y	Y
left	Y	Y	Y	Y
overflow	Y	Y	Y	Y
position	Y	Y	Y*	Y
right	Y	Y	Y	Y
top	Y	Y	Y	Y
vertical-align	Y	Y	Y	Y
z-index	Y	Y	Y	Y

*position:absolute *is buggy in IE 6, but is more stable in IE 7.* position:fixed *is supported by IE 7, but does not work in IE 6.*

Classification

Property	Firefox	Safari	IE 6	IE 7
clear	Y	Y	Y	Y
cursor	Y	Y	Y	Y
display	Y	Y	Y	Y*
float	Y	Y	Y	Y
visibility	Y	Y	Y	Y

*display:table *(and other table-related values) are not supported by IE 6 or 7.*

Table

Property	Firefox	Safari	IE 6	IE 7
border-collapse	Y	Y	Y	Y
border-spacing	Y	Y	N	N
caption-side	Y	Y	N	N
empty-cells	Y	Y	N	N
table-layout	Y	Y	Y	Y

Pseudo-Classes

Property	Firefox	Safari	IE 6	IE 7
:active	Y	Y	Y	Y
:focus	Y	Y	N	N
:hover	Y	Y	Y	Y*
:link	Y	Y	Y	Y
:visited	Y	Y	Y	Y
:first-child	Y	Y	N	Y
:lang	Y	Y	N	N

* :hover *is supported on all elements in IE 7, but only on anchors in IE 6.*

Pseudo-Elements

Property	Firefox	Safari	IE 6	IE 7
:first-letter	Y	Y	Y	Y
:first-line	Y	Y	Y	Y
:before	Y	Y	N	Y
:after	Y	Y	N	Y

Outline

None of these properties are currently supported by Safari or IE, but they are supported in Firefox 1.5 and above.

Property	Firefox	Safari	IE 6	IE 7
outline	Y	N	N	N
outline-color	Y	N	N	N
outline-style	Y	N	N	N
outline-width	Y	N	N	N

Index

You Need the Companion eBook

Your purchase of this book entitles you to buy the companion PDF-version eBook for only $10. Take the weightless companion with you anywhere.

We believe this Apress title will prove so indispensable that you'll want to carry it with you everywhere, which is why we are offering the companion eBook (in PDF format) for $10 to customers who purchase this book now. Convenient and fully searchable, the PDF version of any content-rich, page-heavy Apress book makes a valuable addition to your programming library. You can easily find and copy code—or perform examples by quickly toggling between instructions and the application. Even simultaneously tackling a donut, diet soda, and complex code becomes simplified with hands-free eBooks!

Once you purchase your book, getting the $10 companion eBook is simple:

❶ Visit **www.apress.com/promo/tendollars/**.

❷ Complete a basic registration form to receive a randomly generated question about this title.

❸ Answer the question correctly in 60 seconds, and you will receive a promotional code to redeem for the $10.00 eBook.

2560 Ninth Street • Suite 219 • Berkeley, CA 94710

eBookshop

ASP **Today**

Apress®
THE EXPERT'S VOICE™

Offer valid through 5/27/07.